MARY ANN SHADD CARY

MARY ANN SHADD CARY

THE BLACK PRESS AND PROTEST IN THE NINETEENTH CENTURY

Jane Rhodes

INDIANA UNIVERSITY PRESS / BLOOMINGTON & INDIANAPOLIS

This book is a publication of

Indiana University Press
601 North Morton Street
Bloomington, IN 47404-3797 USA

www.indiana.edu/~iupress

Telephone orders 800-842-6796
Fax orders 812-855-7931
Orders by e-mail iuporder@indiana.edu

© 1998 by Jane Rhodes
First reprinted in paperback in 1999.
All rights reserved

No part of this book may be reproduced or utilized in any form or by any means, electronic
or mechanical, including photocopying and recording, or by any information storage and
retrieval system, without permission in writing from the publisher. The Association of
American University Presses' Resolution on Permissions constitutes the only exception to
this prohibition.

The paper used in this publication meets the minimum requirements of American National
Standard for Information Sciences—Permanence of Paper for Printed Library Materials,
ANSI Z39.48–1984.

Manufactured in the United States of America

Library of Congress Cataloging-in-Publication Data
Rhodes, Jane, 1955.
Mary Ann Shadd Cary : the Black press and protest in the nineteenth century / Jane Rhodes.
p.   cm.
Includeds bibliographical references and index.
ISBN 0-253-33446-2 (alk. paper)
1. Cary, Mary Ann Shadd, 1823–1893. 2. Afro-American women civil rights workers—
Biography. 3. Civil rights workers—United States—Biography. 4. Free Afro-Americans—
Biography. 5. Newspaper publishing—United States—Biography. 6. Women educators—
Canada—Biography. 7. Afro-Americans—Civil rights—History—19th century. I. Title.
E185.97.C32R48   1998
305.48'896073'0092—dc21
[B]   98-19997

ISBN 0-253-21350-9 (pbk. : alk. paper)

2 3 4 5 03 02 01 00 99

For My Parents

Edward C. Rhodes, Sr.
AND
Madelon Battle Rhodes

CONTENTS

CONTENTS

ACKNOWLEDGMENTS

This project represents a twelve-year quest that has been aided by numerous persons and institutions. For all those not mentioned I hope my memory lapse will be forgiven. Manning Marable must be thanked for planting the seed which has flourished in these pages. In the summer of 1986, while chatting about the history of African American journalists, he complained to me that few knew about the legacy of Mary Ann Shadd Cary. I, a black woman journalist anxiously seeking my predecessors, was among the ignorant. Chagrined, I went home that evening and looked up her entry in Gerda Lerner's *Black Women in America*. Since then the pursuit of Mary Ann Shadd Cary's story has been entwined with my own progression from journalist to scholar.

This book began as a dissertation at the University of North Carolina at Chapel Hill. It would not have been completed without the guidance, support, and superb editing of my advisor, Margaret Blanchard. My teachers, including Jacqueline Dowd Hall, Colin Palmer, Jane Brown, and Don Shaw each had a lasting influence on my work. I must also thank the Government of Canada for a Canadian Studies Graduate Fellowship. My first academic employer, The State University of New York College at Cortland, was tremendously helpful through research funding, a leave of absence, and general encouragement. The Indiana University School of Journalism, and Indiana's Research and the University Graduate School, also provided funding for travel and research, and release time. I am particularly indebted to Richard Blackett, now of the University of Houston, for being a friend, mentor, and colleague throughout this process.

The Chancellor's Postdoctoral Fellowship at the University of California at San Diego enabled me to concentrate my time on completing the research, and fleshing out the manuscript. A grant from the UCSD Academic Senate aided in the final preparation of the manuscript. George Lipsitz has become an indispensable mentor and friend who read early drafts and provided crucial feedback. I have also appreciated the support and comments from the community of media historians, including Maurine Beasely, Rodger Streitmatter, Gerald Baldasty, and Hazel Dicken-Garcia. In Canada, Kate McPherson and Michael Wayne willingly shared their research and insights. Carolyn Stefanco and Roslyn Terborg-Penn also gave of their time to answer my questions and/or read drafts.

A number of libraries and archives made this project possible. I must single out Esme Bahn, of the Moorland-Spingarn Research Collection at Howard University, for her assistance and perseverance on my behalf. I am also indebted to the help and generosity of Alice Newby and the staff of the Raleigh Township Centennial Museum in North Buxton, Ontario. The services of the reference and interlibrary loan staff of the libraries at Indiana University and the University of California at San Diego were invaluable, as well. Thanks go to those who aided me at the Ontario Provincial Archives, the National Archives of Canada, the Metropolitan Toronto Reference Library, the Chatham-Kent Museum, the D. B. Weldon Library at the University of Western Ontario, the Library of Congress, the National Archives, the Historical Society of Pennsylvania, the Rare Books Department of Cornell University Library, the Southern Historical Collection at the University of North Carolina, the Chester County Archives, the Delaware State Archives, and the Schomberg Center for Research in Black Culture.

For me, as for many academics, this project would never have been completed without a circle of friends. Cindy Hahamovich and Scott Nelson shared the angst of graduate school and many of the Canadian adventures, the North Carolina "Girl's Club" offered sympathy, sustenance, and good times, and Ellen Seiter has given encouragement during the ups and downs of publishing and relocation. This manuscript was also aided considerably by the friendship of Robyn Wiegman—a scholar from whom I have learned a great deal.

Lynn M. Hudson is a true partner in all realms; my most reliable reader, strongest critic, and steadfast ally. This project would never have been completed without her wit, intellect, patience, and devotion.

* * *

Throughout this text I have used the terms African American, black American, and black interchangeably. Most often the terms black American or black Canadian seemed most relevant for the historical context in which skin color was the primary determinant for one's status in the world, with national identity a secondary factor. Nevertheless, African American is a commonly used designator to avoid redundancy and repetition. When appropriate, I have also used the term Afro-Canadian to refer to persons of African descent living in Canada.

INTRODUCTION

On Independence Day 1856, Frederick Douglass took time out from his agonizing over the violence in "Bleeding Kansas" to praise Mary Ann Shadd Cary as an exemplar. "We do not know her equal among the colored ladies of the United States," Douglass proclaimed in the pages of his newspaper. Shadd Cary, founder and publisher of the *Provincial Freeman,* had toiled away in relative obscurity in the black expatriate communities of Canada. Douglass wanted his readers to know something of her "unceasing industry, . . . unconquerable zeal and commendable ability." Paradoxically, Douglass also saw fit to note in his tribute that "The tone of her paper has been at times harsh and complaining."[1]

This seeming contradiction—that Shadd Cary would be viewed simultaneously as an object of respect and leadership, and as an object of derision—is central to the story of this African American woman. Mary Ann Shadd Cary was clearly an exceptional figure in United States history: first black woman to publish and edit a newspaper, second to become an attorney, champion of black emigration to Canada, educator, orator, feminist, and agitator for civil rights. She devoted her life to using public discourse to advance a range of political and social reforms. In the process she became a consummate communicator who thrust herself into a public sphere where few people of color, especially women, dared to tread.

Such accomplishments could only be attained by someone with a strong character, keen intelligence, and determination. But Shadd Cary was neither a saint nor a heroine in any romantic sense. This was a woman with her share of human faults; she could be headstrong, cantankerous, and abrasive in her personal and public relations. She was motivated by both altruism and self-aggrandizement, by political philosophy and a quick temper. She enjoyed the sports of debate and repartee, and rarely hesitated to strike back at rivals and enemies. These qualities, while often admired in a man, were scorned in a woman, making her both the subject and source of controversy. Mary Ann Shadd Cary was a quintessential dissident; a woman whose life was marked by the numerous ways she transgressed the boundaries of sex, color, and class, and the price she paid for the boldness of her actions.

An evaluation of Shadd Cary's career as a publisher and editor trans-
forms the traditional conceptual framework of nineteenth-century journalism as a white male-centered enterprise where women and persons of
color existed only at the margins. James Carey has suggested that the black
press is more than "a source of data about Black social history," but rather
a means for understanding the cultural milieu of the African American experience. The black press emerged at a particular historical moment during which the partisan press was moving toward commercialization, while
the nation's political and social practices were devoted to denying freedom of expression to people of color. The nineteenth-century black press
played a crucial role in community building, and was an influential forum
for the assertion and dissemination of African Americans' ideas. Shadd
Cary's paper, the *Provincial Freeman,* was one of the longest-operating independent black newspapers of the antebellum period, and was instrumental
in the community debates over abolition and emigration. Shadd Cary's
efforts to keep the newspaper going reveal the tenuous nature of nineteenth-century African American economic institutions, and the barriers
to the articulation of African American political ideas. The *Provincial
Freeman* has been an important resource in the study of African American
history, but Shadd Cary's significance as the driving force behind the paper has been obscured.[2]

The life of this public figure can also be defined, in large part, by her
participation in African American political movements before and after
the Civil War. Yet, it is difficult to place Mary Ann Shadd Cary as an historical subject; she does not fit our contemporary expectations of what a
radical abolitionist, feminist, or black nationalist should be. Shadd Cary
consistently defied the conventions and strategies of the movements in
which she was involved. From her upbringing in an activist family, and
vantage point as a teacher in embattled all-black schools, she developed a
powerful commitment to the cause of black liberation and empowerment.
But she was equally critical of the social and political practices she observed
in black communities. Shadd Cary was an early nationalist who shied away
from masculinist, Afrocentric ideologies; she forged a distinct perspective
on black American autonomy and survival that put her at odds with many
of her contemporaries. Her evolving intellectual positions paralleled the
changing circumstances of African American life— from the hopelessness
of the 1850s, to optimism following the war, and the dismantling of the
gains of Reconstruction. Shadd Cary was an activist who could deeply love
black people, while simultaneously fighting with them over the personal
and the political.

Mary Ann Shadd Cary appears prominently in what continues to be the
definitive study of early black nationalist and emigrationist movements,
and her writing has been reproduced in several documentary sourcebooks.

Recent scholarship has claimed a place for her within the small but vibrant community of nineteenth-century black women activists. But the quest to establish nineteenth-century black women's political identity has resulted in the construction of Shadd Cary as part of a collectivity—an imagined community of activists who shared common experiences of oppression and privilege as part of the black intelligentsia. It is equally important to see Shadd Cary as an activist who was not necessarily part of an established network of antebellum black women. It was not until after the Civil War that she began to participate in women's associational politics through the temperance and suffrage movements. At the end of her life she had developed an appreciation for the potential of black women's collective action, but did not live to see the club movement come to fruition.[3]

Early in her activist life, Shadd Cary became determined to have some control over the public representations of her concepts, ideas, and feelings. She understood the intersection between public discourse and political and social action, and waged a constant battle to be heard. She sought to present herself as an authoritative, learned source who had a valuable opinion about the future of her people. When strategically necessary, she also represented herself as an embattled victim, or as an innocent woman enduring attacks on her virtue. She deliberately manipulated gendered notions of propriety to gain a sympathetic audience or to inspire outrage against her foes. Some considered her a visionary, others saw her as arrogant and presumptuous. But Shadd Cary believed she was fashioning a representative identity that would enable her to have a public voice. Her peers Frederick Douglass and Martin Delany each struggled to obtain the critical authority to call themselves race leaders. Douglass was the most successful in defining himself as the nineteenth-century's representative black man. In this role, Douglass took it upon himself to anoint Shadd Cary as a representative black woman, thus complementing her own efforts at image-making. But Douglass's ambivalent Fourth of July commentary was typical of the representations of Shadd Cary constructed throughout her life. Even her most ardent supporters often expressed discomfort with her political positions and the way she expressed them. Her independence and radical positions did not fit the representative role she was expected to fulfill.[4]

The shifting gender dynamics within nineteenth-century African American communities provide another theme found throughout Shadd Cary's narrative. Several scholars have succinctly described the contradictions between black men's desire to keep women within the cult of domesticity and their encouragement of black women's political labor. The male impulse to privatize women created contradictory—and what Carla Peterson calls liminal—spaces through which female public figures like Shadd Cary had to negotiate. This cannot be reduced to a simple male/female opposition, however. Shadd Cary's closest political allies and defenders were influential men, including Douglass, Delany, William Still, and Samuel Ringgold Ward. At times she seemed to thrive on her singular status in the company of men, and she was often critical of what she considered to be black women's capitulation to the gender conventions that constrained them. We can trace her developing politics from the antebellum era, when she muted her feminist voice in favor of abolition and emigration, to Reconstruction and its aftermath, when women's rights was in the foreground of her political agenda. Throughout this ideological progression, Shadd Cary articulated for herself and for other nineteenth-century women a sense of anger at and frustration with the gender conventions of her times. Ironically, perhaps, she has not always been recognized as a paradigmatic African American feminist.[5]

Shadd Cary left her imprint on many of the decisive issues that shaped the nineteenth century: slavery and abolition, black nationalism, public education, freedom of expression, woman suffrage, and temperance. Yet, her name does not resonate with popular recognition. The folklore surrounding famous nineteenth-century black women like Harriet Tubman and Sojourner Truth originated during their lives. They were heroic, distinctive figures who captured the public imagination. These women were easy to exoticize by a white public preoccupied with their illiteracy and slave status. At the same time, they were venerated by a black public enamored of their deeds and courage. Through the generations, their names have become synonymous with crucial moments in American history.

Mary Ann Shadd Cary, on the other hand, does not easily fit the mythologies that would have facilitated her place in historical memory. She and her contemporaries, Frances Ellen Watkins Harper, Charlotte Forten, and Sarah Parker Remond, were freeborn, educated, and thoroughly European in their outlook and in their bearing. As Nell Painter notes, these women forced whites to "reevaluate their stereotypes about black women" because they lacked the "otherness" that made a figure like Truth such a resilient folk hero. Shadd Cary was a trailblazer and a pioneer in many pursuits, but these activities tended to be outside the realm of folklore construction—hers is less a tale of bravery or cunning, and more a narrative of tenacity, political acumen, and striving for social change under difficult circumstances. There is little room in the pantheon of heroes for a black woman who simultaneously fought for—and with—her people.[6]

Shadd Cary is a lesser known figure for other reasons, as well. A large contingent of the Shadd clan emigrated to Canada in Mary Ann's footsteps, and remained there after she returned to the United States. Many of her descendants—particularly those interested in celebrating their family tree—have done so from an Afro-Canadian perspective. Nevertheless, Shadd Cary was more fortunate than most nineteenth-century black Americans, whose stories have been lost. As a journalist, lawyer, and activist she left behind a collection of writing that provides a window on her life, her political ideas, and the world around her. Few nineteenth-century African American women produced a written record that has survived the passage of time. This lack of documentary sources has been a key obstacle in the writing of black women's history. Only a handful of well-known figures, like Ida Wells-Barnett and Elizabeth Keckley, managed to produce diaries or autobiographies that have survived to the present. In Shadd Cary's case, the gaps in the historical record make it difficult to develop a full profile of her life, but what exists is a rich resource for expanding our knowledge of the nineteenth- century black experience.[7]

Shadd Cary's story offers glimpses into the everyday lives of the northern black elite. The Shadd family, like most of their counterparts, existed in a quasi-free status in which they enjoyed considerable privileges compared with the majority of black Americans. But, as Ira Berlin has noted, they were a despised class who "straddled one of hell's elusive boundaries." Shadd Cary's existence was shaped by discrimination and injustice, a constant struggle against poverty, and intergroup discord. At the same time she enjoyed the rare opportunities to obtain an education, practice several professions, travel extensively, engage in politics, and make independent choices about how to live her life. Both intentionally and unwittingly, her public work exemplified the crises within this aggrieved community, including the divisions between freeborn and former slave, radical nationalist and integrationist, light-skinned and dark, male and female. Her speeches and articles criticized what she saw as the "complexional character" of black American social and political structures, and she fought tirelessly for racial unity and self-sufficiency. Yet, her own actions were at times divisive. Shadd Cary was also among a minority of black activists who openly criticized the racism and paternalism manifest by many white abolitionists and reformers. Despite a growing body of literature, we still know far too little about the northern black experience both before and after the Civil War. Much of this scholarship places male figures like Douglass and Martin Delany at the center. This project seeks to explore this world through the eyes of a decidedly independent woman.[8]

This does not mean that Shadd Cary has been entirely ignored. In the last twenty years several essays and articles on her life have been published in textbooks, encyclopedias, and anthologies. Students of African American and women's history have long acknowledged her importance. We can trace interest in Shadd Cary to several references in women's history texts that sought to identify significant black pioneers. Her image graces the pages of black history month calendars, posters celebrating "great black foremothers," and even a card game of "great women." Recently, her spirit is evoked as a minor character in a novel about another of her contemporaries, Mary Ellen Pleasant.[9]

Some of the contemporary discussion about Shadd Cary originated with a biographical essay written by her daughter, Sarah Cary Evans, in 1926. At the time of publication, Evans was in her seventies, disabled, and hoping to resurrect the story of her mother's accomplishments. As interest in black history surged in the 1970s, the anthology containing Evans's sketch, *Homespun Heroines,* was reissued. In 1988, Oxford University Press included the book in its landmark series on African American women, marking it as an important historical and cultural document, if not an authoritative source. Although many of Evans's recollections are not supported by the historical record, her essay has become a primary source for many interested in Shadd Cary's life.[10]

Scholarly attention to Shadd Cary first emerged out of interest in the Afro-Canadian experience. In 1959 a historian writing about antislavery in Canada stumbled across copies of the *Provincial Freeman* in the library of the University of Pennsylvania. By the 1970s, the *Freeman* had become an important resource for studies of blacks in Canada. As interest in African American and U.S. women's history grew during this period, Shadd Cary became the focus of several brief biographical accounts. Each tended to promote a singular component of her life. One historian proclaimed her "one of the most distinguished Negroes ever born in Delaware," while others celebrated her status as the "first black woman newspaper editor." There was growing recognition by many investigators that she played a significant and varied role in nineteenth-century social movements. But most attention to her broader historical significance was relegated to a few sentences or a footnote. Previous scholars interested in Shadd Cary's life have often been stymied by uneven documentary evidence. Those interested in this story are indebted to the work of Linda Jean Butler and Jim Bearden, who published a slim volume, *Shadd: The Life and Times of Mary Shadd Cary,* in 1977. This book is displayed and sold in black history museums and book-stores throughout Western Ontario, but it is difficult to find in the United States. These two Canadian writers excavated many of the archival materials scattered in the United States and Canada, and synthesized these fragments into a whole.[11]

Much of the primary resources for the present study are derived from Shadd Cary's writing during her Canada years when she published the *Provincial Freeman,* produced pamphlets, broadsides, and speeches, and carried on an extensive correspondence with the American Missionary Association. Shadd Cary's published and unpublished writing during the pre- and post- Canadian periods are incomplete and scattered through several archival collections. Consequently, the pictures that emerge through these sources are often the products of her own self- representations; we know far less about what others thought of her in public and private. In the end, Shadd Cary got her fervent wish to at least partially control her public image. Parts of the story of this early black feminist must be unraveled through the men around her. Besides her own writing, important sources are the texts produced by Douglass, William Still, Henry Bibb, and others. There are no comparable resources from her female contemporaries. Shadd Cary and Frances Ellen Watkins Harper, for example, may have corresponded over the years, but nothing pertaining to this relationship exists in Shadd Cary's papers, and there are virtually no manuscript sources for Watkins Harper. Thus, the assumption of a relationship between the two is purely speculative. In general, there is very little to tell us about the women in her life, particularly her family members. The female bonds and relations of this outspoken woman will always remain a mystery.[12]

I felt the presence of Shadd Cary's legacy on a hot July day, 135 years after Frederick Douglass's proclamation, in the small, dusty town of North Buxton in southern Ontario. This farming community has changed little since its days as a settlement for antebellum African American refugees. Clusters of tidy houses are separated by single-lane roads and railroad tracks. At the end of a quiet street are the boarded-up remains of the Shadd general store—once a symbol of her family's prominence. Residential mailboxes along the streets bear the Shadd name, as well as those of their descendants by marriage— Shreve, Robbins, and Williamson. In the center of town stands the Raleigh Township Centennial Museum where the few photographs, documents, and artifacts from the Shadd clan have been carefully preserved. Pamphlets, guides, genealogies, and local histories proudly tell the story of Mary Ann Shadd Cary as a pioneer who embodied the best attributes of the Afro-Canadian character—ambition, bravery, stamina, and intellect. To anyone who follows the trail from her former residences in Windsor, Chatham, and Buxton to libraries and archives in London, Ottawa, and Toronto, it is readily apparent that Shadd Cary is revered and remembered by Afro-Canadians intent on reclaiming their past.

In the last fifteen years, Mary Ann Shadd Cary has been assigned folk hero status in Ontario. Her work as founder and editor of the *Provincial Freeman,* and as a feminist, educator, and reformer, has been celebrated through the efforts of local historians and her descendants. In 1987, for example, the city of Toronto dedicated a new public school in her name. Writings about her work are prominently displayed in women's bookstores, and avidly discussed in history classes. Shadd Cary's articles and essays have been reproduced in assorted anthologies, and there is even a song in her honor written by Toronto-born folksinger Faith Nolan.[13]

It remains to be seen whether Mary Ann Shadd Cary will receive as much attention in the United States. The story of her life and the world in which she lived reminds us of the halting progress this nation has made to rectify the prejudice and discrimination rooted in its history. At the same time, it reveals how far there is to go. Many of the questions about rights and freedom that she raised more than a century ago are still contested issues. In an 1856 editorial in the *Provincial Freeman,* she challenged the opponents of black emigration to take stock of the nation they refused to abandon. Her words, deemed radical in her day, ring eerily true for the present:

> Cease to uphold the United States government, if it will, and while it does uphold human slavery. Cease to grapple after the shadow while you disregard the substance. "Come out from" a government that begins its depredations upon the rights of colored men, and ends by destroying the liberties of white men: if they will not regard the members of the household, think you they will listen to you?

Several generations in the future, black feminist author Audre Lorde echoed Shadd Cary's sentiments when she proclaimed, "the master's tools will never dismantle the master's house." The ensuing chapters are intended to bring into sharp focus the multiplicity of this once-forgotten life.[14]

MARY ANN SHADD CARY

ONE

The Making of an Activist

Mary Ann Shadd was part of a remarkable family of free-born African Americans who devoted their lives to the fight against racism and inequality in North America. In the years before the Civil War they were active in the movements to end slavery, to promote racial improvement and social reform, and to encourage black emigration from the United States. During and after Reconstruction the Shadds became professionals and public officials, and their descendants would be counted among the black elite in the United States and Canada. Mary Ann grew up against the backdrop of slavery and racial oppression in America and was exposed to the political, social, and intellectual upheaval that shaped the antebellum years. This would prove to be a fertile training ground for the future activist, journalist, educator, and attorney.

Mary Ann Shadd's ancestry provides a narrative of American racial history that can be traced to the founding of the nation. It is a story of the early meeting of black and white—European and African—and the accidents of war. The results were a family line of mixed racial heritage that would contradict the ideologies of racial purity that were the underpinning of legally sanctioned segregation and discrimination. At the dawn of the twentieth century, Mary Ann's descendants understood the significance of this past and began the difficult job of unraveling their heritage. They relied on oral history, genealogical research, and inscriptions in the family Bible of Mary Ann's grandfather, Jeremiah Schad, to discover their roots. There are significant gaps in the historical record, however, which makes it particularly difficult to piece together any details of the Shadds' family life.

Mary Ann's great-grandfather, Hans Schad, was born in Hessen-Kassel, Germany in 1725. The men of this German principality had a special reputation as warriors; one traveler described the Hessian men as stout, strongly built, hardy, and mentally adapted for life as soldiers. By the seventeenth century the Hessians were routinely used as Europe's mercenaries. These soldiers, volunteered by their sovereigns who were paid a subsidy for their services, were favorites of the British and played an influential role in Britain's efforts to control its colonial subjects. Hans Schad was recruited for such duty, and he traveled to the American colonies and joined General Braddock's army in 1755 in the prelude to the Seven Years' War. Schad was among the nearly 5,000 Germans who either deserted or resigned from the British army and settled in the United States. During a deadly attack on Braddock's troops, Hans Schad was injured "in a place called Chads Ford, about thirty miles from Philadelphia and about five miles above the Delaware line." The wounded soldier was left in the care of two free black women who lived nearby, Elizabeth Jackson and her daughter Elizabeth. One of Mary Ann's descendants remembered family descriptions of the younger Elizabeth Jackson as Abyssinian, which she interpreted as "colored." According to family lore, young Elizabeth tenderly nursed Schad back to health and they married in January 1756.[1]

The marriage of Hans and Elizabeth may have occurred out of necessity as well as affection, for their first child, Hans Jr., was born six months later. Thus, a German soldier became the patriarch of a family of people of color. Hans Schad's descendants would be categorized as colored or mulatto in a social order that denied whiteness to anyone with African blood. For a time the Schads lived in Pennsylvania, and in November 1758 their union produced another son, Mary Ann's grandfather, Jeremiah. In the 1770s Hans moved his family across the state line to Mill Creek Hundred, in New Castle County, Delaware, and he worked as a butcher in Wilmington. This move established Delaware, a slave state at the boundary that separated North from South, as the Schads' ancestral home. Delaware was settled by Dutch and Swedes in the 1620s, and Jeremiah grew up amid the throes of the American Revolution. The state's black population grew in the eighteenth century through immigration from Maryland, as well as the slave trade. In the first census of 1790, people of color were twenty-five percent of the state's population. An influx of Quakers into the state helped establish a small but influential antislavery movement during the Revolutionary period. Their influence was sufficient to support a clause in the Delaware constitution, passed in 1776, forbidding the importation of slaves. The politics of race had an undeniable impact on the social and economic contours of the state, and on the lives of the Schad family.[2]

Mary Ann's female ancestors were at least as enterprising as their male counterparts, and their legacy was the stuff of legends. While Hans Schad ran his butchering business, Elizabeth Jackson Schad operated a tea shop in Wilmington in a choice location overlooking the Delaware River. One of the few memoirs written during the period singled out Elizabeth—known locally as Betty Jackson—as a consummate businesswoman and an influential figure. "As the queen of her class, she knew how to rule, and her subordinates were submissive and attentive," remembered a local author. Betty's shop was "celebrated for its nice refreshments, where everything was the best of its kind," and she hosted tea parties and attracted business from miles around. While people of color seemed to be segregated from their white neighbors in some social circumstances, the Schads had no difficulty attracting a white clientele. The memoir noted that "Betty died in old age, much respected, leaving valuable property," but no date of death has been established for Hans or Elizabeth. Hans Schad's name appeared on New Castle County tax lists until 1798.[3]

Mary Ann's grandfather, Jeremiah Schad, continued his father's trade as a butcher in Wilmington, and married twice during his life in Delaware. Local histories indicate Jeremiah was one of the city's principal butchers who built a solid reputation for his cured meats, and was generally well-respected as a businessman. The assorted family genealogies offer conflicting accounts of his two wives, both named Amelia. According to public records, Jeremiah married Amelia Siscoe in 1785, and during the next twenty years they raised twelve children in the family homestead in Mill Creek Hundred. One of these offspring was Abraham Doras Schad, Mary Ann's father, who was born in 1801. Jeremiah began another business as a shoemaker in about 1805. When the first Amelia died in February 1806, Jeremiah wed again and his union with the second Amelia produced three more children.[4]

Some descendants have claimed Amelia Siscoe was Jeremiah's first wife, while some have claimed she was his second. Regardless, Mary Ann Shadd's grandmother—or step-grandmother—reportedly emigrated from Santo Domingo. Amelia Siscoe Schad was apparently a colorful and enterprising businesswoman, much like Elizabeth "Betty" Jackson Schad. Amelia Siscoe became known in Wilmington as "old Mother Shadd" and was described as nearly white and "very Frenchy and polite." If she fled Santo Domingo following the slave revolts of the 1790s, as claimed by the family history, she was very likely part of a privileged, light-skinned, free caste that emigrated to the United States. A large number of this French-speaking group of mulattos settled in the lower South and were quickly elevated to high status within the larger community of free blacks. One informant told a Shadd descendant that Amelia did her own butchering—perhaps having taken over Jeremiah's butcher shop—and sold her sausages, along with coffee and cakes, at a stand in the city's Second Street Market House. Her business was so prosperous that she reportedly bailed out Jeremiah when he was about to lose some property. "Everybody liked her and the money fairly rolled into her place of business."[5]

Jeremiah Schad and Amelia Siscoe Schad maintained and broadened the economic foothold established by the earlier generation of Schads. Jeremiah's status as a free person of color, with a trade and property, enabled him to prosper and leave a financial legacy to the next generation. He was among a tiny group of free blacks in the upper South who accumulated some measure of wealth in the late eighteenth century, and he fit the standard profile: a person of mixed racial origin who was the child or grandchild of whites. When Jeremiah died in 1819 at the age of 61, he left an estate valued at more than $1,300, which included a store and a house. It took four years to settle the estate, which was ordered by the Orphans Court presumably to provide for the five younger Schad children who would have ranged in age from 3 to 16 at the time of his death. The inventory of the estate included luxury items such as silverware, wine glasses and a decanter, china, an eight-day clock, and carpeting, as well as a considerable amount of furniture, tools, and farm implements.[6]

Abraham Shadd, aged 18 when his father died, probably inherited little of Jeremiah's actual wealth but benefited from his family's social position. By the early 1800s, the family name had gradually been Anglicized from Schad to Shad and finally to Shadd. Abraham spent his early life in Delaware, where he followed in his father's footsteps as a shoemaker and married Harriet Parnell. Harriet is a shadowy figure in Shadd family history. All that is known about her is that she was born in 1806 in North Carolina and was identified as mulatto. Between 1800 and 1840, the only Parnells listed in the North Carolina census are white, which suggests several possibilities: that Harriet was born into a slave family, that her father—or head of household—was white, or that her family were among those free people of color ignored by the census. Harriet Parnell and her family may have lived in North Carolina only briefly, migrating to Delaware sometime in the early nineteenth century. Harriet was seventeen years old when she bore her first child, Mary Ann; thus she wed Abraham at a young age. Abraham Shadd owned property and ran a shoemaking business in Wilmington and by the late 1820s he had apprentice cordwinders—or cordwainers—placed in his charge. In the late eighteenth and early nineteenth centuries, cordwainers—artisans who produced a fitted shoe by hand—were often respected and prosperous tradesmen. During the 1820s, young Abraham Shadd had continued the life of relative stability and social mobility begun by his ancestors.[7]

The first of Harriet and Abraham's thirteen children, Mary Ann Camberton Shadd, was born October 9, 1823. Like her parents and grandparents, Mary Ann would reap the benefits of a mixed ancestry that offered certain privileges—they were mulatto, they were free born, they worked in skilled trades, and they owned property. The Shadds escaped the worst of slavery while living in a slave state, and benefited from a color-conscious social system in which light-skinned blacks had more status, wealth, and power than their dark-skinned relatives. Hans Schad's descendants followed a common pattern in this respect; Jeremiah and Abraham Shadd married mulatto women, thereby perpetuating the family's color position. Several studies have borne out the assumption that mulattos in the antebellum North and South were more highly skilled than darker-skinned free blacks, leading them to have greater occupational advantages, be more likely to own and sustain businesses, and to attain at least a rudimentary education. It was from the ranks of this privileged group of free people of color that many of the leaders of the abolitionist movement arose. This would be the case for Hans Schad's descendants, who devoted their lives to the cause of African American liberation at the same time that they enjoyed a degree of economic independence and personal autonomy denied to most of their black brethren. The Shadds had a range of choices in constructing their racial identity—some may have been able to pass as white while others could surely set themselves apart as an elite caste. At least in the case of Abraham Shadd's family, there was a conscious decision to claim an identity as persons of color, and to cast their lot with the darker members of the race.[8]

Despite these advantages, the region of Mary Ann Shadd's birth neither shielded her from the horrors of slavery nor protected her from racial oppression. Indeed, the Shadds were in a position to be radicalized by the experiences of segregation and discrimination, yet not be crippled by them. The number of free people of color in the United States increased dramatically between the Revolutionary War and the beginning of the nineteenth century, so that by 1810 they constituted nearly nine percent of the black population in the South. This social group was caught between the rigid boundaries of the slave's bondage and the white man's absolute freedom. The rise in the free black population was due primarily to the manumission of slaves following the American Revolution, an increase in runaway slaves, and an influx of West Indian people of color like Amelia Siscoe Schad. Less is known about those free persons of color born in the United States who had no slave heritage, but they were clearly a class apart from black Americans both emancipated and slave.[9]

In late eighteenth-century Delaware, large numbers of slave owners, particularly Quakers, found the institution obnoxious and began emancipating their slaves so that by 1850 only eleven percent of the state's black population were in bondage. The federal census did not begin differentiating between black and mulatto until 1850 so we can only speculate on color distinctions in early nineteenth-century Delaware. The number of free blacks in the state leaped from nearly 4,000 to 13,000 in a thirty-year period. By 1810, 76 percent of Delaware's African Americans were free, making them the fastest growing segment of the population. The declining number of slaves, combined with state laws prohibiting the exportation of slaves and against the holding of slave auctions, contributed to the crippling of slavery in the state. In Mill Creek Hundred, where the Shadds made their home, there were 83 free persons of color and 82 slaves counted in 1800; just ten years later the proportions had changed significantly to 426 free persons and 174 slaves.[10]

Delaware's system of slavery did not resemble the flourishing institution of the lower South. Slaves were present in the colony as early as 1639, and were crucial to the cultivation and production of tobacco. Grain crops eventually replaced tobacco, and the need for slave labor diminished as the state's geography and short growing season limited the development of plantation agriculture. Thus, most Delaware farmers owned small numbers of slaves. It has been argued that Delaware's form of slavery was unique among states in the upper South: "Individually, the members of that population bore the status of slaves, but collectively they were simply an alternate source of labor within a system of which slavery was not the organizing principle," notes Barbara J. Fields.[11]

In the years of Mary Ann Shadd's childhood—the 1820s and 1830s—slavery remained a protected legal entity in Delaware, but the majority of African Americans in the state had some degree of control over their lives and labor. This, however, did not translate into the kinds of opportunities for free blacks that were possible in the North. Delaware's free people of color were increasingly thwarted by repressive black codes introduced in the early 1830s, despite their best efforts to become economically self-sufficient and to establish community institutions, including schools, churches, and organizations. These laws, implemented out of fears of slave insurrection, stripped free blacks in the South of most constitutional protections. The Shadds may have enjoyed considerable financial success in Delaware, but they also had to confront "an extensive and moral FEAR of the free colored people pervading the community," as described by William Yates, a black minister representing the American Anti-Slavery Society, in 1837.[12]

Delaware's state constitution had given blacks the right to vote subject to the same property requirements as whites, but this provision was slowly stripped away by the mid-nineteenth century. The new laws prevented African Americans from holding elected or appointed office, and they could be fined or imprisoned if found within a half-mile of the polls on election day. Free blacks in Delaware and other slave states had to carry proof of their status and provide it on demand or risk being jailed or enslaved. Free black men who appeared to be idle and roving the countryside risked being captured and forced into labor. White fear of black retribution became so great that free blacks had to have a license to own firearms and faced severe penalties if found assembled in large groups, especially at night.[13]

Delaware officials were particularly concerned with halting the growth of the free black population, and in the wake of this hysteria laws were passed preventing free blacks from returning to the state if they left for more than six months. Those from other states were denied entry altogether. Employers could be fined five dollars for every day they hired a non-resident person of color. Abraham Shadd may have grappled with this law when accepting black apprentices from out-of-state. Marriage between whites and blacks or mulattos was forbidden, and those violating this law faced a stiff penalty of $100. The state's climate of repression in the 1830s would have deterred Hans and Elizabeth Schad from settling there sixty years earlier. In many respects, life for Delaware's free blacks was precarious at best. The abolitionist Yates concluded that the purpose of the state's black codes was "to degrade, to crush, and to render them ignorant and powerless. Indeed, it has been anything but human, benevolent or liberal."[14]

Delaware's community of free blacks also found themselves excluded from white churches and schools. At the end of the eighteenth century, most free persons in the state attended white-dominated churches, particularly Methodist. As their numbers increased, free blacks found themselves barred from white churches and discriminated against in mixed churches. The establishment of independent black churches occurred in the North, with the formation of the African Methodist Episcopal Church in 1787 in Philadelphia by Richard Allen, who had been born a slave in Kent County, Delaware. But as late as the 1830s, many blacks in Delaware still attended white churches. Jeremiah and Amelia Siscoe were married in Wilmington's Old Swedes Church, founded in 1698.[15]

The first black church in Delaware was Ezion Methodist Episcopal Church, founded in Wilmington in 1805. The congregation later split, and the African Union Methodist Episcopal Church was formed in 1813. African Union was the first black-controlled incorporated body in the state, and it provided social and cultural outlets for the free black community. It sponsored an annual homecoming on the last Sunday of August, the "Big August Quarterly," which blended religious services and street fairs, and has been identified as Wilmington's oldest folk festival. Its leader, Reverend Peter Spencer, was considered an influential figure who presided over twenty-one churches. One writer of the period called Spencer "an exemplary colored man" whose "tact to govern was wonderful, and his influence unbounded." The mother church boasted 175 members and four hundred "hearers" during the early nineteenth century.[16]

The free black community's success in establishing independent religious institutions was not replicated in their quest for education. The handful of integrated schools scattered throughout the South languished by the end of the eighteenth century, and blacks were generally excluded from all-white schools. The commitment to educate free blacks was strongest among Quakers, who, at the American Convention of Abolition Societies meeting in 1794, called for the creation of schools for former slaves. But the African Schools, as they were named, struggled for survival with limited funds and constant opposition from most whites. An African School begun by the Delaware Abolition Society in 1798 offered instruction in reading, writing, and arithmetic one day a week, provided by a Quaker volunteer. The school served about twenty students, and by 1802 plans were made to raise funds and expand. Seven years later, however, the school still remained open only one day a week. By 1816, an African School Society was formed with the purpose of running a school in Wilmington. A black teacher was secured to begin regular daily instruction, and there was a small library. Opportunities for free blacks in Delaware to obtain an education apparently changed little in the next twenty years. In the 1830s, the African School remained the only year-round school for free blacks in the state, supplemented by a handful of church-run Sabbath schools that operated irregularly. By 1837, Reverend Yates wrote in his report on black life in the region that "the free people of color in Delaware are in a most dreadful state of destitution in regard to schools."[17]

Abraham Shadd lacked formal schooling since he was fifteen by the time Delaware's African School was functioning regularly. This likely fueled his determination to educate his children, who should have been able to attend the African School in Wilmington, which continued to operate throughout the 1820s and 1830s. Yet, biographical sketches of Mary Ann Shadd insist there were no schools for her to attend in Delaware, a fact that allegedly propelled the Shadds to move to Pennsylvania. In 1926 her daughter, Sarah Cary Evans, wrote: "She was deprived of obtaining the education of which her early development gave promise." Mary Ann's gender was the crucial factor in this lack of opportunity. In the 1840s, the African School Society petitioned the state legislature for funding, and reported that it only had sufficient funds for a boys' school. A Female African School—operating as a subsidiary of the main school for black youth—failed in the 1830s and did not reopen until 1847. Meanwhile the political backlash against free blacks was intensified in 1831, when public education was established in the state with a caveat expressly forbidding the admission of black students. When the Shadds moved North in 1833, Mary Ann was ten years old, and she had three sisters, ranging in age from two to seven, and a brother Isaac, age four. From the beginning, Abraham and Harriet Shadd demonstrated a commitment to educate their daughters, as well as their sons. The difficulty was in finding a school they could attend.[18]

While Mary Ann may have lacked formal schooling during her childhood in Wilmington, she received an education of another kind at home. The emergence of the American Colonization Society in Delaware propelled her father, Abraham, into the maelstrom of abolitionist politics. The American Colonization Society was founded in 1816 by an odd coalition of northern abolitionists and southern politicians who believed that the United States would never be hospitable to the growing population of free blacks. Abolitionists in the society rationalized that the relocation of free blacks would eventually lead to the end of slavery, while offering them the opportunity to govern themselves and "ameliorate the condition of the African race." Southern colonizationists, led by Kentucky slave owner Henry Clay, assumed that slavery would be preserved once free blacks were repatriated to Africa. By 1830 the society had settled some 1,400 persons in the American colony of Liberia, established in 1822. The society's efforts to reduce the free black population through its "back to Africa" scheme was met with immediate and widespread condemnation by African Americans and white abolitionists. Starting in 1817, conventions of free blacks and former slaves met in Philadelphia and other northern cities to protest efforts to send them into exile. The response to colonization marked the beginnings of an organized black abolitionist movement in America.[19]

By 1824, the American Colonization Society sought to build support in the states of the upper South by establishing auxiliary groups. One of the largest was the Union Colonization Society of Wilmington, formed in 1824 when Mary Ann was a year old. A female auxiliary society was founded in Wilmington at the same time. The Delaware colonizationists, many who were neighbors and business associates of the Shadds, blended abolitionist rhetoric with anti-black sentiment when they declared that the slave population "deprecates our soil, lessens our agricultural revenue, and like the lean kine of Egypt, eats up the fat of the land," at their first annual meeting in 1825. The Wilmington Society sent a representative to the national organization's annual meeting that year, and reported contributions of fifty dollars in its first few months. Colonization fever had caught on in Delaware, despite the state's small number of slaves. The free black population was the obvious target of this agenda.[20]

A goal of the colonization auxiliaries was to gain state government support for their ventures, after objections by some southern states squelched the possibility of federal aid. In February 1827, the General Assembly of Delaware adopted a resolution presented by the Wilmington Union Colonization Society which endorsed the efforts toward guaranteeing whites' safety through the "removal from this country of the free negroes and free mulattos." The colonization project was lauded as "one of the grandest schemes of philanthropy" that would enable "the redemption of an ignorant and much injured race of men." The petitioners' paternalism did not mask their racial animosity, as they argued that the freedmen posed a grave threat to the social order: "Our manners are and must be unfavorable to them as our laws. We will not permit them to associate with us. We will not tolerate any notion of equality with them." In Mary Ann's early years, the state where the Shadd family had grown and thrived was rapidly becoming hostile to their presence. Free people of color had become the enemy.[21]

Three years later, Abraham Shadd publicly lent his voice to the mounting opposition against such sentiments. On September 20, 1830, about thirty African Americans met in Bethel Church, Philadelphia, for a five-day national convention to "devise ways and means for the bettering of our condition." Shadd was among the representatives from seven states, who were later identified as "the most intelligent and leading spirits among colored men in the United States." The delegates composed an address that called for immediate action to combat the legal and social oppression experienced by free blacks. They voted against emigration to Liberia as proposed by the American Colonization Society, and they discussed the possibility of black emigration to Canada as an alternative.[22]

This national convention was prompted by a crisis in Ohio that propelled a group of free blacks to find refuge in Canada. In 1830 mob violence and the institution of rigid black codes in Ohio culminated in the exodus of nearly 2,000 blacks from Cincinnati to land in Upper Canada. The convention delegates debated the merits of a black exodus to Canada and concluded that the formation of black settlements in the British province was a legitimate alternative to the struggles endured by African Americans in the northern states. Canada had four distinct advantages: the absence of slavery and full enfranchisement of black citizens; familiar language, climate and culture; cheap land; and the promise of financial success for farmers there. Canada was idealized as "a land where the laws and prejudices of society will have no effect in retarding their [blacks'] advancement to the summit of civil and religious improvement."[23]

Abraham Shadd was an active participant in the early public discourse on black emigration to Canada. It is conceivable that young Mary Ann was imprinted with ideas of Canada as she overheard discussions among her parents and visitors in their home. The free black conventions that were held on and off for the next thirty years would be preoccupied with the question of emigration, whether to Liberia through the American Colonization Society or to Canada, the West Indies, and other African destinations through independent projects. Emigration would shape the lives of Abraham Shadd and his children for generations.

During the summer of 1831, the thirty-year-old Shadd was once again representing Delaware's free blacks at a national meeting. The First Annual Convention of Free Persons of Colour assembled on June 6, 1831, at Philadelphia's Wesleyan Church on Lombard Street. It was a modest assem-

Abraham Doras Shadd, father of Mary Ann Shadd Cary, entrepreneur and influential black abolitionist, migrated to Canada West where he became one of that nation's first black public officials. (Raleigh Township Centennial Museum)

bly of fifteen persons, and Abraham Shadd rose to a leadership position when he was elected vice president of the convention. On this occasion, barely a word was spoken about emigration to Canada. Several of the established black leaders, including Shadd, expressed skepticism about emigration as a strategy for black survival. Instead, the convention focused on blacks' need for education, and most of the discussion involved plans for establishing a manual labor college for free blacks in New Haven, Connecticut. The organization of the convention movement became solidified, and Philadelphia was identified as the power base for future meetings. At the convention's end, Abraham Shadd was appointed vice president for fund raising in Delaware.[24]

A month later, the threat of colonization became more than an abstract concern to the Shadds when the Wilmington Colonization Union set its sights on recruiting Delaware blacks to emigrate to Liberia. The Union invited free blacks to attend a meeting in Wilmington, where they were solicited by several white clergy and abolitionists with "flattering accounts" of life in West Africa. The colonizationists were met with swift opposition. In July 1831, Rev. Peter Spencer convened a large gathering at Wilmington's African Union Church. They proclaimed the colonization efforts to be "inimical to the best interests of the people of color," and they disavowed any connection with Africa. Abraham Shadd was one of four speakers to address the crowd, and he, along with Spencer, and William Thomas, a former African School teacher, were elected to put the meeting's position into a written declaration for publication. Their statement, published on the front page of the *Liberator*, argued that colonization was a violation of black Americans' constitutional rights and that the agents of colonization attempted to lure participants under a guise of humanitarianism. "We are constrained to believe that the welfare of the people of color, to say the least, is but a secondary consideration with those engaged in the colonization project," they wrote. Shadd and his colleagues also made a powerful plea for African American citizenship when they proclaimed: "We are natives of the United States . . . we have our attachments to the soil, and we feel that we have rights in common with other Americans."[25]

Abraham Shadd played an important role in shaping the abolitionist rhetoric in opposition to colonization. William Lloyd Garrison, among other antislavery activists, used free blacks' expressions of *amor patriae*—love of the land—to support their claims of basic rights to American soil. When Garrison published his *Thoughts on African Colonization* in 1832, he included the address written by Shadd, Spencer, and Thomas as a prime example of this platform. The Shadds' home became a locus for Wilmington's black abolitionist activities as Abraham grew more active in the fight against colonization and in the burgeoning black convention movement. During this period Shadd also became a subscription agent for *The Liberator*, which relied heavily on black support in its early days.[26]

Emigration to Canada stimulated a lively debate at the 1832 convention in Philadelphia, when a proposal was introduced to purchase land in British North America for black American settlers. While some participants manifested a keen interest in emigration, Shadd and others took a more conservative approach, warning that support of Canadian emigration might be interpreted by their enemies as a sign that blacks were relinquishing their claim on the United States as their homeland. A committee on the "Canadian question," supported by Shadd, offered a compromise by suggesting that an agent or society in Canada further investigate the matter, while the convention concentrated on matters closer to home. By 1833, when Shadd was elected president of the Third Annual Convention for the Improvement of the Free People of Colour, there was little discussion of Canada as a safe haven. Although Shadd encouraged the discussion of Canadian emigration at the meeting, the idea was squelched by the convention's majority, who feared that emigration of any sort—whether voluntarily to Canada or involuntarily to Liberia—played into the hands of the colonizationists' agenda.[27]

Shadd's ambivalent stance on Canada reflected a developing ideology among some free black activists, who equated emigration with abandoning the larger cause of abolition. The early black conventions were dominated by the belief "that the slave must be free before the Negro could use his God-given initiative in bettering his condition—by emigration if he saw fit." Twenty years after the convention, Martin Delany, who would become a leader of the black emigration movement of the 1850s, noted that this more conservative position became accepted among free blacks and that individuals could not publicly express support of emigration "without risk of being termed a 'traitor' to the cause of his people, or an enemy to the Anti Slavery cause." Support for Canadian emigration was suppressed within the larger black abolitionist movement, but the idea took hold among many, including the Shadd family.[28]

Delaware's oppressive environment became too much for Abraham and Harriet Shadd, and sometime in 1833 they moved north to relocate their family in West Chester, Pennsylvania, fifteen miles south of Philadelphia. The Shadds settled at the Mason-Dixon line near the border between Pennsylvania and Maryland, keeping them in proximity to friends and family in Delaware while gaining access to the quasi-freedom of the North. Census data suggest that members of the extended Shadd family moved to this location, as well. West Chester was a community of farms and mills, where Quakers had a strong presence and where many residents were active in the Pennsylvania Society for Promoting the Abolition of Slavery. The Shadds hoped their new home town would prove more hospitable than the last.[29]

Mary Ann was ten years old when they moved, and family lore has attributed the Shadds' northward migration to the paucity of schools for black children in Wilmington. Another impetus for their relocation may have been the increasing severity of Delaware's black codes, which could have threatened the family's safety and well being as Abraham became a visible abolitionist leader. Abraham's frequent trips to Philadelphia acquainted him with the advantages of the northern city's thriving free black community. As a resident of a free state he could do more for the antislavery cause. Abraham may have been at least partially motivated by ambition. The free black elite of Philadelphia held a firm grip on the convention movement, and he sought to be part of this inner circle rather than a participant from afar.

By the time the Third Annual Convention for the Improvement of the Free People of Colour was convened in Philadelphia in 1833, Abraham Shadd was a delegate from West Chester, Pennsylvania. Having paid his dues at earlier meetings, Shadd was elected president of the convention, a largely ceremonial role but one that gave him stature and authority. In his convention address Shadd quickly put the Canadian question to rest when he declared that the "unequivocally expressed sentiments" of free blacks were against emigration unless it was voluntary. Rather, black Americans should focus their attention on racial improvement through education and temperance. Shadd revealed his Garrisonian leanings when he called for an immediate end to slavery through an appeal that focused on the immorality of the institution, or moral suasion. At least publicly, Abraham Shadd's rhetoric was moving away from a preoccupation with colonization and emigration, and toward solidifying a black abolitionist ideology.[30]

Shadd was recognized within the ranks of national abolitionists when, in December 1833, Garrison and his followers met in Philadelphia to form the American Anti-Slavery Society. On the final day of the meeting, the sixty-three delegates ratified a Declaration of Sentiments and named a board of managers for the society; among the six African Americans named to this important body was Mary Ann's father. Shadd would attend subsequent meetings of the American Anti-Slavery Society in 1835 and 1836, contributing to the development of a biracial abolitionist movement. But in other arenas, Shadd's influence lessened. He attended the 1834 black convention in New York as a delegate from West Chester, but his role was minimal. Perhaps Shadd's connection with Philadelphia's free black community placed him at a disadvantage as activists from New York and New England became influential in the convention movement. Or it may simply be that he tired of these annual meetings with their predictable opposition to colonization and growing competition for power among regional cliques. Whatever the reason, Abraham Shadd did not attend the 1835 convention held in Philadelphia, and when the meetings resumed after an eight-year hiatus, a younger cadre of black abolitionists, including Frederick Douglass and Henry Highland Garnet, had taken center stage.[31]

The Shadds also actively participated in the dangerous and often heart-wrenching affairs of the Underground Railroad. In her early years Mary Ann likely witnessed the harboring of fugitive slaves, and learned about the role of black and white abolitionists in this shadowy practice. Family conversation and household gatherings undoubtedly included some of the men and women engaged in this subversive action. Canada was more than a theoretical haven to be debated in convention sessions; it was the final destination for hundreds of blacks fleeing bondage. Delaware was ideally situated on the escape route, as a border state at the headwaters of the eastern shore of Maryland. William Still, a Philadelphia-based black abolitionist, collected the narratives of numerous fugitives who escaped the Lower South, as well as Virginia and Maryland, via Delaware. Abraham Shadd was one of a dozen blacks in Wilmington known to have assisted in the flight of escaped slaves. When the Shadds moved north, their exodus paralleled the Underground Railroad path that ran from Wilmington to Chester County. It was no coincidence that the activist Shadds settled in southern Pennsylvania, which had more Underground Railroad routes than anywhere else in the North.[32]

One nineteenth-century chronicler of West Chester noted that the town "was well known far and wide for being friendly to the slave" and for aggressively pursuing their liberation. This quality, it was believed, attracted a sizable black population so that by the end of the 1800s people of color comprised a quarter of West Chester's population. The Shadds' West Chester farm was located on a northern branch of the Underground Railroad leading out of Wilmington. They likely facilitated the passage of fugitive slaves from Delaware through a network of family and friends in their former home town. Abraham Shadd has been identified in assorted local histories as one of three West Chester blacks who assisted Quaker bookseller Samuel Painter in guiding fugitive slaves through the region. The Shadds probably played a more prominent role in Underground Railroad activities than has been acknowledged, but much of the local history written during that era minimized the role of blacks while elevating the deeds of whites to heroic stature.[33]

The Shadds settled into a comfortable, though not affluent, life in West Chester. Abraham was described by one Quaker neighbor as an intelligent and well-educated property owner. He began paying taxes in 1833 and for six years the family lived in a rented house while Abraham continued his trade as a shoemaker. By 1839 Abraham and Harriet had saved enough to purchase a small farm, and they gradually amassed more real estate, purchasing a half-dozen parcels adjacent to their land over a fifteen-year period. By 1850, the Shadds owned property valued at more than two thousand dollars. During the same period, the size of the Shadd family more than doubled—Harriet bore eight more children, bringing the total of Mary Ann's siblings to twelve. Abraham had neither the capital, education, nor profession to elevate his family to the upper classes of African American society in the North. Thus, in the words of one historian, Shadd was "fairly well off but not in a class with [William] Whipper or [Robert] Purvis," two wealthy African Americans.[34]

Mary Ann's family had moved to the outskirts of one of the North's most populous free black communities, enabling them to become part of a new world of class and social relations. Blacks migrated to Philadelphia from a wide terrain in the North and South, but the largest group were, like the Shadds, from Delaware, Maryland, and Virginia. The constant influx of blacks to the city meant that by 1840 there were more than 10,000 free blacks in Philadelphia as compared to 1,600 in Wilmington. The result was a diverse, economically stratified black community. In neighboring

West Chester, there were about 300 free black residents, comprising 13.6 percent of the town's population. Unlike Delaware, Pennsylvania had never profited significantly from slavery. The first legislation to abolish slavery in Pennsylvania—which never had more than 4,000 slaves—was passed in 1780, and the institution gradually died out by the early 1800s.[35]

A distinguishing characteristic of Philadelphia's black population was the presence of a large and firmly entrenched elite—"gentlemen and ladies of colour"—who were as separate from the majority of the city's blacks as they were from whites. This gentry boasted a long-standing tradition of education, entrepreneurship, and participation in skilled trades. They could trace their roots in the city back to the 1700s, and enjoyed national visibility as they established influential social and religious institutions. The African Methodist Episcopal Church, the Negro Convention Movement, and the American Anti-Slavery Society all had their foundation in Philadelphia. It is safe to assume that Mary Ann Shadd came of age on the fringes of this community—West Chester's close proximity to Philadelphia, and Abraham Shadd's participation within some of these institutions, allowed her access to many of the people who formed the backbone of black Philadelphia's political, cultural, and religious world.[36]

Life among the city's black elite was clearly marked by a caste system. One black resident complained in 1841 that Philadelphia's "higher classes of colored society" suffered from snobbery and an inability to muster their forces for the common good of the larger black community. At the same time, these leaders were in the forefront of campaigns for racial justice and enfranchisement. A small number of the elite were the city's richest black residents, like sail-maker James Forten, whose worth was valued at more than $100,000, or William Whipper, a lumber merchant. But most, like Abraham Shadd, were included in this network of power because of personal qualities such as intellect, ambition, and commitment to abolitionism, rather than through real power or wealth. Throughout her life, Mary Ann Shadd returned to Philadelphia often, to visit friends, engage in political activities, and seek support for her assorted ventures. She grew up in West Chester, but she considered the city her home.[37]

Antebellum Pennsylvania was not a particularly hospitable environment for free blacks, especially during the period of Mary Ann's childhood. There was considerable socioeconomic deterioration in the city's black community in the 1830s and 1840s as new European immigrants displaced blacks from semiskilled and unskilled jobs. At the same time, blacks could not vote and had no political voice, a status that would not be altered until 1870. Philadelphia's African American community also encountered the same opposition to their growing numbers that had forced the emigration of Cincinnati's blacks to Canada. Beginning in the 1820s there were numerous instances of riots and anti-black violence in the city, and increasing backlash against abolitionist activities. The year after the Shadds moved to the area, a race riot in one of the city's black enclaves ended with one death, numerous injuries, and considerable damage to churches and private homes. So while there were more tangible freedoms in Pennsylvania as compared to Delaware, there was persistent discrimination as well, even against the black elite.[38]

Education for free blacks was a benefit of living in the North, however, and the Shadd family seized the opportunity. The Quakers, African American churches, and benevolent societies offered an array of limited schooling options in the early nineteenth century. Although state law established free public education in 1818, prejudice and custom generally excluded black children. It was not until 1829 that the first black public school was built in Philadelphia, and by 1830 one-fourth of Philadelphia's 1,200 black students attended private schools with the remainder in public-supported institutions. By the end of the decade more than 1,700 black youth attended twenty-five schools in the city.[39]

Considerably less is known about the opportunities for black education in nearby West Chester. Abraham Shadd reported that one day school and one sabbath school served the small black population of his town in 1837. Black children were apparently excluded from West Chester's eleven public schools identified in the sixth census. Mary Ann's descendants have asserted that at the age of ten she was placed in a Quaker school headed by a Phoebe Darlington, where she was educated for six years. There is little evidence to substantiate this claim. In 1836, when Mary Ann was thirteen years old, Chester County paid for the schooling of her younger siblings Harriet, age eight, and Isaac, age six. We can only speculate that by the time public education was available to Mary Ann, she was too old to benefit from grade-school training. Instead, her parents paid for her private education. It is possible that Abraham offered an exchange or barter to Darlington, who was listed as a client in his business ledger. The Shadds and the Darlingtons apparently had a variety of associations; both families were said to have coordinated a West Chester branch of the Underground Railroad.[40]

Wherever Mary Ann was educated, the clear assumption is that she received a Quaker education that carried with it the connotation that it was the best training available to black youth of the time. She would have received instruction in religion and philosophy, literature, writing, basic mathematics, Latin and French, and the mechanical arts. Mary Ann was also exposed to the values of the Society of Friends, who believed in the brotherhood of man and in education as the means for moral and social uplift. Most important, the Quakers were in the forefront of the nation's antislavery movement and argued that slavery was a moral abomination and anti-Christian. At home and in school, Mary Ann was taught to take the moral high ground in questions of politics and race. She observed that the promotion of social change required active, rather than passive, adherence to one's beliefs, even if action came at a high personal cost. Her formal schooling concluded in her teens; by 1840 she had returned to Wilmington as a school teacher.[41]

While Mary Ann attended school, Abraham Shadd reassessed his involvement in the antislavery movement, shifting his activities from the conventions to a group of Garrisonian blacks who emphasized the universality of the brotherhood of man. At the Philadelphia-based convention of 1835, Shadd joined a splinter organization, the American Moral Reform Society, which formulated a more conceptual—rather than pragmatic— approach to social and political reform. Tired of the racial uplift projects that seemed to go nowhere, the Society fashioned an ideology to eliminate slavery and social ills through a call for brotherly love and equal rights. As one scholar noted, the American Moral Reform Society "set for itself goals well worth working for but almost impossible to attain." They included the abolition of slavery, an emphasis on temperance and moral uplift among free blacks, and the avoidance of color distinctions in their social and political activities. The organization used "Christian militancy" to attack churches that tolerated or supported slavery in any way, and its members urged boycotts of goods produced by slave labor. One of the group's most controversial stands was their insistence on identifying with a universal concept of mankind rather than any racial identity, which was criticized by many black activists. The American Moral Reform Society also vocally supported the ability of women to have an equal role in reform and abolition organizations. This principal would underscore much of Mary Ann Shadd's political life. Abraham attended the society's first meeting and gave a report on the state of the black population in West Chester, but it is unclear how active he was in the group, which met for four years. The leadership of the society was in the hands of Philadelphia's black elite, with Whipper, Forten, and Purvis at the helm. Although the society was short-lived, its rhetoric—especially the emphasis on avoiding "complexional distinctions"—would later resurface in the writing and activities of Abraham Shadd's daughter, Mary Ann.[42]

While her father was absorbed in these reform activities Mary Ann was graduating into adulthood, but we can only guess at how she spent these years. Her adolescence may have been centered around her large immediate family and the small community of blacks in West Chester. There were forty-nine black women and thirty-one men between the ages of ten and twenty-four in Mary Ann's home town, so there were a handful of peers with whom she could establish relationships. Her father's close association with Philadelphia's black elite may have paved the way for her to participate in that world as well. The young women of Philadelphia's black upper class studied painting, needlework, and music, were visited by young men in their circle, attended parties, and heard lectures at the literary societies. There was a range of employment possibilities for black women, as well. Some few among the elite enjoyed lives of relative leisure and did not work outside the home. Indeed, the extent to which black families could reproduce the Victorian ideals of domesticity was an indicator of their upper-class status. But the lack of steady employment for black men meant that regardless of class identification, most black women needed to work. African American women, both married and single, ran small businesses and took in boarders to add to their household income. They might also be engaged in trades, as washerwomen, day workers, seamstresses, cooks, and live-in maids. Less than two percent of the city's black working women were in professional occupations such as teacher or musician.[43]

Mary Ann Shadd was among these fortunate few, as her education enabled her to select a profession and become a teacher. While still in her teens she left her home, family, and friends to return to Delaware and open a school for black children in Wilmington. In doing so, she carried out the expectation articulated by her father and other black leaders that educated members of the race must lend their talents to uplift those less fortunate. Free black women of the antebellum era were encouraged to take an active role in antislavery and social improvement work. They formed benevolent and mutual aid societies, were leaders of the Underground Railroad, were famed lecturers and writers, and were central to the building of black institutions such as schools and churches. Mary Ann's family and environment instilled in her this sense of social responsibility and selflessness.[44]

In Wilmington, Mary Ann returned to a community of friends and extended family who desperately needed a school for their children. The young teacher may have been motivated by her own experience of being denied an education in Delaware and by her parents' urging to go home and "serve her people." While Mary Ann taught in Wilmington, Abraham Shadd was invited there to give a lecture on the anniversary of the abolition of slavery in the West Indies. These "First of August" celebrations were popular social and political events in African American communities before the Civil War. Mary Ann was not present at her father's lecture on July 30, 1840, because the gathering at the town's colored schoolhouse—perhaps her own school—was all male, according to one newspaper account. Abraham Shadd's address, which was published in the black-owned newspaper *The Colored American,* repeated the principles that he had transmitted to his daughter: "It is our imperative duty as well as interest, to use every exertion to elevate the character of the free colored population."[45]

Information about Mary Ann's activities during the 1840s is scant. It has been suggested that she stayed in Wilmington until a public school opened there. But it is more likely that groups like the Delaware Association for the Moral Improvement and Education of the Colored People eventually succeeded in expanding educational opportunities for Wilmington's blacks. One report found there were three "colored schools" in Wilmington by 1849, but by then Mary Ann Shadd had left the area.[46]

During this period Mary Ann also worked as a teacher in Norristown, Pennsylvania, and Trenton, New Jersey. Norristown was a small abolitionist enclave connected to Philadelphia along the Schuylkill River. Well-known activists like Lucretia Mott and Rev. Samuel Aaron made their homes in the town. Several fugitive slaves settled in the area, and it is possible that Mary Ann established a modest school for their children. A rare surviving bit of correspondence also located Mary Ann in Trenton in 1844. She had written her father about a constant sore throat, and complained of having trouble with "the colored population of Trenton." At the age of twenty-one she was a seasoned teacher with strong opinions, and she apparently used harsh words to describe those whom she had encountered. Abraham responded in a paternal tone of concern and suggested she quit her job and return home to convalesce. He cautioned her to resign in a quiet and judicious manner to avoid further conflict with her employers. "Thank God you yet have a home whear [*sic*] you are welcome," Abraham wrote. The bonds of affection with her family remained strong even as she had ventured far from home. But little else is known about how she spent these years, or about her teaching career.[47]

Abraham Shadd's political activism continued throughout the decade. In 1848, he participated in a meeting convened to protest Pennsylvania's laws denying blacks the right to vote. Shadd, William Whipper, Robert Purvis, and four others prepared an address that called for the state legislature to give African Americans the franchise by repealing a portion of the Pennsylvania Constitution, ratified in 1838, that specified only white males could vote. Prior to that time, state laws accorded all free men the vote, and on several occasions blacks had exercised this right. The committee also addressed a statement to Pennsylvania's black residents urging them to live up to the standards expected of voting members of society. "We should be careful to present a manly bearing by the exercise of politeness and good manners, and avoid all unnecessary display and ostentation," wrote Shadd and his colleagues. This discourse was representative of the cultural divide among free persons of color—the "respectable society" of the black elite sought to change the attitudes and behavior of lower-class blacks in the struggle to prove their fitness for citizenship. Despite their efforts, this and subsequent campaigns failed, and blacks did not vote in Pennsylvania until after the Civil War. Nevertheless, this ideology clearly influenced the thinking of Shadd's daughter, Mary Ann, who put her ideas in print for the first time the year after the Pennsylvania convention.[48]

In January 1849 Mary Ann Shadd introduced her own voice into the spirited discussion on racial uplift. She penned a long letter to Frederick Douglass in response to his request for suggestions on how to improve the "wretched conditions" for free blacks in the North. The letter, which was published in the *North Star*, articulated her views on the best course for African American liberation—opinions culled from her ten years of teaching black children in all-black schools, and influenced by her father's ideas. She was highly critical of free blacks' apparent inability to implement the programs they devised during fifteen years of convening meetings and establishing organizations. Yet she counted herself among those who had been ineffective. "We have been holding conventions for years—have been assembling together and whining over our difficulties and afflictions, passing resolutions on resolutions to any extent; but it does really seem that we have made but little progress, considering our resolves." Shadd suggested that action should take precedence over rhetoric: "We should do more, and talk less."[49]

Some of Mary Ann Shadd's solutions to the "negro problem" were consistent with mainstream black abolitionist thinking, particularly her argument that agricultural investment should be a priority if blacks were to become producers rather than consumers. If black Americans reduced their economic dependency on whites, she reasoned, "The estimation in which we would be held by those in power would be quite different." She also promoted education and interracial political organizing. "What intellectually we most need, and the absence of which we most feel, is the knowledge of the white man," she wrote. Shadd moved beyond these homilies to fire a caustic attack against the "influence of a corrupt clergy among us, sapping our every means, inculcating ignorance as a duty, superstition as true religion." She seemed especially outraged by the widespread influence of black ministers both as community leaders and as teachers. In her view, "their gross ignorance and insolent bearing, together with the sanctimonious garb, and by virtue of their calling, a character for mystery they assume, is attributable more of the downright degradation of the free colored people of the North, than from the effect of corrupt public opinion."[50]

These were strong, audacious words for an unknown black woman. Shadd's identification with the educated classes, and her labors as a teacher, led her to resent the black clergy's dominant role in schooling. This may have been the source of the discord she hinted at during her tenure in Trenton, New Jersey. But her treatise also revealed a deep skepticism about religion and its role in African American communities. The ecclesiastical teachings that encouraged blacks to think only of the afterlife enforced a doctrine of submission among a people who needed to become more assertive and self-sufficient. Blacks gripped within the trappings of black churches were "prevented from seeing clearly," she argued. Shadd stepped into even more dangerous territory by charging that black ministers were often motivated by money rather than good will, and that they had a vested interest in keeping their flocks in the dark. She did not reject Christian spirituality, but rather saw a clear demarcation between the role of the church and of the school, the latter being her terrain. During this period Shadd had apparently joined the African Methodist Episcopal church, but would later claim she left it because it was intentionally segregated. Her arguments echoed the work of Lewis Woodson, a black minister from Pittsburgh, considered by many the ideological forebear of nineteenth-century black nationalism. In the 1830s Woodson wrote a series of articles for *The Colored American* in which he criticized disunity among blacks and complained about the influence of the clergy on African American thought. Mary Ann Shadd shared his disdain.[51]

At about the same time that her letter appeared in the *North Star,* Mary Ann also published her developing theories about black self-help in a twelve-page pamphlet entitled *Hints to the Colored People of the North.* No complete copy exists, but excerpts published in the *North Star* revealed a strong-willed, confident approach in asserting her views. Her goal was to arouse her readers with a direct analysis of the condition of northern blacks, regardless of whether it might offend. She claimed the authority to speak out on the subject "as one who, by assent, if not by actual participation, has aided in this complexion of things." She proclaimed that "my destiny is that of my people" and argued that it was part of her duty to the race to "expose every weakness, to exclaim against every custom" that she believed contributed to black Americans' oppression. She denounced the "processions, expensive entertainments, excursions, public dinners and suppers, a display of costly apparel, and churches on churches, to minister to our vanity," reminding her readers that most blacks were too poor to afford such luxuries. Fundamentally, she found little usefulness in these distractions: "How does that better our condition as a people?" she asked. Shadd was particularly critical of low-brow fashion and ostentation among people of color: "Negroes and Indians set more value on the outside of their heads than on what the inside needs. They [blacks] are glad when one of their number dies, that they may walk in procession, and show their regalia." It is possible that Shadd placed these arguments in a broader context that was not entirely critical, but the *North Star* correspondent chose these comments as representative of the larger work.[52]

Mary Ann Shadd was, in these two essays, crafting an ideology of racial uplift deeply rooted in her class identity, upbringing, and political socialization. Education, moral refinement, and economic self-sufficiency were, in her view, inextricably connected to the fight against racism and slavery. Black Americans could not hope to attain any social mobility or political recognition until they wholly embraced the values and behaviors that would make them appear less deviant and threatening to white society. In criticizing black ministers and funeral celebrations, she was denouncing the cherished institutions of the black church, which she associated with the uncultured lower classes. This position, which may have stemmed from her Quaker education and her family's middle-class associations, can be interpreted as a form of internalized racism. But it was also a pragmatic ideology which constructed some behavioral strategies for black Americans to act upon in the struggle against oppression. Shadd presented a stern and austere manifesto, overlooking the pleasures and social importance of these rituals and institutions. The impulse behind these first public communications was didactic—to teach the masses to choose activities that might bring long-term material changes over those that gave immediate satisfaction. Over the next decade, Shadd would often repudiate the African Methodist Episcopal Church and other black religious institutions in favor of more staid, and therefore more acceptable, Christian denominations. By singling out clergymen for criticism, Mary Ann also foreshadowed her willingness to challenge male authority. This was an ambitious, perhaps even presumptuous, undertaking for a twenty-six-year-old black schoolteacher.

The pamphlet received little recognition at first. In April 1849, a friend in Philadelphia wrote to the *North Star* that although it had been published for several months only a handful had been sold. The author of the letter speculated that while the document had been widely circulated in Philadelphia, local writers had not taken notice, suggesting that perhaps Shadd's writing contained "too much truth." Three years after its publication, black nationalist Martin Delany referred to Mary Ann's pamphlet and praised her work as "an excellent introduction to a great subject, fraught with so much interest." Delany, who was becoming an increasingly influential figure as an abolitionist and emigrationist, called Mary Ann "a very intelligent young lady, and peculiarly eccentric," probably an apt description for the outspoken and controversial young activist. Delany's comments suggest how she may have been viewed by other black leaders. On one hand she was clearly bright and on target in her assessments; on the other hand her strident, uncompromising positions marginalized her as strange and controversial.[53]

By the end of the 1840s Mary Ann Shadd had carved out a path that would direct her activities for the rest of her life. Teaching would always be an important part of her identity and the way that she earned a living. But writing and public expression would become increasingly important as a means to have a political voice. As a young man, Abraham Shadd fought valiantly for black Americans to be granted the fundamental rights of equality and enfranchisement. He believed that the best hope for free blacks was to improve themselves intellectually, morally, and socially. He implemented these ideals in the education and training of his children, and his eldest daughter embraced these principles in her own work. On the eve of the Civil War, he was remembered for his "earnest, dignified, logical demeanor . . . as a debater, and public spirited man" during the convention movement. As Abraham Shadd gradually faded from the public limelight, Mary Ann Shadd began to take his place. But unlike her father, she would be influenced by an emerging black nationalist ideology and would be more willing to consider radical solutions to racial inequality—in particular, emigration to Canada.[54]

TWO

Emigration Furor and *Notes of Canada West*

At the start of the tumultuous decade of the 1850s, Mary Ann Shadd had accumulated ten years' teaching experience in African American schools across the North. By making education the centerpiece of her life's work, she took the course of many free women of color. Fostering mental improvement and combating ignorance were crucial components in the doctrine of racial uplift. Education was believed to be synonymous with black liberation since the days of the early black conventions, and the black elite were obliged to transmit the riches of their knowledge to the less fortunate. But the lofty rhetoric of uplift belied the reality; black teachers were poorly paid and often worked in deplorable conditions. Undaunted, Mary Ann and her contemporaries made education the frontline of the racial battlefield. In the classroom they carried out their responsibilities to the race in a profession that gave them status, and that was deemed socially acceptable for their gender. Women like Frances E. W. Harper and Sarah Mapps Douglass used teaching as a launching pad from which to carry out reform activities including public speaking, writing, and organizing community institutions. Mary Ann Shadd also sought to catapult herself into the public sphere through her work as a teacher.[1]

By 1851, Mary Ann had left the familiar environs of Pennsylvania and New Jersey for a position at Primary School No. 1 on Center Street in New York City. The school, located in the basement of a black church, served close to 900 students in humble facilities. It was one of three schools formed by the Society for the Promotion of Education among Colored

Children to improve the limited educational opportunities for black youth in the city. While public education became the norm in the nation's urban centers, free blacks were consistently excluded from these institutions. Thus, the responsibility for educating the city's black children was on the shoulders of black self-help groups and white philanthropists. But antebellum black communities had to stretch their limited resources to address all human needs, including housing, food, and clothing. Schools could only be maintained on a subsistence level, despite the urgent need for education. The uncertainty of life as a teacher led Mary Ann to change jobs frequently during the first decade of her career. Teaching may have enabled Shadd to make an important contribution to her people, but it was a frustrating endeavor as well.[2]

Mary Ann Shadd was typical of the teachers in New York's all-black schools. Ninety-seven percent were black, 69 percent were female, and about half had a normal school education. Her race and gender meant that her income was among the lowest for teachers in the state, requiring her to exist on a meager salary with little job stability. She undoubtedly took advantage of the networks of free blacks that stretched from Philadelphia to New York and Boston, to aid in her transition to this new setting. Friends and associates of the Shadd family could aid her in finding a suitable boarding house and direct her to the churches, mutual-aid societies, and small businesses that embodied northern black communities. Mary Ann could have made contacts during her years teaching in Delaware, Pennsylvania, and New Jersey that helped in securing employment in New York. The black press, antislavery societies, and personal contacts formed an elaborate system of communication that eased free blacks' transition to new communities and provided them with a measure of security in hostile surroundings. This was particularly important in locales where educated free blacks were a small and embattled group.[3]

New York in the 1850s was an unfriendly home for many of its black residents. The city's nearly 14,000 free people of color comprised only 2.68 percent of the total population, a significantly smaller proportion than Philadelphia or Wilmington. Although nearly three-quarters of the city's black men found some form of employment, the overall wealth of New York's blacks did not come near the prosperity of their compatriots in cities like New Orleans, Cincinnati, or Philadelphia. But there was an old and well-established community of black abolitionists, including Charles Reason, James McCune Smith, Samuel Cornish, and Rev. James Pennington. New York boasted several black newspapers, antislavery societies, vigilance committees, and civil rights groups. New York had been the site of numerous racial disturbances, including fierce riots against blacks and white abolitionists in the summer of 1834. By the time Mary Ann arrived in New York, discrimination against blacks in employment, education, and public transportation was at an all-time high. Little is known about Shadd's time in the city, but one incident related by black activist William J. Watkins became part of local folklore:

> In New York, and coming down Broadway at a time when colored women scarcely dared to think of riding in the stages, Miss Shadd threw up her head, gave one look, and a wave of her hand. There was such an air of impressive command in it that the huge, coarse, ruffianly driver, who had been known to refuse colored ladies as though suddenly seized with paralysis, reined up to the curb, and she entered, and, without hindrance, rode to the end of her journey.[4]

The conditions in New York were characteristic of the worsening state of affairs confronting free blacks in the North in the 1850s. There were some tangible social and economic gains at mid-century; for example, the number of free blacks who owned property increased gradually in many northern cities. Yet, by most indicators, free African Americans had little to celebrate. Only a handful acquired the education and capital to become professionals or entrepreneurs; in northern cities like New York and Philadelphia as many as 90 percent of all employed blacks worked in menial and unskilled jobs. By the 1850s, black Americans in the North were leaving the agrarian life for the cities, where discrimination and hostility forced them into segregated communities.[5]

Black Americans also found little redress in the nation's political system. The push for black suffrage started in the black state conventions of the 1840s and spread from Pennsylvania—where Mary Ann's father, Abraham Shadd, was a leader—to Ohio, New Jersey, Connecticut, and Illinois. But by the mid-1850s none of these efforts was successful. By 1860 the five states that granted the vote to black males contained only 6 percent of the free black population in the North. In addition, four midwestern states passed measures during the 1850s that prohibited African Americans from migrating across their borders.[6]

But the event that constituted the greatest crisis for African Americans in the North was passage of the Fugitive Slave Act in September 1850. The law was part of a larger effort to lessen sectional strife in the decade before the Civil War—the Compromise of 1850—and both slaves and free blacks suffered the brunt of its effects. The compromise tried to deal with several issues: among them, California would be admitted to the Union as a free state, Texas would not be restricted regarding the presence of slaves in the state, the slave trade—but not slavery—would be abolished in the District of Columbia, and the federal government would respond to slaveowner demands for a more effective fugitive slave law.[7]

The act was a frightening development for northern blacks who had escaped from slavery via the Underground Railroad, and for free blacks who might be mistaken for fugitives. For many black Americans, the law signaled the extent to which proslavery forces influenced public policy and the national economy. The law empowered federal commissioners to grant certificates for the return of fugitive slaves. Claimants who could prove ownership would be allowed to take possession of and remove fugitive slaves from the state where they were seized. But under no circumstances would a fugitive's testimony be accepted as evidence on his own behalf, and the process no longer had to be tried in a judicial hearing. Stiff penalties were levied against anyone harboring fugitives or seeking to obstruct the law.[8]

The Congressional debate over the compromise was followed carefully in the abolitionist press, and its passage was met with a swift and angry outcry. Frederick Douglass called the measure "The Bloodhound Bill" and denounced it in his newspaper, *The North Star.* "The Legislature of the United States in adopting so monstrous a measure, will place law in direct antagonism with some of the noblest and strongest feelings of human nature," Douglass declared. Rev. Jermain W. Loguen, a former slave and antislavery activist, asked how it was possible that Congress could pass a law that would "endanger the liberty of an American citizen who, for twenty years before it was enacted, has stood upon free soil, inhaling and exhaling the air of freedom?" His words voiced the fears that were causing a ripple effect in black communities across the North.[9]

Meetings were held in northern cities to protest the measure, and free blacks and their white supporters formed vigilance committees to rescue captured fugitives in open defiance of the law. But the majority of white Northerners tolerated or openly supported the measure in the hope that it would placate southern politicians. For many African Americans, the Fugitive Slave Act served as a catalyst to revive interest in black emigration to Canada, the West Indies, and Africa as the United States became increasingly inhospitable. Others, although frustrated with the new law, held fast to their claim on the United States as their homeland. Frederick Douglass led the latter ideological camp and made a strong case against emigration: "It is idle—worse than idle, ever to think of our expatriation, or removal. We are here, and here we are likely to be . . . this is our country; and the question for the philosophers and statesmen of the land ought to be, What principles should dictate the policy of the action towards us?" Douglass demanded.[10]

Such bravado was overshadowed by the fact that the new law was prompting hundreds of black Americans to seek refuge in Canada. There had been a steady trickle of former slaves to Canada for more than twenty years, but the Fugitive Slave Act precipitated an exodus from every northern city with a sizable black population. Forty former slaves fled Boston within days of the bill's passage; 112 members of the Baptist Colored Church in Ro-

chester and 100 from the Colored Baptist Church of Buffalo rushed across
Lakes Erie and Ontario; in Pittsburgh 200 blacks headed north, followed
quickly by hundreds more of their relatives and friends. One newspaper
account estimated that 3,000 fugitive slaves arrived in Canada within weeks
of the passage of the Fugitive Slave Act. Mary Ann Shadd, who grew up
amid the convention movement debates on emigration, was profoundly
influenced by these developments.[11]

Persons of African descent had been present in Canada since the first
slave was sold in New France around 1628. By the early eighteenth century,
there was little need for slave labor in the colony, whose economy focused
on the fur trade, and only a few wealthy families had black servants. By the
middle of the eighteenth century there were only about 1,100 persons of
African descent—mostly slaves—living in Montreal or its environs. When
the British took over Canada in 1763 following the Treaty of Paris, British
law supported the continuation of the slave trade. This had little effect on
what had become a relatively mild system of slavery in comparison with the
United States; harsh punishment, separation of families, and abject deprivation were frowned upon in Canadian society. During the early days of
British rule, slavery spread into the colony of Nova Scotia, and a handful of
black slaves were imported to develop agriculture in Quebec. These small
numbers were bolstered by the migration of British loyalists from the United States following the Revolutionary War. Many of the slaves arriving with
the loyalists were quickly emancipated, creating a new class of free black
citizens. Yet, the fact remained that most of the early blacks in Canada arrived on the continent as someone's property.[12]

The loyalists became the driving force behind growing antislavery sentiment in Canada. The institution of slavery was associated with the most
repugnant aspects of United States policies, rather than with French and
British colonialism. In 1793 Upper Canada's legislative assembly passed a
bill that halted the importation of slaves and called for gradual emancipation. Canada's Imperial Emancipation Act of 1833 was the final blow to an
institution that had virtually died out by the time the bill was passed. By the
early decades of the nineteenth century, Canadian blacks had been emancipated and enjoyed full equality under the law. Blacks in Canada faced
little of the virulent racism and legal oppression suffered by their counterparts to the south, although they often remained on the bottom rungs of
Canadian society. Black men could vote, serve on juries and in the military,
and own property—privileges that were out of the reach of blacks in the
United States. Not surprisingly, Canada became an increasingly attractive
haven for African Americans as conditions for them worsened at home.[13]

American slaves fled across the border to Canada as early as the Revolutionary War period, but their numbers remained minuscule until the
1820s. During the period when Mary Ann Shadd was growing up in the

United States, blacks in Canada generally settled in towns close to the border and were encouraged by the Canadian government to farm, cultivate tobacco, build roads and aqueducts, and serve in the militia as laborers and foot soldiers. The black American fugitives rarely mixed with the Canadian-born blacks, and they slowly formed their own communities. On occasion the Canadian government offered cheap land to fugitive slaves as an enticement for this pool of black labor. In the 1820s, a black settlement near Toronto, Oro Township, was established for this purpose. Generally, however, separate black communities were established through the efforts of abolitionists and philanthropists in the United States as well as Canada.[14]

The first large influx of freeborn American blacks to Canada was in 1830, caused by the flight of 1,000–2,000 refugees from Cincinnati. About 200 settled near Lake Huron on lands that became the Wilberforce Settlement, and hundreds more took off on their own throughout the region. At Wilberforce, the migrants built farms, a sawmill, churches, and a school, but the settlement mainly survived on contributions from white donors in the United States. The organization behind Wilberforce crumbled by the mid-1830s, but this planned settlement served a symbolic purpose in demonstrating to American blacks that land and autonomy were possible in the Canadian haven. It was not long before more self-contained communities were established in Canada West to respond to the needs of the swelling black population.[15]

Another such community was founded near Chatham in the 1840s with the goal of providing land for new black immigrants and establishing a manual labor school. It would develop the skills and knowledge they so desperately needed for survival in their adopted homeland. The school, known as the British-American Institute, was founded in 1842 by a former slave and traveling preacher, Josiah Henson, and Hiram Wilson of the American Missionary Association. At its peak, the Institute provided an education to scores of black emigrants denied access to public schools. A settlement called Dawn grew up around the Institute, and its residents— mostly fugitive slaves—owned 1,500 acres of productive farmland and started a lumbering business. About 500 people of color settled at Dawn, providing a dramatic model for African American self-sufficiency. However, poor leadership and management hampered this community as well, and it died out by the late 1860s. By contrast, the Elgin settlement, founded in 1849 near Chatham by Irish missionary William King, was considered a success. King began the planned community with the fifteen slaves he inherited through marriage and subsequently freed. In ten years Elgin grew to a thriving enclave of 300 families living on ten thousand acres. But King and the settlers had to weather considerable anti-black sentiment from local whites opposed to the creation of a black community in their midst.[16]

There have been widely varying estimates of the black population of

The only existing photograph of Mary Ann Shadd Cary. (National Archives of Canada, C29977)

Canada during this period because of inaccuracies in the early Canadian censuses, and because abolitionists often inflated the numbers of fugitives in their reports to emphasize the urgency of their cause. The 1851 census for Canada West reported 4,669 blacks while an antislavery convention in New York claimed there were 20,000 fugitive slaves in Canada a year earlier. As a compromise, one scholar suggested there were approximately 10,000 blacks in Canada by 1850, a number that would swell to perhaps 40,000 by the eve of the Civil War. More recently, however, another historian has argued that relatively few black Americans—either fugitive slave or free— actually relocated in Canada during this period. In this new assessment, it is estimated that there were between 17,000 and 20,000 blacks in the country by the time of the 1861 Canadian census. Blacks were always a tiny fraction of the Canadian population—never more than one percent—but their presence had an influence on the national fabric that far exceeded their numbers.[17]

Mary Ann Shadd learned about this black migration northward from the pages of the abolitionist press and through the far flung network of black antislavery activists in the North. The published accounts of black life in Canada varied from romantic stories of freedom and prosperity to tales of of privation among poor and unskilled fugitives, depending on the writer's agenda. Missionaries and supporters of black migration often extolled the advantages of life across the border. The superintendent of the Canada Mission, established by the American Missionary Association, wrote a series of letters that were reproduced in antislavery newspapers during the winter and spring of 1849. He described Canada's black residents as engaged in "honorable employment" and said most Canadian whites spoke of their black neighbors in complimentary terms. There were prosperous farms and a bright future for people of color in British North America: "They are destined, in the country to which they have fled, to become just what the people of that country is—not what they are now, but what they will be, when the resources of that great country become fully developed—a wealthy, learned, influential, and highly civilized community," he proclaimed. These observations were welcome encouragement for American blacks contemplating the move North.[18]

The reports from the Canadian frontier were vital propaganda for the abolitionist movement's campaign to counter proslavery discourse with tangible examples of black progress. The dispatches also justified pleas for financial and material support for the fugitive slaves. The antislavery press reported that the black exile communities in Canada West were in desperate need of skilled personnel—particularly teachers. Hiram Wilson, a white missionary and one of the founders of the ill-fated Dawn settlement, reported that Canada had proven to be a receptive haven for black Americans but that educational opportunities for the new emigrants was lacking: "What they most need is instruction, as they generally come into Canada deplorably ignorant of letters," he wrote. Superintendent Smith, of the Canada Mission, called on abolitionists and philanthropists to donate funds to support schools: "What an object to educate the youth of such a number, and prove the colored man's capability of moral, civil, intellectual and religious elevation." Such rhetoric portrayed the black migrants as needy and dependent, reinforcing the abolitionist paternalism which fueled so much white philanthropy of the era. The chained, prostrate slave reaching out to white reformers for redemption had become the symbol of abolitionist beneficence. Indeed, coming to the aid of Canada's black fugitive population became the central focus of abolitionism in Canada West.[19]

This rhetoric about the fugitives' plight also struck a chord with black abolitionists like Mary Ann Shadd, who found racial progress inextricably linked to education and morality. Since early in the nineteenth century, abolitionists argued that blacks' ability to prove their intelligence and citizenship was essential to win public opinion over the slavery question.

Education and self-help were also vital for strengthening free black communities. Racial uplift had a dual goal: to literally raise the slave out of bondage and into freedom, and to boost the actual and perceived character of black Americans. The growing communities of ex-slaves in Canada were a bold experiment in the implementation of uplift ideologies. So when the abolitionist press published a call for a "Great North American Anti-Slavery Convention," to be held in Toronto, Mary Ann decided to attend so that she could investigate these issues firsthand. The meeting's organizers—black emigration proponents Henry Bibb and James Theodore Holly—hoped to initiate a formal discussion of the virtues of emigration to Canada, and to bring together American and Canadian blacks in a unified agenda. The renewed call for black emigration rekindled a political direction that had absorbed the Shadd family for decades. Abraham Shadd was a visible participant in the Toronto convention, and although her name does not appear in the meeting's proceedings, Mary Ann Shadd was there, as well.[20]

On September 11, 1851, fifty-three delegates assembled at St. Lawrence Hall in Toronto for a three-day meeting that recalled the earlier days of the black convention movement. The city's black population of less than a thousand was swelled by hundreds of people of color who converged on the city for the event. Until the 1850s, Toronto's blacks only numbered in the hundreds, yet they were effective in establishing successful businesses and community institutions including churches and benevolent societies. Toronto appeared, at least on the outside, to be a receptive haven for American blacks as well as other immigrants. A new black political establishment emerged in this meeting. Instead of the customary elite from Philadelphia, Boston, and New York, most of the delegates were lesser-known activists from the cities, towns, and hamlets of Canada West. As an American, Abraham Shadd, one of seven participants assigned to organize another convention, was in the minority. Among those attending the convention were representatives of the independent black settlements, and veterans of the abolitionist movement in the States, as well as local black entrepreneurs and artisans. Mary Ann met some of the central figures in Canada's black communities, and she was introduced to the city of Toronto, the center of Canada West's black cultural and political life. Little did she know that many of those present at the convention—like delegates George and John Cary, Samuel Ringgold Ward, Martin Delany, and convention President Henry Bibb—would have a profound influence on the rest of her life. It was this diverse group who laid out a radical solution to racial oppression and slavery—black emigration to Canada. Resolutions were passed touting Canada as the best site from which to assist in the flight of fugitive slaves, and at the same time in close proximity to the abolitionist organizations in the States. The delegates rejoiced over the availability of Canada's "free soil" and proclaimed that Canada West was "by far, the most desirable place of resort for colored people, to be found on the American continent." Mary Ann found these arguments irresistible. A few days later, father and daughter traveled back across the border to attend a meeting at Buffalo's African Methodist Church, where several participants from the Toronto convention spoke on the topic of Canadian emigration. Mary Ann Shadd was elected secretary of the meeting, and her minutes were published in several antislavery newspapers.[21]

Within a few days, Mary Ann Shadd's life had taken a dramatic turn. At the age of twenty-eight she decided to leave her native country and join the emigration movement in body as well as spirit. She wrote her younger brother Isaac that this new land seemed to offer as much promise as the published accounts suggested. Gripped with Canada fever, she encouraged him to emigrate, as well. "I have been here more than a week, and like Canada. Do not feel prejudice and repeat if you were to come here or go west of this where shoemaking pays well and work at it and buy lands as fast as you made any money, you would do well." In the protective tone of an older sister, she instructed Isaac to learn about Canadian life by observing, to avoid associations with "swearing company," and to seek out a respectable boarding house. "If you come be particular about company—be polite to everybody—go to church, everybody does to be respected," she instructed. Mary Ann's first destination was Sandwich, Canada West, where she hoped to open a school. Although she had been offered a position in Toronto, Mary Ann was determined to tackle the needs and problems of a more remote black community. Sandwich was at the westernmost edge of the province on the shore of the Detroit River, making the town a popular stopping off point for blacks crossing the border from Michigan. Since it was early autumn and the weather was still warm, it is likely that she made the 250-mile trip across Lake Erie by steamboat. During the winter months when the lakes were frozen, the trip entailed a combination of railroad and stagecoach rides, a longer journey that she would undertake frequently in the ensuing years. Mary Ann Shadd was persuaded to take this trip into the Canadian frontier by one of Canada's most influential black leaders, Henry Bibb.[22]

Henry Bibb was born a slave in Kentucky in 1815, having been fathered by a white slave owner. Throughout his youth he suffered from the worst horrors of American slavery: separation from his mother, cruel owners, physical abuse, and denial of all but a rudimentary education. After several unsuccessful attempts to escape slavery with his family, Bibb finally fled to the North in 1841 after being permanently separated from his wife and child. During the 1840s, Bibb attended school briefly and then settled in Detroit where he became active in the antislavery movement. In 1848 he married a free black woman, Mary Miles, who worked as a teacher and abolitionist. Bibb became a well-known antislavery lecturer and itinerant preacher, and published the account of his life in the *Narrative of the Life and Adventures of Henry Bibb, an American Slave,* in 1849. Following passage of the Fugitive Slave Act, the Bibbs fled across the border and established new lives in Canada, where they emerged as community leaders.[23]

The Bibbs settled in Sandwich, on the Detroit frontier, opened a school for fugitive slaves run by Mary Bibb, and became key players in a black settlement project called the Refugee Home Society. They also founded Canada's first black newspaper, the *Voice of the Fugitive*. The majority of Canada's newspapers refused to support the country's nascent abolitionist movement, and some openly sided with proslavery forces. In the 1850s, the *Toronto Globe* was the solitary voice in favor of abolition. Publisher George Brown worked valiantly to educate the public on the evils of slavery and he condemned discrimination against the fugitive population. *Voice of the Fugitive,* launched in January 1851, was a badly needed voice for Canada's black community, with a circulation both in Canada and the United States. It was also a forum for discussion of the black emigration and colonization programs advocated by the Bibbs. In the paper's first issue, the editors announced their agenda to be the abolition of slavery, the emigration of blacks to Canada, and the support of education, temperance, and moral reform: "While we intend this to be a mouth piece for the refugees in Canada especially, yet we mean to speak out our sentiments as a FREEMAN upon all subjects that come within our sphere."[24]

The first issue of the *Voice of the Fugitive* also reported on the dire need for teachers in Canada West, noting that there was no school in the nearby Township of Windsor, where a sizable number of fugitives had settled. Henry Bibb, one of the principal organizers of the Toronto convention, found the perfect teacher at the meeting—Mary Ann Shadd. Bibb invited Mary Ann to travel with him to Sandwich where they arrived by mid-September; Mary Bibb may have accompanied them as well, although her name does not appear in the convention's proceedings. Once in Sandwich, Mary Ann met other teachers, missionaries, and activists and began to learn about the realities of life in her new country. She did not linger long in Sandwich, apparently moving the few miles north to Windsor by late September where she was invited by the local residents to start a school.

Windsor was at the terminus of the Great Western Railway and at the westernmost edge of the province directly across the river from Detroit. In 1854 the abolitionist Benjamin Drew would estimate there were one thousand residents in the village, including fifty black families living in "comfortable homes." But in 1851, what Mary Ann Shadd found on arriving in Windsor might have discouraged a more faint-hearted soul; privation and illiteracy were abundant. An article in *Frederick Douglass' Paper* painted a dismal picture of this frontier community: "The vast barracks erected during the last war [1812] may be seen there rapidly falling to decay. They are now occupied by fugitive slaves, and among them both poverty and suffering are visible." Mary Ann was determined to open a school, and she quickly spread the word through the town. She announced that it would be open to all children—black and white—if she was guaranteed at least twenty-five pupils whose parents could pay one shilling per week for their education. Shadd promised Windsor's residents that she would accept children even if their parents had no money. She found that there were far more anxious students than parents who could afford to pay. So she opened the school in a room in the drafty barracks, which she shared with a small Methodist congregation, and began to look elsewhere for financial support.[25]

One of Mary Ann Shadd's first associates in Windsor was a white Congregational minister named Alexander McArthur, who advised her that the recently formed American Missionary Association (A.M.A.) was looking to hire teachers for their Canada Mission. The A.M.A. was organized to collect donations to benefit the fugitive slaves and it hired several missionaries and teachers for the Canadian field beginning in 1848. The A.M.A. was the first and largest organization from the United States to minister to the needs of the Canadian fugitive population, but Canada was not the association's top priority. Shadd wrote George Whipple, corresponding secretary of the A.M.A., to apply for an appointment. Over the next three years, Mary Ann's letters to Whipple would offer a window on black life in Canada West, as well as on her observations and frustrations. Mary Ann's new school was clearly tottering on the brink of failure, and she appealed to Whipple's missionary sentiments when she reported that Windsor was "the most destitute community of colored people known in this province." Of her twenty-five students, twenty were unable to pay tuition and she suspected that an equal number did not attend school at all because of poverty. Mary Ann feared that if she waived the tuition for the poorest students, the remaining families "might not feel inclined to pay at all," and she would have to abandon the project.[26]

To bolster her request, Mary Ann noted that the Bibbs, who also urged her to contact the A.M.A., faced similar circumstances at their school in Sandwich. Mary Bibb had received only ten dollars in eight months of teaching, and had to carry firewood long distances just to heat her schoolroom. Mary Ann was already having doubts that she could maintain the school under such conditions. It was November, the harsh Canadian winter approached, and she was living on charitable contributions and money sent from her family to supplement the meager tuition. Added to her financial woes were the complicated politics of black education in Canada. In her zeal to open a school in Windsor, Mary Ann had not fully understood that she was stepping into the middle of the debate over whether

Canada's black children should be educated in segregated or integrated schools.

Despite the myth and promise of the Canadian Canaan, equal education was not universally available to the country's black citizens. Most were educated by missionaries, although small numbers attended public or "common" schools. Yet black citizens paid taxes to support the common schools even if their children did not attend them. An 1840s law supported separate schools based on religious denomination, but in Canada West, where there was a growing black population, the law was used to justify racial segregation. The Common School Act passed in 1850 empowered blacks to establish their own schools with government support, which reinforced whites' efforts at segregation. By the time Mary Ann Shadd arrived in Canada West, most black children attended schools in the planned settlements like Elgin and Dawn or those supported by the A.M.A., or they obtained no education at all. Canada's black leaders, as well as the A.M.A., generally condemned separate schooling in principle, but in reality that was the only educational opportunity available for the swelling black population.[27]

In keeping with this rhetoric, the A.M.A. quizzed Mary Ann about whether her new school promoted segregated education. Whipple asked Shadd to provide a rationale for establishing a private school and asked her why Windsor's children were not attending the local common school. Mary Ann replied that she was "utterly opposed" to segregated education, and that she was well aware of the A.M.A.'s position in this matter. "I beg you will not consider my effort here, an attempt to encourage the spirit of caste," she wrote. "Whatever excuse may be offered in the states for exclusive institutions, I am convinced that in this country, and in this particular region, (the most opposed to emigration of colored people I have seen), none could be offered with a shadow of reason, and with this conviction, I opened school here with the condition of admission to children of all complexions."[28]

Mary Ann's response echoed the A.M.A.'s critique of separate schooling, which was also consistent with the political positions she had taken in the United States. She had been denied schooling until the age of ten because of race and gender segregation in Delaware, and black education was severely circumscribed in Pennsylvania, as well. As a teacher, she observed firsthand how state governments legally sanctioned the lack of educational opportunities for African Americans. The American Moral Reform Society, in which her father was an active participant, advocated color-blind institutions as the best course for racial advancement. Mary Ann's own developing ideology argued that people of color could and should benefit from contact with whites, while simultaneously promoting racial pride and autonomy. In Canada, the potential existed for integrated education. Although separate schools were increasingly the norm in Canada West, this occurred because of community prejudice rather than legal mandate. Shadd reasoned that in a community like Windsor, where schooling was needed for both black and white, racial prejudice might be overcome.

Windsor's black residents would have to take legal action to gain access to government schools, but Mary Ann found parents unable or unwilling to pursue this course. Thus, she argued, there were at least forty school-age children and some adults who sought an education but could not pay for it. An A.M.A.-supported school was the best alternative. She told Whipple that she would need at least $250 a year to keep the school going, particularly if there was any hope in improving the physical accommodations. "If I should receive foreign aid, my dependence on parents would be at an end," she wrote. "At present, parents furnish fuel, and take room rent out of it, the consequence is, a very cold, open apartment, unfurnished & objectionable in every way, and a scanty supply of fire-wood."[29]

Mary Ann remained determined to keep the school going, despite the hardships she encountered. The local missionary, Alexander McArthur, had become her ardent supporter, and he wrote a glowing letter of recommendation to Whipple on her behalf. He provided a rare physical description of Shadd during her first year in Canada: "Miss S. is a young (light colored) lady of fine diction, refined address, and christian deportment; and possessing an energy of character & enlargement of views well fitting her for the work of teaching amongst such a people as this," wrote McArthur. In 1851 the A.M.A. supported the work of nine white missionaries in Canada West, all but one of whom were clergymen. Mary Ann's race and occupation made her application exceptional. She listed some of New York City's most prominent black abolitionists as references, including Rev. Charles Ray and Charles Reason, whom she identified as personal friends, and James McCune Smith and Samuel Cornish, who were board members of the Society for the Promotion of Education among Colored Children. As an evangelical organization, the A.M.A. wanted to determine Mary Ann's suitability for the appointment. When asked about her religious leanings, she professed no religious affiliation, stating that she left the African Methodist Episcopal Church "because of its distinctive character." She also confirmed that she was unmarried. Mary Ann's disdain for black ministers included one of the largest, and most influential, black institutions. She and McArthur referred to the African Methodists as a "complexion church," and she wanted to disassociate herself from any local segregated institutions. Inadvertently, perhaps, Mary Ann's lack of evangelical credentials would make her vulnerable as her relationship with the A.M.A. continued.[30]

McArthur also took this opportunity to lobby on his own behalf. He sought an appointment from the A.M.A. to continue his missionary work, explaining that the Wesleyans could no longer support him in Canada. Suspecting that the A.M.A. would be impressed with Mary Shadd's credentials, he attempted to present the two of them as a team: "An efficient missionary with the cooperation of Miss Shadd as a teacher could do much for the moral and intillectual [*sic*] advancement of the fugitives at this point." There was only the African Methodist church to minister to the throng of fugitives in Windsor, said McArthur. "Seven boys and girls—all of one family landed on our shores last week, thus adding to the responsibility of the christian publick to furnish these poor spoiled ones "christian education," he reported.[31]

Despite the combined efforts of Shadd and McArthur, the A.M.A. was slow to respond to their requests for aid. Mary Ann maintained her school on a shoestring budget throughout the early winter of 1851–52 and became a visible figure in Windsor. Henry Bibb's *Voice of the Fugitive,* which provided a weekly chronicle of events among local blacks, reported that there were plans underway to construct a new building for her school. At a fund-raising event in November, a speech by the new teacher was the evening's highlight. Bibb's paper was effusive in its praise of Mary Ann, calling her "a lady of high literary attainments," and claiming that she was the evening's main attraction. Mary Ann's talk stressed the importance of education, and she revealed a growing admiration for the power of the press. According to the *Voice of the Fugitive,* Mary Ann returned Bibb's compliments when she referred to his paper "as being one of the most important publications now in circulation, for the elevation of our people in North America, but especially in Canada." The *Voice* concluded that the audience was "well paid for coming" to hear Mary Ann's address. Clearly, she had made a favorable first impression on this community of black American exiles. She received more welcome publicity in January, when the *Voice* reported that "Miss Mary Ann Shadd, a worthy colored lady" was running a private school for eighteen to twenty students "whom she is teaching in a private house." The report was optimistic, noting that Windsor's black residents had pooled their resources to buy land for Mary Ann's school. In reality, the future of the school was precarious.[32]

Meanwhile, Mary Ann's advocate, Rev. McArthur, urged the A.M.A. to speed up their response to her application before she abandoned the school. "Miss Shadd ought to be sustained here if possible. She is doing much good," he wrote. In February, a letter from the A.M.A. finally arrived. The association's cautious administrator, George Whipple, offered some hope, but indicated that funds were limited and that they could only offer the minimal salary necessary to sustain a teacher in the field.[33]

Mary Ann responded with gratitude that the A.M.A. was interested in supporting her and the school, and she explained that her estimate of $250 a year operating expenses was based on her assumption that Windsor's parents would stop paying tuition if she received funds from outside sources. Uncharacteristically, she was at a loss for words to describe her financial situation. "The limits of this sheet are insufficient, to present a clear statement of the difficulties to contend against at this point," she told Whipple. Some parents and students had failed to pay the promised tuition, others were too poor to even make such a commitment. The two dollars she had earned in the last month were "not nearly equal to a support." Just five months into her tenure at Windsor, Mary Ann was frustrated and distraught. Instead of being welcomed in the town with open arms, as she had expected, there was some resistance to her efforts. She explained to Whipple that she was forced to reduce the tuition price and offer free instruction to the indigent after some unnamed competitors attempted to open a segregated school in the town. She seemed doubtful that she could count on the good will of local residents: "I do not know how far to depend upon the people, my first experiment with them having failed." In a last-ditch plea, she lowered her price and pledged that she would "cheerfully engage for the year," if the A.M.A. would pay her half of her estimated expenses.[34]

Finally, four months after Mary Ann's initial application, the A.M.A. agreed to pay her $125 a year to keep the Windsor school open, making her the association's only black missionary in Canada West. By April she had received her first paycheck and was able to report considerable success running a day school for twenty-three children and an evening school for about ten adults. Attendance had dropped in February and March because of bad weather but as spring approached there was a steady stream of students, especially among the adults. Like most nineteenth-century teachers, Shadd had to teach fundamental skills to a diverse group—in this case, her students ranged in age from four to thirty-three years old. In the one-room school, she taught reading at three levels, geography, and arithmetic. She proudly reported that "the progress thus far, has been encouraging: the fugitives are anxious to learn, and are not inferior in capacity to those brought up under more favorable circumstances." This was an especially difficult task as many of her students stayed in Windsor temporarily. "This being very near to the U.S., the fugitive population has been of a transient character, many remaining, only so long as they can make further arrangements for the interior," she told Whipple.[35]

The financial support from the American Missionary Association, as well as the end of winter, had cheered Mary Ann considerably. She counted "sickness, bad roads, and want of suitable accommodations" among the obstacles she faced. Yet her letter exuded confidence about the school and her students, and her description of her relationships with her students and their parents showed a shift from uncertainty to mutual support as the months passed. But she reported there were rumblings of discord from "pretended sympathizers in this vicinity" who she believed resented her growing success. When her school was "but an experiment, or a doubtful probability," there was consistent support for her efforts. But now that it was a reality, she was sensing "much indirect opposition" to the project.[36]

Mary Ann's troubles may have been exacerbated by her endorsement of Alexander McArthur. She implored the American Missionary Association to hire Rev. McArthur before he left Windsor for more receptive locales. She had relied on McArthur's counsel and support, and he was probably one of the few residents of Windsor with whom she could share her intellectual and political interests. But by joining forces with a white minister she was beginning to alienate herself from Windsor's black establishment. Opposition to white missionaries was spreading through many of Canada West's black communities. Part of the strife was sectarian; black ministers who had no affiliation with white denominations resented the presence of the white clergy. Some of the missionaries were openly racist, others mildly paternalistic, and many viewed black preachers as illiterate and unable to transmit the proper intellectual and moral teachings to their congregations. Mary Ann was determined to act independently of these racial factions, and was unwilling to forge alliances based solely on color. But she was about to pay a price for her actions.[37]

By the spring of 1852 it was becoming apparent that there was resistance to Shadd and McArthur's work in Windsor, although none of the correspondence specifies the exact nature of these activities. The earlier amicable relationship between the Bibbs and the new schoolteacher had soured, and Mary Ann revealed that her former friends were part of the opposition. She went so far as to accuse Henry Bibb of orchestrating the push for a rival school. Bibb also had close friends in the A.M.A., and Shadd guessed that the association's reluctance to hire McArthur was rooted in this growing discord. At the heart of their differences was an ideological split over what constituted the appropriate strategies for black survival in Canada. Shadd and McArthur were committed to aiding the fugitives from American slavery, but increasingly they became viewed as unwelcome interlopers who might siphon off some of the precious philanthropic aid targeted for the community. This argument became particularly rancorous in the case of the Refugee Home Society (R.H.S.). The society was formed in 1852 from the merger of two antislavery groups—one based in Michigan and the other in Canada West—to create another black settlement in Canada West. The Refugee Home Society planned to purchase 50,000 acres of farm land near Windsor, which it would then sell to refugees in

25-acre parcels rather than creating one large community. The R.H.S. was controlled by whites in Michigan and administered locally by the Bibbs and David Hotchkiss, an A.M.A. agent in Amherstburg. The *Voice of the Fugitive* became the official organ of the Refugee Home Society, and the Bibbs were the standard-bearers for the project.[38]

From its inception the Refugee Home Society spurred controversy at home and in the United States. Among many African American intellectuals, projects such as this symbolized the ideological distinctions between black assimilation and black separatism. Since the early part of the century, black Americans had grappled with the meaning of black nationalism. David Walker's *Walker's Appeal in Four Articles* (1830) angrily denounced racial oppression but refused to endorse black separatism. Nationalists who followed him formulated an ideology that called for the creation of autonomous, self-sufficient black communities based on a collective racial identity. Mary Ann's approach combined both impulses; she believed in the quest for self-sufficiency but, like Walker, opposed racial separatism or "complexional distinctions." In Canada, critics charged that the R.H.S. encouraged segregated black settlements, schools, and churches—a policy that Mary Ann Shadd, McArthur, and others felt ran counter to the interests of the refugees. Bibb defended this position, maintaining that while the R.H.S. did not support the separation of the races in principle, it was a logical strategy in practice. It was quite natural, Bibb argued, "that strangers in a foreign land, no matter of what country or color they may be, experience a greater degree of happiness in being associated with those who may have come from the same region as themselves." Mary Ann Shadd, however, believed that blacks needed to function beyond their own insular communities so that they could benefit from exposure to the culture, education, and moral refinements of western society.[39]

Mary Ann Shadd and the Bibbs also disagreed about the relationship between white philanthropy and projects to develop black self-sufficiency in Canada. Shadd became a vocal critic of the Refugee Home Society's fund-raising efforts—derisively labeled a "begging system" by some abolitionists—in which whites in the United States were urged to contribute clothing, supplies, and money to help the "impoverished fugitives." The Anti-Slavery Society of Canada, established following the passage of the Fugitive Slave Act, placed its main emphasis on relief for fugitive slaves. But the society was small and often overshadowed by abolitionists and missionaries in the United States who sent aid on the fugitives' behalf. Shadd resisted the impulse to construct an image of the former slaves as helpless and needy. She also hoped to encourage blacks to develop entrepreneurial skills rather than subsisting as clients of a welfare economy. The Refugee Home Society's supporters, on the other hand, saw nothing wrong in seeking donations in this way and saw Shadd's position as hypocritical since she was being supported in part by white philanthropy through the American Missionary Association. These differences soured any hopes of a collegial relationship between Mary Ann Shadd and the Bibbs.[40]

Bibb and his supporters were equally disturbed by Mary Ann's independence and her refusal to be submissive to Canada's more established black, male leadership. Mary Ann committed the ultimate act of defiance when she took it upon herself to write and publish a pamphlet on black emigration to disseminate her ideas to an audience beyond Windsor. Shadd compiled her observations, research, and recommendations into a forty-four-page essay that was published in June 1852, nine months after her arrival in the region. Titled *A Plea for Emigration or Notes of Canada West, in its Moral, Social and Political Aspect, with Suggestions Respecting Mexico, W. Indies and Vancouver's Island, for the Information of Colored Emigrants,* the little book catapulted Mary Ann Shadd into the public arena and into the heart of the emigrationist debate.[41]

Notes of Canada West was an encyclopedic compilation of agricultural, economic, political, and social data about life in the region. This was a significant accomplishment, since Mary Ann had lived in Canada for less than a year, during which time she was working long hours in a constant struggle to run her school. Despite the demands on her time, she managed to produce a detailed study that emphasized the advantages of Canada West and downplayed the problems. Underlying her account was a deeply rooted optimism about, and love for, her adopted country. Some of the pamphlet took on the tone of a travel guide, as she described "the most beautiful lakes and rivers on the Western Continent." Shadd spent several pages dispelling the notion that Canada's weather was too harsh, an idea that emigration opponents used to dissuade African Americans accustomed to a southern climate. "The climate is healthy and temperate; epidemics are not of such frequency as in the United States owing to a more equable [*sic*] temperature, and local diseases are unknown," she asserted. Such claims were nothing new; the *Voice of the Fugitive* often reported on the mild climate of Canada West as an enticement for potential migrants. But to claim that Canada was "healthier" than the United States went beyond hyperbole.

Shadd's pamphlet also reported that Canada West's soil and timber were superior to that found in the United States, and farming and raising livestock could be profitable enterprises. Land in the western reaches of the province could be bought for $1.62 an acre for uncleared land to as much as $100 an acre for improved land. From her own observations Shadd found that emigrants owning small parcels of land were "independently dragging along miserably" because their income was insufficient, thus she advocated investing in large parcels when possible. *Notes of Canada West* was an unabashed propaganda tract that exaggerated the benefits of the Canadian haven while ignoring many endemic problems. In Shadd's zeal to promote Canadian emigration, she declared that "land is cheap, business increasing, with the steady increase of population, no lack of employment at fair prices, and no complexional or other qualification in existence."

Most controversial were her assertions that racial prejudice was rare in Canadian life, despite the segregated circumstances she encountered in Windsor and environs. She argued that segregation of the races often occurred as a result of blacks establishing separate institutions, rather than because of exclusion by whites. Shadd was convinced that the integrated communities she observed in the eastern sections of the province, especially in Toronto, proved that the same was possible in the less developed West. She wrote that she was "forcibly struck" by an integrated church in Toronto, where "the presence of colored persons, promiscuously seated, elicited no comment whatever." This was, from her perspective, the embodiment of the Canadian dream; that blacks could participate unnoticed and unfettered in public institutions. Shadd's view of Canadian integration was not entirely novel. Fifteen years earlier, the American abolitionist James G. Birney had rejoiced over the integrated congregation of a Toronto Episcopal church. This was contrasted with Mary Ann's contempt for black clergy and churches, which had not softened in the years since she published *Hints to the Colored People of the North*. Her assessment in *Notes of Canada West* was equally harsh: "Aside from their caste character, their influence on the colored people is fatal. The character of the exclusive church in Canada tends to perpetuate ignorance, both of their true positions as British subjects, and of the Christian religion in its purity," she argued.

Notes of Canada West consistently romanticized British rule, and elevated white institutions to the pinnacle of civilization. She insisted that the black churches fostered anti-white prejudice and that what was needed were more missionaries—ostensibly whites, or blacks who were integrationists—to minister to the needs of the fugitive population. She also painted an optimistic picture of educational opportunities, refuting claims in the abolitionist press that Canada's segregated schools were no better than those in America. In Shadd's view, Canada's blacks—unlike those in the United States—had the ability to obtain an integrated education if they used the political options at their disposal.

Notes of Canada West also gave a broader platform from which to critique begging for charity on behalf of Canada's black immigrants. In one section she reprinted documents to support her assertion that the majority of Canada's blacks opposed the practice. Though she may have been enamored of elite culture, Shadd was equally suspicious of whites' motivations in assisting blacks. She stepped into controversial territory by disparaging the donations that were so prized by aid workers in Canada West. She undoubtedly offended white philanthropists when she asked if it was "really a benevolent act to send old almanacs, old novels, and all manner of obsolete books" to the fugitives. She mercilessly suggested that vanity motivated the benefactors to empty "the useless contents of old libraries" so that they could congratulate themselves for their selflessness. "Why not give, when gifts are *needed,* of that which is useful?" she asked.

Shadd's discussion of black settlements added more fuel to her feud with Henry Bibb. She gave a generally glowing account of Elgin and Dawn, but her discussion of the Refugee Home Society was less flattering. Shadd argued that the Refugee Home Society's policy of selling land only to former slaves discriminated against freeborn blacks and was divisive for the black community. She gave a lengthy defense of free blacks—herself included—who sought greater freedom and opportunity in Canada. Her focus on this issue hinted at another source of the discord between herself and Bibb. "The Fugitive Bill makes insecure every northern colored man— those free are alike at the risk of being sent south," she explained. "They arrive in Canada destitute . . . but may not settle on the land of the Refugees' Home, for the accident of nominal freedom." Mary Ann's indignation was understandable, but her argument seemed to ignore or minimize the abject status of the slave. Her goal was to erase the boundary between slave and freeborn to promote a unified racial identity. In her view, the Refugee Home Society defeated the nationalist ideal of collective purpose and action by artificially dividing the black community. The Bibbs and other missionary workers in Canada West were more pragmatic and less visionary. They sought—often unsuccessfully—to solve the immediate problems of the black Americans flooding their towns. Bibb and other escapees from slavery may have viewed Mary Ann as a light-skinned, privileged, elite who had little understanding of the hardships they had encountered. Despite the difficulties of living as a free black in America, the needs of the slave were more critical. Shadd softened her critical stance when she reported that Bibb and "other able men" published the only black newspaper in Canada, and she predicted that "there is no good reason, why they should not prosper."

The last nine pages of *Notes of Canada West* were devoted to a brief examination of the British West Indies, Mexico, and South America as alternate destinations for African American fugitives. Having no firsthand experience in these countries, Shadd's discussion was far less detailed and more ideological. She preferred emigration to the British provinces in the West Indies and Vancouver, arguing that they were important strongholds against slavery. South American countries were rejected because of their ties with Catholicism—"the Romish Church"—and Mexico had coalitions with southern slaveholders. Shadd essentially ignored Africa, aligning herself with those who considered African colonization as part of a pro-slavery agenda. The pamphlet concluded with Shadd's declaration that free blacks who remained in the United States were waiting for "a powerful miracle for the overthrow of slavery." In her estimation, the antislavery agenda in America was futile and did little to develop blacks' self-esteem or autonomy.

We may never know all of the factors that motivated Shadd to publish this tract, but *Notes of Canada West* performed several political functions. It was an elaborate piece of propaganda that established Mary Ann as the authoritative voice on Canadian matters. Her enthusiastic descriptions of the Canadian haven responded to the opponents of emigration, who sought to discourage the northward exodus. At the same time, the pamphlet was designed to supplant Henry Bibb and other abolitionists in Canada who claimed an expertise on the subject. *Notes of Canada West* was a curious mix of empiricism and polemic; it contained authentic material gathered by observation and experience, while using persuasive language to make the case that Canada West was a far superior destination for those oppressed by American slavery. *Notes of Canada West* began with her obser-vation that African Americans contemplating emigration needed practical information, and that her goal in moving to Canada was to collect and distribute this material. This was the beginning of her role, described by Carla Peterson as a "colored tourist," in which Shadd's writing reflected her position as a simultaneous insider and outsider in Canada West's black communities. Through this journalism, she appointed herself the inter-preter of the black Canadian experience for audiences in the United States.[42]

The pamphlet also gave Mary Ann a public voice and a means of expression that was under her control, especially as her relationship with Bibb worsened, limiting her access to the *Voice of the Fugitive*. For reasons that will remain a mystery, Shadd did not write for abolitionist newspapers in the United States during this period, or if she did, they did not publish her contributions. So she took an alternative route to public communica-tion, independently writing, editing, publishing, and distributing her ideas, as she had done three years earlier in *Hints to the Colored People of the North*. Both of these publications showed the consistency of her racial uplift ideology, which emphasized blacks' accumulation of land and capital as the basis from which to become economically and politically self-sufficient. In her developing emigrationist logic, African Americans had little hope of accomplishing such goals in the United States, so it was logical that they should migrate to a new location where such opportunities were possible. If emigration meant acquiring a new national identity as well, blacks should align themselves with a system that had outlawed slavery. Through these ideas we find Shadd's emerging thoughts on black nationalism, in which she conceptualized black Americans as a distinct, mobile entity who could relocate and shift national allegiances to ameliorate the problems of the race. With time and hard work, she believed that Canada West would be a hospitable site for institutions devoted to blacks' moral and intellectual improvement.

A reaction to *Notes of Canada West* appeared in the *Voice of the Fugitive* as soon as the pamphlet was published. The brief article reported that Shadd was "getting out a little work of some thirty or forty pages" and credited her "ability and experience as an authoress" but then criticized her for having the pamphlet printed by a white publisher in Detroit. Bibb considered this a personal affront since he also operated a printing business, and a political mistake since she was not spending her money in her own community. We will never know why she made this decision, but Shadd may have been motivated by her growing dislike of Bibb. Her actions clearly contradicted her anti-American/black self-sufficiency rhetoric, giving Bibb ample ammunition to attack her. The next issue of the *Voice* continued this treatment; at the same time that Shadd was lauded as an "accomplished and talented authoress," she was chided for printing errors. Bibb's review seemed kindly on the surface, but reeked of smugness. On the one hand, *Notes of Canada West* was based on "extensive correspondence, personal examination of society, and reference to the laws of the Province," but he was careful to taunt Mary Ann for the typographical errors which caused "deep chagrin that we know the precise authoress feels."[43]

Such commentary typified the bittersweet relationship between Shadd and Bibb. The article certainly aided in publicizing Shadd's work. It reported that the price was twelve and a half cents a copy and it gave an address for orders. Bibb also overlooked Mary Ann's attacks on him and the Refugee Home Society, choosing instead to promote it as a useful source of information that upheld the emigrationist agenda. In the same issue of the *Voice of the Fugitive*, however, Bibb made a more personal stab at Shadd that further exacerbated their worsening relationship.

In an article titled "Schools in Canada," the paper reported on the success of Shadd's school in Windsor. But the article also announced that she was receiving support in the amount of $120 a year from the American Missionary Association because the tuition paid by parents was insufficient (the article was off by five dollars; she was actually paid $125). On the surface the article seemed innocent enough, but its underlying premise was that Shadd was both collecting tuition and a regular salary from the A.M.A., disputing her claims of poverty. Not surprisingly, Shadd was infuriated by this public disclosure of her finances, combined with the criticism of her pamphlet. Mary Ann must have stormed through Windsor in a state of fury, but she chose to vent her frustrations in her correspondence with the A.M.A. She continued the refrain that the Bibbs were jealous of her success with the Windsor school and her financial support from the A.M.A. For the first time, she made it clear that this was not a minor squabble, but rather a matter of survival." I am made to feel their bitterness and the truth must be told," she wrote to Whipple. Mary Ann was careful not to implicate the fugitive slaves, who made up the bulk of Windsor's black populace, but she maintained that "the vicinity of Henry Bibb and wife will ever be a hindrance to both teachers and preachers stationed here, unless creatures of their own." In a moment of conciliation she offered to let the Bibbs have the Windsor field of operations because "I do not know any other way for peace."[44]

But Mary Ann Shadd had no intention of "giving up the field" or giving in to the desires of her enemies. Rather, she sharpened her pen and launched into a bitter attack on the Bibbs' character and abilities. In particular, she complained that Henry Bibb was another among the uneducated black ministers who failed to properly serve his flock. She told of how a Bible class taught by Bibb was halted by the fugitives because of his inadequacies, adding, "You see he did not know, but did no doubt the best he could." Shadd was less charitable in her references to Mary Bibb, whom she described as immoral and "a profane swearer and drug taking woman." While Mary Ann seemed inclined to give Henry Bibb the benefit of the doubt, she did not do so for his wife: "If Rev. H. Bibb had been trained when young he might have become a great man, but it is too late now. His lady is an incorrigible woman and rules him and all within her influence."[45]

Mary Ann Shadd's hostility toward Mary Bibb may have been due to several factors. Shadd made it plain that she believed Mrs. Bibb, who was also a teacher, had designs on the school in Windsor once it became viable. Before Shadd arrived in Canada, the Bibbs had sought financial support from the American Missionary Association for their own school in the nearby town of Sandwich. The A.M.A. responded by endorsing the Refugee Home Society, sending more missionaries to the area, and making donations of Bibles and other materials, but no money was given directly to the Bibbs. In 1852 the Bibbs' school in Sandwich was struggling, thus setting the stage for jealousy and competition between the two. By 1854, true to Shadd's predictions, Mary Bibb would be operating a school in Windsor. Mary Ann also suspected Mary Bibb of being the actual author of the damaging articles in *The Voice* since she considered Henry Bibb to be barely literate and his wife to be the controlling influence in his life. Other scholars have made a similar assessment. Mary Bibb had become an officer of the Refugee Home Society several months earlier, and took it upon herself to defend the organization's practices against Mary Shadd's charges. Thus, Mary Bibb was probably the architect of the attack on Shadd, while remaining shielded by her husband's public status as editor of the *Voice*.[46]

From outward appearances, Mary Bibb and Mary Ann Shadd would seem to have had a great deal in common. The two women were just three years apart in age, both freeborn and raised in the North, both were reasonably well educated, and both came to Canada with the purpose of teaching and aiding fugitive slaves. But there were keen distinctions, as well. Mary Bibb was happy to function in her husband's shadow, while Mary Ann Shadd was defiant in the face of male authority. Shadd presented herself as pious and above reproach; Mary Bibb was, perhaps, more crude. Shadd was the newcomer in the community, yet she achieved a measure of success where the Bibbs had failed. Mary Bibb reaped the benefits of marriage in the nineteenth century, including social status and personal protection, which Mary Ann Shadd did not enjoy. Indeed, Mary Ann Shadd was on her own and believed she had to fight for recognition and any personal gain—and fight she did.

Shadd continued to promote and distribute *Notes of Canada West* to anyone who cared to read it. She sent a copy to the American Missionary Association, apologizing for the typographical errors. She believed the errors were intentionally inserted by the white printer who was so influenced by the "spirit of slavery" that he wanted to discredit her writing. She told Whipple that she hoped to publish a second, error-free edition of the pamphlet. She sent copies of the tract to other antislavery groups, as well. A brief review in the *Pennsylvania Freeman* praised Shadd's writing, research, and commitment to the cause of the fugitives, but refused to endorse her call for emigration. "We are not convinced by her reasoning that an extensive emigration of our free colored population is called for by the circumstances in which they are placed," it noted. Other prominent antislavery newspapers, including the *Liberator* and *Frederick Douglass' Paper,* gave no notice to the little book. With sales proceeding slowly, Mary Ann Shadd may have had to rely on friends and relatives to help her pay for the book's publication. On one occasion, Rev. McArthur paid twenty-five dollars to the printer on her behalf. *Notes of Canada West* was both a political risk and a financial sacrifice.[47]

Across the border in Pittsburgh, an angry black physician and activist was also toiling to attract attention to his new book advocating black emigration. In what now seems a profound coincidence, Martin Delany wrote and published his nationalist treatise, *The Condition, Elevation, Emigration, and Destiny of the Colored People of the United States Politically Considered* in the spring of 1852, as well. Delany's book was a despairing look at black Americans' status after centuries of being "the bones and the sinew of the country." Like Shadd, Delany called for blacks to stop waiting for whites to grant them freedom, and instead to forge an independent black nation. Emigration was the best course for black Americans, argued Delany, just as it had been for the Jews in Egypt and the Puritans in Great Britain. But

Delany advocated settlement in Central or South America because "the Canadians are descended from the same common parentage as the Americans on this side of the Lakes." Delany's endorsement of a southern migration won him no more favor than Shadd's Canadian claims; the abolitionist press in the States either ignored his work or rejected the logic of his emigrationist appeal. Undaunted, Delany peddled his tract to abolitionist audiences in the North. Years later, it would be recognized as a classical text of black nationalism, while Shadd's *Notes of Canada West* would quickly lapse into obscurity. Delany and Shadd had probably met by this time, either in Wilmington or in Toronto at the emigration convention. Delany praised Mary Ann's *Hints to the Colored People of the North* in his book, but was apparently unaware that she was also publishing a work on emigration. Almost simultaneously, Delany and Shadd had produced crucial manifestos for the emigrationist cause that captured the tenor of the times. While the two initially disagreed on the best destination for black relocation, they would eventually form a close alliance and friendship that found firm ground in Canada West.[48]

THREE

Trouble in "Paradise"

The Detroit River communities of Windsor, Sandwich, and Amherst-burg, where Mary Ann Shadd spent the early 1850s, were little more than dusty hamlets on the edge of the Canadian frontier. When William Lloyd Garrison traveled through the area in 1853, he described Windsor as a "rude and impoverished village." The western portion of the province had been settled by French traders, who were joined by British loyalists after the American Revolution. One nineteenth-century observer suggested that Windsor's economy was based, in part, on the smuggling of British goods across the river to circumvent American tariffs. Unlike the bustling commercial centers of Toronto, Hamilton, and other cities in the East, the western region grew slowly. Most of the roads were rough and unpaved—often impassable in mid-winter. Transportation gradually improved as the Great Western Railroad was extended across Canada West, in the process providing jobs for as many as twenty-five hundred black workers. Until the railroad was completed in the mid-1850s, residents relied on horse-back and stagecoach to traverse the province by land, or on steamer ferries that crossed the Detroit River and Lake Erie. Manufactured goods from Britain and the United States were expensive and often unavailable, thus the inhabitants of these communities still existed as pioneers—either locally producing what they could consume, or doing without the luxuries taken for granted elsewhere. For Mary Ann Shadd, life in Canada West was far more difficult than she could have anticipated. Nevertheless, she remained a consistent booster for black emigration.[1]

The hardships in Canada did not deter free blacks from joining the exodus across the border. The *Voice of the Fugitive,* Shadd's pamphlet *Notes of Canada West,* the regular correspondence in the antislavery press, and word of mouth were all carrying the emigrationist appeal to a wider audience. Mary Ann Shadd's family were among the more prosperous free black Americans who decided to seek their fortunes—both political and economic—in Canada West. The Shadd clan had been trickling into the region for several years. Her sister Elizabeth and husband George Shreve moved to the Elgin settlement in Buxton sometime in 1850. Her brother Isaac was living in Canada West, as well. Early in June 1852 Abraham Shadd visited Canada for the first time since the Toronto convention nine months earlier. The *Voice* reported that "the father of the accomplished and talented Miss Mary A. Shadd" was touring Canada "to obtain some necessary information preparatory to the removal of his family, and a large number of others, from Pennsylvania to settle on the Queen's Free Soil." A newspaper from the Shadds' home town of West Chester also reported that the family planned to relocate.[2]

The elder Shadd was still active in Pennsylvania's antislavery movement. In February Abraham Shadd and two associates sent a petition to the state legislature protesting a proposed bill that would prevent the immigration of blacks into Pennsylvania. Although the law was not passed, it reflected the increasingly hostile environment for free blacks in the North. "Already we are prevented by reason of inhuman laws passed by a neighboring State, from visiting our friends without the liability of being heavily fined or sold into Slavery," the petitioners argued. Perhaps this was the last straw in the litany of injustices that Abraham Shadd had encountered in the United States. The announcement of his impending departure was a clear expression of alienation and betrayal. By the end of the year, Abraham Shadd had purchased two plots of land in Raleigh Township, near the Elgin settlement in Buxton, about forty miles from Windsor. It was a long road from the convention debates over emigration in the 1830s, to the act of packing up the family and making the trek northward, but now the Shadds and their relations would call Canada home. Abraham Shadd did not retire from public life, but instead seized the political opportunities of British citizenship. He became the only person of African descent to win elective office in Canada West before the Civil War when he was seated on the Raleigh Town Council in 1859. Abraham and Harriet Shadd lived out the remainder of their lives in Canada, as did most of Mary Ann's siblings and their descendants.[3]

The black emigration movement was coalescing in Canada West as seasoned activists arrived from the United States. Among them was James Theodore Holly, who moved to Windsor in the summer of 1852 and joined forces with Bibb to become assistant editor and proprietor of the *Voice of the Fugitive.* Holly was born free in Washington, D.C., devoted himself to the abolition of slavery, and worked as a bootmaker in Vermont. He became involved with the black emigration movement following passage of the Fugitive Slave Act, and he collaborated with Bibb in organizing the 1851 Toronto convention. Holly was a passionate supporter of the Canadian haven, and a regular contributor to the *Voice*. He exhorted black Americans to "vigorously pursue this project, and swarm in a ceaseless tide to Canada West, and hang like an ominous *black cloud* over this guilty nation" until the abolition of slavery was achieved. He called for the formation of a North American League, which he envisioned as centralizing efforts to unite and then "mould the destiny of the whole Afro American race." This young and energetic visionary also supported the Refugee Home Society and was a loyal ally of Henry Bibb, whom Holly referred to as "the central authority" on Canadian emigration. Holly labored to recruit subscribers and funding to keep the *Voice* solvent, and he gave new vigor to Bibb's efforts to silence Mary Shadd's opposition.[4]

Mary Ann Shadd's challenge to the established black leadership in Canada West laid bare the many fractures in the fragile structure of their insulated communities. The fugitive slaves and free blacks who gathered in these small outposts behaved like many who live in aggrieved and segregated circumstances—they took out their pain and frustration on each other while they remained heavily dependent on their oppressors. Class, color, slave status, gender, and religion were all contested categories that pitted black against black in what William and Jane Pease termed a "series of criminations and recriminations." The war between Shadd and the Bibb faction was rooted in philosophical differences over what was the best direction for building and sustaining Canada's black communities. It also reflected divergent positions on black identity. Bibb and the Refugee Home Society focused their attention on urgently needed relief to the fugitive slaves. In this view, "begging" for support was a means to an end intent on bettering the condition of Afro-Canadians. Shadd and her supporters were also concerned with the fugitives' needs, but wanted to establish a pattern of autonomy and self-sufficiency as soon as they set foot on Canadian soil, in the process creating a new national identity. In her view, long-term survival might mean short-term sacrifice.[5]

These debates were exacerbated because they also became a struggle over power and gender. Who was to be the spokesperson for black emigration to Canada? Whose strategies should win out in the formulation of policies and institutions? And was it reasonable, or acceptable, that a woman should have the authoritative voice on these matters? Throughout the antebellum period, black Americans seemed to encourage—and even require—women's participation in the public sphere as necessary for racial progress. At the same time, black women were expected to adhere to the

MARY ANN SHADD CARY

Henry Bibb, from the
frontispiece of *The Narrative
of the Life and Adventures of
Henry Bibb* (New York, 1850).
(Metropolitan Toronto
Reference Library)

cult of domesticity, with its emphasis on the home and childrearing. As
James O. Horton has noted about northern black institutions, "men dominated their leadership but women played key roles." Shadd's behavior in
Windsor ran afoul of these assumptions, and Bibb and his followers responded by treating her as a hated foe. In July 1852, the *Voice of the Fugitive*
ran an article that, on the surface, appeared to be a status report on schools
in the region. But the article accused Shadd of teaching only black children—an assertion she had consistently denied—and admonished her for
reacting angrily to the paper's revelation of her salary. "Miss Shadd has said
and written many things which we think will add nothing to her credit as a
lady, for there should be no insult taken where there is none intended," the
Voice noted. Women, the paper seemed to be suggesting, should be seen
and not heard.[6]

Many women would have taken this public admonishment as sufficient
warning that they had overstepped their bounds. In the case of Mary Ann
Shadd, the chastising in the pages of the *Voice* simply made her more angry.
Five days later, Shadd "laid before the public a detailed account of her

school, and of the relation she holds with the American Missionary Association" at a public meeting in the Windsor barracks. The chair of the meeting was Coleman Freeman, a black farmer and local activist who served on the executive committee of the Refugee Home Society, but was among those disenchanted with the organization. The meeting's secretary was Shadd's friend, Rev. Alexander McArthur. It was a sympathetic gathering at which Shadd could mount her defense. As the proceedings became tense, Mary Bibb tried to persuade Windsor's black residents to apply for a government-supported school rather than supporting Shadd's private one. The Bibbs' jealousy was obvious, and they had forced Mary Ann to publicly respond to the accusations published in the *Voice*. But the resolutions passed at the meeting were a vindication of her efforts. The group thanked the A.M.A. for its funding, expressed appreciation for Shadd's labors, approved her decision to withhold the details of her salary, and supported her goal of an integrated school for the village.[7]

Shadd celebrated a hollow victory, however. In the pages of the *Voice* her critics continued to accuse her of running a segregated school, and she told the A.M.A. that while she had no intentions of leaving Windsor, the recent events convinced her that Bibb intended to drive her out of town. Then she learned that her opponents were operating behind the scenes to weaken her and Rev. McArthur's ties to the American Missionary Association. Thus began several months of intrigue, accusations, and castigation that eventually spelled disaster for Mary Ann's school. By midsummer, McArthur learned from a colleague that the A.M.A. had denied his application for a missionary appointment. The A.M.A. was under siege by blacks opposing its presence in Canada West. The association's 1852 Annual Report noted that "a class of ignorant preachers, and self-constituted collecting agents . . . are laboring . . . to drive every white missionary from the colony." The A.M.A. reasoned that McArthur would be another white minister who would not be accepted by the fugitives in Windsor, and that his style of preaching was over the heads of his flock. Since A.M.A. Secretary Whipple had never been to Windsor and had never heard McArthur preach, these observations had probably been passed along by a local informant—perhaps Dawn's Hiram Wilson, who was a friend of Bibb's and a supporter of the Refugee Home Society, or A.M.A. missionary David Hotchkiss, who was also affiliated with the R.H.S. McArthur's fate was sealed; his support of Shadd and criticism of Bibb and the Refugee Home Society shortened his tenure in Canada West, and Mary Ann Shadd would lose an important ally.[8]

Shadd was surprisingly naive about the relationships and motivations of some of the actors in this controversy, or she made it appear so in her letters to Whipple. For example, she admitted that she "spoke freely to his [Bibb's] partner Mr. Holly about the shallowness of such publications and explained to him the reasons of my former silence and of having sent to you their article." She was equally unsophisticated about pouring out her anger and frustrations to her employers—an organization with diverse loyalties and connections. Shadd failed to understand that the small, closely knit network of white missionaries and abolitionists who supported the black communities in Canada West might not side with her in the debate, even though she seemed to share their ideological principles. Board members of the American Missionary Association were also affiliated with the Refugee Home Society and other targets of Shadd's criticism. Some were covertly racist—Hotchkiss was known for calling blacks "depraved and inferior"—and were unlikely to have much patience for an upstart black female. Other missionaries simply felt it was more important to remain united in the goal of serving the fugitives' needs. Shadd's brash comments, such as, "the minutiae I have not dwelt upon, they would be too revolting and almost incredible to detail," offended the A.M.A. and their colleagues, and gave the impression that she was obsessed with this controversy and was blowing it out of proportion. Her candor and openness did her more harm than good.[9]

What becomes clear through Shadd's letters is an almost desperate desire to be heard. Her correspondence with the A.M.A. had become a vital means of public expression. Mary Ann Shadd had developed a great appreciation of the power of the press—and she was envious of the *Voice*'s influence: "What a vast amount of mischief a man like *H. Bibb* can do with an organ of his own to nod, insinuate and "fling" away the reputation of others and how *much he* has already done to persons who have had no means equally extensive at their control to counteract it is appalling [*sic*]," she complained. A few days later she wrote Whipple to report on the meeting of Windsor's residents and to send a copy of the resolutions they passed. Again she expressed frustration with not having her own vehicle of expression: "I have not a paper of my own and must leave the result with God," she lamented.[10]

Mary Ann faced a formidable opponent. Although she had a low opinion of Bibb and his newspaper, he was an influential figure in the American and Canadian antislavery communities, and the *Voice of the Fugitive* was considered to be a reliable and important source of information about blacks in Canada West. Clearly, Shadd's pamphlet *Notes of Canada West* had not made her a visibile expert as she had hoped. Much of the content of abolitionist newspapers were articles, speeches, and letters lifted from other periodicals. It was often assumed that material in one paper would appear elsewhere. Stories from the *Voice* were reprinted frequently in the abolitionist press as authoritative accounts of the region, and the *Voice*'s editors functioned as gatekeepers on a variety of issues. On one occasion, a *Voice* article noted disapproval of "beggars from Canada who did not come recommended through the *Voice of the Fugitive*." Henry Bibb's success as a lecturer and organizer, and the popularity of his published slave narrative, made him a powerful spokesperson for the fugitives' cause and won him the support of white abolitionists. His status as a former slave gave him additional credibility, as a comment from the Anti-Slavery Society of Canada illustrates: "The *Voice of the Fugitive* is published here. It is edited by Mr. Henry Bibb, a colored man of respectable talents and who, though young, has suffered much from Slavery." His work on behalf of the fugitives and the intensity of his emigrationist ideology earned him the respect of many black abolitionists as well. Bibb seemed to be surrounded by an impenetrable shield of influential supporters.[11]

The *Voice* delivered mixed messages about gender roles. On some occasions, black women's contributions to the abolitionist movement were encouraged, such as when the paper published a letter from Chatham blacks calling for "the aid and cooperation of our sisters in the elevation of our race." But the scope and manner of women's involvement in the public sphere was often left open to interpretation. Bibb and Holly regularly published Victorian homilies—usually lifted from other periodicals—about women's domestic role. One such article noted that "the most powerful and beneficial of the influences ordinarily at work in the formation of human character is that of woman," and extolled the guiding power of a mother's hand in raising great men. Another piece published in the spring of 1852 seemed almost deliberately placed for Shadd's benefit. Titled "Advice to the Girls," the article asked "Girls, do you want to get married? And do you want good husbands? If so, cease to act like fools." Such advice was a regular staple of the antebellum black press. Frankie Hutton has argued that the editors of these papers consciously reinforced the cult of true womanhood to dispel prevailing negative images of black women. But there was an instructional component to this discourse, as well. Bibb and his fellow editors saw their papers as instrumental for teaching the black masses the values and expectations of bourgeois society. It is likely that Mary Ann's marital status, as well as her outspoken personality, were discomfiting for Bibb and others in Windsor. All around her were messages that she was exceptional, and not necessarily accepted.[12]

Unwisely, Mary Ann took the offensive by writing a series of unsigned letters in the *Western Evangelist* that outlined her criticism of Bibb and the Refugee Home Society. Little is known about this newspaper but its articles were reprinted frequently in the *Voice of the Fugitive*, the *Liberator*, and other abolitionist sheets. The articles elicited an angry, mean-spirited response from the editors of the *Voice*, who identified Shadd as the culprit without printing her name. The paper called her "an insignificant scribbler in this village" who was alone in her criticism of the Refugee Home Society. While admitting that the *Voice* had "inadvertently" accused her of lying about her arrangement with the A.M.A., the paper also said that its revelations had "brought out a public acknowledgment of some secret, and underhanded measures" of Shadd's doing.[13]

The *Voice* excoriated Shadd and sought to turn Windsor's blacks against her: "Such an individual merits the contempt, indignation, and execration of the whole community, and should not be allowed to eat bread amongst a people, whose interest is thus abused," proclaimed the editorial. What angered her enemies the most was that Shadd had published her claims in the *Western Evangelist,* a paper that was read by abolitionists and white missionaries. Every charge by Bibb and his followers was intended to reduce or minimize Shadd's influence, suggesting that her power in Windsor was indeed meaningful. Mary Ann's criticism of the Refugee Home Society was tolerated when it appeared in *Notes of Canada West;* "knowing the limited circulation that this pamphlet would have, could not effect much injury," wrote the *Voice* editors. "But when we perceive the same slanders magnified, and anonymously propagated through a more extended medium," Bibb felt justified in launching his attack. The *Voice* labeled Shadd and her supporters "vile creatures," and vowed that it would "crush to the dust such pygmy opposition."[14]

Shadd's decision to write anonymously clearly backfired. It allowed the *Voice* to be especially nasty in assaulting her without appearing to publicly insult a well-known woman. Shadd may have sent her letters to other newspapers as well, but they were never published, nor were excerpts reprinted in the largest abolitionist papers in the United States. So, whatever margin of protection she gained from this ploy was offset by the fact that her views were not circulated beyond the readers of one small periodical. Perhaps the greatest significance of this exchange was that in discarding the veiled compliments and patronizing tone of the earlier *Voice* articles, Bibb openly revealed his hostility and malice toward Shadd. The debate over the Refugee Home Society had degenerated into a petty, almost juvenile, exchange of insults. But for Mary Ann Shadd, this was no trivial matter. Henry and Mary Bibb, Holly, and others were doing their best to sully her reputation, suppress her public voice, and wrestle away the school she had worked so hard to establish. Shadd found herself in a bitter struggle for survival.[15]

The controversy in the pages of the *Voice* gave Mary Ann's school some visibility that worked to her advantage. The influential Unitarian abolitionist Rev. Samuel J. May visited her school that summer as part of his investigation of conditions for fugitives in Canada. Although Shadd worried that Mary Bibb, who accompanied May on his tour of Windsor, had turned him against her, May's impressions of Shadd's work were favorable. He told another prominent abolitionist, Lewis Tappan, that "Miss Shadd is a very capable young woman. I visited her school and inspected several exercises of several classes, all of which were well performed." May was also persuaded by the opponents of begging and his evaluation of the situation closely echoed Shadd's position. He saw ample evidence that the fugitives could support themselves, and told Tappan that it was "better to leave the fugitives after they get into Canada, to take care of themselves, than to perpetuate their helplessness or inactivity by sending clothes and food." Mary Ann certainly found May's observations a small vindication for her insistence that Canda's blacks needed to be autonomous and self-sufficient.[16]

The internecine squabbling in Windsor was eventually overshadowed—at least for a time—by life and death matters. The daily rigors of life on the frontier were highlighted in the summer of 1852 when a cholera epidemic swept through Windsor. Mary Ann was among those stricken with the disease, and parents were so worried about it spreading that Shadd closed her school for a month's vacation. By mid-August cholera was rampaging through the town, and several children were among those hit hardest. A month later the school was still closed and physicians visiting the area determined that the barracks where many fugitives lived were not fit for habitation. Windsor was in the midst of a crisis. Shadd predicted it would be weeks before school opened again, and that there had been several deaths from the epidemic: "Heads of families have been taken away, and in one instance a member of the school; and in view of the general unhealthiness, persons who have small children talk of moving to the country," she told the A.M.A. Among the visitors to Shadd's school during the epidemic was a black Congregational minister named Samuel Ringgold Ward, who toured the barracks on behalf of the Anti-Slavery Society of Canada and deemed them a health risk. Shadd and Ward may have met at the Toronto convention the year before, and he had undoubtedly read about the bitter war of words in Windsor through the pages of the *Voice of the Fugitive*. During his visit Shadd and Ward found they agreed on many of the contentious issues facing blacks in Canada West.[17]

Samuel Ringgold Ward was born a slave in Maryland in 1817, but his parents escaped to freedom when he was three years old, and he was educated by Quakers in New York. In 1839 he became a licensed Congregational minister, and he led two all-white churches in upstate New York. Ward also studied medicine and law during the 1840s, but his reputation came from his success as an antislavery lecturer and organizer. Like many antislavery activists, Ward also turned his energies to journalism. He founded an abolitionist paper, *The True American,* in Cortland, New York, in 1847. The paper folded within a year, and he joined another editor, Stephen Myers, who published *The Northern Star and Colored Farmer* in Albany. In early 1849, the paper, having been confused with Frederick Douglass's

North Star in Rochester, also folded, and Ward and Myers founded *The Impartial Citizen* in Syracuse. The *Citizen* moved to Boston in 1851 and was halted abruptly when Ward fled to Canada that year.[18]

Ward's lecture tours and newspapers earned him a reputation as an outstanding thinker and orator, second only to Frederick Douglass in stature among black public figures. On occasion he was a maverick and engaged in controversial debates. In May 1849, for example, he challenged Douglass to a debate over the constitutionality of American slavery. But Ward was a reluctant emigrationist, and he moved to Canada out of necessity. By his own account, Ward and his wife became disheartened by the rise in gruesome slave captures following passage of the Fugitive Slave Act. As he described it, "We concluded that resistance was fruitless, that the country was hopelessly given to the execution of this barbarous enactment, and that it were vain to hope for the reformation of such a country." But he also admitted facing financial problems and few employment prospects at home. Ward's decision was accelerated when he aided in the escape of William Henry, a fugitive who was captured and held in Syracuse. As a participant in what became known as the "Jerry Rescue," a warrant was issued for Ward's arrest, and he quickly escaped to Canada.[19]

In October 1851 Ward moved his family first to Montreal, and then to Toronto, where they settled. The prominent black minister was a welcome addition to the abolitionist cause in Canada. He was appointed to the Executive Committee of the Anti-Slavery Society of Canada and he became its official traveling agent. Like Mary Ann Shadd, Ward applied to the A.M.A. for a missionary appointment soon after arriving in Canada, explaining that he had a family of six to support. But such an appointment was never made. For two years, Ward traversed Canada West to promote the antislavery cause and fight the rising tide of Canadian racism. He became a regular correspondent to the *Voice of the Fugitive,* in which he wrote a series outlining his observations on what he termed "negrophobia." His advocacy and organizing were widely considered successful, and his work was the highlight of the Anti-Slavery Society's activities during this period. The *Voice* spoke of Ward in glowing terms—"distinguished gentleman" was a common salutation—and Ward initially supported the Refugee Home Society although he denounced segregated institutions and the practice of begging for donations.[20]

While in Windsor, Ward joined the fray over the Refugee Home Society. He organized a public meeting to discuss complaints lodged against the society, and he offered criticisms that placed him squarely in opposition to the Bibb faction. Ward's gathering prepared a statement condemning the R. H. S as "unrighteous and despotic," and they maintained that the society's methods of land distribution and ownership restrictions were "insulting to our manhood." As a newcomer to these controversies, it was clear that Ward sided with Shadd and the R.H.S. opposition. Several years later, Ward would write that he opposed blacks' self-imposed segregation in Canada West, and that he found black churches and ministers to have a "degrading effect" on the populace. Thus, Shadd and Ward were natural allies, holding the same opinions on matters they considered crucial to black progress.[21]

Bibb and Holly were also present at the meeting and, as expected, opposed the resolution. Facing such harsh criticism from the influential Ward must have been a source of anger and embarrassment for the pair. It is unclear whether Mary Ann Shadd attended the meeting, although it was held in her school room and the outcome reinforced her hostility toward the R.H.S. The meeting made it public that Ward—a powerful abolitionist spokesman—was part of the growing group of dissidents. Not surprisingly, there was no report of the meeting in the *Voice,* but stories appeared in several abolitionist papers in the United States, including the *Pennsylvania Freeman.* The Windsor battles were beginning to spill into the American antislavery press.

A week later, another meeting was held in Windsor to continue the critique of the Refugee Home Society. This time, Ward was absent and the initiative was led by local residents including Mary Shadd, who served as one of two secretaries. The group adopted five resolutions that, among other things, condemned begging and asked abolitionists in the United States to stop sending clothes and money because the donations rarely reached those who were most needy. At the meeting's end, the majority agreed to send the proceedings to the Toronto *Globe* and to antislavery papers in the United States. Broadening their audience beyond the borders of Canada West, the Shadd faction succeeded in having their strongly worded denunciation published in the *Liberator.* "We do not regard the Refugees Home Society as a benevolent institution," Shadd and her allies resolved. The society was nothing more than "an exceedingly cunning land scheme" that encouraged a system of begging that "will materially compromise our manhood, by representing us as objects of charity." This was a stance on which Shadd, Ward, Tappan, and other abolitionists had harped. Canada West's experiment in black self-sufficiency worked best when the fugitive slaves did not rely on the benevolence of others. The resolutions also charged local missionaries and fund raisers for the Refugee Home Society with taking "pecuniary advantage" of the donations they collected. This accusation was at the core of local opposition to white missionaries. One A.M.A. missionary in Amherstburg, Isaac Rice, had been replaced after he was accused of numerous fund-raising infractions. Similar charges had been leveled against the A.M.A.'s Hiram Wilson. No individual was singled out by these latest complaints, but they helped to taint the image of the R.H.S.[22]

The varying accounts of this gathering illustrate the almost riotous nature of the political culture in Canada West's black communities. Henry and Mary Bibb and James Holly were present, and, along with an unnamed supporter, were the only ones to oppose the resolutions. The *Voice of the Fugitive* reported that many of the participants were uneducated fugitives who did not understand the proceedings, and that the meeting ended when "the whole house was thrown into a mad confusion" that almost led to a fist fight. In Mary Ann Shadd's version, the "confusion" was caused by Bibb, who "after having *commanded* the reading of the resolutions, insisted, then and there, on taking the names of the officers, preparatory, he said, to their prosecution for holding what he was pleased to call an 'illegal meeting.'"[23]

The decision to distribute the proceedings to the antislavery press was symptomatic of Shadd's frustration with the dominant role of the *Voice of the Fugitive* in the public dialogue concerning Canadian emigration. She wrote a letter to William Lloyd Garrison to clarify the group's reasons for airing their grievances in this manner, taking pains to assure him that she was speaking on behalf of Windsor's black residents. The Refugee Home Society, she explained, had "been a source of great uneasiness" for the fugitives who found the "false reports of their destitution" both "hideous" and "decidedly objectionable." They were disturbed that while the *Liberator* had published numerous articles and notices about the society, there had been no revelations of the discord in the communities of black exiles. The society's opponents were "resolved to speak but the great difficulty is to get the public ear," she wrote. Shadd sought to convince Garrison that fairness required the publication of their complaints. At the same time, she was gaining greater visibility for the emigrationist cause, despite the R.H.S. scandal. Even opponents to emigration like Garrison and Frederick Douglass could no longer ignore these debates. Garrison published the resolutions in the next issue of the *Liberator* with the title "No More Begging for Farms or Clothes for Fugitives in Canada," and it set off a lively discussion both in Canada and the United States.[24]

Readers of the *Liberator* took note of the resolutions from the Windsor meeting, and at least one inquired whether they described the true condition of Canada's fugitives. The paper's editors were cautious not to assume that Mary Ann and her cadre spoke for all of Windsor's blacks. The *Liberator* was also reluctant to endorse the request that charitable donations from northern abolitionists be stopped. Few who worked to raise donations for the fugitives from slavery were likely to acknowledge that their efforts were not wanted. But the *Liberator* did congratulate the group for promoting self-sufficiency in the black community, a gesture that Bibb considered a repudiation of the Refugee Home Society. "We confess, however, that we greatly like, and applaud, the spirit of the Windsor meeting, and of the resolutions passed by them. It is manly, and cannot fail to ensure respect," said the *Liberator*.[25]

Mary Ann Shadd was quite comfortable with evoking masculinity as the ultimate symbol of black power and authority, at the same time that she openly challenged black male supremacy. For abolitionists, the masculine ideal was equated with the freedom for black men to exercise control over their lives, openly display both physical and intellectual strength, and protect their families. Twenty years earlier, another black feminist, Maria Stewart, had urged black men to fight oppression by exerting their manhood. "But where is the man that has distinguished himself in these modern days by acting wholly in the defense of African rights and liberty?" Stewart had asked. Similarly, Shadd clearly differentiated between the gender ideals of racial uplift and the gendered authority claimed by individuals like Henry Bibb. She relied on Victorian femininity to shield her from the attacks of her enemies. While Bibb, Holly, and others wanted her to behave according to gender conventions, she argued that they violated these conventions by refusing to treat her in a "ladylike" fashion.[26]

Bibb took several swipes at his opponents in the pages of the *Voice* but generally painted them as powerless and insignificant. They were labeled "some feeble opposition" and "a set of half cracked, hot headed individuals" who criticized the Refugee Home Society because, as freeborn persons, they were ineligible to purchase lands from the society. But it was Mary Bibb who uncharacteristically moved from her husband's shadow to challenge the Shadd faction. In a rebuttal published in the *Liberator,* she repudiated begging and advised potential contributors not to give funds to anyone on behalf of the fugitives unless their claims were legitimate. Mary Bibb also struck at the claim that the quantity of land sold by the Refugee Home Society was too small and suggested that industrious farmers could easily live off of the twenty-five-acre parcels. Like her husband, Bibb maintained that the opposition to the R.H.S. was led by whites and free blacks who resented the fact that they were excluded from purchasing land from the society.[27]

Canada's influential white abolitionists weighed in to the controversy in late October in a refutation of the Windsor group's charges. The Anti-Slavery Society of Canada was particularly disturbed by the resolutions, which contradicted their claims of extreme deprivation among the fugitive population. Its members believed there was a continued need for charity for the fugitives and worried that the debate would have its intended effect, which was to stem the flow of contributions. Michael Willis, president of the society, declared that "there is no sufficient reason to believe that the allegations made in the resolutions . . . are founded in fact," and that the charges were "the result of erroneous judgment; if not of prejudice or jealousy." Although Samuel Ringgold Ward—a critic of the Refugee

Home Society—was an emissary for the Anti-Slavery Society of Canada, the organization clearly sided with Bibb and his supporters. Others in the antislavery establishment took a similar position. The editors of the *Pennsylvania Freeman* asserted that the Windsor group were presumptuous to claim that they represented all of Canada's blacks. The paper also argued against withholding aid from the fugitives in Canada: "We cannot believe that in such a population there is not real, pressing want, which must be supplied by benevolence."[28]

In November 1852, the officers of the Windsor meeting made one last attempt to defend their position. In a lengthy letter written by Shadd that was published in the *Liberator,* they pressed their claim that there was unanimity in the criticism of the Refugee Home Society among Canada's blacks. To bolster their argument they reported that similar meetings had been held in other towns and villages in the province. The letter stated that Canadian—as opposed to American—benevolence adequately served the needs of the fugitives. And it revealed what was to be Shadd's new agenda when it proclaimed that the *Voice of the Fugitive* "is not the voice of the colored people in Canada." For the first time in print, Shadd suggested that another newspaper was needed to counter the *Voice*'s influence: "Character, weight, ability are needed in a journal proclaiming itself the voice of fugitives."[29]

During this period, Shadd also became a central figure in the formation of the Windsor Anti-Slavery Society, which was initiated by Samuel Ward's visit that summer. The first official meeting of the Windsor chapter was held in October 1852, and the large, interracial gathering approved a constitution that stated as its purpose "the abolition of chattle [*sic*] Slavery, and the elevation of the colored population of North America." Despite their bitter differences, both sides of the R.H.S. debate gave their support to the new organization, and Henry Bibb was elected as its first president. At the second meeting of the society, Mary Ann Shadd agreed to serve on a committee to investigate the needs of newly arrived fugitives. On the surface, at least, Windsor's black community was working together for the common good.[30]

It is a wonder that Shadd still found time to operate the Windsor school while she was consumed with these local politics. The cholera epidemic had finally subsided, but many parents were reluctant to send their children to school until well into October. Shadd was teaching an average of twenty-five children during the day and a dozen adults at night. In addition, she was continuing the Sunday school classes and Bible classes previously taught by Rev. McArthur, and she reminded her employers that Windsor remained without clergy, "a privation seriously felt by many who cannot well afford the expense of crossing to Detroit to worship." Money was a concern for the teacher as well. Shadd provided a detailed accounting of her receipts, as if to protect herself against further charges of financial malfeasance. She reported $40 in tuition and $50 in outside contributions, in addition to the support from the A.M.A. This, she told her employers, was not sufficient to sustain a teacher for very long. But she had few employment alternatives. Not surprisingly, Shadd blamed Henry Bibb's article for making it difficult to collect tuition. On the optimistic side, Shadd reported that the frame for a new schoolhouse had been built, and she hoped the building would be completed before winter set in. Her hopes were dashed when, in a letter to Whipple a month later, she reported no progress on the schoolhouse but said she had found two rooms for her classes during the winter.[31]

Worse than the approaching cold and snow was the continued enmity toward Shadd from the ranks of the Refugee Home Society. A white Presbyterian minister, Rev. Charles C. Foote, who was the principal fund-raising agent for the R.H.S., launched the most insidious and damaging attack against Shadd. It was Foote, more than any other individual, who was the target of the Windsor group's complaints. Foote became well known for raising thousands of dollars in donations through exaggerated claims of their destitution, although he maintained that his intentions were based on his concerns for the fugitives' welfare. Publicly, he wrote a long defense of the society and his fund-raising practices in a letter to the *Liberator.* He refuted the Windsor meeting's resolutions in typical fashion, declared the opposition a "small faction of colored persons, in and about Windsor (most of whom have never been slaves)," and defended the integrity of Henry and Mary Bibb.[32]

But Foote was also active behind the scenes. Samuel Ward learned from a colleague in Philadelphia that, unknown to Shadd, Foote was trying to discredit her within American antislavery circles. Ward warned George Whipple that "Rev. C. C. Foote is directly or indirectly seeking to cast censure upon Miss M. Shadd of Windsor," and he urged the A.M.A. to investigate before heeding Foote's charges. Rev. Alexander McArthur also came to Shadd's defense in a letter to the A.M.A. that did not mask his outrage. McArthur was no longer seeking a job with the A.M.A., and he discarded his earlier conciliatory tone and got right to the heart of the matter. He was anxious to assure the A.M.A. that Mary Ann's complaints were not exaggerated. "She has been very much abused here in public meetings and through the columns of the 'Voice of Fugitive' by the senior Editor of that paper," he wrote. He was particularly disturbed that Bibb "has frequently impeached her honesty and what is worse, questioned her virtue publicly." Despite the attacks, Mary Ann continued to "enjoy the confidence of the entire colored people of Windsor," he said.[33]

Although McArthur expressed concern for Shadd's plight, he was also confident that she could defend herself against Foote's claims that she slandered the Refugee Home Society. "If Mr. Foote calls this slander, it must be on the principle of English law, which declares 'the greater the truth, the greater the slander.'" McArthur was blunt in his criticism of the R.H.S., saying it did not promote the interests of the fugitives and was "another of those bottomless pits which have opened their mouths on this fugitive mission and swallowed so much of the peoples charitable contributions." Foote and other members of the Refugee Home Society had spent little or no time among the fugitives in Canada West and were least able to judge Shadd's assertions. "If he [Foote] had sat by their firesides, and mingled with them in social life, and gathered his news from their conversation as I have he would not have evinced so much feeling at the statements of Mary Shadd. Short stays at Mr. Bibb's was not the way nor the place to obtain the requisite information," he wrote.[34]

As Christmas 1852 approached, Mary Ann was teaching an average of thirty children aged four through twelve, while battling bouts of measles and cholera, a lack of books and supplies, and the fact that her pupils often left school to work in the fields or at home. Shadd tried to be an innovative teacher and added history and botany to the daily regimen of grammar, arithmetic, and geography studied by her older students. And she was proud that although her school was comprised mostly of the children of fugitive slaves, there were "children of all complexions in appearance, from African to Caucasian" among them.[35]

Shadd's success as a teacher and public servant, however, was overshadowed by the political strife that seemed to engulf her. While Bibb continued to assail Shadd in the pages of the *Voice*, Foote sent a stream of charges against Shadd to the American Missionary Association. In a series of letters, Shadd tried to clarify her criticism, explaining that while many officers of the Refugee Home Society were committed abolitionists, others were primarily interested in their own gain. She declared that "Henry Bibb has hundreds of dollars belonging to fugitives," that he was "dishonest," and that she felt it her duty to expose him. Mary Ann had learned to bolster her arguments with the evidence she amassed, and she offered an extensive list of Bibb's financial activities. She claimed that during 1852 Bibb had "built a house, bought a vessel, bought a house and lot, on which he lives, leased another, and Mrs. Bibb has purchased a farm," and that they had business holdings in both Detroit and Canada. What disturbed her most was that Bibb decided how the funds should be distributed, "and sends from his door naked fugitives," because donations were made at his discretion. Mary Ann also bluntly questioned the gender politics of the attacks, and asserted that being a women made her an easier target for a smear campaign since Ward and other male critics were not receiving the same treatment. "[Foote] may partly succeed in crushing a mere woman like myself, but . . . it is certainly not brave neither is it christian-like in Mr. Foote . . . to pounce upon one he thought *easy* to crush, and cautiously avoid allusion to able and weighty *men*, whom he knew to be actively opposed to his scheme," she asserted.[36]

To make matters worse, a letter Shadd wrote to one of her allies, the Philadelphia abolitionist William Still, somehow fell into Foote's possession. The content of that letter made its way to Whipple of the American Missionary Association in New York, who seemed to be seeking some way to mediate the controversy. He suggested that Shadd meet with Horace Hallock, a white officer of the R.H.S. living in Detroit, to discuss her grievances. She defiantly refused, saying that although she would continue to defend herself, she suspected that she would not be believed. Shadd argued that portions of her letter to Still were taken out of context and exaggerated and she repeated her mistrust of Foote and his colleagues. "I am not personally acquainted with Mr. Hallock, but, as himself and others in Detroit have willingly listened to false reports concerning me from Henry Bibb, and have given Mr. B. instructions on which he has acted, I cannot subject myself to the degradation of an interview with him," she replied.[37]

Mary Ann's suspicions of Hallock were correct. He had aligned himself with Bibb and Foote, and had no intentions of mediating a solution. To the contrary, when he corresponded with the American Missionary Association, he made it clear that Mary Ann was viewed as an enemy who had to be silenced at all costs:

> Regarding Miss Shadd and the malign influence she is seeking to exert against our *Sy.* [society] I know not what may grow of it, but of this I feel well assured, that she is not only a busy body in other men's matters, but a notorious mischief maker to the extent of her ability—if half that I hear of her efforts in that line be true. . . . We propose soon to do something through a Com. [committee] and if no *truce* can be declared shall take such action as we trust may at least weaken her power for *evil* against our *Sy.*[38]

Mary Ann Shadd had hit a vital nerve in the corps of abolitionists and missionaries stationed in Canada West. This lone black woman, with her vociferous criticism, detailed investigations into wrong-doing, and relentless energy for confrontation, had unleashed an ugly side of the antislavery establishment. It is possible that Shadd's complaints were rooted in personal dislike for the Bibbs, Foote, and the others. But evidence suggests that she had uncovered questionable and unethical activities that were doing more harm than good to the cause of black emigration to Canada. Like most whistleblowers, Shadd paid a dear price for her revelations.

The American Missionary Association Committee on Canada Missions met in mid-January and voted to "withhold aid from her when it can be done without violating our obligations to her." Since Shadd's one-year contract with the A.M.A. had begun the previous spring, she could expect to be paid only through April or May. The brief minutes of the meeting give little information about the discussion among the committee's members, all influential abolitionists, at least one of whom—Samuel Cornish—knew her personally. Also present were New York anti-slavery leader and former A.M.A. treasurer Lewis Tappan, and John Scoble, a British abolitionist who headed the controversial Dawn settlement in Canada West. The meeting's minutes, written by A.M.A. secretary George Whipple, said only that her lack of Christian evangelism violated Act 3 of the A.M.A. Constitution, thus providing grounds for her dismissal. In later correspondence, Shadd accused the two blacks on the A.M.A. Committee, either Cornish or Rev. Charles Ray, of suggesting that her views were not sufficiently evangelical to meet the criteria of the A.M.A.[39]

Ironically, the Annual Report of the A.M.A. issued just a month earlier had praised Mary Ann as an "experienced colored teacher," whose reports were "full and satisfactory." Her dismissal had nothing to do with the effectiveness of her school, or her abilities in the classroom. Her lack of evangelical views was simply a smoke screen—at least the matter had never come up during the months she had been employed by the A.M.A. Rather, the members had to find some way of extricating the association from this acrimonious debate, and she had offended too many closely allied with the A.M.A. In particular, Horace Hallock of the Refugee Home Society had strong ties to the association, and he became its vice-president in the 1860s. While some of the committee members may have felt sympathy for Shadd and her political position, they closed ranks against her in a show of public support for Bibb, Foote, Hallock, and the Refugee Home Society.[40]

Mary Ann was devastated by the news. She immediately saw through the ruse that her religious views were at fault and chided the A.M.A. for its hypocrisy. She penned her response in a letter to the association:

> I regard this as the most severe *blow* I have received this year—not the order to leave so much as the reasons your Committee are pleased to assign. I say to leave, because a school cannot, yet, be supported here without aid foreign to this place. Had your Committee decided to cut me off because of views I hold of the R.H.S. I should feel it a light matter in one sense, but by this action (which if I understand your letter is certain beyond reasonable doubt) I am placed in the unenviable and ridiculous light of having sought support from your Society at the expense of peculiar religious views I am *supposed* to entertain or of having concealed my views or of having kept up the deception the entire year. This is not so.[41]

In a calm and measured tone, Shadd brushed aside the charges that she lacked an evangelical commitment, noting that she had undergone considerable personal and intellectual changes during her shift from Catholicism to the Methodist Church. She said it was presumptuous that her "friend" spoke as an authority regarding her religious views without her permission.

"I hope you will allow me to ask if it is a custom of your Committee to review at the beginning of each year the opinions held by missionaries, and their testimonials, or was your action in my case of a special character?" she asked. Mary Ann made it clear that she felt singled out for unfair treatment. "I have been puzzled to determine what phase purely evangelical views must take to deserve to be called heterodox; but the whole thing involves an absurdity."[42]

Shadd continued to correspond with the A.M.A. over the next few months, holding fast to her criticism of the Refugee Home Society. But she knew that her cause was hopeless and that the school she had struggled to maintain for over a year was doomed without outside funding. Windsor's residents came to her defense, holding a large meeting where more than forty-five persons signed resolutions denouncing Foote's charges and appointing Shadd to write a response on their behalf. By the time Shadd's letter was published in the *Liberator*, it was too late to salvage her job, but it helped to give her greater public visibility. She declared, "Since the formation of the Refugees' Home Society, there has not been a meeting held in its favor in Canada" and that Foote's letters to the abolitionist press were "a strange medley of false statements, curious comparisons, stale recommendations of the Fugitives' Home by gentlemen who have never examined the scheme in working order." Now there was nothing to lose from the rhetorical battle.[43]

Mary Ann Shadd closed her little school in Windsor on March 23, 1853 after spending eighteen months fighting for financial and political support to educate the community of black American expatriates. The tuition paid by the parents failed to cover the school's expenses, much less her salary, and she reported that "the rent for a month . . . has been greater than receipts for three." Without a more secure commitment of financial aid for the school, the prospects were dim and the community discouraged. "So long as there is uncertainty in regard to support for the school, not much will be done by the people," she wrote. This must have been both painful and humiliating for Shadd. Teaching had been her life for ten years, and her school reports indicate that she was fond of many of her pupils. The closing was also public acknowledgment that she had lost the war to run an integrated school on her own terms. She received her last paycheck from the A.M.A. on March 25 and hinted that she might reopen the school in the future, but there is no evidence that she ever did.[44]

FOUR

"We Have 'Broken the Editorial Ice'"

Mary Ann Shadd may have lost the battle for her school in Windsor, but she refused to give up the fight over public communication in Canada West. By the end of 1852, she took the offensive and began to rally public support for establishing a newspaper that would counter the influence of the *Voice of the Fugitive*. At a mid-December meeting of Windsor's black residents, she publicly denounced the *Voice* and called for the creation of an independent journal. Mary Ann had been wounded by the attacks on her virtue and femininity, and she deployed an elaborate—though unsuccessful—strategy to create the illusion that she was not overstepping acceptable gender boundaries. When Shadd had an idea to promote, she would discuss the matter with a few close allies, and then a meeting would be called with someone else—always male—serving as chair. The gathering would seek public approval for Shadd's initiative, thus insulating her from charges that she was a solitary oppositional voice. It is clear that the impetus for starting a newspaper lay with Shadd, but she was careful to surround herself with male supporters.

But the editors of the *Voice* were not fooled. The newspaper's hostile report of the meeting presumed that the project was Mary Ann's idea: "We suppose the lady in question is to have employment in begging, and at the same time to have a vent to pour out her vituperation" in the pages of the new journal. Her opponents also ridiculed the claim that the meeting was a collective effort, saying that "it would have been more proper to have called it 'Mary Ann Shadd's and Thomas Jones' meeting.'" The paper called Jones, who served as chair, "a mere tool and lackey of the former [Shadd], who uses him in seeking public notoriety by taking advantage of his ignorance." Bibb discredited Jones's leadership, maintaining instead that he "brings a pocketful of resolutions in her handwriting, not a word of which he is able to read, and she, as usual, is appointed assistant secretary of the meeting, and called upon to read her own writing and make a long speech in support of the same." While there was a kernel of truth in these accusations, Jones was by no means an ignorant minion. He was a fugitive slave with a rudimentary education, who would write and publish his narrative a year later, and give antislavery lectures across New England. Bibb was correct on two points, however: Shadd was the driving force behind the proposed paper, and it would serve as an uncensored forum for her point of view.[1]

Beyond the public limelight, Mary Ann invited Samuel Ringgold Ward to join an editorial group that would include herself and Rev. Alexander McArthur. She proposed publishing the paper in Windsor and asked Ward's advice about how to run such an operation. Ward indicated that he was pleased by the invitation, but cautioned her that publishing a newspaper was more costly than Shadd realized. "My opinion is that the expenses for such a paper would be $30 a week," Ward explained. "The first two years a paper of the sort would not support itself. Hence a friend would be needed to keep [it going]." He advised against publishing in Windsor, arguing that Toronto was a more influential locale and that few blacks in the underdeveloped western parts of the province would read the paper. He also cautioned Shadd that publishing outside a large city would increase postage costs. Ward was reluctant to make a commitment to a venture beyond Toronto, saying, "To edit a paper from 250 miles distance would be out of the question." Mary Ann would eventually heed many of these recommendations. In subsequent correspondence, Shadd and Ward sorted out the details of the paper, which they intended to model after the *Pennsylvania Freeman,* published by the Pennsylvania Anti-Slavery Society. She asked his advice on whether the words Canadian or Provincial should appear in the paper's title, and she asked him to write a publication prospectus and send it to prominent abolitionist newspapers in the States.[2]

Samuel Ward was a powerful ally in Shadd's struggle for a public voice in Canada West, and in the beginning she bowed to his experience and authority. He had firsthand knowledge of the glory and disappointment inherent in publishing a black newspaper in North America during the antebellum years. His most successful paper, the *Impartial Citizen* (1849–1851), published in Syracuse and Boston, had been widely praised in abolitionist circles and the daily press. On announcing the founding of Ward's paper, one journal described the editor as "a nervous writer and

72

very effective speaker on all matters of reform" while Horace Greeley's *New York Tribune* called the *Impartial Citizen* "an able and radical anti-slavery paper, holding to the doctrine that the United States Constitution is an anti-slavery instrument."[3]

Yet the *Impartial Citizen* had succumbed to the financial problems that plagued all but the most famous abolitionist sheets: lagging subscriptions, limited advertising, and insufficient capital to keep the publication afloat. Articles complaining about deadbeat subscribers were common. "We shall be compelled to send bills to many of our subscribers, immediately," Ward wrote in an early issue. The paper folded by the time Ward fled from the United States to Canada. "The *Impartial Citizen* breathed its last, after a lingering illness of the spine, and obstructions, impurities and irregularities of the circulation," quipped Ward in an article in the *Voice of the Fugitive*. Charges of improper handling of the paper's finances haunted Ward for another year. In response to the accusations, Ward said that the *Impartial Citizen* had "run hopelessly into debt after spending all I received from subscribers, and from my own personal labors . . . to keep the paper afloat" and that he was arrested for debts and forced to file for bankruptcy in Massachusetts. With such a difficult history in publishing it is not surprising that although Ward agreed to serve as editor to lend prestige and credibility to Shadd's proposed newspaper, he made no financial commitment to the enterprise.[4]

In a letter to the *Pennsylvania Freeman* Ward publicly announced that he had agreed to edit the new publication in Canada West. He complained that the *Voice of the Fugitive* consistently silenced oppositional voices, and he promised that the new paper "shall never contain an indecent article, except such as shall be taken from the *Voice,* as specimens of Bibb and Hollyism." At the same time, Mary Ann's friends and family worked to attract both political and economic support from the United States–based anti-slavery establishment. Mary Ann's father, Abraham Shadd, traveled frequently between his new home in Buxton and Pennsylvania, and during one trip he organized a meeting in West Chester to endorse the proposed journal. The *Pennsylvania Freeman* reported that an unnamed group in Canada West sought funds "to establish a newspaper that will correctly represent their conditions and express their views; as the Voice of the Fugitive, a paper thought by many to express the views and represent the condition of the Refugees in Canada, does not do so, but on the contrary misrepresents them, and has refused to publish their sentiments." The momentum was building for Shadd's newspaper to materialize.[5]

These events infuriated the editors of the *Voice,* who unleashed a new barrage of insults against Shadd. Mary Ann Shadd was made to embody the most despised characteristics of Victorian womanhood: the temptress, the contaminator, the evil yet shrewd manipulator who could not be

Samuel Ringgold Ward, from the frontispiece to his *Autobiography of a Fugitive Negro* (1855). (Metropolitan Toronto Reference Library)

trusted. The paper referred to her as "a designing individual whose duplicity is sufficient to prove a genealogical descent from the serpent that beguiled mother Eve, in the Garden of Eden." As she became increasingly demonized, Mary Ann Shadd was invested with real or imagined powers. If masculinity was commonly equated with political activism and influence, then how could Shadd's detractors explain her rapid ascent in the public sphere of this small community? A woman with political influence had to be reconstructed as deviant and wicked, someone to be shunned and reviled. Bibb and his followers wanted to believe that Samuel Ward and other male critics of the Refugee Home Society had been lured or tricked into their position by "Shadd-as-Eve-the-Evil," as they called her. Ward had shifted his allegiance after he was "prevailed upon by evil counsel, spoken by a *syren* voice." Mary Ann Shadd was blamed for any controversy or unfortunate event in Windsor. On one occasion, a meeting of a Debating Society organized by supporters of Shadd's newspaper ended in tragedy. Two young men in attendance began an argument that erupted into a fight in which one was killed. The *Voice* seized on this as an opportunity to blame Shadd and her colleagues for the murder. Under a headline "A Deed of Blood," the *Voice* claimed that those planning the newspaper were holding illegal meetings with an intent to incite violence. Despite their best efforts, however, Shadd's and Ward's detractors could not stop the rival newspaper from appearing.[6]

The first issue of the *Provincial Freeman* was published on March 24, 1853, the day after Mary Ann Shadd closed her school in Windsor. Samuel Ringgold Ward was listed as editor, Rev. Alexander McArthur as corresponding editor, and a seven-member Committee of Publication was named, which included some of Canada's most prominent black leaders. Since Ward lived in Toronto, McArthur lived in Amherstburg and was on a three-month tour of fugitive settlements, and half of the publication committee's members lived hundreds of miles from Windsor, it is clear from the outset that the tasks of writing, editing, and production were in Shadd's hands. Yet, only one sentence under the masthead indicated who was the real power behind the newspaper: "Letters must be addressed, post-paid, to Mary A. Shadd, Windsor, Canada West." It was not unusual for one or two individuals to conduct the myriad operations of an antebellum newspaper. The small press was a labor-intensive business, with all aspects— from writing, editing, setting type, and printing—done by hand. It is possible that Shadd paid others to do many of these tasks, or she enjoyed the help of volunteers. But this prototype issue did not reveal the actual division of labor.[7]

The timing of the paper's debut was important because it demonstrated that the opposition to Bibb and the Refugee Home Society had not been silenced. Instead, Shadd and her allies had gained a vigorous new medium for their protests. Even the selection of the paper's name was symbolically useful. Shadd and Ward sought to represent Canada's black population as independent and autonomous "freemen" rather than as dependent and oppressed "fugitives," as portrayed by the opposition. Under the nameplate was the phrase "Union is Strength," an ironic motto given that the paper's founders were engaged in a bitter and often vicious controversy that had caused deep divisions among black and white abolitionists in Canada and the United States.

On the front page, the *Provincial Freeman*'s editors explained that this first issue was a prototype for a future publication that "shall be issued weekly after a sufficient number of CASH subscribers, at 7s. 6d. currency ($1.50) per annum, shall have been obtained." Ward's earlier experiences with financially ailing newspapers had likely persuaded Shadd and her colleagues not to begin regular publication until there was a solid base of capital available for its operation. The *Provincial Freeman* resembled most newspapers of the period. It was a four-page broadsheet with seven columns on each page. Editorial material was offset by small headlines or titles. There were no ads or illustrations in this first issue, but it was filled with articles, essays, letters, prose and poetry that foreshadowed the paper's later content.

Samuel Ward wrote an "Introductory" for this issue that admitted his reluctance to take on the editorship. "It was my intention not to connect my name with the Press ever hereafter," said Ward, as he explained that he agreed to serve as editor for only one year and that he had made no financial investment in the paper. Following this first issue, Ward noted that the paper would be moved to one of Ontario's larger cities, either London or Toronto, and would be issued on a weekly basis. Ward pledged the *Provincial Freeman*'s service to abolitionism, temperance, and racial uplift. The *Provincial Freeman* would be an autonomous voice without allegiance to any religion or political party. "The religious influence of this Journal shall be free from sectarianism," said Ward. "As to politics, the *Freeman* is the organ of no party." Most important, this new newspaper would champion black emigration, and would be a resource for those considering relocation in Canada West. "The refugees from the southern plantations shall be made welcome and pointed to means and measures for such improvement and development, as shall make them independent, self-sustaining laborers," Ward proclaimed.[8]

Accompanying Ward's introduction on the front page were reprints of the letters from Ward and Foote which had been published by the *Pennsylvania Freeman* in February. The *Freeman*'s editors resisted the temptation to lash back at the *Voice* with their own mean-spirited assault. Instead, they enabled their readers to see both sides of the argument over the Refugee Home Society, in the process indicting the overt censorship in the pages of their rival. A lengthy editorial written by Ward on the second page critiqued pro-slavery sentiment and "negrophobia" in Canada and declared, "As long as these exist, we shall want anti-slavery labors, organizations, agitation and newspapers in Canada."

This is the most that Samuel Ringgold Ward would ever write for the *Provincial Freeman*. A brief "apology," probably written by Shadd, followed his editorial and indicated the tenuous nature of Ward's association with the paper:

> This number of the Freeman is published under very unfavorable circumstances. Mr Ward is either traveling, or at his residence more than 350 miles from Windsor, where this number is printed; and, as Mr. W. is obliged to perform other [illegible] for a livelihood, it is impossible for him to give the attention to the paper that he would were his pecuniary interests connected with it.

Ward traveled continuously on behalf of the Anti-Slavery Society of Canada, and beyond the pieces written for the first issue, his most significant contribution as editor was in the use of his name and reputation to attract readers and supporters. Ward was in considerable demand in abolitionist circles. He had also agreed to serve as corresponding editor for another fledgling black newspaper, *The Aliened American,* published in Cleveland by William Howard Day. A letter from Ward figured prominently in its first issue, which appeared on April 9, 1853, less than two weeks after the *Provincial Freeman*'s first issue. Ward wrote that his commitments to several antislavery newspapers might appear to be fickleness, but it really demonstrated his lifelong quest to "serve my own people, to the extent of my very limited ability." Meanwhile, Ward's employers, the Anti-Slavery Society of Canada, were preparing to send him on a lecture tour of Great Britain, a fact that may have hastened the appearance of the *Provincial Freeman.* Ward barely had an opportunity to observe the reaction to his collaboration with Shadd, because on April 18, just three weeks after its publication, he embarked for England.[9]

Not surprisingly, Shadd and Ward's opponents reacted angrily to the appearance of the *Provincial Freeman.* Bibb and Holly organized a meeting in nearby Sandwich just two days after the paper was published and introduced a series of resolutions condemning the editors and the idea of a rival newspaper. They were outraged and frightened by the prospects that the *Provincial Freeman* might become viable, and their anxiety was not masked in their report, which was distributed to antislavery papers across the United States. They mocked the *Freeman*'s motto—Union is Strength—arguing that the faction behind the new publication were a divisive lot. After more statements in defense of the Refugee Home Society, Bibb and Holly came to their main concern—that a newspaper competing for readers among the small network of black and white abolitionists in Canada would seriously hurt the *Voice*'s circulation. In their view, the creation of a rival newspaper was the ultimate act of disloyalty toward the cause of black survival in Canada. "Resolved, That as the *Voice* is not as extensively patronised as its merits demand, there is no necessity for another paper devoted to the interests of the colored people of Canada," they argued. The *Provincial Freeman* "is unworthy of the support of the well wishers of our race."[10]

This desperate and selfish plea was not well received by abolitionists in the United States. Frederick Douglass seemed especially annoyed by all the fuss and said so when his newspaper published Bibb's resolutions. One can envision Douglass shaking his head in disgust at Bibb's tactics as he wrote: "We think Mr. Bibb and his friends manifest entirely too much sensitiveness and apprehension on account of the proposal to establish a paper in Canada. For our part, we should welcome the establishment of a dozen newspapers in our neighborhood, "devoted to the interests of the colored people," for it would require quite that number to meet the wants of all classes." Few blacks in Canada read the *Voice*, Douglass sniffed, "Only fifteen copies of it are taken in Toronto, and one copy in Hamilton." Bibb and Holly's mean-spirited commentary had not enhanced their paper's credibility.[11]

The editors of the *Pennsylvania Freeman* were similarly annoyed by Bibb's outcry and published only one paragraph summarizing his "strongly partisan resolutions." This occurred three weeks after the Pennsylvania paper welcomed its namesake, calling the *Provincial Freeman* "a large, fair, and readable sheet" and praising Ward's experience as an antislavery publisher. The *Anti-Slavery Bugle*, published in Ohio, also welcomed the arrival of the *Freeman* in a front-page article and reprinted part of Ward's editorial on pro-slavery sentiment in Canada. There was no notice taken by the *Liberator* other than to reprint Bibb's protests.[12]

By the end of April, the furor and excitement over the first issue of the *Freeman* had subsided, and Mary Ann Shadd had to make some decisions about what to do next. There was no money to continue publishing the paper, she was tired and "worn in health," and the protracted battle with Bibb, Foote, and the Refugee Home Society had left her dispirited. Her exhaustion showed in a final letter to the A.M.A. that was plagued with errors, but she was strong enough to complain about the gendered nature of her treatment in Windsor. "A regular and well executed series of attacks might be resisted by a man of strong physical condition, but I am not equal to it—I confess." If she was pleased by the appearance of the *Freeman*, Mary Ann failed to say so. But she remained defiant about having a public voice, and declared "I hope, ever to have unrestricted liberty of opinion on all matters of general interest."[13]

She instructed Whipple to send future correspondence to Hamilton, at the eastern edge of the province on Lake Ontario near Toronto, where she planned to rest for several weeks. Her vacation was short-lived, however, because the following month she was in Philadelphia, where she gave lectures promoting black emigration to Canada. It was a homecoming of sorts for Mary Ann, who returned to the familiar environs of Pennsylvania where she had friends, family, and political supporters like William Still, one of the city's best known black abolitionists and Underground Railroad operator. Philadelphia was a hotbed of antislavery activism, and many African Americans including Still, Robert Purvis, and Frances E. Watkins (later Harper), were in the forefront of these efforts.[14]

Shadd turned to the lecture hall as a mode of public expression which enabled her to press a political agenda while securing subscribers and contributions for her nascent journal. By the mid-nineteenth century, public lectures had emerged as a popular form of instruction and entertainment in both white and black communities in the northern United States. Lecturing enabled professionals and intellectuals to display and legitimate their career aspirations, and signaled the speaker's "possession of wisdom, general learning, or . . . 'man thinking.'" Mary Ann's public speaking was a natural outgrowth of her work as a teacher and community activist. She saw her role as both imparting information and advancing a protest rhetoric that would rally support for abolition and emigration. The next few months would give her the opportunity to develop a style of oratory that was part didactic, part polemic, in front of listeners who were accustomed to hearing the best-known antislavery lecturers. In May 1853 she gave talks at two Presbyterian churches in Philadelphia. William Still, who was contributing regularly to the *Pennsylvania Freeman,* was in the audience on one of these occasions. He wrote a review for the newspaper praising Shadd's knowledge of Canada and her persuasive abilities. "Miss Shadd is well known and highly respected here, and her lectures were listened to with great interest by all whom I have heard speak of them," wrote Still. Among the other listeners that night was the influential A.M.E. Bishop Daniel Payne, who endorsed Shadd's comments on Canada as factual and enlightening.[15]

Shadd recited many of the observations and data she had compiled in *Notes of Canada West,* as she championed the Canadian haven for black Americans. She used a map of North America to aid her presentation of the geography and climate of Canada, as well as its political advantages. If Mary Ann had suffered any great disappointments or sorrows during her time in Canada, they were pushed to the background as she commanded her best arguments to persuade American abolitionists generally opposed to black emigration. She also used these lectures as a forum for her ongoing critique of the Refugee Home Society. She told stories of the "various tricks and plans which had been resorted to by certain leaders in the begging movements," and she did not spare the *Voice of the Fugitive,* which she declared had been "unceasing in its shameful assaults upon all who have exposed the duplicity of the agents." This was a powerful forum through which Mary Ann hoped to influence public opinion about the black experience in Canada. The fact that she had firsthand experience in the Canadian frontier lent credibility to her assertions. Unlike the meetings and debates in Windsor, there were few, if any, in this audience who shared her intimate knowledge of conditions in Canada West. Here, she did not have to confront the reproach and scrutiny of the opposition. The lecturer's podium, like her newspaper, gave Shadd an unfettered vehicle to disseminate her point of view.[16]

She continued her lecturing later that summer when, in August, she and her father, Abraham, visited their former home town of West Chester, Pennsylvania. The Shadds were the featured speakers at a meeting organized by several black leaders, including Robert Purvis, to argue against the African colonization movement's growing momentum in Pennsylvania.

It was organized after two white colonization agents went on a door-to-door campaign in West Chester and succeeded in attracting the interest of local clergy and black residents. This so alarmed some of the area's black activists that they organized a meeting and called on the expertise of Abraham Shadd, who had championed the anti-colonization cause for nearly twenty years. One of the meeting's organizers described the elder Shadd as "a man of reading and reflection" who "gave his views clearly and forcibly." However, it was Mary Ann who controlled the program until nearly ten o'clock that night. The published report of her talk focused on her demeanor and technical skills, rather than the content of her arguments. "She appears quite young, but has a fine spirit, a noble independence; and expresses herself with astonishing facility," noted the observer. "Her ideas, indeed, crowd upon her too fast for expression, as a consequence she is too rapid in her elocution." The article combined compliments with paternalism in reviewing Shadd's performance, particularly in contrast to her father's polished delivery. Her youth and inexperience were referred to repeatedly—in the summer of 1853 she was twenty-nine years old. She was portrayed as overwrought with excitement at speaking to a home-town audience, but "with some more discipline as a public speaker, [she] would be excelled by very few." Mary Ann Shadd was not a novice public speaker—she was an experienced teacher who had addressed numerous gatherings in Canada West. But in an era in which few women played an active role in public, "promiscuous" gatherings, her presence was an oddity to be explained by diminishing her age and her abilities, and by ascribing to her various feminine frailties.[17]

Mary Ann Shadd was still a relative newcomer to the antislavery lecture circuit, an arena in which few African American women ventured—or were allowed. As Mary Ryan has explained, the exclusion of women from the nation's political domain was a fait accompli by the 1850s. Abolitionist women who dared to speak in public were often rebuked, threatened, or literally run off the stage. Sojourner Truth, who became the embodiment of the exotic and the eccentric, began her speaking career in the early 1850s and often encountered hostile crowds as she forcefully campaigned on behalf of abolition and women's rights. Frances E. Watkins, who also made her antislavery lecturing debut in the early 1850s, combined a powerful articulation of abolitionist principles with a genteel delivery that included readings of her poetry. Although Watkins was characterized as unthreatening, she encountered violence and animosity when she toured beyond the safe confines of her home town of Philadelphia.[18]

However, some in the West Chester audience were sufficiently impressed with Mary Ann's oratory to invite her to speak at a larger anti-colonization meeting down the road in Philadelphia a few days later. Advertisements in several local newspapers announced that Purvis and Shadd would speak and Frances E. Watkins would read her antislavery poetry. This may have been Shadd's and Watkins's first meeting, but they would cross paths often in the years to come. On August 30, a large crowd assembled at Brick Wesley Church in Philadelphia, and among them were William Still and Lucretia Mott, founder of the Female Anti-Slavery Society of Philadelphia. Before this stellar gathering, Shadd reprised the themes of her earlier talks by launching a stinging critique of the colonizationist position. She argued that their "professions of sympathy for the colored man" were the height of hypocrisy, when their primary goal was to rid the nation of its free black population. Part of her task was to differentiate between colonization and emigration for an audience suspicious of any removal of blacks from American soil. Shadd fiercely advocated emigration to Canada as a hospitable destination that African Americans reached of their own free will. By comparison, she voiced opposition to Africa, where blacks were coerced into seeing the continent as their legitimate homeland. She maintained that "owing to the excessive heat of the climate, and other natural disadvantages, Africa was utterly unfit as a place of colonization and elevation of oppressed Americans." This position not only repeated the common anti-colonization stance, but also placed her in conflict with other black emigrationists like Martin Delany, who preferred Africa and Latin America over Canada.[19]

We see in this series of lectures the evolution of Shadd's oratorical technique in which she combined the rhetorics of equality—a central theme of black abolitionism—with what has been called the black jeremiad. Since the early days of the convention movement, black abolitionists appropriated the American values of equality, liberty, and property to make a universal claim for liberation. The colonizationist position represented the denial of equal rights and equal protection to a group because of their race. Black resistance to colonization—as articulated in Mary Ann's speeches—denounced the role of race in determining entitlement to rights. Her rhetoric was also squarely in the tradition of the black jeremiad as she condemned the colonizationists' use of racial bigotry and negative stereotypes. Wilson Moses defined this protest rhetoric as "the constant warnings issued by blacks to whites" of the dire consequences of their adherence to racism. This was a political tirade that had its origins in the pulpit but was used widely by black abolitionist speakers including Frederick Douglass. But Mary Ann's task was not only to argue the logics of black liberation, but also to utilize the techniques of persuasion and disputation to advance the marginalized position of emigration within the mainstream of black abolitionism. Mary Ann's problems in Windsor had not lessened her enthusiasm about the benefits of Canadian citizenship. By the end of this lecture tour she was anxious to return to Canada where she planned to resume publication of the *Provincial Freeman*.[20]

Getting the newspaper back in operation was a daunting task. To run a paper successfully—even a small abolitionist sheet—she would have to find financial backing and develop a list of reliable subscribers. She would have to recruit traveling agents who would sell the paper on her behalf in cities across Canada and the United States—and not pocket the proceeds. Shadd would need to learn about advertising and its growing influence on the financial health of newspapers. But most of all, she needed to find reliable patronage, as Samuel Ringgold Ward had suggested months earlier. Subscriptions and advertising alone did not support most antebellum newspapers. But without an official affiliation with a political party or organization, she would have to solicit individual donations. Mary Ann would also have to learn how to work with printers, and decide whether to set up her own print shop, as did several antislavery publishers, including Henry Bibb.[21]

Freed from the demands of running her school, Mary Ann spent the summer and fall of 1853 working toward these goals. She followed Ward's advice and decided to pack her belongings and move the *Provincial Freeman* 250 miles across Canada West, from Windsor to Toronto. In the early 1850s, Toronto was the province's largest city with a population of nearly 50,000, and it is estimated that from 500 to 1,200 were black. As the numbers of fugitive slaves in the city increased, abolitionists and more established black residents set up a network of service and freedmen's aid societies to respond to their needs. Unlike Windsor, Sandwich, and Amherstburg, in the West, Toronto boasted integrated schools and churches and a number of successful black businesses. This prompted Ward to declare that he had yet to see "a more intelligent, enterprising and independent class of coloured people" than those living in the city. Toronto was home to the Anti-Slavery Society of Canada, the staunchly abolitionist Toronto *Globe,* and many prominent antislavery activists, including the family of the *Freeman*'s nominal editor, Samuel Ward, who was still touring Great Britain. Here, Shadd decided, was the best location for building a loyal readership for the *Freeman.*[22]

Shadd's plans were encouraged by the fall of her bitter rival's newspaper, the *Voice of the Fugitive.* The vicious battle between Henry Bibb and Mary Ann Shadd virtually disappeared from the pages of the antislavery press once Shadd and Ward left Canada in the spring of 1853. But Shadd continued to level charges of impropriety against Bibb and the Refugee Home Society during her lectures in the United States, while Bibb and his coeditor Theodore Holly struggled to keep their paper going. The final blow to Bibb's dynasty occurred on October 9, 1853, when the building in Windsor that housed the paper and his printing presses burned to the ground. William Lloyd Garrison, on a tour of Windsor at the time, reported that Bibb's "office was entirely destroyed by fire—press, types, everything." It was a strange coincidence that the fire occurred on Mary Ann Shadd's thirtieth birthday. Garrison noted: "The fire is supposed to have been an incendiary act on the part of some of his [Bibb's] enemies." Bibb may have suspected that some of Shadd and Ward's allies were behind the arson, but no further mention is made of the incident. The *Voice* did not fold instantly after the fire, but staggered on for a few more months. By November, James Holly was no longer associated with the paper, and it was being printed across the river in Detroit. Ironically, Bibb had criticized Shadd for publishing *Notes of Canada West* in Detroit two years earlier. Bibb told his readers the paper "is not dead," and he solicited support and sympathy through a brief article in *The Liberator*. Bibb tried to enliven his paper with new typefaces and the claim that the *Voice*'s news was transmitted by telegraph. The paper's new creed, "This Journal is Independent of Party or Sect, and Shall be Devoted to Human Liberty, Mental Culture and Progressive Reforms," was similar to pledges in the first issue of the *Provincial Freeman*. But these lofty ideals could not hide the fact that the *Voice* was smaller, had few ads, and carried no illustrations, which were expensive to reproduce. By early 1854, the *Voice of the Fugitive* was gone.[23]

Mary Ann Shadd moved swiftly to fill the void. By the winter of 1854 she was living in Toronto and had announced intentions to resume publication of the *Freeman*. William Still wrote Shadd from Philadelphia to report that backing for the paper was beginning to grow: "I am glad the Prov. Freeman is likely to appear soon. Mr. McKinney has some money and names for you which he offered me some weeks back, but I thought he had as well hold on to them not knowing at that time what your prospects were." Still's letter indicated that Shadd's contact with Samuel Ward was limited, and he offered to send her a copy of Ward's latest speech made on his British tour.[24]

Shadd also found a new colleague closer to home who would help get the paper underway. Her associate was John Dick, an Englishman who had helped Frederick Douglass run the *North Star* before moving to Toronto in 1850. Dick learned the printing trades in England and oversaw the production of Douglass's paper for nearly two years. By the time Shadd met him, Dick had his own business in the city's commercial district and he understood the particular needs of a small antislavery newspaper. During her first months in the city, Shadd was busy lining up financial support for the newspaper, as well. She formed the Provincial Freeman Association and sold stock through the corporation, using Ward's Toronto contacts when she could. The stockholders, known as a Board of Trust, had the responsibility of overseeing the paper's operations. Among her investors were Rev. John B. Smith, a black Baptist minister from the United States, and Thomas F. Cary, a local black businessman who was close friends with Samuel Ringgold Ward.[25]

Shadd's prospects were apparently good enough to allow them to set up shop at No. 5, City Building on King Street East, in downtown Toronto, where they rented offices for £18 annually. King Street was the city's main commercial district, filled with shops "decorated in the English style" that attempted to recreate London's Regent Street. She and her associates purchased the printing equipment and materials from a local business-man for £250. They had raised enough money through stocks, subscrip-tions, and the loan from Rev. Smith to make a £100 down payment with the balance due in a month. They decided to launch the paper on March 25, 1854, exactly a year after the prototype issue of the *Provincial Freeman* appeared. On the surface, the *Freeman*'s leadership remained unchanged, with Samuel Ringgold Ward still listed as editor, Alexander McArthur as corresponding editor, and M. A. Shadd as publishing agent. Added to the original masthead were new contributors, subscription agents, and John Dick, who was listed as the printer. But Ward remained in England, and McArthur was on his way to a post in Scotland, leaving the daily operations to Shadd. Nevertheless, readers were led to believe that this situation was temporary: "All letters, whether intended for publication or on business, must, during the absence of the Editor, be adressed [*sic*] *post-paid* to M. A. Shadd, Toronto, C.W."[26]

A prominent article on the front page reported on Ward's tour in England and hailed his efforts to raise funds for Canada's fugitive slaves. An editorial probably written by Shadd on page two gave further glow-ing testimony to Ward's successful work in England, and highlighted his agenda of promoting self-reliance and autonomy for blacks in Canada. This piece also underscored the distant nature of their relationship. Shadd was receiving only second and third-hand news about Ward, and the "editor" had been gone for nearly a year. Regardless, it was important to keep the myth of Ward's editorship alive as his reputation was the main selling device for the fledgling newspaper. In fact, another editorial made clear the expectation that Ward's celebrity would benefit the paper: "the increasing of his influence, will all tend to make him the more useful, as the Editor of our Journal."[27]

Shadd's persistence in using collective terms like "the proprietors" or "our journal" contradicted the fact that in most respects she controlled the paper's editorial content, circulation, and business matters. It is clear that part of her motivation was based on her fear that the *Freeman*'s fi-nancial success would be jeopardized if it was revealed that a woman was at the paper's helm. Mary Ann's suspicions proved to be accurate. Shadd continued to walk this gender tightrope for many months by symbolically placing men in positions of authority while she remained in the back-ground. This was a familiar pattern for nineteenth-century women writ-ers, many of whom used pseudonyms to mask their gender and shield themselves from public scrutiny. As one scholar has noted, "She was to stand in the background, out of the way. Even her exercise of moral, social, or personal influences was to be indirect, subtle, and symbolic." Shadd's later writing indicates that she was acutely aware that her role as publisher and editor of the *Provincial Freeman* was a groundbreaking step for black women in the world of journalism. In this early stage of the newspaper's life, however, Mary Ann professed little need for a prestigious title; it was simply enough to have a medium of expression at her disposal.[28]

A small ad in the *Freeman* announced that "the proprietors" sought jobs printing cards, labels, handbills, show bills, circulars, books, and other materials. It is safe to assume that these activities fell to John Dick since Shadd had no experience as a printer. The ad claimed that the *Provincial Freeman* was fully equipped to carry out such activities and that the business had been purchased from a Mr. Stephens. Dick's exact role at the newspaper is unclear, but it is possible that he was either a major stockholder or partner, or he may have merged his own printing business with the *Freeman*'s, or he was simply an employee. He wrote a brief apology for the assorted typographical and writing errors in this first issue, and proclaimed the lofty goal that the *Freeman* "will be found to have attained to a high, if not to a first rank among the stars that bedeck the firmament of literature on our Western Hemisphere."

The opening editorial of the "new" *Freeman,* written by Shadd, offered a lengthy rationale for the paper's existence. Foremost among these reasons was a common creed of journalism—to provide "some cheap, reliable means of information furnished by persons on the spot." The intended audience were both supporters and opponents of black emigration. The *Freeman* was also needed as a persuasive medium to counteract the opposition—namely Henry Bibb and his supporters—despite the fact that the *Voice* had folded. For the first time, Shadd could advance her political agenda unhindered by Henry Bibb's editorial control. Although the *Voice of the Fugitive* was gone, Mary Ann was still smarting from the vilification she had received in its pages. Repeatedly she made thinly veiled references to Bibb and his influence over the discourse on blacks in Canada: "To be always at the mercy of the demagogue of the hour is neither safe, dutiful, nor in any sense becoming. We must allow our fellow subjects to know who we are and what we want, through our own authorized mouthpiece."

Her efforts to establish a group identity for the newspaper reflected Shadd's political commitment to a racially integrated community of like-minded activists in Canada West. Readers, contributors, stockholders, and traveling agents could all feel a sense of ownership about the *Freeman* even if they were unable to invest in it financially. This new periodical devoted to the interests of Canadian blacks was intended to facilitate and enliven intergroup communication. Shadd was providing a medium they could use to reach each other for commerce, politics, and pleasure, especially in

Toronto. In the few months since she arrived in the city, Shadd had begun to build a network of friends and supporters who played multiple roles
in this imagined community. Thus, contributor A. B. Jones also advertised
his grocery business in the pages of the *Freeman,* as did barber Thomas
Cary, a key investor and brother of contributor John Cary. Announcements
for traveling agent Smith's lectures on slavery and intemperance were
included among the assorted ads that were purchased by Shadd's and
Ward's friends in the United States. Publicly, at least, Mary Ann was delighted with the growing interest in the *Freeman,* and she envisioned the
paper's role in facilitating a trans-Atlantic abolitionist network: "Should
the *Freeman* survive the critical period of its early childhood, it will be no
unimportant medium of communication between the friends of the down-
trodden on both sides of the Atlantic," she declared.[29]

Shadd intended for the *Freeman* to invigorate the small antislavery
movement in Canada. In this inaugural issue, she declared that the newspaper was designed to "create a sentiment in Canada, and out of Canada, that
shall tell against slavery." Mary Ann articulated a classical moral suasion
ideology as she argued that "If a sound moral and religious influence,
when exerted by individuals, can accomplish great good, surely the influence of large communities, such as this, for instance, in its character of a
liberal, powerful, well sustained Province, can do more." A number of
scholars have included Shadd among the ranks of the Garrisonians because of her uncompromising call for the end of slavery, as well as her
attempts to blend other reform issues—including women's rights and
temperance—into the abolitionist appeal. But Shadd considered herself
to be an independent voice, and pledged that the *Provincial Freeman*
would not align itself with a particular branch of American abolitionism,
such as the Garrisonians or Free-Soilers. Instead, she called for a distinct-
ly Canadian movement in which those living under the British crown,
where slavery was outlawed, would serve as a model for racial tolerance and
justice in America, and exert an antislavery influence internationally.[30]

The *Provincial Freeman* would argue mightily for Canadian emigration,
and fill the void left by abolitionists in the United States who ignored or
denigrated the cause. "None of the papers published by our people, in the
States, answer our purpose," she wrote. "They either pass us by, in cold
contempt, ignore us altogether, keep themselves or their readers, or both,
ignorant of what Canada is, or in some other way, by opposition or neglect
disparage us, as much as convenient." Shadd argued that by demonstrating that black Americans were "fit for freedom," Canadian emigration
could be a potent force for antislavery activism. She maintained that "the
development, education and progress of Canadian colored men, will do
more to stamp those two Anglo-Saxon assertions with their native falsity,
than anything else this side of Heaven, can do."[31]

Shadd also wanted to fashion the *Freeman* as the standard-bearer of black emigration. Despite her opposition to emigration beyond Canada, she published a call for a National Emigration Convention to be held in August 1854 in Ohio. The convention was the brainchild of Martin Delany, and its purpose was to discuss emigration to Central America, South America, and the British West Indies. The *Freeman* publicized the convention announcement although Shadd was skeptical about its lack of attention to Canada, and of the fact that two of her former enemies, Henry Bibb and Theodore Holly, were among the twenty-six activists who endorsed the call. She penned an editorial that took the organizers of the convention to task for virtually ignoring the community of blacks in Canada who also considered themselves part of the emigration movement. Yet, she demonstrated there was a growing alliance among the different factions of emigrationists who found themselves rebuffed by mainstream black abolitionism.[32]

In the United States, Frederick Douglass and other black leaders were infuriated by the proposed convention. They considered the emigration movement to be playing into the hands of colonizationists, and they believed that the fight for racial equality should be carried out on American soil. Douglass offered a particularly harsh denunciation of the idea, stating, "Whatever may be the motives for sending forth such a call, (and we say nothing as to these,) we deem it uncalled for, unwise, unfortunate, and premature." Douglass echoed the concerns of many black abolitionists who denied emigration's potential for community improvement and self-sufficiency when he declared, "Our enemies will see in this movement a cause for rejoicing." Shadd's harangues about the convention's agenda eventually elicited a response from Delany, who hastened to reassure her that "it was not the case that delegates to the convention are restricted," and he urged Canadian emigrationists to attend.[33]

The differences of opinion among black emigrationists, spurred by Martin Delany's convention proposal, were discussed regularly in the early issues of the *Freeman*. This debate enabled Shadd to sort out fundamental aspects of her nationalist ideology. She was particularly disturbed by two elements of Delany's emigration plan: that Canada was considered an easy candidate for annexation by the United States, and that it called for a separate black nation. In an editorial titled "A Word about, and to Emigrationists," she suggested that blacks were no better equipped than whites to govern a segregated nation—an observation undoubtedly born of the enmity and rancor she had repeatedly encountered in Canada's black communities, as well as in the United States. Shadd refused to adhere to notions of black superiority or nobility, arguing instead that "colored men are as merciless as other men, when possessed of the same amount of pride, conceit, and wickedness, and as much, if not more ignorance." She wondered what kinds of people would be attracted to an "exclusive nation," and suggested that emigrationists should consider the opportunity to be "*part of the Colored British nation.*" Shadd offered a pragmatic rationale, as well: blacks would be exploited in the sugar cane fields of Latin America and the Caribbean, just as they were in the United States, and that no nation would readily accept dominance from a group of African Americans. Life in the tropics seemed particularly loathsome to Shadd, who suggested that black men's zeal for the climate might not be shared by their women. "What will you do, or what will your women say, for they must go along, when surrounded by big spiders, lizzards, snakes, centipedes, seorplugs and all manner of creeping and biting things?" she asked.[34]

During the three years since Mary Ann Shadd's arrival in Canada West, she had cultivated a black nationalist ideology that was dependent on an identification with a nation-state—in this case British North America. Traditionally, the ideological basis of nationalism has its roots in a people's ties to a geographical region which they feel entitled to possess. Black nationalism, as it evolved in the nineteenth century, was less connected to a particular nation-state than to the unifying ties of skin color and culture. Shadd's nationalism blended these two impulses: blacks could not hope to possess and control Canada, but could claim their rightful place within a nation-state that promised them equality and citizenship. At the same time, she believed that the political, social, and cultural unification of black people was essential for their survival. Shadd shared Martin Delany's advocacy of an autonomous black political force that could fight white supremacy from beyond the borders of the United States. But she was fundamentally at odds with Delany's romance with Africa as the "Fatherland," and his assertions of black hegemony.[35]

The *Freeman* settled into a weekly publication schedule with the paper issued every Saturday. Besides Shadd's editorials, much of the paper was filled with articles lifted from other antislavery newspapers, dailies, and religious periodicals. Shadd, Dick, and assorted correspondents reported on local events and political issues, as they sought to construct and enlarge the imagined community of black Canadians. Within a month, as much as a page in each issue was devoted to letters from readers in Canada and the United States, attesting to the paper's growing audience. "Our Correspondents have this week been so liberal with their contributions, that our table is literally groaning under the weight of their favours," she wrote. "What we want chiefly, however, from our friends in Canada, is items of news reporting the doings and progress of the colored people." Mary Ann wanted to control the tone and direction of this community discourse, instructing correspondents to "deal as severely as you please with the measures and motives of other papers or Editors, if you know them to be wrong. If you do not do so, we will." In her zeal to exercise her new-found editorial authority, however, Mary Ann was exceedingly harsh in publicly criticizing the paper's contributors. Her efforts to set high standards for the *Freeman* undoubtedly offended or alienated some of those she hoped to reach. She explained that paper would not publish every letter it received, and on another occasion complained that "the crabbed writing and higgledy-piggledy character of the arrangement dispose us to pass them by as a waste of time."[36]

Shadd's criticism did not stifle the flood of letters and articles to the *Freeman,* which was testimony to the need for a black newspaper in Canada and to readers' enthusiasm about having such a medium at their disposal. But readers' excitement would not pay the bills. Mary Ann hoped to attract 3,000 paying subscribers and announced that both friends and opponents were encouraged to take the paper. She solicited traveling agents to sell subscriptions, and promised "a liberal discount" or a 20 percent commission for successful sales. The paper's reach lengthened with each issue, and agents appeared in Detroit, Philadelphia, Pittsburgh, and Cincinnati, and other American cities. In one instance, Shadd agreed to pay agent Abraham McKinney $400 in four installments if he delivered 1,000 subscribers from New York, New Jersey and Pennsylvania. This was an ambitious, and perhaps naive, plan for building a readership, but Shadd forged ahead with vigor.[37]

Her friend William Still was more worried about the paper's financial prospects and he urged those who professed support of the *Freeman* to back up their words with cash subscriptions. Still, a keen observer of the black press, knew that Shadd would have great difficulty getting African Americans to support her newspaper while "the Pro-Slavery Presses of the land, are liberally patronised by us." He accused blacks of being frivolous —of spending money "on an excursion; to a picknick; fancy Ball, sumptuous supper, etc."—rather than on practical items like newspapers that would help them engage in a political culture. He expressed frustration that "this great waste of money, this foolishly impovering ourselves, adds largely to the capital of our oppressors—the whites." This would soon become Mary Ann Shadd's headache, as well.[38]

It wasn't long before Shadd was also using the *Provincial Freeman* to probe the failings of abolitionism in the United States and Canada. No longer confined to her pamphlets or the editorial decisions of other journals, she was free to expand her critique of a political movement tolerated by black activists despite its failings. In an editorial titled "The Humbug of Reform," she complained about the hypocrisy of whites who championed the antislavery cause because of self-interest, while they ignored the suffering and injustice endured by the slaves. She scoffed at the antislavery rhetoric that highlighted slavery's "evil to the white classes." Many abolitionists had lost sight of the "inherent wickedness" of slavery, as they devised political strategies that would appeal to white voters, she argued.[39]

Part of her attack on mainstream abolitionists was aimed at Frederick Douglass, an opponent of emigration, who was considered the most powerful black antislavery spokesman on both sides of the border. Mary Ann created a stir when she wrote an editorial suggesting that the *Freeman*'s supporters hold "bazaars, festivals, tea-meetings, and similar gatherings" across Canada to supplement the revenues slowly trickling in from subscriptions. She noted that the tradition of annual bazaars organized by women's groups in Boston and Rochester played an important role in sustaining *The Liberator* and *Frederick Douglass' Paper*. She argued that Canadian abolitionists should be doing the same so that the *Freeman* "may be regarded as connected with the soil—a paper for the Canadas, as well as other parts of the world."[40]

Before the paper went to press, however, Shadd learned that the Toronto Ladies' Association for the Relief of Destitute Colored Fugitives was planning just such a bazaar—but for *Frederick Douglass' Paper*, not the *Freeman*. Shadd lashed out in print, demanding to know why Canadian abolitionists labored to support Douglass while ignoring the work of blacks in Canada. "Are the abolitionists of Canada, or, rather of the Toronto Society, opposed to free colored people coming into the Province to settle? and are those the initiatory steps to a public endorsement of Anti-emigration views?" she asked. Shadd said that she looked forward to the day when Douglass would change his mind and emigrate to Canada rather than taking money away from Canadian blacks. She employed a sarcastic, if not jealous, tone to describe Julia Griffiths, a white Englishwoman who aided Douglass with the publication of his newspapers for more than six years. But most of her anger was targeted at the Toronto Anti-Slavery Society, the umbrella agency of the Toronto Ladies' Association. She claimed that Canadian abolitionists were ignoring the *Freeman* because "Mr. Ward has unfortunately fallen into disgrace with Lewis Tappan, Esq., and the right wing of the Toronto Society."[41]

The editorial sparked a controversy between the *Freeman* and the Anti-Slavery Society of Canada that continued for over a month and probably did more to hurt than to help the paper. Thomas Henning, secretary of the society, responded angrily that his organization had no connection with the bazaar and that the Ladies' Association would be glad to sponsor an event for the *Freeman*, "If that hitherto well-conducted paper should condescend to make application." He said that Ward was not out of favor with the society and offered patronizing advice to Canada's black citizens, which added fuel to Shadd's anger. "Such a spirit is not one likely to conciliate, or to gain that respect and confidence, to which the colored man is equally entitled with his white brother; and which, amongst Britons, he will ever ultimately gain, when he is really worthy of them," Henning asserted. His attitudes gave Shadd further evidence of racism and arrogance among some white abolitionists.[42]

The first regular
issue of
the *Provincial
Freeman*, published
in Toronto, March
1854. Samuel Ward
and Alexander
McArthur listed
as editors.

Interestingly, Henning believed that the author of the editorial was the only black male member of a committee of the Anti-Slavery Society, since it was unsigned like all those in the *Freeman*. Perhaps he could not imagine a woman composing the assault, or he knew little about the newspaper's leadership. At any rate, Shadd took pleasure in exploiting Henning's mistake—and highlighted both his racial and gender prejudice—in her editorial response. With a tone of outrage, she asked, "Has he yet to learn that colored men are men, and that they will not ask respect from Britons who give such clear evidence of prejudice as himself, *when* they are worthy? . . . You have been wasting precious time and much 'powder,' not upon a brother Committee member . . . but upon one who would not be *admitted* to a seat in your committee."[43]

Mary Ann was finding it difficult to obtain the assistance from local abolitionists that she had expected would materialize. After much cajoling, she did succeed in getting a group of the newspaper's supporters to plan a fund-raising event, and she used the editorial column to announce it—a tea meeting or festival to be held in two weeks at St. Lawrence Hall in Toronto. Local dignitaries would make speeches, refreshments would be served, and Shadd hoped Toronto's abolitionists would generously contribute to the fledgling newspaper. However, Shadd was to be disappointed with the scanty attendance at the event, and she remained bitter about what she saw as disproportionate support for Douglass's newspaper among Canadian abolitionists in light of his firm opposition to emigration.[44]

The early issues of the *Freeman* established the paper as a forum for Shadd's growing interest in women's rights, especially within the context of anti-slavery and other reform movements. Unlike the *Voice of the Fugitive,* which rarely carried articles or letters regarding women's rights, the *Provincial Freeman* regularly published material on the subject. The lead story on the front page of the March 25, 1854, issue was a reprint of a speech given by Harriet Beecher Stowe, "An Appeal to the Women of the Free States of America on the Present Crisis in our Country," which exhorted white women to become active in the fight against slavery. Similarly, the lead story on May 6, titled "Women's Rights," was a report on the debate in the New York State Assembly on the question of suffrage. On the same page was an excerpt of a letter recounting the exploits of a woman traveling through rural upstate New York, titled "Extraordinary Performances of a Lady." Thus, at the same time that Shadd was masking her gender by using her initials, not signing her editorials, and identifying men as the editors, she was championing women's concerns in her newspaper.

In one exchange, a meek letter signed by "Henrietta" asked whether the *Freeman* would accept correspondence from "the weaker sex." The letter prompted a lengthy response from another reader, Dolly Bangs, who criticized Henrietta's timidity and the gender constraints of the time. "The idea that now, 'in the afternoon of the nineteenth century,' a woman should have to ask that question, seems ridiculous," Bangs lamented. Taking a page from early feminist rhetoric, Bangs argued that women's talents were divined by God and should not be hidden under the burden of gender prejudice. Shadd must have been quietly delighted when this correspondent asserted that "no one has a right to hinder her from doing that which God has manifestly commanded her to do." Unwittingly, Dolly Bangs had articulated Shadd's position while believing the editor was a man—letters to the editor were usually addressed to "Mr. Shadd" or "Mr. Editor." Bangs ended the letter by warning that Henrietta should "never take such exposed positions as the columns of a newspaper," a message that Shadd herself heeded since she was careful not to make her gender visible in print.[45]

In fact, Shadd rarely addressed gender directly in her editorials, choosing instead to publish other's opinions that seemed to support her own. The attacks on her morals and virtue during the months in Windsor had made her especially cautious about taking a public stance in favor of women's rights. Yet, her actions in the public sphere made it clear that Shadd believed she had a right to participate in political discourse and to play an active role in community affairs. She was particularly interested in the debate over woman's proper place and devoted considerable space to the topic. The *Freeman* reprinted several articles by the feminist-abolitionist journalist Jane Swisshelm. In a front page article published in September 1854, Swisshelm criticized the assumption that men were the best judges of proper behavior and activities for women. "It is not enough that she please her own husband, fathers or brothers, but every scribbler and stump orator in the community demands that the entire sex conform their actions to his taste," Swisshelm wrote. Why not reverse these roles so that women require "them all to consult her wishes about what is proper to be done." On another front page, Shadd reprinted an article from the *New England Farmer* titled "Make Your Girls Independent," that called for equal education for young men and women to prepare them for enterprises outside the home, and argued that women ought to be equipped to teach, run businesses, or engage in trades or manual labor. "Education for all, according to the capacity of each, is the true law of love and of progress," proclaimed the author in the best reformist tradition. Shadd seemed to delight in providing space for women journalists like Swisshelm and Fanny Fern, the pseudonym of the prolific writer Sara Parton, and for the poet Frances E. Watkins, whom she had met in Philadelphia the previous summer. These articles served a dual purpose: to keep the women's rights issue at the forefront of the paper and to support Shadd's increasing visibility as editor. In the years after the Civil War, Shadd would concentrate much of her political energies on these feminist themes.[46]

Despite Shadd's efforts at masking her identity, at least some readers and contributors were well aware of who was editing the paper, and this fact invited criticism. One writer lashed back at Shadd after reading her harsh comments about his writing, and reminded her that she was not the "real" editor of the *Freeman,* but only operating on Ward's behalf. Mary Ann's tactless critiques of the paper's contributors invited one to assert that "the paper should not suffer because of its present captious Editors—it will be a paper, soon—Rev. Ward will take it in hand." But editor Samuel Ringgold Ward was barely visible in the first few issues until a writer using the pen name "Cannuck" wrote a letter praising Ward's tour in England. Accompanying the letter was a brief note from Shadd that openly showed her pleasure at the connection between the newspaper and Ward's celebrity abroad. In reality, this connection remained distant.[47]

By early summer, it was becoming increasingly apparent that Shadd was running the newspaper on her own, a disquieting fact for some readers and contributors. Where was the famous Rev. Ward upon whose reputation the *Freeman* relied? After three months of the paper's existence, Shadd was relieved to publish a letter Ward sent from London, noting that Ward's absence "has been the subject of remarks, no way favorable to those connected with the *Freeman,* who have said all along that he would write. This letter will put them at ease on that point." Shadd's credibility was at stake, and in this instance, Ward came through just in time with a letter that thanked the paper's supporters for keeping the *Freeman* afloat. The next issue carried a three-column review of a speech by Ward at a British antislavery meeting. This kept the hounds at bay, at least temporarily.[48]

Shadd launched herself into greater visibility when she announced in June 1854 that she was embarking on a fund-raising tour throughout the western portions of the province, prompted by the limited success of the Toronto tea meeting. As a public spokesperson for the paper, she could no longer hide her gender. Throughout the summer she sent regular accounts of her travels that were published each week, and she began to sign her correspondence "M. A. Shadd," the first time she attached her name to her writing in the *Freeman.* While she was away, few editorials appeared in the paper, lending further credence to the assumption that Shadd was the primary author of the *Freeman's* opinions. Mary Ann's substitute was her younger sister, Amelia, who had arrived in Toronto several months earlier. Amelia Shadd was to become an important figure at the paper, filling in for her sister when she traveled and later writing her own editorials. So, even in Mary Ann's absence, a woman remained a central figure at the *Freeman* offices.[49]

Mary Ann's letters, written in mid-July, offer a glimpse at how Shadd was received as the *Freeman's* spokesperson. She described her trip as "a hurried and rapid journey by steamboat, a railroad and waggon" with the first stop at the Dawn settlement, about eighteen miles from Chatham. There she was welcomed by friends and supporters, and she provided a lengthy account of the success of local black farmers and businesses in the nearby village of Dresden. She reported that there were many supporters of the *Freeman* among them and that the people both read and paid for the newspaper. Her enthusiasm was tempered two weeks later when she reported that at a "respectable gathering" on behalf of the *Freeman,* she was publicly attacked by John Scoble, the British administrator of Dawn. According to Shadd, Scoble told the audience that they risked loosing the support of abolitionists if they continued to patronize her newspaper, and that publication of the *Freeman* should be stopped. Scoble aimed directly at Shadd when he stated that, in Shadd's words, "the paper was edited by persons of no position, and comparatively unknown," an accusation that Shadd claimed did not influence the audience but deeply insulted her.[50]

Mary Ann used the double standard of gender to respond to Scoble's attack. "Mr. John Scoble . . . trying to do battle against a negro *woman, in a log schoolhouse at Dawn!* Conflict of Russian and Turk, how comparable with it!" Shadd hoped to provoke outrage that Scoble would stoop to so affront a woman in public. But Scoble's enmity toward Shadd was long-standing. He was an ally of Henry Bibb, and was part of the American Missionary Association committee that decided to withdraw her salary and missionary appointment. She did not dwell on such hostilities in her travelogues, but rather maintained a sanguine attitude about the other communities she encountered.[51]

Shadd returned to Toronto in time for the Emancipation Day, or First of August, celebration, an important occasion for the community of fugitive slaves and African American expatriates. Yet, all was not cheerful on that day when local residents learned that Henry Bibb had died following a long illness. She graciously announced Bibb's death in the paper, avoiding any of her customary negative commentary about her former enemy. But Bibb's death did signal the end of an era and the arrival of a new one in which Shadd would seek a more prominent role in abolitionist politics.

The first step in this direction occurred the following week, when a large group of Toronto's black activists met in the Sayer Street Chapel to form the Provincial Union, an organization concocted by Shadd and her associates. Rev. William P. Newman, an influential black Baptist minister, presided over the meeting and was appointed secretary. Mary Ann Shadd read the constitution of the Provincial Union, which she wrote and printed at the *Freeman* offices, and she was assigned as a special agent to organize auxiliaries—a euphemistic term for female volunteers. Indeed, while Shadd had organized the Union, all activities were divided by gender: the officers were all well-known men of the community, while women served in a separate committee for which Shadd acted as treasurer. Samuel Ward was elected president of the Union in absentia, while his wife served on the Ladies' Committee. Others leading the Union were Thomas F. Cary, Mary Ann's future husband, and Wilson R. Abbott, one of Toronto's most established and successful black residents.[52]

The Provincial Union was the antidote to Shadd's disgust with the Anti-Slavery Society of Canada. Here a group of blacks pledged themselves to the common purposes of self-help, racial uplift, and abolition without the involvement with white antislavery leaders. The Union's goals were to fight slavery, oppose segregated black settlements, encourage black education, and perhaps most important, support the *Provincial Freeman,* which would be designated as the official organ. The main responsibility of the Ladies' Committee was to sponsor an Annual Fair in Toronto and other Canadian cities to raise funds for the newspaper. If the Anti-Slavery Society of Canada would not support the *Freeman,* Toronto's black community would do it alone.

The formation of the Provincial Union inspired Shadd to travel again to organize auxiliary groups in other towns and cities that would operate on the *Freeman*'s behalf. Just a week after the Union's first meeting, she was off to Niagara, a short steamer ride away along Lake Erie. Niagara's black residents met to plan a tea meeting for the paper, and Shadd signed up members for a subsidiary union. She recommended Niagara to new emigrants because it offered "great inducements not just to men of small capital, but to those who prefer pure air, cheap rents, and abundance of labor, to the unhealthy atmosphere, and uncertain chances of a large city."[53]

After this flurry of activity, Shadd seemed less reluctant to reveal her identity in the paper. If anything, she was growing increasingly annoyed with her self-imposed anonymity. In late August, she finally snapped when a correspondent from Michigan wrote a letter to Mr. M. A. Shadd praising the *Freeman* and the fact that "a colored man publishes such a paper." In a brusque response, Shadd said "we do not like the Mr. and Esq., by which we are so often addressed," and she gave her full name to avoid any future "misapprehension when addressing us." Readers immediately took the hint, and by the next issue, letters were addressed to Dear Madam under the heading "To the editor of the Provincial Freeman." Shadd must have been pleased that one such letter gave her the credit she deserved for guiding the newspaper. "I am proud to behold the independent manner in which you conduct the *Freeman,*" wrote James Wentworth, of nearby Hamilton, as he supported her for taking a critical position against Frederick Douglass and Douglass's Canadian allies.[54]

As the summer 1854 came to a close, more than 100 African Americans gathered in Cleveland to attend the National Emigration Convention of Colored Peoples, which had inspired Shadds' ire months earlier. Among the four Canadian delegates was Mary Bibb, who sought to carry on her late husband's work. Visibly absent from the meeting was Mary Ann Shadd or any members of the Provincial Union. Ironically, this was one of the first national black conventions in which women's participation was encouraged, and there were 29 accredited female delegates in attendance. Despite Henry Bibb's death, his legacy was still evident at the meeting. The first resolution passed observed his death, and Martin Delany delivered an emotional eulogy. The dominant group of emigrationists were reluctant to recommend Canada as anything other than a temporary haven and the meeting concluded with calls for black emigration to the West Indies, Central or South America. The convention participants also discussed the need for a periodical to represent all African Americans. *Frederick Douglass' Paper* was considered and rejected because of his opposition to emigration, but the *Provincial Freeman*—the only black newspaper among the three or four being published at the time with a strong emigrationist position—was ignored.[55]

Mary Ann Shadd may have stayed home to protest the convention's positions or to continue her efforts to improve the *Freeman*'s finances. She gave minimal coverage to the convention in the pages of the *Freeman*. Instead the paper focused on matters closer to home, such as the availability of cheap government land for new immigrants. In September she was back on the road, traveling throughout Canada West to rally support for the newspaper and the Provincial Union. A brief story in the *Freeman* reported that funding for the paper was increasing and that citizens in Brantford, London, and other small towns were forming auxiliary unions and planning tea meetings. Shadd's correspondence to the paper gave accounts of her successful organizing and praised the industry and commitment of the men and women living in the communities she visited.

But Mary Ann grew unhappy with the response from Toronto's antislavery community. In particular, she was disappointed with the women of Toronto who escaped into the safety of traditional gender conventions to avoid helping the *Freeman*. Since the membership of the Provincial Union was largely black, it appears that the main targets of her disdain were local black women:

> If there is any one thing that tends to intensify one's contempt for the *muslin* multitude, it is the nothingness the delicate creatures display when invited to aid in a work for the general good. You would be surprised at the pains they take to impress you with their "feebleness." They "would" probably do *something*, but would not for the world "join with others." Why? you ask. "Would have to associate with the circle. Goodness!" Must not think of helping without getting Mr. _____'s consent.[56]

This outburst hinted at the undercurrent in Toronto black society that resisted supporting the *Freeman* in the manner that Shadd had anticipated. It was also evidence of Shadd's inability to hide her contempt for those whose politics she found dubious, even if she would benefit from maintaining their assistance. It was not only the white antislavery establishment that held her at arms length; she also perceived that black women were uncomfortable with her visibility as a publisher and activist. Mary Ann faced a wide gulf between herself and her black female peers who led more traditional lives. She may have been exaggerating their opposition. But it is also likely that at least some of these women considered any single, youthful woman as a potential temptress to their husbands, and resented her professional associations with "their men." Or they saw her public visibility as a repudiation of their own life choices. This was a painful realization that would soon prompt Mary Ann to return to the shadows.

During her fall fund-raising tour, Mary Ann's sister Amelia Shadd and John J. Cary ran the *Freeman* in her absence and wrote many of the editorials and local articles. Shadd's tours became a regular activity as she grew confident about leaving the newspaper in others' hands, at the same time that she became more desperate for funding. She finally dropped the charade of Ward's role at the paper when, in the October 28, 1854, issue, his name no longer appeared on the front page. The duration of Samuel Ward's tour of Europe had extended far beyond anyone's expectations—he had been gone for eighteen months—and he sent little correspondence or funds to the *Freeman*. And despite Shadd's denials, Ward was falling into disfavor with the Canadian and British antislavery organizations that had sponsored him. In the fall of 1854 Shadd revealed her disappointment with Ward's involvement in the paper when she wrote that he had failed to attract subscribers or donations for the paper during his tour in Great Britain. The *Freeman* had "not one English or foreign subscriber, nor had one copper ever been collected abroad, or been sent to America for this paper," that had borne his name, Shadd complained. In mid-winter, she published a brief article stating that Ward had donated four shillings to the Provincial Union, but had declined to serve as president of the organization. She was weary of the inquiries about Ward's activities, and made it plain that she knew nothing of his whereabouts. The era of Ward's absentee editorship was over, and Mary Ann Shadd emerged as the true force behind the newspaper, although she continued to use the title of general agent rather than editor. Disappointed and feeling abandoned by Ward's lack of involvement, Shadd no longer defended Ward's actions, and his writing rarely appeared in the *Freeman* after this period.[57]

The onset of winter did not stop Shadd's ceaseless travels to solicit subscribers. During a brief respite, she announced that interested persons could invest in the *Provincial Freeman* press at eight dollars a share and that she had successfully organized Provincial Union branches in several communities. There were occasional reminders in the paper for subscribers to pay their bills, and readers were induced to solicit subscriptions with a promise of cash or free copies. From November through January, Shadd crossed the border to lecture in Michigan, Ohio, and Pennsylvania on the subject of black emigration to Canada. She had exploited the pool of potential Canadian subscribers and began looking to the United States for new readers.[58]

In March, another member of the family arrived in Toronto to assist with the newspaper, which was about to enter its second year of publication. The *Freeman* announced that Isaac D. Shadd, Mary Ann's oldest brother, was authorized to sell subscriptions. Like sister Amelia, Isaac became a central figure at the newspaper and would remain so for many years. On the *Freeman*'s second anniversary, William Still praised Mary Ann Shadd for keeping the paper afloat and establishing it as a credible voice for Canada's black community, at a time when most black-owned periodicals were short-lived. In a few words he epitomized the complex role Shadd had played at the *Freeman*. "That you have had formidable difficulties to contend with, in relation to your enterprise, none will doubt who have the least idea of how much labour, activity, and ability that is required to fill the post of Editor, Publisher and Financier, all at the same time," Still noted. "How you have thus long and well succeeded, to me is a matter of wonder."[59]

Still was quite perceptive in his suggestion that the pressure of maintaining the paper under mounting criticism was too much for Mary Ann Shadd to bear. In early June 1855 she announced she was giving up the editorship, which she assumed would be welcome news to her detractors. It is unknown what was the exact catalyst for this decision for she clearly had no intention of relinquishing her control of the newspaper. But the constant stress of finding capital to keep the paper published, and Shadd's perception that many in Toronto's black community were reluctant to support her efforts, were a source of great dismay. The paper had barely broken even in its first year so that stockholders had no return on their investment. But she maintained that the greatest obstacle was her gender, and that her role as editor was threatening the newspaper's very existence. Shadd did not hide her bitterness and anger toward those who had disappointed her, but she hoped that they would not turn their backs on the *Freeman*: "With Editors of the unfortunate sex, who never, in their most ambitious moments aspired to the drudgery; it has had to struggle harder than the interest of my people require, if they too will not put their shoulder to the wheel." But she was willing to forgo any measure of celebrity so that her newspaper could continue. "The *Freeman* must not be discontinued because obnoxious persons have it in charge," she said pointedly.

The contradictions of masculine privilege were too much for Shadd to bear. She could not hide her resentment that male figures like Frederick Douglass and Samuel Ringgold Ward were allowed to muster "a most necessary amount of puff" to promote their careers, while she was expected to function quietly in the background. Men were accustomed to behaving "peacock-like" as they called "public attention to their individual merits, and high importance," Shadd asserted. She wondered out loud why women were denied the same opportunities. If the *Freeman*'s audience was so offended by her public visibility, she would give them a new "gentleman" editor. But in doing so, Mary Ann did not hide her pain at being rebuked by other women. "The ladies will be pleased, and assist to sustain it, which they will not do while a colored female has the ugly duty to perform; then, it is hoped that the childish weakness, seen in some quarters, will disappear altogether." She pleaded with the paper's readers to overlook their prejudices and "to make the Agent's tour profitable, and the *Freeman* prosper."[60]

A few weeks later, Mary Ann Shadd officially turned the editorship over to William P. Newman, the Baptist minister who had played an active role in the Provincial Union. Newman was to assume the editorial responsibilities, while she would concern herself with finding new subscribers. It was left unsaid who would oversee the paper's financial operations. Shadd wrote an editorial announcing the transition, continuing her public discourse on the obstacles she had encountered as editor. She could not relinquish her objection that she had suffered from misguided and unfair gender conventions.

> To its [the *Freeman*'s] enemies, we would say, be less captious to him than to us; be more considerate, if you will; it is fit that you should depart your ugliest to a woman. We feel confident few, if any, females have had to contend against in the same business, except the sister who shared our labors for a while.

Mary Ann's self-representation as the embattled reformer thwarted by gender prejudice was a self-serving strategy that allowed her to advance a political critique without taking responsibility for her own failings. Her harsh, often abrasive, style of commentary had undoubtedly offended some readers who might otherwise have been more generous with their support. It is also safe to assume that this aspect of her personality was not an asset when she was trying to organize volunteers, such as the women's auxiliary of the Provincial Union. Subtlety was not one of her personality traits. We will never know if the women who became the object of Shadd's contempt were responding more to her personal conduct, or to what she represented as a public figure. But, as William Stills's sympathetic correspondence indicates, Shadd clearly experienced substantial resistance to her role as editor and publisher.

In leaving her office, Shadd reminded readers of the contributions she had made to the liberation of blacks and women through the pages of the *Freeman*. She hoped that Newman might elicit a more tolerant audience, and she urged them to continue supporting the paper. Though Mary Ann was exceedingly frustrated by what she perceived to be the reticence of black women, she encouraged them to loosen their gendered shackles and follow in her footsteps. "To colored women, we have a word—we have 'broken the Editorial ice,' whether willingly or not, for your class in America; so go to Editing, as many of you as are willing, and able, and as soon as you may if you think you are ready." Mary Ann Shadd would not soon forget the opposition to her editorship that forced her to make this declaration. But this transition was more symbolic than real. She would remain a driving force behind the *Provincial Freeman,* and her name would again appear on the masthead.[61]

FIVE

The Chatham Years

Wait till you get to Chatham, and you'll see heaps of our people ... William Wells Brown[1]

The appointment of a new editor was only one of the changes that occurred at the *Provincial Freeman* during the summer of 1855. Mary Ann Shadd's faith in Toronto as a mecca for black political activity had been soured by the opposition to her editorship. She had succeeded in coaxing the *Freeman* through its first year, and in establishing a formal organization of black activists to solidify support for the venture—the Provincial Union. But these accomplishments were tempered by her knowledge that many did not want her—or any black woman—to serve at the helm of a newspaper.

Mary Ann Shadd was also confronting some harsh economic realities. As Walter Lippmann noted almost a century later, newspapers were entirely dependent on the loyalty of their readers, and publishers had little recourse if reader interest waned. This was especially true for black-owned periodicals that relied on the small proportion of the black community that was literate and had the financial means to purchase subscriptions and/or advertising. The only black newspapers that survived this period in the United States were those with strong support from white abolitionists and philanthropists, like *Frederick Douglass' Paper*, or from established institutions like the A. M. E. Church, which published the *Christian Recorder*. Although Toronto was Canada's largest city, Shadd constantly traveled elsewhere to find the financial support that was not forthcoming from the *Freeman*'s home base. As the list of agents representing the *Freeman* grew in smaller Canadian towns and cities, only Isaac Shadd remained as a canvasser for Toronto and vicinity.[2]

Mary Ann Shadd seemed at a loss for a reason to explain why there were so few reliable subscribers for the paper. "Can there not be 5000 readers to it in Canada, alone, to say nothing of the many thousands we hope to have in the United States?" she asked. Shadd began to realize that her own aspirations and labor were insufficient to keep the *Freeman* going. There had to be a constituency committed to the enterprise—an audience who understood the importance of maintaining a vital avenue of communication. Shadd bared these frustrations when she wondered out loud, "Why keep up a rickety existence, and be obliged to dunn and coax and flatter to get sums legally due, or to invite an increase of favour from mainly those whose best interests are promoted by its continuance?" This was the complaint of most small-town newspaper publishers in the nineteenth century. Subscribers often failed to pay for the privilege of reading, pushing the press to became a servant of business rather than politics.[3]

The combination of her disappointment with Toronto, and the need to boost the paper's circulation and cut costs, prompted Shadd to move the *Freeman* 170 miles to the town of Chatham, not far from her former home of Windsor. She returned to the less developed, westernmost region of the province where she had traveled during the last year to solicit contributions and subscribers. The encouragement she received from residents in this area led Shadd to believe that the growing population was more committed to the goals and purpose of her newspaper. Her old nemesis Henry Bibb was dead, and time had healed the wounds created by her earlier political battles in the region. By the mid-1850s Chatham was a bustling frontier town on the Thames River, which flowed into the Detroit River at the United States border. It was within a few miles of Canada's largest black settlements, including Dawn, Elgin, and Raleigh Township, leading Shadd to declare that "all are beautiful and thriving towns; but Chatham is a grand central point for the Counties of Kent, Essex, Lambton, and Middlesex." Varying accounts suggest the town's 800 blacks were 20–25 percent of the total population, making them a potent economic and social force. In 1855, the abolitionist Benjamin Drew found the towns' black residents to be particularly industrious, running shops, engaging in trades, and farming.[4]

Mary Ann was also drawn to the region because her parents and other relatives had settled on 200 acres in North Buxton just a few miles from Chatham. Her father, Abraham Shadd, had become involved in local politics and was in the forefront of establishing black fraternal organizations in the region. Her sister Amelia Shadd remained in the Toronto area, where she settled and married David T. Williamson, a former slave. Amelia continued to be a regular correspondent for the newspaper, writing about events in the Toronto area. Another sister, Emaline Shadd, also lived in Toronto where she attended normal school. But brother Isaac Shadd joined his elder sister for the long trek to Chatham, where he took over as publisher of the *Provincial Freeman*. The new editor, William P. Newman, stayed in Toronto where he was a Baptist minister, so the day-to-day responsibilities for running the paper were shared by the Shadd siblings. This continued the pattern that kept others in visible leadership positions while Mary Ann Shadd and, increasingly, her brother Isaac, shouldered the daily burdens of publishing.[5]

Publication of the *Freeman* was suspended for nearly three months while the move was under way. The only glimpse of this arduous journey was provided by a brief article that apologized for the long time between issues. The printing press and type were damaged during the move, and once the equipment arrived in Chatham, the *Freeman*'s offices had to be set up. They moved into Charity's Brick Building at the corner of King and Adelaide Streets in the heart of the town's financial district. During the first weeks, the paper sometimes came off the printing press late "owing to the scarcity of hands, and other unavoidable circumstances incidental to moving," as Isaac explained. Finally, publication resumed on August 22, 1855. The front page was almost identical to the Toronto version of the paper; there was a large ad for the *Freeman*'s printing business and a column of advertisements mostly from Toronto supporters. The editors hoped to encourage timely payment of bills with a humorous poem titled "Pay the Printer," which warned, "The cats will mew between your feet, The dogs will bite you on the street" if the printer's bills were ignored.[6]

This issue carried a long, front-page article highlighting the features of Chatham. The town was described as a thriving community of 3,500 that boasted ten churches, six schools, numerous mills, shops, foundries, and stores (including three printing shops), fertile land for agriculture, and proximity to other commercial areas via the Great Western Railway and Lake Erie. Chatham appeared to be an ideal location for the paper. A growing population and new businesses would be untapped sources of subscribers and advertisers. Indeed, this seemed to be the editor's expectation in an announcement that asked that local residents consider the *Freeman* "for an equal share of the publishing business of the community."[7]

But there were several other newspapers in this developing region of Canada West, including the Chatham *Planet,* the *Kent Advertiser,* which served the county, and the nearby *Windsor Herald.* The *Planet* fashioned itself as a champion of the black fugitives and a supporter of abolitionism, and it occasionally published information about Chatham's black residents. The other newspapers were generally hostile to the large black presence in the area. The *Freeman* received an especially chilly welcome from the *Kent Advertiser*, which dreaded the arrival of new competition. After learning of the Shadds' plans to relocate in Chatham, the *Advertiser* carried an editorial that reflected the paper's anti-black sentiments. The editorial charged, among other things, that Chatham's black citizens were prone to criminal activity, that a newspaper like the *Freeman* would promote lawlessness among the black populace, and that having a woman editor made the *Freeman* an inferior journal. Infuriated by these charges, the *Freeman* carried a fiery response defending the paper and making it plain that Mary Ann Shadd relinquished the editorship only because of gender prejudice. The editorial, written by either Isaac or Rev. Newman, characterized Mary Ann as "one of the best Editors our Province ever had if such did wear the petticoats instead of the breeches." The only reason she relinquished the title of editor was because of "the folly of adhering to a wrongly developed public sentiment that would crush *a woman* whenever she attempts to do what has hitherto been assigned to men, even though God designed her to do it." Previously, Mary Ann had claimed that her calling to journalism was inspired by politics and social responsibility; now her quest was attributed to divinity. But her writing was far from evangelical.[8]

The criticism from the *Kent Advertiser* would not go unanswered. Mary Ann lashed out at the paper for attempting to harm the *Freeman*'s reputation just as it was getting established. For two columns she methodically refuted the claims made against the *Freeman* and suggested the whole matter reflected white Canadians' ambivalence about abolitionism. She closed by asking how much the *Advertiser* had done to eradicate prejudice and promote the needs of Chatham's black residents. "Do something for them, besides trying to sow discord among them for your paper's interest, before you take the *Provincial Freeman* to task, and be able to understand it before you attempt to dictate to it," she challenged. This exchange typified the race relations of the Shadds' new home.[9]

Despite Mary Ann's optimism about Chatham, the town had a reputation for being notoriously racist. "Among that portion of the whites who put a high value on their prejudices . . . there seems to be a dread that some terrible and unpardonable crime, termed 'sauciness' may yet become rife among the blacks," noted Benjamin Drew as he traveled through the town. Chatham, unlike the more cosmopolitan Toronto, had churches, schools, and social institutions firmly separated by race and religion. Mary Ann carried on a regular battle with local editors who allowed their racial ideology to spill into print. On one occasion, for example, the Chatham *Planet* published an article accusing local blacks of drunkenness, and suggesting that a law should be passed to prohibit the sale of alcohol to "the sons of Ham." Mary Ann did not deny that some blacks drank too much, but also noted that local whites—even community leaders—could

Isaac D. Shadd emigrated to Canada West in the 1850s and shared the burdens of publishing the *Provincial Freeman* with his sister. After the Civil War he returned to the United States where he became involved in southern politics, serving as Speaker of the Mississippi Legislature, 1874–76. (Raleigh Township Centennial Museum)

be intemperate, as well. "Who patronize the saloons, taverns &c in this place? Indians and colored men only?" she asked. Shadd supported the idea of a prohibition law that would "not only prevent Indians and colored men from getting drunk, but will stop white men from drinking as well and not only the 'inferior' classes about Chatham, but a drunken Editor occasionally."[10]

William Newman quietly assumed the role of editor, graciously accepting the unpaid position to "push along the *Freeman*." From his home in Toronto, Newman contributed editorials which often reflected his religious interests and support for Canada's Conservative Party. Other editorials published in the paper during this period were written by Isaac Shadd. Meanwhile, Mary Ann Shadd moved further into the background of the newspaper's public affairs. She retained her official title of agent —a position she considered "less responsible, but more congenial"—and she ran occasional announcements for *Freeman* business, such as stockholder's meetings and fund-raising events. But she had no intention of remaining silent. Shadd began to contribute an extensive correspondence to the paper that expressed her views as if she were an independent entity rather than a officer of the *Freeman*. Once again, as she had done with *Notes of Canada West*, Shadd wanted to represent herself simultaneously as an insider and outsider in the affairs of these black communities. Belatedly, perhaps, Shadd also realized that the paper could still function as her public forum without it becoming embroiled in her assorted crusades.[11]

Once the paper was being published regularly in Chatham, Shadd shifted her attention to a political debate brewing over the Dawn settlement, a 1,500-acre black community in the nearby town of Dresden. In the first Chatham issue of the *Freeman* there was a call for a convention to investigate the affairs of the settlement and to elect a new board of trustees. It is possible that the publication of this first issue of the *Freeman* was deliberately planned to advertise the convention. The meeting, to be held at the end of August in Chatham, was organized by a group of blacks disgruntled with Dawn's leadership. They wrote: "The Land is ours, and it is ment [*sic*] that we should control it, and make it useful to us in the way designed. Its affairs are now in a confused state." An upheaval was in the works, and Mary Ann Shadd would be in the middle of the controversy, just as she had been when she marshaled opposition to the Refugee Home Society. The *Provincial Freeman*'s new editor, William Newman, had a particular interest in Dawn because he lived and worked there in the 1840s, leaving after he accused the settlement's founders, Josiah Henson and Hiram Wilson, of mismanagement. Newman returned to Dawn briefly in 1850 as an administrator, but was replaced by the British abolitionist John Scoble, who had run afoul of Mary Ann Shadd on several occasions. By the mid-1850s, Wilson was gone, Henson was reduced to a figurehead, and Dawn's black population was frustrated with the white leadership. From the editor's chair in Toronto, Newman was in a prime position to encourage the growing dissent at the settlement.[12]

By the time the *Freeman* began publishing in Chatham, Scoble and Henson had been accused of deceit, slander, extortion, and alienating Dawn's black residents. This set the stage for another run-in between Mary Ann Shadd and Scoble. Now, with the full power of her newspaper and the local black community behind her, Shadd could effectively attack this white abolitionist whom she believed embodied the worst hypocrisy and paternalism of the movement. It was also a perfect opportunity to take revenge for his participation in her firing by the American Missionary Association, as well as their other contentious encounters. Just a few weeks after settling in her new home, Mary Ann made her presence known at the convention of Dawn's residents, where the minutes noted that "Miss M. A. Shadd, also, dissenting from the Rev. Mr. Scoble, addressed the meeting for a few minutes, in a very lucid and appropriate manner." Rev. Newman had also traveled from Toronto to attend the meeting and lent his voice to the opposition. The *Freeman* published the minutes, several accounts of the meeting, and an editorial that provided a scathing critique of Henson and Scoble. At the end of the convention, a committee was organized to solicit funds for a lawsuit to wrest control of Dawn away from Scoble and his associates. Mary Ann Shadd was recruited for this task: "This lady has our entire confidence in this mission, and as it is for the furtherance of your interests, we trust she may have yours," announced the committee. This gave Shadd an influential voice in the Dawn controversy, which she put to immediate use.[13]

In the first of a series of letters Shadd wrote to the *Freeman* about the issue, she revealed that she had not forgotten Scoble's earlier deeds. When one of Scoble's supporters accused her of being an infidel, she referred to the American Missionary Association decision to withdraw support for her school in Windsor: "The latter [Scoble], I remember, made a similar charge against 'that Miss Shadd' to a Yankee Society once, and they cut off her 'bread and cheese' for the same charge, not for the truth of it, for they had satisfactory evidence to the contrary." Shadd accused Scoble of being patronizing and obsessed with control over his black charges at Dawn. Scoble, whom she dubbed the "master man," relished his power and authority at the black settlement. In her report Shadd charged Scoble with making comments that were "lengthy, self-laudatory, disparaging to the colored people." Scoble's black supporters, particularly Josiah Henson, were compared to "nigger drivers" ready to do the white man's dirty business. She called the Dawn administration's behavior "most despotic, insulting and reprehensible, and leaves us as much to fear from the high-handed conduct of such 'friends' in Canada," and she cheered on the efforts of blacks to take control of their community. Scoble was so incensed by the Dawn convention—and probably by Shadds' commentary—that he refused the group entry to the settlement's schoolhouse, and they had to move their assembly to a nearby church.[14]

From Toronto, where Shadd began her correspondence, she traveled to London, St. Catherines, and Niagara to raise funds for the *Freeman* and the Dawn committee. Her written travelogues enhanced her authoritative position for her readers; they had to rely on her eyes and ears to learn about the vast terrain that comprised Canada's black imagined community. Her success at fund raising was varied: in Niagara, the *Freeman* was praised and contributions were made; in London, she found an embattled community in which the black residents fought among themselves and the British missionaries were "distinguished for their colorphobia." In St. Catherines, a tea meeting held for the *Freeman* was hampered by bad weather, yet the small turnout "gave liberally of their substance on the occasion." Shadd reported raising eight pounds, eight shillings, a successful take for one evening. One pound was donated to the Dawn committee and one pound covered her own travel expenses. She was becoming weary of this double duty, however, and may have suspected that her efforts on the Dawn committee's behalf were hurting rather than helping the newspaper. She questioned why the Dawn Committee did not send out an agent solely devoted to its cause, thus relieving her of the responsibility.[15]

The battle over Dawn would drag out for almost a decade. Scoble seemed unable to defend himself, and the British and Foreign Anti-Slavery Society was drawn into the unflattering controversy. Scholars have agreed that Scoble made no improvements at Dawn during his tenure and his only accomplishment was to distance himself from all but a few blacks connected with the settlement. Mary Ann Shadd continued to canvass for the Dawn committee for several months before her attention was diverted elsewhere. It would not be until the 1860s that a lawsuit would be settled, allowing the black residents to take legal and financial control of Dawn.[16]

Meanwhile the *Freeman* was struggling to keep afloat, and Mary Ann Shadd remained on the road in her never-ending search for financial support. Each week the paper published reminders for subscribers to pay their bills, and by early October the entire editorial column was devoted to this subject. Moving and setting up shop had added to the *Freeman*'s debts, and although there were new advertisements from Chatham merchants, there was a desperate need for more subscribers. "So much being true, it must be the *duty* not only of the colored people, but also of the whites, to give the paper a *liberal support!*" wrote Newman. Although the newspaper appeared to have numerous readers, the bills were not being paid while expenses mounted, and the editors went so far as to invite payment from farmers in the form of "their 'hog and hominy,' their bread and cheese, and wood, or the winged tribe. But remember, we would much rather have the cash!"[17]

The new editor also attempted to smooth over the ruffled feathers of white abolitionists who were insulted by Mary Ann Shadd's attacks on Scoble and others. Many in Canada West's black communities viewed these men as essential for attracting international attention and philanthropic support to the fugitive slaves, despite their shortcomings. White abolitionists were also an important part of the *Freeman*'s readership. Yet it seemed that few white missionaries escaped Shadd's pen. Her muckraking journalism constantly went after the underside of Canadian abolitionism. While visiting St. Catherines she accused Rev. Hiram Wilson of profiteering when she discovered him building a "large brick mansion for his own use" which she suspected was financed by donations for the fugitives. "Mr. Wilson's prosperity only confirms one in the irresistible conclusion, that no missionary field is more *profitable* than that in which the fugitives of Canada are the *victims,*" she charged. The corruption she found endemic to those working for the fugitives' aid led her to the conclusion that "no people need such missionaries less than the said fugitives."[18]

In direct contradiction to Shadd's sentiments, Newman's editorial in the same issue declared that the *Freeman* was not opposed to the work of white missionaries. This was followed by a long sermon on the Christian principle of universal brotherhood and the necessity for persons not to be evaluated on the basis of skin color. For the first time, there was an attempt in the pages of the *Freeman* to soften Mary Ann Shadd's rhetoric, if not to dissociate the paper from her views. It is unclear whether this reflected a difference of opinion between Shadd and Newman or rather an attempt to reassure readers who might be present or future subscribers.

While Rev. Newman penned the editorials, Isaac Shadd shouldered the responsibility for getting the paper out and keeping creditors at bay, especially in his sister's absence. Isaac was plagued with logistical problems, from a broken press to readers who refused to pay for their subscriptions and left their papers languishing at the post office. Mary Ann Shadd may have been attracting new readers for the paper, but she was also canvassing a population that had varying degrees of education and financial security. Many may have been caught up in the fervor and enthusiasm of supporting the black-owned journal while attending her fundraising meetings. But when confronted with a bill for the subscription, either they could not afford to pay it or were unwilling to donate their limited resources to such a luxury.[19]

On the completion of this Canadian tour, Shadd left St. Catherines, crossed Lake Ontario, and headed south to Philadelphia, where she could always find an hospitable audience. She arrived on October 13, four days after her thirty-second birthday, "wearied with fatigue and exposure" from a long journey marred by rain and transportation delays. But she regained her strength sufficiently to attend the Colored National Convention that began in Philadelphia three days later. This meeting was the follow-up to a convention in Rochester, New York, two years earlier at which a National Council of African American leaders was formed to provide a platform for their views and to establish a unified political agenda. The 1855 convention sought to continue the movement toward black autonomy and collective action, calling on free blacks to "disencumber themselves from whatever tends to impede their march" so that they might "take upon them the responsibility of doing and acting for themselves—of laying out and directing work of their own elevation."[20]

On the surface, at least, Mary Ann's commitments to racial uplift and black nationalist identity seemed well represented by the convention's agenda. But the National Council was dominated by Frederick Douglass and other prominent blacks who rejected the growing emigration movement. Thus, Mary Ann Shadd could not expect widespread support for her exhortations about Canada. But now that she was relieved of many of the daily pressures of publishing the *Freeman*, she had the time and energy to join the larger forum of black political activism in the United States. This was relatively easy for Shadd to accomplish in Philadelphia, where she had friends and an established reputation.

Mary Ann Shadd was the sole Canadian delegate to the convention and one of only two women, which created quite a stir. The official minutes reported that on the first day, Charles Lenox Remond, "the handsome, spellbinding pioneer among full-time black abolitionist lecturers," supported Shadd's participation with a motion to admit her as a delegate. "This question gave rise to a spirited discussion, after which the motion was passed," noted the proceedings. That night Frederick Douglass, among others, endorsed Shadd's presence while several delegates spoke in opposition. After a lengthy debate, Mary Ann Shadd was admitted to the convention with thirty-eight votes in her favor and twenty-three opposed. The vote reflected the tension between men like Douglass and Remond, who supported women's public role in the abolitionist movement, and others who thought it improper for women to participate in or address male-dominated gatherings. Mary Ann Shadd's historic presence at this meeting was a victory for black women who had toiled behind the scenes for black abolitionism. Her role as a delegate was tolerated, but she was not quoted in the proceedings, appointed to any committees, or a signer of any resolutions.[21]

Yet, a correspondent to *Frederick Douglass' Paper* wrote that Shadd was an active participant at the meeting and gave a forceful speech on Canadian emigration that virtually rocked the convention hall. "She obtained the floor and proceeded to, and succeeded in making one of the most convincing and telling speeches in favor of Canadian emigration I ever heard. It was one of the speeches of the Convention," he wrote. The audience was so riveted by Mary Ann's oratory that she was granted a ten-minute extension after her first ten minutes expired. And then, the gathering allowed her more time to complete her comments, as the afternoon session came to a close: "The House was crowded and breathless in its attention to her masterly exposition of our present condition, and the advantages Canada opens to colored men of enterprise. Herein consisted the charm and potency of her speech."[22]

The author, Brooklyn abolitionist William J. Watkins, was clearly dazzled and awestruck by Shadd's performance as a lecturer. He wrote "She is a superior woman; and it is useless to deny it; and, however much we may differ with her on the subject of emigration," typifying the mixed reception to Mary Ann's political work. Her articulateness and bearing made her symbolically useful for the project of racial uplift, but few were receptive to her nationalist/emigrationist ideology. Watkins's description of Shadd's elocution was reminiscent of earlier reports of her lectures. He seemed as preoccupied with her physical appearance and technique, as with her ideas. As a black woman public speaker, she was a rarity who required a detailed report. "Miss Shadd's eyes are small and penetrating, and fairly flash when she is speaking," wrote Watkins. "Her ideas seem to flow so fast that she, at times, hesitates for words; yet she overcomes any apparent imperfection in her speaking by the earnestness of her manner, and the quality of her thoughts." The years of lecturing across Canada and the United States on behalf of the *Freeman* had developed Mary Ann Shadd into a mature and charismatic orator. Yet the power of her speech failed to persuade those in her audience opposed to emigration, and she described the convention as "the great failure" that brought out the ugly side of her opponents.[23]

Nevertheless, Shadd had become a minor celebrity, and she gave several talks while in Philadelphia. On November 6, she was featured in a debate against Isaiah Wears, a prominent local black abolitionist, on the topic "Shall the Free Colored People of the United States Emigrate to Canada?" Wears was free born, just a year older than Shadd, and a longtime fixture in Philadelphia's black conventions and vigilance committees. The debate took place at the Banneker Institute of Philadelphia, a society devoted to African American intellectual activities that was named for the black mathematician and astronomer. A letter in the *Freeman* described Wears as "one of our most able debaters, and, withal an unflinching opponent of emigration to Canada, or elsewhere" and said the event attracted a large and enthusiastic audience. Wears presumed that he would "demolish all her en masse emigration notions" and told the audience that he would treat Shadd like any male opponent because she was "too high spirited to crave any special favor or courtesy." But despite his confidence, Wears was no match for the persistent and well-prepared Shadd, who was voted the winner by a panel of three judges.[24]

Mary Ann had beaten a man at a man's game, in the process enhancing her reputation as a powerful adversary in political matters. Her growing reputation as a vigorous antislavery lecturer finally brought her some small yet tangible financial gain, as well. When she addressed an antislavery meeting at Philadelphia's Shiloh Church, several in attendance noticed that Shadd had always given such presentations for free. The group voted to organize a fund-raising gala "in view of her faithful services in the cause of Reform." The event, which was packed to overflowing, featured a performance by Elizabeth T. Greenfield, a popular singer often called "the Black Swan" or the "colored Jenny Lind." There were refreshments and short speeches from Shadd and prominent black abolitionists including James Miller McKim, John C. Bowers, and H. Ford Douglass. The tribute to Mary Ann was not without controversy, however. Bowers, a veteran of the black convention movement and a member of Philadelphia's black elite, took exception to her emigrationist pleas. After Shadd made a few remarks, he took the stage to speak in vigorous opposition to Canadian emigration. Even at this social gathering on her behalf, Mary Ann had to fend off political challengers.[25]

William Still wrote an account of the event for the *Freeman,* in which he gave tribute to Shadd's pioneering role as a journalist: "As she stands connected with the press, she is justly entitled, doubtless, to the credit of being the *first* colored woman on the American continent, to Establish and Edit a weekly newspaper," he proclaimed with obvious pride. Still described the emotional and physical stresses inherent in publishing a newspaper, offering a glimpse at the lengths she went to keep the *Freeman* afloat. There were ceaseless travels on "burthen trains" and the open upper decks of steamboats "in the most inclement weather, even when in delicate health," he noted. Worse than the physical discomfort were the numerous indignities, insults, and injuries she suffered at the hands of "insolent conductors and others, on the score of prejudice." Meanwhile, she relied on selling copies of her pamphlet *Notes of Canada West* and subscriptions to the paper to cover expenses. On this occasion, however, the proceeds of the event were given directly to Shadd.[26]

Buoyed by this warm reception from her friends and followers, Shadd returned to Canada West to continue her quest to find new subscribers for the *Freeman.* If she went home to Chatham it was only for a brief visit, because by early December she was in Windsor. This return to her former home town brought out Shadd's acid pen, which she aimed at proslavery Canadians and other enemies. Shadd's next letter to the *Freeman* was tinged with anger and ethnic prejudice when she described supporters of Canada's Reform Party, which sought to democratize elements of the British-controlled government and take control from the Anglican aristocracy. Shadd insisted that the Reformers used anti-black sentiment as part of their political platform, calling them "enemies to the colored people of the most contemptible kind." There were white Yankees who were "true to their inferior training, and dirty instincts," French immigrants who were "stupid to the last degree, beyond improvement or progress of note, dressed in their moccasins, and glorying in their 'dogcarts,'" and the Scotch and Scotch-Irish "from whom better things should be expected." The *Freeman* was an important tool for politicizing the black populace, and Shadd urged them to vote for the rival Conservative candidate in the next election, which was in keeping with editor William Newman's endorsements. Shadd also ran into her old enemy from her Windsor days, Rev. C. C. Foote, whom she delighted in calling a "defunct beggar for the absolete [*sic*] Refugees' Home, Old Clothes Agent for the fugitives, and Religious Nothing-arian." She found Foote interfering with local plans to build a school for black children and declared that "such meddlesome scourges ought to be stopped."[27]

From Windsor Shadd traveled a few miles south along the Detroit River until she reached Amherstburg, a town that, like Chatham, was one-quarter black and considered by many to be Canada's most active point on the Underground Railroad. She wrote a brief report for the *Freeman* about this "time-worn" town, which she likened to a "singed cat." Mary Ann provided an optimistic assessment of the town's progress, noting that local residents were working to improve race relations and build the economy. Her main target was a white missionary—Isaac Rice—whom she considered to be engaged in self-serving activities. Rice was once of the region's first missionaries for the African American fugitives. He established a school in Amherstburg in 1838 and represented the American Missionary Association until 1850. But by the mid-1850s he had fallen into disfavor with many local blacks, who determined that his fund raising was lining his own pockets instead of benefiting the needy. They formed the first of several "True Band" societies in the region devoted to community improvement and self-help, and published a letter in the *Freeman* opposing Rice's efforts. The group publicly declared that Rice and his associations were "completely destroying the character and prospects of the colored people of this entire district." As a result they independently raised the money to aid "all who are suffering." Mary Ann Shadd lent encouragement to the True Band, which carried out her goals of black self-sufficiency, and in turn they praised the good work of the *Provincial Freeman*.[28]

By the end of December 1855, Mary Ann Shadd had carved out a reputation as a rugged, persistent and capable advocate. A. M. E. Bishop Daniel Payne heard Mary Ann give one of her last emigration lectures of the year on a visit to Chicago. Payne's memoirs recalled Shadd as "that extraordinary young woman" whose "power did not consist in eloquence, but in her familiarity with facts, her knowledge of men, and her fine power of discrimination." He praised her editorship of the *Provincial Freeman*, noting that she also functioned as traveling agent and financier. "Her editorials compared well with those of the sterner sex, some of whom she often excelled," Payne remembered. Having made such an impression, Mary Ann finally came home to Chatham for a rest and to spend the holiday season with her family. She had been on the road constantly since August.[29]

In the new year, Mary Ann took time out from her hectic schedule to make a significant personal transition. On January 3 she married Thomas F. Cary at her sister Amelia's home in St. Catherines. There are few sources on Cary's background. It has been assumed that he was older than Mary Ann, but the 1860 census reported that when they married, Mary Ann was thirty-two and Thomas was thirty. Cary was a black man born free in the United States, and emigrated to Canada in the early 1850s, along with his brothers George, Isaac N., and John J. Cary. He ran a barbershop in Toronto, was a partner in the city's first ice business, and was an active opponent to slavery. The marriage abruptly thrust Mary Ann into the role of stepmother, as Thomas had three children from a previous marriage: Ann, age 14; Thomas, Jr., age 11; and John, age 7. We know virtually nothing about the nature of their courtship and marriage; only a few letters from Thomas Cary remain to provide any insight into this companionate relationship.[30]

Mary Ann and Thomas had several mutual friends, including Samuel Ringgold Ward, who stayed with Cary when the Wards first arrived in Canada. Thomas had been an early supporter of and investor in the *Freeman* and was a founding officer of the Provincial Union. Thus, the two had worked together for several years, and their political association may have paved the way to courtship. Knowing Mary Ann in this context, Thomas Cary was fully aware of her fierce independence and disdain for traditionally feminine roles. The physical descriptions of Mary Ann Shadd indicate she was attractive, youthful, and poised, qualities likely to attract male attention. She may have turned down numerous marriage proposals, both in the social whirl of black Pennsylvania and in the small communities of Canada West where eligible women were often scarce. Whether it was for love, security, or a nod to social convention, Mary Ann Shadd finally decided to marry well past the conventional age. Perhaps with Thomas Cary, unlike other suitors, Mary Ann shared a sense of common purpose that allowed her to continue her life in the public sphere.

Thomas kept his home in Toronto while Mary Ann lived in Chatham, but they traveled frequently between the two residences to be together when they could, and two children were born from their union. Their letters reveal the affection and respect the two felt for each other, although there was little of the romance or thinly veiled eroticism often found in Victorian-era correspondence. It has been suggested that the Carys' marriage was an example of a relationship that defied nineteenth-century gender conventions because Mary Ann continued her active public career with her husband's support and approval. It was clear from the outset that marriage did not hinder Mary Ann's public activities. This was a quiet, personal decision that received little fanfare or attention. There was no mention of the marriage in the *Provincial Freeman,* and it took six months before Mary Ann began to use her married name in print. She apparently spent little time occupying herself with a wedding, honeymoon, or other frivolities. Her frequent absences during the fall of 1855 had created considerable instability at the editorial offices of the *Free-man,* and she focused much of her energy to get it back on track.[31]

The first transition occurred in November, when William Howard Day's name appeared on the masthead as corresponding editor. Day, a college-educated, free-born African American, had spent a good deal of his professional life working for newspapers. He began his journalism career in 1850 as a reporter for the white-owned Cleveland *True Democrat,* where he eventually became editor. Day was associated with several black newspapers, and in 1853 he founded the *Aliened American,* for which Samuel Ward agreed to serve as corresponding editor. The paper foundered within a year because of Day's inability to secure financial backing. Just two years earlier Day had opposed black emigration as a member of the National Council and allied himself with Frederick Douglass. But he became increasingly disgruntled with Douglass's conservatism and dissatisfied with conditions for free blacks in the North. In early 1854 the Ohio Senate denied Day's request to cover the body's proceedings as a reporter, and afterward he became increasingly sympathetic to the emigrationist's call. So, in September 1855, Day and his wife purchased a farm in Dresden, near the Dawn settlement, to begin their lives anew in Canada West.[32]

The *Freeman's* management leaped at the opportunity of having this well-known and experienced black activist and journalist associated with the paper. However, although Day's name appeared on the *Freeman's* front page in November, there was little evidence of his involvement with the paper until January 1856, when William Newman was no longer listed as editor. The following week there was a brief editorial column noting that Newman had resigned and that "Mr. Day or some other suitable person" would be selected to fill the editor's post. In the meantime, the former editor, Mary Ann, and the publishing agent, Isaac, would take over the editorial responsibilities. The Shadds had jumped to the wrong conclusion, however. William Howard Day did not become editor, despite the coaxing from the *Freeman.* In fact, he never had more than a cursory relationship with the newspaper. He wrote occasional letters to the paper while he earned a living as an antislavery lecturer and became increasingly involved in black Canadian politics. However, another African American active in abolition and social reform—H. Ford Douglass—arrived to fill the gap.[33]

In February 1856 a brief editorial announced that ownership of the paper was being transferred to Isaac Shadd, H. Ford Douglass, and Louis Patterson. It is unclear exactly what this transition entailed, but stockholders were reassured that their interests would not be damaged. Little is known about Patterson; he lived in Chicago and was described by Mary Ann Shadd as "a young person of fine talents." H. Ford Douglass was a self-educated escaped slave who lived in Cleveland and became an important fixture in Ohio's abolitionist community before moving to Chicago. He was a solid supporter of the emigration movement, had been active at the 1854 National Emigration Convention, and had been a speaker at the fund raiser for Mary Ann Shadd in Philadelphia a few months earlier. It was at this event, perhaps, that he began to consider a more active role with the *Freeman.* Douglass had also battled with William Howard Day over the emigration question at the black state conventions in Ohio. Douglass's involvement with the *Freeman* during the early months of 1856 was primarily financial. Meanwhile, Isaac supervised the paper's daily operation and Mary Ann went on the road once more.[34]

Within days of her marriage Mary Ann Shadd Cary was traveling in her endless quest to find financial sustenance for the paper. Her first destination was Chicago, home to the *Freeman*'s new proprietors Douglass and Patterson. Despite the bitter cold—she wrote that the temperature dipped to 30 degrees below zero—she found a thriving African American community with pockets of support for her newspaper. She even had time for some fun, including a sleigh ride through the countryside with some young residents. She was in good humor when she described the hostility she encountered from opponents of emigration, who forced her to "suffer from partial torpor, induced by hearing of the wicked machinations of the enemies of the *Freeman.*"[35]

Isaac Shadd was still struggling to keep the paper's financial problems at bay, and there was talk that someone was waiting for the paper to collapse so it could be bought out. Mary Ann heard the rumor during her stay in Chicago and confronted it publicly. "Who in Canada hopes to play 'hide and seek' with the *Freeman,* until they hope to see it *hopelessly* involved so as to buy it off 'stock and flute,' by paying the new debts only?" she wondered. On one hand, she called such opportunists "crazy dolts" for wanting to take on the precarious newspaper. But Mary Ann was also outraged that anyone would have designs on the project that had been her lifeblood, and a crucial component of her public identity. She promised that if she could identify "the moral monsters" she would reveal their names for public scrutiny.[36]

It is not surprising that the rumor was circulating given that each issue of the *Freeman* carried a more desperate plea for subscribers to pay their accounts. By late February, an editorial warned that the paper might fold if payments did not start coming in, despite Mary Ann's constant fund raising. The newspaper's managers hoped to avert the crisis with a plan to turn from subscriptions to payment on delivery after Shadd Cary returned from her canvassing tour. "The *Freeman* has now kept its head above the stern ripple of the troubled waters of adversity from week to week, having no other agencies at work for its sustenance, than the single efforts of a young woman, out of the office," Isaac wrote, in another plea for support. It was clear that the paper could not go on this way indefinitely.[37]

This new distribution plan brought Shadd Cary a month's rest in the middle of winter, but did little to increase revenues. By March she was back in Chicago, where she was joined by H. Ford Douglass for a late winter tour through the region. For two months the pair, sometimes together and sometimes on their own, visited towns and cities in the Midwest, including Waukegan and Palmyra, Illinois, and Kenosha and Racine, Wisconsin. Transportation to the most rural areas was often primitive, and Shadd Cary recalled considerable hardships. On one occasion "having made a bitter cold journey, by sleigh, of many miles, and having 'roosted' for one night on a very narrow platform at the Geneva station in company with several belated snow-delayed mortals of both sexes," she finally reached her destination north of Chicago. Yet in a series of letters to the *Freeman*, Shadd Cary and Douglass put the best face on their exhausting travels.[38]

The response to a woman as a public speaker was varied in these small communities. In Palmyra, Mary Ann preached a sermon on slavery to a large congregation at the Baptist Church and was warmly received. But her efforts to speak in Rockford, Illinois, were blocked and she was only permitted to address a group of young women, prompting Shadd Cary to declare: "The advocates of Women's Rights should go there, as the citizens are so conservative on the question as not to tolerate lectures from women." She found "staunch friends of freedom" at Wheaton College in Illinois, but in a nearby hamlet "the Congregationalists do not let their church hold anti-slavery meetings" and the hotels refused to serve black women. In one town she found that black men as well as white resisted women's independence. "The cause of 'Women's Rights' does not flourish as it should do and strange enough, the monkey tricks of such colored men are said to injure it," she wrote. Racism and sexism followed Mary Ann Shadd Cary throughout her journeys, but she treated them as little more than annoyances. Along the way there was always an abolitionist family, black or white, who provided lodging for the night, energetic men and women who helped canvass for new subscribers, and enthusiastic audiences who attended her talks. These bright spots sustained her until she returned to Chatham in May 1856.[39]

Shadd Cary arrived at home just as the *Freeman* celebrated another anniversary and began a third year of publication. She and her colleagues made yet another decision about the paper's leadership, and this time it would be accurately represented on the front page. Beginning with the May 10, 1856 issue H. Ford Douglass, Isaac Shadd, and Mary Ann Shadd were all listed as editors. Those who had shared in the work of keeping

the paper going would also share in the public recognition—or antagonism. Perhaps with two equally ranked colleagues, less attention would
be focused on Mary Ann's gender; after all, she was not in solitary control
of the newspaper. It may also be that the black community of Chatham
was more tolerant of her public role and that her increasing stature as a
public speaker mitigated other concerns. The editors explained that the
new masthead would enable readers to identify individual's written opinions with the author so that "each one may be made responsible for his
own sentiments, and sins." Ultimately, Douglass's editorial contributions
were limited although he continued to travel extensively to raise funds
for the *Freeman* for several years. So, despite the fanfare, little about the
paper's editorial control had changed.[40]

Shadd Cary's emigrationist appeal was clearly reaching black activists
in the northern states, as several important figures migrated north to
Canada. Among them was emigration movement leader Martin Delany,
who moved his family to Chatham in February 1856 after spending twenty-five years in Pittsburgh. Delany's move signaled a coalescing of the
black emigration movement. The previous August, Delany had abandoned
his criticism of Canada as a refuge for black Americans in a report to the
emigration movement's National Board of Commissioners. Undoubtedly
pleased with his ideological shift, the editors of the *Freeman* prominently displayed Delany's endorsement of Canadian emigration on the front
page. At the same time, Shadd Cary had softened her earlier hostility
toward Delany's notions of a black nationality as she realized that both
camps faced persistent challenges from anti-emigrationists like Frederick Douglass. Delany's arrival in Chatham reinforced Mary Ann's claims
that emigration to Canada was a core tenet of black nationalism. This
was not Delany's first contact with Canada. He first visited the country in
1851 on the invitation of Henry Bibb, and he was an early correspondent
for the *Voice of the Fugitive*. But now Canada West would be the staging
ground for his dream of an independent black nation.[41]

The Delanys moved into the black-owned Villa Mansion Hotel, not far
from the *Freeman*'s offices. He set up a medical practice to treat women
and children, which he promptly advertised in the *Provincial Freeman*. Once
he was settled in Chatham, Delany became a popular lecturer, and in May,
the *Freeman* announced that he would become a regular contributor. Delany's journalistic experience as well as his political prominence would
be a boost for the *Freeman*. He had edited his own newspaper, the *Mystery*,
in Pittsburgh between 1843–47, and he was a cofounder and editor of
the *North Star* with Frederick Douglass between 1847–49.[42]

Shortly after his arrival, Delany gave a speech at a local church to
announce the arrival of Amelia Freeman, a free-born black teacher and
antislavery activist who had been educated at Oberlin College. Delany

had become acquainted with Freeman during the days when she taught art and music at several schools in Pittsburgh. She moved to Chatham to open a school for black children, and the *Provincial Freeman* heralded her arrival with great fanfare. One of those particularly impressed with the new teacher was Isaac Shadd, who wrote a long editorial commending her "fine literary and artistic attainments." Within a few months Amelia Freeman married Isaac Shadd and became a regular fixture at the newspaper in addition to running her school.[43]

Another new associate for the Shadds was Osborne Perry Anderson, who became a subscription agent for the paper in June 1856. Anderson had moved to Canada West to manage the farm of Mary Ann's uncle, Absalom Shadd. Later he became a printer, and he worked for the *Freeman* in several capacities. Anderson also became active in the struggle over control of the Dawn institute. In a few years Anderson would become known as one of the surviving members of John Brown's raiding party at Harpers Ferry, Virginia.[44]

During the spring and early summer of 1856 the *Freeman* seemed to have a new vitality. Gone were the desperate requests for payment of bills. The familiar asterisk signaling Mary Ann's authorship appeared in the editorial column once more, and she resumed her practice of taking on the sacred cows of American abolitionism. In May, she criticized noted black abolitionist minister Jermain Loguen for suggesting that the free-born blacks he observed while traveling through Canada West were lazy and given to drunkenness and depravity. Loguen had ignited one of Shadd Cary's pet peeves—the double standards of behavior for free blacks and slaves. "Neither all fugitives, free-born colored men nor white men, behave as they should do and we protest against this special reference to men of free birth only," she wrote. Loguen had fallen into the trap of pro-slavery ideology, she argued, by his assumptions "that slavery makes a better man of the colored man, than freedom can possibly do."[45]

But this concern was a momentary preoccupation. Shadd Cary was far more incensed by an upcoming visit to Canada West by Harriet Beecher Stowe, which was being heralded by some of the loathed white missionaries. Since the publication of Stowe's influential book *Uncle Tom's Cabin* in 1852, black abolitionists had both praised and criticized the novel. For some, including Frederick Douglass, Stowe's work was a powerful abolitionist tool that evoked widespread sympathy for the slave's plight. Others like Martin Delany, complained that the book capitalized on gross racial stereotypes and gave support to the American Colonization Society's exportation of blacks to Liberia. Shadd Cary made plain her dislike of Stowe's colonization stance, but her main complaint was that the visit was sponsored by "our Canadian 'locusts.'" With tongue in cheek, Mary Ann said she would welcome Stowe to Canada because the tour would provide "abundant evidence of the fallacy of her expatriation theory." But she feared nothing good would come of the event: "Should she submit, as is likely[,] to the 'Missionaries' we foresee evil to the colored people, and only evil from the visit," Shadd Cary insisted.[46]

Within a few weeks Mary Ann shifted her attention to the second Emigration Convention, which was announced in the *Freeman* in late June. The convention would be held in August in Cleveland, and with Delany now living in Chatham, she expected the Canadians to play a more visible role than they had two years earlier. Shadd Cary wrote an editorial endorsing the convention without qualification and urged all participants to engage in an open forum on the emigration question. Such positive commentary revealed a considerable shift in her relationship to Delany and the larger black emigration movement. "Let men who clamor for free thought, speech and action, from their oppressors, tolerate their brethren in the exercise of these necessary rights," she declared. In an accompanying article Shadd Cary called for the election of Martin Delany to the presidency of the Board of Commissioners of the emigration convention. Delany and Shadd Cary had now publicly affirmed their political alliance.[47]

Delany wrote a series on American and European politics for the *Freeman* as he paved the way for the upcoming emigration convention. In one article Delany took Frederick Douglass to task for paying a long overdue compliment to the editors of the *Provincial Freeman*. "The press became a necessity and was bravely supplied by Miss Mary Ann Shadd," wrote Douglass. "This lady, with very little assistance from others has sustained *The Provincial Freeman* for more than two years." Douglass had gradually shifted his stance on emigration during the mid-1850s. Although he still opposed black flight from the United States, Douglass on occasion praised the advances made by Canadian blacks, and he credited emigrationist activists with their commitment to antislavery and racial uplift. Frederick Douglass had also been impressed by Mary Ann Shadd's performance at the National Convention in 1855. In Delany's view, however, Douglass's article, titled "Canada—Liberia—H. Ford Douglass—Mary A. Shadd," was evidence of hypocrisy and paternalism. This was yet another sore point that fueled the debates between the two former allies. Delany was irritated by Douglass's attempt to give Shadd Cary his stamp of approval, when just a few years earlier Douglass "never deigned to notice but to disparage" her in print. "Miss Mary Ann Shadd (now Mrs. Cary), is made the special subject of his compliment," Delany fumed. "Is this a recent discovery? Are the talents and acquired ability of Miss Shadd just beginning to develop themselves that this great keen eyed expositor of our 'awakened mental abilities' has just discovered them?" Delany made it known that he and his emigrationist colleagues sought no special favors from the influential Mr. Douglass. Delany's article inadvertently revealed Mary Ann's marital status for the first time in the pages of the *Freeman.* Perhaps it was the push she needed to make it official, for the next week she began signing her editorials "M. A. S. Cary."[48]

Things seemed to be going well at the *Freeman* during the summer of 1856 when the paper mysteriously stopped publishing in August, with no advance notice. The staff ran into some unexplained difficulties when the *Freeman's* operations were about to be moved to a different building in Chatham. But readers were simply left in the dark until the paper resumed publication four months later in November. Nevertheless, the *Provincial Freeman* was present, at least in name, at the emigration convention held in Cleveland that summer. The only person representing the Canadian contingent was Isaac Shadd. Mary Ann chose to remain at home, and Delany could not attend because of illness.

The convention decided to move its headquarters to Chatham, and the *Freeman* was designated as the official organ of the emigration movement. During the convention Mary Ann Shadd Cary was appointed one of eight corresponding editors for a proposed literary journal called the *Afric-American Quarterly Repository,* which was never published. Delany was elected president of the movement's National Board, and among the members were Isaac Shadd, H. Ford Douglass, and Thomas F. Cary. The Chatham contingent of activists who had converged around Shadd Cary's *Provincial Freeman* were now at the center of the movement. The minutes of the convention were not published in the *Freeman* until November, after its long hiatus. Perhaps Mary Ann chose to spend the time with her new husband and stepchildren, or perhaps she and Isaac were consumed with trying to get the *Freeman* back in operation. The record for this period, however, is lost.[49]

On November 25, the *Freeman* finally appeared again. The paper's office had been moved to King Street West opposite the town's market, a location the editors hoped would attract more business. Shadd Cary apologized for the long absence and made it clear that the paper was in dire financial straits. The combination of the move, lack of revenue, mounting bills, and a worsening economic recession had forced the suspension of publication. The paper was also facing several legal challenges. Thomas Smallwood of Toronto had taken the *Freeman* to court on behalf of a group of subscribers who were angry about not receiving their paper. The dispute ended when the Smallwood faction gave a verbal assurance that they would allow the *Freeman* to resume publication without taking further action. Hiram Wilson also threatened a lawsuit, claiming he was libeled in an article written by Mary Ann's sister, Amelia Shadd Williamson, under a pseudonym. Wilson demanded to know the author's identity, and Isaac Shadd publicly challenged Wilson to carry out his threat of legal action. The author's name was made public, Wilson's letters were published in the paper, and the controversy died out.[50]

The paper's editors had avoided the courtroom but were left feeling under siege and disheartened. Shadd Cary believed that the *Freeman* had endured "wicked opposition" causing her to wonder if "it could not exist another week." What kept them going was the conviction that there was no other "*real* anti-slavery paper in the Canadas" and there continued to be a "great need of a paper through which our mis-represented people can speak their sentiments." Valiantly, Mary Ann, Isaac, and H. Ford Douglass were determined to continue the paper as long as possible.[51]

Isaac wrote a brief plea to local merchants to give a share of their business to the *Freeman*'s printing operations. He complained that without government support, such as revenues from public notices, the *Freeman* was unable to compete in the local market because it was consistently underbid by other printers who had other sources of income. Thus, he tried to appeal to the goodwill of Chatham's business community, a risky proposition in a racially divided city in which the *Freeman* often took controversial and unpopular stands. Months later, there was a minor victory in the editor's struggle to find other sources of revenue when the *Freeman* finally acquired some of the government support it had been seeking. In February the paper began publishing the minutes of the Chatham Town Council as the official town printer.

Mary Ann stayed close to home through the end of 1856. She broadened her editorial scope to decry the election of James Buchanan as president of the United States, which she viewed as evidence of the control of pro-slavery forces in the government. She anticipated a war between North and South when she declared that it would be "be hard and bloody work, before the struggle terminates." She also focused attention on local concerns when she called for the establishment of a "good boarding house" that prohibited alcohol to counteract immoral and corrupt influences in Chatham. In her first editorial of 1857, Shadd Cary explored the problems facing black Canadians. Her criticisms had changed little since she published "Hints to the Colored People of the North" almost a decade earlier. The greatest obstacle to racial progress, she believed, lay in the black community's lack of collective action. "Instead of being like the Jews, who unite the more because of oppression, unlike every other people, the more the division the better," she found. Blacks' inability to work together, said Shadd Cary, was a "free invitation" to their enemies who sought to exploit their weaknesses.[52]

The doctrines of black abolitionism as expressed by Frederick Douglass and other leaders generally embraced an optimistic belief in progress and retribution for the oppressed. But Mary Ann Shadd Cary, Mar-

One of the last extant issues of the *Provincial Freeman*, published in Chatham in 1859. Note the ads for William Stills's boarding house and Martin Delany's medical practice, as well as other black-owned businesses. (Cornell University Library, Division of Rare Books and Manuscript Collections) tin Delany, and others in the emigrationist camp were extreme pessimists. Shadd Cary saw blacks' only hope for salvation in pragmatic action and self-reliant activism. But increasingly, she believed most people of color had not overcome the legacy of slavery and racial discrimination, preventing them from developing a black nationalist sensibility. What has been accomplished by the colored people of Canada in the last thirty years, she asked? Community fragmentation, "colored beggars," and immoral behavior too often dominated black life, she contended. In an interesting bit of self-irony, she indicted the "caucuses, conventions, and resolutions" in which she had played a central role. "Pretended leaders of the people" returned to Canada West's towns and cities "'like the dog to his vomit, or the sow to her wallowing in the mire,'" doing more harm than good.[53]

Shadd Cary's commentary reflected the tensions in her roles as both observer and participant in this social experiment. Like those she scolded, Shadd Cary was accused of not getting along with many in the black community in Canada West. Similarly she, along with others, was active in many of the meetings and conventions that failed to lead to substantive action. As a teacher she accepted support from the white missionaries she reviled, and although she vehemently condemned begging practices, she had to engage in similar fund-raising strategies for the *Freeman* and other causes. The problems that plagued her community—poverty, discrimination, illiteracy, and dissension among them—negatively affected the *Freeman,* as well.

When Frederick Douglass reduced the size of his newspaper because of similar financial problems, Shadd Cary praised his fiscal prudence. But she also wondered what the fate of the *Provincial Freeman* would be if even the famous Frederick Douglass was struggling to make ends meet. "A few good men and women, here and there, among them, act nobly, but their subscriptions cannot support and pay the printer," she noted. "What must be the condition of a 'weakling' like the *Freeman,* think you gentle reader, young as it is in years, and feeble in support in comparison? ready to 'keel' over at every breath because of the non-substantials of which the older paper in the States so forcibly complains?"

The *Freeman* tottered on the brink of a similar tragedy. In February the editors made a desperate appeal through a circular that was printed on the *Freeman's* press and distributed in Chatham and throughout Canada and the United States. The message was simple: if the *Freeman* did not receive an infusion of funds, it would not survive. This appeal was colored with Shadd Cary's disappointment as she watched her prized newspaper decline:

> We have never appealed to you before, as we had hoped by severe self-denial and untiring exertions, to succeed without aid except from the

> sale of the papers, but, after having labored long and being obliged to
> support ourselves by *other* means (for not one cent do we realize toward
> support from the papers as yet), the indifference of many indebted to us,
> and the little sympathy from friends of the slave arising from non-acquain-
> tance with our enterprise, make our efforts to meet our liabilities impos-
> sible as yet.[54]

The circular was followed by an editorial in the *Freeman* titled "Pay us
what you Owe," repeating the all-too-familiar complaint about tardy or
nonexistent payment for subscriptions. Shadd Cary reported that bills
totaling hundreds of dollars had been mailed out, but only one had
been paid. Mary Ann lashed out at the *Freeman*'s audience, complaining
that local blacks did not believe in the newspaper's crisis and had no loyalty to the race. "Yes, colored people will generally pay white men *first,*" she
wrote. The constant state of crisis was pushing her to the peak of anger
and desperation.[55]

Mary Ann was not entirely consumed with the *Freeman*'s troubles, however. Her husband Thomas Cary was spending more time in Chatham
where he became active in the Dawn Institute controversy and joined in
the fund-raising activities for the newspaper while his brothers kept his
business going in Toronto. By February Mary Ann was four months pregnant and caring for Thomas's three children. Isaac Shadd and H. Ford
Douglass took over the traveling duties while Mary Ann spent more time
at the editorial desk.

She had clearly grown weary of the endless canvassing that seemed
to yield few tangible benefits. But she never tired of taking swipes at
the Refugee Home Society and its main representative, Rev. C. C. Foote.
Shadd Cary's ire was inspired by an article in the *American Missionary* that
reported on the value of goods donated by well-meaning Americans to
aid the fugitives in Canada. She wrote that the begging that Foote employed to attract donations was designed to "degrade and crush" the
refugees rather than to help them. She accused Foote of stockpiling many
of the donations in Detroit rather than sending them to Canada and
then earning a twenty-five percent commission for his efforts. She charged
the Refugee Home Society with failing to sell its land to the fugitives and
with providing them with "miserably poor conditions" in which to live.
Shadd Cary concluded by calling for an investigation of the practices of
the Refugee Home Society, similar to the investigation of Dawn she promoted a year earlier.[56]

Shadd Cary's article elicited an angry response from David Hotchkiss,
the white missionary who had done so much to discredit her during
her struggle for the Windsor school. Despite the *Freeman*'s financial woes,
it still had considerable clout in Canada West, and Hotchkiss saw Shadd
Cary as the ringleader of the opposition. Mary Ann was still regularly

vilified by the corps of white missionaries she attacked in the pages of the *Freeman*. Hotchkiss's correspondence with the American Missionary Association revealed the true extent of his disdain for and fear of Shadd Cary. She was "reaching her dirty fingers out after your association" Hotchkiss warned A.M.A. secretary George Whipple, and "She is reaching after me as your missionary here in C.W." He probably expressed the sentiments of many who had been accosted by Mary Ann's persistent journalism when he wrote, "I wish you or someone would tell her lady-ship that I choose to mind my own business." He advised against send-ing her further copies of the *American Missionary* and wished out loud that she would leave the issue alone. The editorials in the *Freeman* had served to unnerve many in the Canadian antislavery establishment. The following month Hotchkiss told Whipple that he suspected Shadd Cary would "fight it out every inch of the way" and that her influence should not be underestimated.[57]

Hotchkiss's prediction was accurate. Like a pit bull gripping its prey, Shadd Cary alternately weighed in against Dawn or the Refugee Home Society during the spring of 1857, in her campaign to rid Canada West of begging and opportunistic missionaries. Since the R.H.S. was "the mor-al pest of Canadian refugees," she questioned why antislavery leaders in the United States persisted in supporting Foote and the R.H.S. She criti-cized Josiah Henson for raising funds for the defunct manual labor school at Dawn. Throughout the year, Mary Ann's writing for the *Freeman* was preoccupied with local matters. But the U.S. Supreme Court decision in *Dred Scott v. Sanford* did not go unnoticed. The court opinion, which stated that persons of African descent could not claim the rights of citizenship under the U.S. Constitution, was further evidence of the hopelessness of the abolitionist cause in the States, she argued. "Colored Northern State men" were "little superior in condition to the slave," said Shadd Cary. Those black leaders like Frederick Douglass who had maintained a claim on the United States, and at the same time condemned emigration, "should have remained in such utter darkness, in hope of surmounting the machi-nations of the pro-slavery people of the S[outh]." Mary Ann felt vindicat-ed by the high court's decision: "The contention for rights, then must end in talk, and the few great Orators, Journalists, &c. . . . must come down to the earth to find a permanent resting place."[58]

Isaac and H. Ford kept Mary Ann abreast of their fund-raising ef-forts, and their reports were discouraging. From Cleveland, Douglass wrote that he had collected a few dollars but no new subscribers: "I tell subscribers why frankly that when we have no funds we intend to stop until we get some," he revealed. Isaac Shadd wrote of a "lengthy and discourag-ing" trip to Toronto, where a combination of rain and scant notice from the local press resulted in cancellation of their lecture at St. Lawrence

Hall because of a poor turnout. Members of the Coloured Regular Baptist Church in the same city refused Shadd and Douglass access because of their antislavery theme. And Isaac almost reached his limit when a known abolitionist wished him luck but declined a subscription to the *Freeman* because he took so many other newspapers. Shadd lamented, "If I could see less profession and a little more practice I would look for a more happy demonstration in the end."[59]

Douglass and Isaac Shadd ventured as far south as the slave state of Delaware—the Shadds' birthplace—to gather support for the *Freeman*. Word of the newspaper's troubles reached Philadelphia, where Lucretia Mott encouraged the Philadelphia Female Anti-Slavery Society to send ten dollars to the *Freeman*. The editors were so encumbered by financial problems that Douglass wrote a brief apology on behalf of Isaac and Mary Ann, who had begun turning down speaking engagements:

> We are sorry that our pecuniary circumstances and the many embarrassments under which we labor at this time in our efforts in connection with the earnest labors of Mr. I. D. Shadd and M. A. S. Cary to sustain a Paper among our exiled fellow countrymen in Canada, has prevented us from complying with the numerous invitations we have received from various sections of the West, to address Societies, Masonic Celebrations, 1st of August Anniversaries, &c.[60]

The *Freeman* had fulfilled Mary Ann's dream of being the authoritative voice on black emigration and the Canadian haven. And she, Isaac, and H. Ford Douglass had become sought-after representatives for the cause. But local support for the *Freeman* was fragmented at best. The paper had succeeded in sowing seeds of discord throughout Canada West, and was now suffering the consequences. An article in the June issue of the *Christian Messenger*, the organ of the Baptist Church of Canada, charged *Freeman* editor H. Ford Douglass with slander for accusing the church of supporting pro-slavery churches in the United States. The black members of the First Colored Baptist Church of Chatham were sympathetic to the *Messenger* and allegedly joined in the attack on the *Freeman*. Douglass responded with a challenge for the Canadian Baptists and the *Messenger* to disavow their connection with the American Baptists. The lawsuit never materialized but it left bitter feelings among some blacks in Chatham.[61]

This incident was quickly followed by opposition from other quarters. In the July 18 issue of the *Freeman*, Mary Ann Shadd Cary wrote that blacks and whites in the town were using intimidating tactics to force the paper to "take the popular side" in supporting the Reform party rather than the Conservatives. Some black Canadians were attracted by the Reform Party's call for universal suffrage. But the *Freeman*'s editors were convinced that support of the Conservative Party was a show of loyalty to the British crown. In Shadd Cary's nationalist view, blacks should pledge their allegiance to Britain in exchange for the freedoms they enjoyed in Canada West. She took a hard line against those supporting the Reform Party, noting that endorsing a popular position had not ensured the survival of other black newspapers and was unlikely to do so for the *Provincial Freeman*. Black American newspapers had consistently failed, she argued, "killed either from excess of popularity—neglect by the people, or from trying to keep pace with the popular cry instead of defending the right only, 'though the Heavens fall.'"[62]

She suggested that competing newspapers—particularly the *Kent Advertiser*, which was pro-Reform—as well as unscrupulous whites and "unprincipled, knavish or stupid colored people" were to blame for the criticism over the *Freeman*'s political allegiance. The wear and tear of the *Freeman*'s constant battles was evident when she concluded: "What shall we do? Do nothing at present, the weather is too warm! But the *Freeman* will be '*kilt*' they say; die of popularity. Can't help it."[63]

The *Freeman*'s decline was also due in part to a depression that was crippling the Canadian economy. Thomas Cary returned to Toronto to tend to his barbershop and other business so that he could send money to his wife and children. The times were so harsh that to supplement his income he began selling oil lamps on the streets of Toronto and through the newspaper's offices in Chatham. A small notice in the *Freeman* advertised "lamps of superior kind and patent" and fluid at $1 per gallon. He sent Mary Ann small bits of money when he could, along with instructions for marketing the lamps and oil. In his absence Mary Ann was the sole parent to his three children, and his inquiries revealed an intense longing for his family. The Carys did have time for rare moments of affection. Separated for extended periods, Thomas asked Mary Ann to write "a long letter so that I will get it on Sunday morning and it will be food for me on that day as I keep in my shell all of that day."[64]

On August 7, 1857 Mary Ann gave birth to her first child, Sarah Elizabeth Cary, an event that diverted her attention away from the *Freeman*. Isaac Shadd and H. Ford Douglass continued to write editorials and kept the paper going for a least another month, when a brief notice hinted that the end might come at any time: "And as a paper,—an organ is a necessity when we can not get on without, we shall be obliged to suspend till we make such collections and then on again; for the debts must be paid!!"[65]

It is unknown whether any more issues of the *Freeman* were published in 1857; if so, no extant copies now exist. Mary Ann and Thomas Cary were likely preoccupied with caring for their growing family, and H. Ford Douglass continued to travel to raise funds to pay off the newspaper's debts. In November he wrote Mary Ann that Canada's worsening economic depression was making his job almost impossible. "We have the hardest of times here for money I have ever seen. Men won't even go to an anti-slavery meeting much less give," he complained. Isaac Shadd remained in Chatham to run the printing business, deal with creditors, and assist Amelia with her new school.[66]

As winter set in, Thomas Cary was back in Toronto, seemingly anguished about the separation from his family. "I live with you altogether and I shall try and be up if I can by Chrismus [sic] day the loard [sic] knows wheather [sic] I will be able," he wrote. A month later he was considering closing his barbershop or selling it to his brother because business was so slow. He reported that local merchants were meeting in Toronto to consider closing their shops at seven in the evening to save gas for lighting. "Times is hard and money scarse [sic]," Cary proclaimed, as he worried about his and others' futures.[67]

The word was beginning to spread that the *Freeman* had halted publication. Mary Ann's close friend William Still wrote her a warm and engaging letter in the new year to inquire about the paper, and he expressed concern for her health. Childbirth and caring for an infant undoubtedly put new strains on Mary Ann's time and energy. "The Freeman I presume is no more," Still wrote. "Without its care I trust your health is much better. At the same time I hope you will find a field of labor and usefulness in which your mind can be profitably engaged without having to say for [illegible] such oppression as fell to your lot while in the editorial chair."[68]

Unbeknownst to Still, however, Mary Ann was already planning to revive the *Freeman* once more. H. Ford Douglass would no longer be a part of the newspaper's management. He had become disillusioned with black separatism in Canada West and was planning to return to Chicago. Instead, Thomas Cary would take a more active role in the paper's operations as co-publisher with Isaac Shadd. He temporarily closed his business in Toronto and was living in Chatham with his family. In March 1858, Mary Ann, Isaac, and Thomas hoped to resume publication and sought the support of Chatham's local officials. A petition recommending the *Freeman* was signed by the Mayor, members of the town council, and other local officials and circulated around Chatham:

> For three years, Mr. Shadd and sister, have published the paper, independent of the support usually given to papers and Institutions advocating the interests of this class; and have unflinchingly held up the standard to incite the colored people to progress, both mentally and morally.
>
> We take, or have patronized the paper and consider it to be a great and efficient means of improving their condition and prospects, and also feel

satisfied that wherever it has circulated it has not only been found improving, but has reflected credit upon the colored people generally. Consequently, we can in good faith, recommend it to the philanthropic every where, and ask in its behalf their warmest support.[69]

The petition was no guarantee of subscribers or revenue from the town, but it was a vote of confidence after a stormy year of opposition. It is difficult to determine exactly when the *Freeman* reappeared. The only extant copies remaining from the period are from January and June 1859, but the volume and issue numbers indicate the paper may have begun again on a bi-monthly basis in June 1858. Isaac Shadd wrote that he mailed out the revived *Freeman* on June 21, 1858, and he apparently got the paper out somewhat irregularly, but at least twice a month. A year later the newspaper's new title, the *Provincial Freeman and Semi-Monthly Advertiser,* suggests a compromise between the cost of issuing a weekly paper and the editor's desire to keep it going.[70]

Although the *Freeman* was on hiatus for nearly a year, it was a busy time in Chatham. Mary Ann Shadd Cary continued to maintain a visible presence in local politics, as typified by an address she gave to a local gathering on a Sunday evening in early April. Rarely did Mary Ann specifically address women's rights during the antebellum years, although she was keenly aware of the discrimination that she and other women routinely experienced. This talk, which was infused with religious rhetoric, laid out a moral argument in favor of gender equality. Those who insisted on the inferiority of women were not principled and virtuous individuals, she argued. "We cannot successfully Evade duty because the suffering fellow woman is only a *woman!* She too is a neighbor." She insisted that Christians should not use religious doctrine as a rationale for oppressing women. "The spirit of true philanthropy knows no *sex.* "[71]

Despite Shadd Cary's quest to eliminate gender boundaries, especially among abolitionists and other reformers, strict divisions remained, especially at an important convention in Chatham the following month. John Brown, a white antislavery activist who considered himself on a mission from God, traveled to Canada West during the spring of 1858. He hoped to enlist support among the African American expatriates and fugitive slaves for his plan to end slavery through armed revolt, and set up a provisional U.S. government. His final destination was Chatham, where he arrived on April 29 to arrange a quiet meeting ostensibly to discuss new routes on the Underground Railroad. The men in Mary Ann's world were all active in this event. Martin Delany and Osborne Anderson called a gathering to prepare for Brown's convention. Word spread quickly through the town, and the convention was held on May 8th and 10th at the First Baptist Church under the guise of organizing a Masonic Lodge. Among the twelve white and thirty-four black men present were Del-

MARY ANN SHADD CARY

The Charity Block house in Chatham, Ontario, first home to the *Provincial Freeman* and the reported site of John Brown's Canadian headquarters. (Chatham Kent Museum, Chatham Cultural Center)

any, Isaac Shadd, Anderson, and Thomas Cary. Although several women, including Mary Ann Shadd Cary, actively supported Brown's efforts, none attended—or were allowed to attend—this momentous meeting.[72]

Nevertheless, Brown's radical plans made a profound impression on Chatham's network of activists. Brown was elected commander-in-chief and Anderson was elected a member of Congress for the proposed government. A constitution, drafted and printed by William Howard Day, was distributed among a handful of blacks sworn to secrecy, and on May 29, Brown left Chatham having enlisted Osborne Anderson as one of the raiding party members. Brown's agents returned to Canada West in the summer of 1859 to enlist further support, but they found little enthusiasm beyond those who had participated in the convention.[73]

There are hints that Brown stayed at the home of Isaac Shadd and had extensive contact with Mary Ann and her father Abraham during his time in Chatham. Anecdotal accounts suggest Mary Ann Shadd Cary provided Brown with whatever aid she could, given the limitations gender placed on her role. Years later William Wells Brown understood her frustration well when he wrote, "Had she [Shadd Cary] been a man, she would probably have been with John Brown at Harper's Ferry." History may be better served, however, because instead of losing her life in the ill-fated raid, Shadd Cary made a lasting contribution toward preserving the memory of this event as editor of Osborne Anderson's memoirs, *A Voice from Harpers Ferry*, published in 1861.[74]

During the months when the *Freeman* lapsed, at least one competitor sought to fill the gap. Encouraged by his work with John Brown, William Howard Day tried to start his own paper in St. Catherines. He wrote abolitionist Gerrit Smith for help in starting a newspaper, which he suggested would replace the moribund *Freeman*. But Day found it impossible to raise the necessary funds, and the project remained only an idea.[75]

Perhaps aware of the lurking competition, the *Freeman*'s editors got out an issue shortly after Brown's convention. But the paper immediately ran into trouble. Mary Ann was out of town and Thomas was back in Toronto trying to revive his barbershop when the local sheriff seized the printing press and supplies, probably for non-payment of bills. Isaac wrote Thomas of his worry that the sheriff's racism and his dislike of the *Freeman* would make things difficult. "If the sheriff was a conservative I would stand a better chance for time but he is such a negro hater and yank reformer that I do not hope for many days grace, besides M.A.S.C. gave him cuts last year."[76]

Somehow Isaac managed to regain control of the *Freeman*'s property, and he continued publishing. Mary Ann traveled across the Midwest during the summer of 1858, delivering lectures and making a desperate attempt to raise funds for the paper. While in Michigan she wrote Thomas of her encounter with the author and abolitionist lecturer Frances Ellen Watkins, to whom Shadd Cary uncharacteristically took a back seat. There was a hint of envy when she told Thomas, "Why the whites & colored people here are just crazy with excitement about her. She is the greatest female speaker ever was here, so wisdom obliges me to keep out of the way as with her prepared lectures there would just be no chance of a favorable comparison." Mary Ann was keenly aware that while she was sought after as a speaker, the reviews of her oratory were mixed. Some did not find her particularly eloquent, and as a champion of emigration her politics were marginalized. She confided to Thomas that she knew the importance of promoting Watkins's success. "I puff her as strongly as any body in fact it is the very best for me to do so as otherwise it would be put down to jealousy."[77]

Back in Chatham, life took on a mundane sameness after the excitement of John Brown's convention. The summer was unusually hot— Isaac wrote that it hit 93 degrees for several days—and the Shadd Cary household functioned with the help of relatives. With both parents away, Mary Ann's young sister Sarah watched the Cary children and "managed the house with perfect ease," Isaac reported. Thomas continued to be in financial straits, and Mary Ann worried about his health. His smoking caused her great concern and she offered her husband advice. "You smoke an old clay pipe. Some one has said that a Meershaum [*sic*] absorbs the oil in the tobacco and prevents it from doing smokers so much injury. Do not you think you had better get a Meershaum as you will smoke?" she asked. Mary Ann also worried endlessly about the fate of the *Freeman*. She instructed Thomas to "tell Isaac to put in as much reading matter as he can crowd into the Freeman as that is the only way to get up an interest in it. Douglass and those men put in more than we do."[78]

The third National Emigration Convention met in Chatham in August, but the gathering was a shadow of the movement's earlier meetings. Many emigrationist leaders were absent, and William Howard Day, who had recently moved to Chatham, was elected president. Isaac Shadd attended the convention and likely gave it significant coverage in the *Freeman*, but it is unclear whether Mary Ann Shadd Cary was there as well. The convention platform was softened to reflect Day's and others' ambivalence toward emigration projects beyond Canada. It seemed that the era of Delany's militant call for general black emigration was over. Symptomatic of this shift was the new name proposed for the convention: "Association for the Promotion of the Interests of the Colored People of Canada and the United States."[79]

Chatham, with the help of the *Provincial Freeman*, had emerged as the center of Canadian black activism, and African Americans continued to move there throughout the late 1850s despite the worsening economy. Several local residents were members of the Chatham Vigilance Committee, which organized to save fugitives from being returned to slavery. In September 1858, the Committee rescued Sylvanus Demarest, a black youth who had been seized by a white man claiming to be his owner. More than 100 concerned citizens—some with weapons—stormed the train carrying Demarest and rescued him from the claimant when it stopped in Chatham. Demarest found refuge in the home of Isaac and Amelia Shadd. Once again, a Canadian antislavery group was dominated by those associated with the *Freeman*. William Howard Day was the chair, Isaac Shadd was vice-chair, Mary Ann Shadd Cary was secretary, and other members included Thomas Cary, Osborne Anderson, and Martin Delany. When the railroad brought charges against the committee, seven participants were arrested, including Isaac Shadd. Mary Ann prepared a circular to raise funds for the defendants and made it clear that this constituted one more blow against her newspaper. "The editor of the *Freeman* (organ of the fugitives) holding the boy in his care, in spite of pro-slavery officials, is the most responsible party to the Court, yet he, the conductor of a struggling paper, must suspend it to meet the exigencies of the case," she explained.[80]

When news of Isaac's troubles reached the United States, at least one relative could not suppress her fear for his safety and questioned whether Canada was really such an advantageous haven for black Americans. "I was struck panic on looking over the Standard of last saturday to see it anounsed [*sic*] that I. D. Shadd had been sent to prison," wrote her Aunt Elizabeth. "It made me so sick and so bewildered that I could scarcely attend to my duty. I am much afraid that Canada is not going to prove what it was cracked up to be."[81]

Mary Ann's efforts to raise funds for Isaac's defense must have been successful, because, although the Demarest case temporarily halted publication of the *Freeman,* the paper was appearing again by the end of 1858. In January of the new year, Isaac and Mary Ann were listed as the paper's editors, and little had changed except they reduced the subscription price by fifty cents. Most of the advertisements were several years old, indicating that Isaac was having little success attracting new patrons. Indeed, many of the ads represented the personal connections in the Shadds' world; Martin Delany still advertised his medical practice as well as his new book *Blake or the Huts of America,* Thomas's brothers, Isaac and John Cary, solicited business for their bathhouses in Toronto, and Isaac Shadd, who entered the real estate business, sold land through the paper.

By 1859 the *Freeman* was shifting its focus to give limited support to emigration to Africa and the West Indies, projects Isaac and Mary Ann had roundly criticized just a few years earlier. Delany had succeeded in at least partially convincing the Shadds that his dreams of an African homeland had merit. After the disappointing Emigration Convention in August, Martin Delany had turned his attention to planning an expedition to the Niger Valley of West Africa. In January, Isaac wrote an editorial describing the African Civilization Society of Canada, the brainchild of Delany, which included several Chatham residents. The short-lived society was formed "for the purpose of aiding in promoting the civilization of Africa, and thus destroying the slave trade," he explained.[82]

The June 18 issue carried a notice of the formation of Delany's Niger Valley Exploring Party. This issue of the *Freeman* also contained the last extant editorial by Mary Ann Shadd Cary, who railed against efforts to carry out a separate justice against three black men from neighboring Brantford, who were imprisoned on charges of hijacking a train and committing murder. Just as her aunt had feared, Canada West was becoming increasingly hostile to the black populace. "There are certain ignorant, and low conditioned white men in Canada, just stupid enough to think they know a great deal, who are not only constantly restive under the immunities guaranteed to colored emigrants by British Law, but who have conceived the foolish notion that colored men reside here by their special grace," argued Shadd Cary. These "negro haters" included several public officials who used their influence to blatantly discriminate, she charged. But Mary Ann refused to relinquish her belief that despite the hardships, life in Canada was preferable to that in the United States, and she blamed anti-emigration proponents for deterring many blacks from settling in the British province.[83]

Her loyalty to Canada would not save the *Provincial Freeman*, however. In the final existing copy of the paper, the Scottish-born abolitionist John Linton wrote a tribute to the paper and its founders in a fitting epitaph for seven years' hard work:

> We would wish to awaken an attention to the exertions of Messr. Shadd and Sister [Mrs. M. A. S. Cary] and crave aid from all humans and Christian people to support their exertions in their publications. They know how the fugitives and others from the land of bondage arrive—where they arrive at in Canada—and what help they receive, and who it is who help them in an honest and liberal way; and we hope that British solicitude and sympathy and monied help will also be extended to those who are and who reside on British colonial soil and who promote the interests on the spot of those who flee for liberty dearer than life.[84]

These were trying times in Canada's black expatriate communities. The raid at Harpers Ferry in the fall of 1859 had been a miserable failure, and John Brown and most of his accomplices had been swiftly captured. Osborne Anderson was one of the few to escape to freedom. By late 1860 Brown would be executed, and was martyred by many abolitionists. But little had improved in the political, social, or economic conditions of blacks living on either side of the border.

SIX

Civil War and the End of the Canadian Sojourn

The 1860s was a decade that brought intense personal and political disarray to Mary Ann Shadd Cary's life. The *Provincial Freeman* staggered into 1860 as Shadd Cary and her brother Isaac desperately sought new subscribers and a last-minute infusion of funds. But their efforts were to no avail. Chatham was slow to recover from the 1857 depression, which had gripped Canada and much of Europe. Construction ceased on extension of the Great Western Railroad, which was a significant employer of blacks and other new immigrants. Local banks closed, businesses failed, and few—particularly among the region's black residents—had the funds either to advertise in or purchase a newspaper. By the summer of 1860, the *Weekly Anglo-African,* based in New York City, stopped carrying ads for the *Freeman.* No more issues of the *Freeman* appeared, and Isaac eventually sold off the printing business as well. The newspaper, into which Shadd Cary had poured so much of her energy and resources for six years, quietly slipped away.[1]

Mary Ann's attention was diverted by another crisis—her husband's serious illness. Since their marriage, she had beseeched Thomas to rest and change his smoking habits. Her worst fears were realized when Thomas Cary died on November 29, 1860. At the time, Mary Ann was pregnant with their second child and they had been married less than five years. In the 1861 census, Mary Ann reported that Thomas was just 35 years old at the time of his death. His front-page obituary in the *Weekly Anglo-African* hints at the unconventional nature of their relationship. Thomas died at his brother George Cary's home in Camden, a day's horseback ride from Mary Ann's home base in Chatham. There is no evidence that Thomas and Mary Ann ever maintained a home together. Until the final months of his life, Thomas continued to work in Toronto and visited Mary Ann and the children as often as he could. Perhaps his early death was hastened by the rigors of endless traveling during the long and frigid Canadian winters, as well as his constant battle to earn a decent living for himself and his family.[2]

Thomas Cary's funeral in Chatham attracted many friends and admirers. Their long cavalcade accompanied his remains through the town and into the countryside until they reached his burial site on land at the Dawn Institute. Thomas had been an active participant in the efforts of fugitive slaves to wrest Dawn from white control. Dawn's de facto leader Josiah Henson spoke at Thomas's funeral despite Mary Ann's deep dislike for him. It is unclear, in fact, if Mary Ann played any role in the funeral. Afterwards, she retreated from public view for several months until the birth of her son, Linton. With an infant and a four-year-old, as well as three stepchildren, Mary Ann Shadd Cary faced an uncertain future. Gone were the intimacy, companionship, and sense of shared purpose that her marriage provided, even at a distance. And in a society oriented around the patriarchal nuclear family, Mary Ann was once more without the symbolic protection of or public identification with a man.[3]

While Mary Ann grappled with these personal challenges, dramatic events were shifting the political landscape in the United States. The expansion of slavery into the western territories became a central issue in the 1860 presidential election. Republican Senator Abraham Lincoln won a narrow victory while standing firm against slavery's extension. Lincoln refused to negotiate when southern leaders in the Senate tried to push through a compromise on the issue. Less than a month after Thomas Cary's death, South Carolina led the way among southern extremists when the state legislature voted to secede from the Union. Six other southern states rapidly followed suit. By the time Lincoln was inaugurated in March 1861, he faced the dilemma of how to maintain the integrity of the Union without provoking the South into declaring war. The answer came when Confederates fired their guns on the federal garrison at Fort Sumter in April 1861.[4]

The outbreak of the Civil War sent reverberations throughout the black communities of Canada West. The war renewed fears of Canadian annexation by the United States, and public opinion across the country was split between abolitionists and Canadians sympathetic to the South's quest for independence. Some fugitive slaves in Canada worried that a victory for the South would mean their extradition back to bondage, and many blacks worried about the impact of the war on the friends and family they left behind. Yet there was also enthusiasm about the possibility of the South's defeat. When news of the skirmish in Charleston harbor reached Chatham, a meeting was hastily organized and several black men prematurely announced their intentions to join the Union army. But the Lincoln administration was not yet prepared to enlist black troops and their actions were ignored. Groups of black men in several states formed militia units and prepared for military service, while black activists debated their positions on the growing conflict.[5]

African American leaders like Frederick Douglass urged the black populace to support the Union, and called on President Lincoln to make slavery the main issue of the war. Ignoring the President's resistance to this position, Douglass hailed the war as a signal that slavery would be abolished. "Drums are beating, men are enlisting, companies forming, regiments marching, banners are flying, and money is pouring into the national treasury to put an end to the slaveholding rebellion," he gleefully announced in the pages of *Douglass' Monthly*. But many African Americans were not convinced that the sectional conflict would ultimately benefit their position. A correspondent to the *Weekly Anglo-African* advised black men to be cautious about volunteering to fight in the war, arguing that it was senseless to risk their lives "with no promised future in store for us."[6]

The black emigration movement found a momentary catalyst in free blacks' ambivalence about the war and their heightened anxiety about its outcome. Canada West was a staging area for renewed debate over emigration and nationalism, and these developments drew Mary Ann Shadd Cary back into the political arena. This activity was sparked, in part, by Martin Delany's return to Chatham in December 1860 after successfully negotiating a treaty with Egba chiefs in Abeokuta, Nigeria, that would provide land for what Delany hoped would become a resettlement project for African Americans in Africa. Although Delany had found a relatively comfortable and safe haven in Canada West, he had not relinquished his dream of an autonomous black nation outside the boundaries of Europe and North America. "My duty and destiny are in Africa, the great and glorious . . . land of your and my ancestry," he wrote to James Theodore Holly. Delany was filled with optimism when he returned to Canada to reunite with his family and move the project along. He traveled across the province to give lectures on "The Regeneration of Africa" and "Africa and the African Race," while he toiled to drum up recruits and additional resources.[7]

But Delany's scheme found limited support from American blacks and white abolitionists, who equated emigration to Africa with the hated American Colonization Society's efforts in Liberia. While he was abroad, Delany canvassed Great Britain where he and other black emigrationists promoted the formation of the African Aid Society, an odd alliance of British capitalists and philanthropists. The group endorsed Delany's ideas for Christianizing Africa, cultivating cotton as a cash crop, and exploiting the region's resources, and they agreed to provide loans and materials to support the plan.[8]

Martin Delany's brand of black nationalism was based on the assumption that a select group of educated African Americans would use their knowledge and skills, and their devotion to Protestantism, to civilize and uplift Africans. It was hoped that well-meaning whites would finance his venture. This black chauvinism, as Wilson J. Moses has called it, exemplified the contradictions in black emigrationist ideology that led, in part, to the movement's demise. African Americans' own Eurocentrism and expressions of manifest destiny reflected the colonial mentality of their oppressors. The emigrationist agenda also ignored the majority of free blacks in the United States and Canada who had neither the education nor the financial means to participate in or benefit from such project.[9]

Apparently undiscouraged, Delany's nationalist community on African soil was to be inaugurated by a handful of black Canadians who were won over to his cause, including Mary Ann's brother Isaac Shadd, her sister Amelia Shadd Williamson, and her friend and colleague Osborne Perry Anderson, the survivor of the Harpers Ferry raid. Mary Ann was also swayed by Delany's appeal and her family's interest in African emigration. After years of criticizing emigration projects beyond Canada, she apparently considered reversing this position and explored the possibility of going to Africa. In February 1861 she wrote to the American Missionary Association asking for an appointment as a teacher at its Mendi Mission in West Africa. Delany's rhetoric resonated with her own leaning toward missionary work as a means for racial uplift and her paternalistic attitude toward "uncivilized" blacks. She hoped time had healed her old animosities with the association. "I would be delighted to instruct the heathen and preach to them . . . to tell them of a more acceptable way than bowing to idols or trafficking in their fellow men," she offered. But it was a futile attempt to secure employment. During the 1850s the A.M.A. maintained several missions in West Africa near Sierra Leone, but as the American Civil War heated up, the organization shifted its emphasis to aiding the freedmen and women in the South. There is no evidence that she ever received a response to her request, and the idea was quickly cast aside.[10]

Publicly, Shadd Cary remained lukewarm to the idea of African emigration. Although she helped publicize Delany's 1856 Cleveland emigration convention in the pages of the *Provincial Freeman*, she only embraced the African agenda as part of a larger emigrationist ideology. In 1859, Delany had persuaded Isaac Shadd and a handful of Chatham blacks to form the short-lived African Civilization Society of Canada, which was announced in the pages of the *Freeman*. But the group did little more than proclaim that emigration to Africa would promote racial improvement and the destruction of the slave trade. Until the paper folded, the *Freeman* published notices and progress reports about Delany's exploration of West Africa, but there was never a clear endorsement of his project. By early 1861, the Niger Valley plan fell apart. The treaty that Delany had secured for land in Nigeria dissolved when the Egba chiefs and several opponents of the plan called it into question. The Civil War's disruption of shipping routes and the cotton market made emigration to Africa seem impossible. Throughout most of 1862, Delany continued to tell audiences he was relocating to Africa, but like many black Americans in Canada his attention gradually shifted toward the developing war in his homeland.[11]

Shadd Cary took a much stronger—and more hostile—position against the revitalization of the idea of black emigration to Haiti. This scheme, which had been simmering among a small group of black emigrationists since the mid-1850s, was spearheaded by one of Shadd Cary's earlier foes, James Theodore Holly. Holly, along with Henry Bibb, had been party to the vitriolic attacks on Shadd Cary in the *Voice of the Fugitive,* a fact she undoubtedly never forgot. She considered him a traitor to the cause of Canadian emigration when Holly shifted his interest to Haiti in 1855. Holly traveled to the Caribbean island and was the main organizer of various Haitian emigration support missions in the United States. Holly, who was ordained an Episcopal priest in 1856, intended to Christianize Haiti's inhabitants with the usual missionary zeal.[12]

In early 1861, there was increasing visibility of the Haitian agenda in Canada West, which prompted Shadd Cary's ire. She was particularly outraged because the Haitian government had hired James Redpath, a white journalist and abolitionist, to run its Haitian Emigration Bureau in North America. And she was equally annoyed that several prominent black activists, including William Wells Brown and William J. Watkins, were campaigning in Canada West on behalf of Haiti. Shadd Cary was revived, if not invigorated, by the ensuing battle with the Haitian agents. She dusted off her pen and leaped into the fray. Between September 1861 and April 1862 she wrote numerous letters to the *Weekly Anglo-African* reporting on the debate in Canada West and articulating her position.

Shadd Cary was deeply distressed that the black press was being appropriated to promote the Haitian emigration program. In the spring of 1861 Redpath purchased the *Weekly Anglo-African*—one of the three remaining African American newspapers of this period—with financing from the Haitian government, and renamed it the *Pine and Palm.* This gave the Haitian supporters an official organ and eliminated the major voice of opposition to the movement. Although the new publisher, George Lawrence, Jr., was black, the paper was largely controlled by Redpath, who had been a reporter for the *New York Tribune* and had published his observations of slavery in *The Roving Editor; or Talks with Slaves in the Southern States,* in 1859. By the summer of 1861, however, a new *Weekly Anglo-African,* published by Robert Hamilton, was back in print with the support of several black abolitionists. Writing for the revived newspaper, Shadd Cary made it plain that she had little use for Redpath's politics or his journalism. "Who, may I ask, is this James Redpath, in the hollow of whose hand lies trembling the destiny of our people?" she asked. The *Pine and Palm,* in her view, was the "great Mogul newspaper" and a vehicle for the "itinerant mercenaries—the paid Agents of the Haytian government." Shadd Cary ignored, or perhaps was unaware of, the fact that Redpath was a committed radical who had served as an intermediary between John Brown and the abolitionist establishment. In her criticism of Redpath's pro-Haiti propaganda, Shadd Cary underscored her own frustration with the demise of the *Provincial Freeman* and other black-owned newspapers. Her anger was reminiscent of her opposition to Henry Bibb and the *Voice of the Fugitive* ten years earlier. Redpath's advocacy had "succeeded in throwing glamour over the optics of all our friends," as he transformed the once-hated agenda of colonization into "a sweet morsel to hundreds of devotees of the god *Palm,*" she complained.[13]

Shadd Cary recast the argument that emigration to Haiti was replicating the model of white colonizationists who sought to rid North America of free blacks by sending them to uncivilized and dangerous locales. The fact that Redpath was white and a lesser-known abolitionist bolstered her attacks. But in reality, there were few ideological or practical differences between Delany's African emigration project, which she tacitly supported, and the Holly-Redpath Haitian project, which she abhorred. In her characteristic fashion, she insisted that Haiti and other tropical destinations spelled only disease and death for those who traveled there. Her litany of drawbacks read like a biblical invocation of hell: "pestilential fevers, licentiousness, drunkenness, heathenism and superstition abound," she maintained. By comparison, she argued that Canada had proven to be a hospitable asylum for African Americans. Ignoring her own flirtation with African emigration, she asserted that it was folly for African Americans to migrate south rather than north.[14]

Shadd Cary was particularly distressed that small cadres of blacks across Canada West, including the elderly and the destitute, were being enlisted into the Haiti plan with the lure of a warm climate and tropical delights. Despite the realities of prejudice and hardship that were her daily life in Canada, her public enthusiasm for her adopted home had not diminished. She urged blacks seeking asylum to reconsider Canadian emigration.

> Canada is just as large as ever, and though they may suffer a little for a time, the people will rally to help them; our government will give them one hundred acres of land, in a region where now she gives the same to Norwegians, Irish, English and Scotch, and where colored men can get it if they will, or they can settle down readily, and do well in this western section, with friends and relatives to help them along.[15]

Shadd Cary also took her anti-Haiti campaign to the meeting halls of Chatham, where she addressed crowds and submitted resolutions against the "specious representations" of the Haiti proponents. She was careful to uphold the "right of individual emigration," but challenged the Haitian plan as not in "the best interests of a once sorely oppressed people." She also complained that the Haiti agents were earning a commission for the emigrants they attracted—an average of twenty dollars per recruit—and thus were motivated by greed. "They preach, lecture, write, doctor a little, and to repeat a lady of the Baptist persuasion at the last Haytian meeting here, 'How they do lie!'" she reported in the *Weekly Anglo-African*. No Haiti supporter was exempt from her scorn.[16]

William J. Watkins, a black abolitionist lecturer who had rejected the emigration movement throughout the 1850s, jumped on the Haiti bandwagon and arrived in Canada West to promote the cause. Watkins, cousin of author Frances Ellen Watkins Harper, had written a flattering review of Shadd Cary in 1855 for *Frederick Douglass' Paper*. Nevertheless, when Shadd Cary learned of Watkins's arrival, she predicted that "free speech among the colored citizens of Chatham will be stifled" because announcements of the meeting instructed the opposition to hold a separate session to express their views. Undaunted, Shadd Cary attended Watkins's lecture at the Town Hall, and stood up in the audience to argue with him over the merits of Haitian emigration. Watkins retaliated with what Shadd Cary called "a string of second-hand charges and personalities upon your most humble servant." The meeting erupted into an uproar during which, according to Shadd Cary, Watkins was shouted down by the audience. This event gave her an opportunity to employ her favored strategy of turning gender conventions against her opponents. She took pleasure in criticizing Watkins for overstepping the boundaries of proper behavior by picking on the weak and powerless. How "these Haytian agents like to call names, make mischief, fight old men with broken arms, or women," she wrote. Ironically, Watkins's endorsement of emigration was feeble, and when the Haitian movement died out, he returned to the United States from Canada without ever setting foot on the island.[17]

Another Haitian agent, William Wells Brown, was also an object of Shadd Cary's contempt. Brown, unlike Redpath, was a highly regarded black abolitionist—one who had resisted the emigrationist impulse until the 1860s. When he toured Canada West in the Fall of 1861 on behalf of the Haitian Emigration Bureau, Shadd Cary was particularly disturbed. Brown brought credibility to the hated emigration plan, and he attracted large audiences in towns stretching from Toronto to Windsor. He reported on his observations of Canada's black communities in a series of seven articles that were published in the *Pine and Palm*. The articles tried to balance an appreciation of the accomplishments of blacks in Canada with arguments in favor of black emigration to Haiti. Brown, who had encountered Shadd Cary during her lectures and fund-raising tours across the North, briefly praised her as "the most intelligent woman I have met in Canada." By the end of his four-month sojourn in Canada West, Brown realized that she was also his most formidable opponent. She took particular delight in castigating Brown in the pages of the *Anglo-African* for luring emigrants with tales of enormous sweet potatoes and bananas grown in Haiti. Her stinging, relentless attacks on the Haitian agents continued until they retreated back to the United States.[18]

So chaotic and disturbing were these early Civil War times for African Americans that even the staunchly anti-emigrationist Frederick Douglass gave limited support to the Haiti project and apparently toyed with the idea of relocating to the island. He advertised the activities of the Haitian Emigration Bureau in *Douglass' Monthly,* and admitted that he found many aspects of Haiti appealing. Shadd Cary may have been pleased that the influential Douglass finally endorsed African Americans' right to emigrate, but his kind words about Haiti only added to her consternation. In the early stages of the secession crisis, Douglass was so frustrated with Lincoln's conciliatory gestures toward the South that he announced plans to spend two months in Haiti. Douglass's fits of anger and disappointment over the President's failure to condemn slavery caused him to seriously consider abandoning his strident claims to the United States. But he belied these sentiments in print, as he urged his readers to have faith that abolition's moment had arrived. "We shall stay here and watch the current of events, and serve the cause of freedom and mankind," Douglass wrote. When he learned that war had broken out at Fort Sumter, he expressed renewed faith that the slaveholding states would be overthrown. The plans for visiting Haiti were abandoned as he placed all his energies into the war effort, but Douglass's interest in Haiti gave a strong boost to the movement.[19]

There was also a personal component to Shadd Cary's enmity toward Haitian emigration. Among Redpath's agents and supporters were her brothers-in-law, Isaac N. Cary and George Cary. Isaac was hired as a recruiting agent by the Haitian Emigration Bureau, and he sought emigrants in Windsor and later in Washington, D.C. In October 1861 Shadd Cary wrote that her brother-in-law supervised the departure from Chatham of 116 black emigrants en route to Haiti, an event she described as "in every sense humiliating." Although Isaac Cary briefly sold subscriptions for the *Provincial Freeman* in 1857, it is unlikely that he and Shadd Cary enjoyed a very cordial relationship. Not only were they on opposite ends of the Haiti issue, but he was also married to one of Shadd Cary's worst enemies, Mary Bibb.[20]

George Cary, on the other hand, figured more prominently in her life since he had been close to her husband Thomas and was caring for her three stepchildren. In the midst of the Haiti controversy, George Cary organized a group of blacks who planned to leave the "damning prejudice" they suffered in Canada to grow cotton in the new promised land of Haiti. Shadd Cary's opposition to the scheme was to no avail. In December 1861 George Cary and other members of the Cotton Growing Association sailed to Haiti. Three weeks after he landed in Haiti, George Cary was dead. It is unknown what happened to Shadd Cary's three teenage stepchildren; they may have been shuttled to other relatives in Canada, or they may have also been part of the ill-fated expedition.[21]

Mary Ann Shadd Cary turned out to be a prophetic critic of the Haitian movement, because death and disaster seemed to be its only result. Four members of James Theodore Holly's family died within a year of arriving in Haiti, including his infant daughter and his mother, along with 38 other members of his party, and the *Weekly Anglo-African* published numerous reports of casualties among the immigrants. By early 1862 opposition to Haitian emigration was also coming from African Americans who had traveled to the island and found conditions there intolerable. After protests in Boston, the Haitian Emigration Bureau closed its office in that city, and enthusiasm for the movement quickly dissolved across the rest of the North and in Canada West. Meanwhile, the Civil War was deflecting the attention of would-be emigrationists.[22]

Shadd Cary's persistent rhetoric and oppositional activities helped to dampen the fire that fueled emigration to Haiti, but did little to help her own cause. In many ways, her shifting allegiances epitomized the confusion and eventual disintegration of the black emigration movement. Yet she was more tenacious in sticking to her hopes for Canada than were many of her contemporaries. Unlike the failed projects to Africa and the Caribbean, Canada had been home to thousands of African Americans for more than a decade, and Shadd Cary had a tremendous personal and political stake there. Thus, even as she was drawn closer to events in the United States, she clung to her identity as someone who was in the forefront of building a black presence in British North America.

The realities of life for blacks in Canada West, however, were vastly different from the rosy picture she painted in her articles in the *Weekly Anglo-African*. The relentless racial hostility that blacks encountered propelled many, like her brother-in-law George Cary, to flee white Canadian dominance despite the promise of equality and the absence of slavery. It has been suggested that African American migrants to Canada were always unwelcome guests who were tolerated as long as their numbers were small, but were increasingly ostracized as they became a distinct segment of the Canadian polity.[23]

The threshold of racial intolerance and expectations changed over time for both whites and blacks in Canada West. The Canadian government initially welcomed the fugitives from oppression as a demonstration of British North America's moral superiority over the United States. In 1830, one official hailed the plans of Cincinnati blacks to move across the border by proclaiming, "Tell the Republicans on your side of the line that we do not know men by their color." But widespread antislavery sentiment did not translate into a true desire to bring blacks into the social and cultural matrix of Canada. As demographic and political circumstances changed, the fears and prejudices of the white populace were exacerbated. In the 1840s, the American philanthropist William King had to struggle mightily to gain sufficient white support for the purchase of land that became the Buxton settlement. One local town councilor petitioned the government in opposition to the project, arguing that whites felt "disgust and hatred" at the thought that blacks should be allowed to live nearby. In the town of Chatham, where the black population grew rapidly and the races lived in close proximity, whites' expressions of racial hatred were a daily occurrence. An Anglican missionary visiting the town in 1854 noted that "prejudice against the coloured people prevails here" worse than anywhere else in Canada West. The presence of such numerous vocal and persistent black activists in Chatham as Mary Ann Shadd Cary and Martin Delany, and the publication of the *Provincial Freeman* in the center of the town's business district, heightened the visibility of and backlash against Chatham's black community.[24]

African Americans, particularly fugitive slaves, sought freedom from bondage and the opportunity to be counted as full citizens. On their arrival in Canada, they acknowledged that racial prejudice existed in the new homeland, but were optimistic that it could be eradicated. In the early 1850s Samuel Ringgold Ward wrote several articles about Canadian "negrophobia," in which he related numerous personal indignities such as being denied a cabin on a steamer crossing Lake Ontario. "The boast of Englishmen, of their freedom from social negrophobia, is about as empty as the Yankee boast of democracy," Ward observed. But like many black emigrationists, he naively believed that Canada's racism was less tenacious, less ingrained than that which existed in the United States. Ward expected that "universal agitation by the press and the tongue, church and at the polls," would change racial attitudes and behaviors in Canada.[25]

Time proved Ward wrong. In the years leading up to the Civil War, blacks found themselves increasingly segregated and isolated from the main institutions of Canadian life—churches, schools, business and politics. While they may have enjoyed owning a plot of land, black employment opportunities were confined to work on railroad gangs or menial service as waiters, cooks, barbers, and whitewashers. Their progress was profoundly impeded—and their resentment brewed. From Windsor to St. Catherines, the towns and villages of Canada West which had been deemed a sanctuary years before, had become for many an intolerable hotbed of anti-black sentiment.[26]

Conceptions of race in Canada West were rooted in the dual influences of British Anglo-Saxonism and North American racial formations. As part of the British empire, Canada was settled under the dictates of manifest destiny based on the assumption that Anglo-Saxon superiority justified the conquering and eradication of inferior races. Canada's ruling class was closely tied to such British intellectuals as Thomas Carlyle, who argued that history had predetermined that the Saxons were the bearers of civilization to the lesser races of the world. Carlyle's tract "Occasional Discourse on the Nigger Question" stated that there was little of cultural, moral or intellectual value among all of the blacks inhabiting the British West Indies. Other influential writers of the period, such as Charles Kingsley and Robert Knox, easily rationalized the elimination of the "degenerate races"—including blacks and Native Americans—who would inevitably be overwhelmed by Anglo-Saxon power and accomplishment. These ideas took firm hold in the science, literature, and politics of mid-nineteenth century Britain.[27]

African Americans tended to blame the worsening racial climate in Canada West on racism in the United States. In their view, Canadian racism was derived from contact with whites below the border. "Copied aped deviltry is always meaner than the original diabolism," said Samuel Ward. "But the negrophobia of Canada, is a poor pitiable, brainless, long eared imitation of Yankeeism." Eight years later, Mary Ann Shadd Cary echoed his thoughts when she wrote that "with all this evident aping of American pro-slavery customs, Canada is better for colored men than the United States." Their reasoning was weak, however, because immigration from the United States was a relatively insignificant factor in Canada's growth. With the exception of fugitive slaves, Canadian officials often discouraged American immigration. And Canadians generally eschewed any influences from their neighbors to the south. Said one Montreal editor, "The Canadian's birthright and duty was to hate the Yankee," who was always viewed suspiciously. The few white Americans who were welcomed in the Canadas tended to be entrepreneurs and manufacturers from New York and New England, who found the young country ripe for industrialization. An influx of immigrants from the southern United States did not occur until the outbreak of the Civil War. On the other hand, there was a regular outmigration of Canadians into the United States during this period as farmers sought greater expanses of land in the developing American Midwest. The scattering of white Americans on Canadian soil could not have been the solitary influence on racial attitudes.[28]

Racial formations in Canada West did seem to parallel the conditions that exacerbated discrimination and prejudice in the northern United States. In particular, the arrival of poor, unskilled immigrants from Europe, coupled with an increasing demand for land and jobs, spelled trouble for the tiny black minority. Between 1840 and 1860, 600,000 British immigrants—most of them refugees from the Irish potato famine—emigrated to Canada. The Irish immigrants frequently arrived in British North America with no resources, and they relied heavily on the same kinds of assistance provided to the fugitive slaves—philanthropic aid, government loans and land grants. Many sought farmland with which to start a new life, placing pressure on the shrinking agricultural pool in Canada West. In the less developed regions of Canada West near Chatham, Amherstburg, and Windsor, where many of the black migrants had settled, population growth outpaced agricultural production. Industrial development was limited to the urban areas to the east near Toronto and Hamilton, thus there were few manufacturing jobs for the hopeful migrants. The Roman Catholic Irish immigrants, ostracized because of their religion and class, competed directly with blacks for scarce land and menial jobs, and the latter group usually came up short.[29]

Canada's low-paid white workers developed cultural and ideological mechanisms that forged their racial identity in a manner similar to that of their relatives in the United States. In both countries, Irish Catholics and blacks shared many of the same negative insults and injuries. But as David R. Roediger has suggested, Irish workers sought to distance them-selves from blacks through a construction of "whiteness," rather than to find solidarity with oppressed people of color. Vulnerable black competitors in the job market were easy targets for victimization and vilification. Mary Ann Shadd Cary described the kinds of indignities heaped on blacks at the hands of their white neighbors: "They . . . pull down the fences, injure the crops, lay claims to the hogs, and steal horses and butcher cows belonging to colored farmers out of sheer envy at their prosperity, or hatred of color," she wrote. If white workers were to shed their lowly association with "nigger work," as one historian has noted, they "had to drive all Blacks, and if possible their memories, from the places where the Irish labored." Indeed, Canada's small black population hovered on the margins of the nation's workforce as they experienced routine harassment in their communities.[30]

The failure of the black settlement projects at Wilberforce, Dawn, and the Refugee Home Society, helped to fuel Canadians' jaundiced view of black immigrants. African Americans as a group were to blame for the dismal record of these utopian experiments, argued whites—not faulty leadership, lack of capital and experience, or racially motivated opposition. White Canadians were also gripped by the full spectrum of fears and prejudices regarding black sexuality and the threat of miscegenation. In the inaugural issue of the *Voice of the Fugitive*, Henry Bibb perceptively observed that fear of "amalgamation of the races" stoked the fires of prejudice. By framing blacks as incompetent and ignorant, on the one hand, and debased and immoral on the other, Canadians, like their counterparts in the United States, felt justified in denying them the rights and privileges owed to them as British subjects. This black "child/savage" ideology created a pattern in which discrimination against blacks prevented them from reaching the intellectual, economic or political attainment that was part of the promise of emigration. The full brunt of these negative conceptions was not revealed until after the Civil War, when Canadian newspapers shed all guises of benevolence and openly subscribed to a thoroughly prejudiced and contemptuous view of blacks. During Reconstruction, newspaper depictions of blacks as lazy, lacking in intelligence and initiative, and of bad character were commonplace as Canadians' adherence to abolitionist ideology quickly slipped away.[31]

Mary Ann Shadd Cary's flirtation with African emigration was rooted, in part, in her disillusionment with life in Canada West. The racial discord she experienced on a daily basis was a far cry from the democratic society she championed publicly. But her letter to the A.M.A. was also inspired by financial need. A missionary appointment in Africa held out the possibility of a reliable income, something that seemed beyond her grasp even before Thomas's death. Shadd Cary had few financial securities as a widow in Victorian-era Canada. Under English common law women's property was transferred to their husbands upon marriage, and it was unusual for wives to inherit farms or businesses from deceased husbands or share in the proceeds of the sale of their husbands' property. While there were some provisions in the law for widows to receive a portion of their husband's estate, it was rare that wives were provided for throughout their old age. The sexual division of labor in Shadd Cary's marriage was clearly atypical—she continued to work outside of the home and did not rely exclusively on Thomas's economic contributions. Nevertheless, without her husband's income, Mary Ann and her children were faced with significant financial loss. Any money or worldly goods left behind by Thomas Cary were likely inherited by his brothers or male heirs, and since their son Linton was not born until after his death Mary Ann's family unit was unlikely to have benefited in this way.[32]

Widows in nineteenth-century Canada were generally assisted by their extended families, and they had one of two options: remarry quickly or earn their own living. Shadd Cary was also encumbered with two children who required resources but could provide none to the family earnings. Although widowhood often provided women, especially black women, with a greater measure of social independence, it also required them to develop elaborate strategies for survival. Following Thomas Cary's death, Shadd Cary lived in Chatham with her daughter Sarah and son Linton, and she relied heavily on assistance from her parents, brothers, and sisters who lived nearby. The 1861 census listed her daughter Sarah Cary as part of her grandfather Abraham's household in Raleigh Township, as well as Mary Ann's own home in Chatham, indicating that her children spent considerable time with their extended family.[33]

Although the *Provincial Freeman* was gone, Mary Ann identified her profession as editress when the 1861 census-taker came to call, suggesting she still hoped to resurrect the newspaper once more—or hated to relinquish that part of her identity. In reality, her main source of income was from the school founded in Chatham by her sister-in-law Amelia Freeman Shadd in 1856. By 1858, the school became a joint venture between Mary Ann and Amelia. Teaching was one of the few options for women's wage labor across nineteenth-century Canada; most women working outside of the home were engaged in service work, in trades or in factories. The options for black women were even more closely circumscribed. One study of black women on Vancouver Island found them employed mainly as maids, with a few working as cooks, nurses and teachers. Research on black women in Nova Scotia also reported that the vast majority of working women were confined to domestic service. A handful of black female teachers were found in rural communities where the need was constant. In Canada West, the rapid feminization of teaching between 1851–71 meant that female teachers were low-status and low-paid. This was especially true for the black female teachers who served the black students shut out from the public schools.[34]

Amelia Shadd's school was intended to be a coeducational program where Chatham's more prosperous residents paid for their children to study such refined topics as painting, drawing, and music. Chatham had one local black public school, a crude log building where Alfred Whipper—brother of the Philadelphia abolitionist William Whipper—was the teacher. The school was woefully inadequate and overcrowded and the Shadds eventually sought to fill that void. They hoped to provide a superior education, and to break down the climate of racial animosity and segregation that permeated the community. In the late 1850s, Amelia and Mary Ann advertised that all children would be admitted "irrespective of race, creed or color" for a modest fee. In fact, their school was mostly populated by the children of fugitive slaves, many of whom could not afford the tuition. Mary Ann's brother-in-law George Cary described the black community's anguish over the schooling dilemma, noting that while blacks paid school taxes and the laws mandated an education for all citizens, "They [whites] will not permit a colored child to enter a school where white children are taught." By 1861 the Shadds' school served sixty-five students and was being partially subsidized by the American Missionary Association. A year later Isaac Shadd, who had taken an active role in the school's administration, reported it was in "flourishing condition," and that among the new students were contraband from Kentucky and Alabama—young former slaves newly liberated by the Civil War.[35]

Mary Ann took on the job as principal fund raiser for the school to supplement the limited tuition payments. It was easy to revive her role as traveling agent, an activity she seemed to enjoy and for which she was well suited. But she had to swallow her pride and her animosity when she went to Michigan to ask the Refugee Home Society for financial assistance, and she later reported that her old enemy Rev. C. C. Foote was one of the school's benefactors. Initially her requests for funds were ignored, but she finally pressured the society into pledging $100 to pay a teacher's salary for the 1862 school year. Although Foote and others persisted in calling it "Mrs. Carey's [sic] school," Mary Ann insisted that the school was run jointly by Amelia and herself.[36]

Mary Ann had a dream of establishing a high school and "permanent literary institution" in Chatham, and she declared it would be built if "only [a] brick at a time." Like Chatham's primary school, the local secondary school was ostensibly open to everyone but admission was determined by an entrance exam which few black children could pass. Shadd Cary believed that racial improvement would only occur if Canada's black populace was able to obtain more than a rudimentary education. Toronto's normal school, which Shadd Cary's sister Emmaline Shadd attended, was one of the only secondary institutions in Canada West that was open to black students. Shadd Cary's vision for a new high school was consistent with her plans for black Canadian self-sufficiency and assimilation. Yet, after more than a decade of struggling to provide a decent education for black children, she—like other African Americans in Canada—was beginning to publicly express her rage over the country's unyielding racism. In a circular she prepared to solicit support for the Chatham high school, her faith in British North America as a home for blacks was clearly in doubt. "*The history* of education among the colored people of Kent, *Essex* and *Lambton Counties* is a chapter of wrong, ignorance and prejudice which reflects severely upon the *British name* and the present disabilities in this respect cry aloud for a remedy," she declared.[37]

Mary Ann also managed to get the Mission School, as she called it, embroiled in her quarrel with proponents of Haitian emigration. Haiti supporters retaliated against Shadd Cary's fervent attacks on their project by mustering opposition to the Shadds' Mission School. At a meeting in Chatham they criticized Shadd Cary's plans for building a high school and suggested that the Shadds were hopelessly in debt and could not pay the lease on the school's land. Characteristically, Mary Ann refuted the charges in letters to newspapers in Canada and the United States, and blamed the strife on "a wicked scheme being prosecuted for the purpose of decoying colored people to Hayti." But the squabble highlighted the fact that even in a small and embattled black community, there was a diversity of interests and perspectives. Not all of Chatham's black populace were enamored with Shadd Cary's schemes. A second all-black public school was established in Chatham in 1861, and while it did not respond to the demands for integrated education, it likely siphoned away some of the Shadds' students.[38]

The small donations from the A.M.A., the Refugee Home Society, local clergy, and philanthropists in Canada and the United States barely sustained the existing elementary school much less provide the capital for the construction of a new facility. The Civil War was diverting the attention and funds customarily provided by benevolent societies, and the needs of the freedmen were quickly superseding the needs of the fugitives in Canada West. As early as late 1862 the American Missionary Association began to close its former missions in Canada, replacing them with projects to feed, shelter and educate the masses of former slaves in the South.[39]

The A.M.A.'s waning interest in the plight of the Canadian fugitives was indicative of the deepening impact of the Civil War. As Shadd Cary remained immersed in the doings of the Chatham Mission school, two issues were being hotly contested across the boarder: the role of slavery in the war agenda, and the use of black troops in the Union Army. The exclusion of blacks from the military was standard policy during the first eighteen months of the war, when the Union still felt confident that it could overpower the Confederate forces. It was a "white man's war" and the presence of African American soldiers would undermine the morale of white troops, it was argued. By the spring of 1861, Frederick Douglass was pounding away at government resistance to arm black men on behalf of the Union in the pages of *Douglass' Monthly*, and white abolitionists and some military leaders were questioning the soundness of ignoring the potential benefits of black troops. But in these early stages of the war, President Lincoln was most concerned with appeasing the sensitive slaveholding border states of Maryland, Kentucky, Missouri, and Virginia. The Union government considered the recruitment of black soldiers an incendiary act that would subvert the political and military objectives of the war.[40]

But the stalwart position to keep African Americans out of the war effort, both politically and physically, began to weaken. As the war raged on and casualties mounted, Congress made a symbolic concession when it passed the Militia Act of 1862 which allowed the recruitment of black soldiers for "any war service for which they may be found competent." Yet there was no immediate movement in that direction. Indeed, President Lincoln signaled his ambivalence on the matter when he said in September 1862, "If we were to arm them, I fear that in a few weeks the arms would be in the hands of the rebels." Nevertheless, newly freed slaves were serving as laborers, and increasingly as soldiers, in several southern military theaters as a handful of Union officers bucked the official policy.[41]

Slavery took center stage in the war when President Lincoln issued the Emancipation Proclamation, effective in January 1863, which proclaimed that slaves in Confederate states and territories would be "forever free." The proclamation sanctioned the use of blacks in the armed forces for limited duty, but the courage and ability of black soldiers quickly led to their expanded role. Six months after the Emancipation Proclamation, more than thirty black regiments had been organized and recruiting black troops became a military priority. In Canada West, the Emancipation Proclamation tended to exacerbate already strained race relations, as whites wrongly anticipated an influx of blacks into the province.[42]

True to her stubborn and skeptical nature, Mary Ann Shadd Cary initially viewed the Civil War as a distant event. The rhetoric of Lincoln and other public figures in their attempts to dissociate the war from the central problems of race and slavery did little to convince her that change in the United States was imminent. In 1862 she told the editor of the *Weekly Anglo-African* that "there is a great war going on in your country at this time," as if it would have little impact on her life. That year she applied for and received Canadian citizenship, suggesting that she had relinquished any claims on the United States as her homeland. But

Shadd Cary could not continue to remain detached from the very events which promised to fulfill her lifelong aspiration to see slavery abolished.[43]

Following the Emancipation Proclamation, African American leaders became unified in the view that the Civil War provided an opportunity for blacks to win the respect and equality that had eluded them on American soil. Robert Hamilton, publisher of the *Weekly Anglo-African,* exhorted free blacks in the North to do all they could to aid the Union. "If we rise in tens of thousands, and say to the President, 'here we are, take us!' we will secure to our children and children's children all that our fathers have labored and suffered and bled for!" he wrote. In particular, Hamilton encouraged donations of clothing for the freedmen, and the work of teachers and doctors to aid in the settlement and training of the freedmen. But it was the role of black troops that became the focus of black abolitionism. Perhaps no one stated the case better than Shadd Cary's friend Sattie Douglass, wife of H. Ford Douglass, when she wrote that military service provided black men the opportunity to "strike the blow that will at once relieve them of northern prejudice and southern slavery."[44]

African American men finally got their chance to prove themselves when, in January 1863, Gov. John Andrew of Massachusetts was authorized to raise a regiment of black soldiers. A prominent New England abolitionist named George Stearns was hired to find these soldiers, and he turned to black leaders like Douglass, Martin Delany, William Wells Brown, and Henry Highland Garnet, to recruit troops across the North. These activists, who had spent years debating the merits of abolitionist tactics and emigration, now took advantage of their reputations and access to black communities to build a black Army to defend the Union. Douglass, in particular, enjoyed this long-awaited victory, and his two sons were among the first to volunteer for military service. Delany and Douglass were instrumental in raising the 54th Massachusetts Infantry, which marched toward the battlefield in May 1863 and symbolized a powerful new role for African Americans.[45]

But the small cadre of black recruiters faced a daunting challenge, as black men hesitated to sign up, while the need for Union soldiers for the bloody war increased. The economic expansion spurred by the Civil War had created new opportunities for blacks in the North which were more attractive than the risks and rigors of military service. At the same time, many black men feared they would be used as cannon fodder by the Union Army. The military openly discriminated against the black troops, as well. Until 1864, blacks were paid smaller bounties and salaries than whites and were denied advancement into the officers' ranks. By the summer, several more northern states, including Ohio, Rhode Island, Connecticut, Maryland, and Pennsylvania, obtained authoriza-

Martin Robeson Delany
in Civil War uniform, from
I. Garland Penn, *The Afro-
American Press and Its Editors*
(Springfield, Mass., 1891).
(Metropolitan Toronto
Reference Library)

tion to establish their own regiments of black troops. In late 1863 Martin Delany reported to the Secretary of War that more black recruiting
agents were desperately needed: "The agency of intelligent, competent,
black men adapted to the work must be the most effective means of
obtaining black troops; because knowing and being of that people as a
race, they can command such influences as is required to accomplish the
object," he wrote.[46]

Among those Delany had in mind was at least one competent black
woman. In December 1863 Delany invited Mary Ann Shadd Cary to
join him in the field. Following the success in organizing the 54th Massachusetts regiment, he had been hired by the State of Connecticut to
"raise colored troops," the first African American to secure a state contract for this purpose. Delany offered Mary Ann $15 for every slave and
$5 for every free-born African American she could muster for the 29th
Regiment Connecticut Volunteers. As Delany was well aware, Shadd
Cary's experience in traveling across the North, her widespread contacts
in the abolitionist community, and her proven abilities at persuasive oratory made her an ideal candidate for the job.[47]

The war's urgency gradually forced Shadd Cary to reconsider her contentious relationship with the United States. Her adherence to an emigrationist ideology was predicated on the belief that there was little hope of a free and unfettered life for blacks in the United States while slavery dictated the nation's economic and political framework. Once the slave question became part of the Civil War agenda the rationale for emigration became less relevant. Shadd Cary's acceptance of Delany's invitation gave her an opportunity to earn a living and aid in the war effort. At the same time she could maintain a home base in Chatham and continue her fund-raising efforts for the Mission School.

The Civil War began to have a direct impact on the lives of African Americans living in Canada West, including the Shadd family. Most scholarship has contended that the war depleted the black male population and contributed to the beginning of an exodus of blacks back to the United States. One estimate notes at least 700 people left Buxton; another claims several dozen black men from Elgin immediately volunteered for military service. More recently, this argument has been countered with evidence that suggests only a small number of blacks in Canada were propelled across the border during this period. Nevertheless, many Canadians, both black and white, felt compelled to join in the conflict. Among them were Mary Ann's brother Abraham W. Shadd, age 19 in 1863, who enlisted and served in the 55th Massachusetts Colored Infantry, along with their cousin Gabriel Jackson Shadd. Another young recruit was the son of Martin Delany, Toussaint L'Ouverture Delany, who left school in Canada West at age 15 to join the Massachusetts 54th. Many of Shadd Cary's contemporaries joined the fighting as well, including former *Provincial Freeman* editor H. Ford Douglass, who became one of the few African Americans to serve in a white Army unit when he joined the 95th Illinois Regiment of Infantry Volunteers. Martin Delany would eventually become the highest ranking black officer in the Union Army when he was commissioned as a Major in the waning days of the war.[48]

While some blacks in Canada, like Osborne Perry Anderson and Josiah Henson, helped fill the Union Army with recruits found on Canadian soil, Mary Ann Shadd Cary crossed the border and traversed widely across the United States. Customarily the agents set up recruiting stations in towns and villages where they would give speeches, visit prospects at home, and distribute circulars. They might be found in a church, a pub, or standing on street corners to round up their quota of soldiers. Delany's contract covered the Midwest, and all troops were to be delivered to him at his headquarters in Chicago. Armed with a certificate of authorization which empowered her as Delany's agent, Shadd Cary likely canvassed for recruits across Ohio, Pennsylvania, Michigan, Wisconsin, Illinois, and Indiana, in some of the same states where she had given countless pro-Canada abolitionist lectures the decade before.[49]

Shadd Cary joined the ranks of scores of American women who often defied the gender conventions of the era to engage in wartime efforts. As one postwar chronicler noted, "We may safely say that there is scarcely a loyal woman in the North who did not do something in aid of the cause." The vast majority served the war through domestic activities— sending food, clothing, and supplies to troops, fund raising for freedmen's aid societies and sanitary commissions, and nursing wounded soldiers. Abolitionist women continued to give lectures, write newspaper commentary, and establish organizations like the Woman's National Loyal League to press for complete emancipation. And some determined women went to the front as "daughters of the regiment," as spies, or disguised themselves, took up arms, and engaged directly in battle.[50]

African American women were, like their white counterparts, involved in every aspect of the war. Many free blacks like Charlotte Forten traveled south to open schools for freedmen and women in Union-occupied areas. The exploits of some women became the stuff of legends —such as Harriet Tubman's activities as a Union army spy, and Susie King Taylor's service as a laundress and nurse for the 54th Massachusetts Infantry. More common was the work of women like Elizabeth Keckley, personal servant to Mary Todd Lincoln, who organized the Contraband Relief Association of Washington, D.C., to coordinate the acquisition and distribution of aid to the freed people. Well-known black abolitionist women continued their crusade during the war. Frances Ellen Watkins Harper gave patriotic lectures while Sojourner Truth housed and collected food for black soldiers in Michigan, and gave pro-Union speeches. Truth lamented, "If I were ten years younger, I would go down with these soldiers here and be the Mother of the Regiment."[51]

The exact extent of women's role in the recruitment of black troops is unknown. Sojourner Truth and Josephine St. Pierre Ruffin, among others, are credited with encouraging black men to join the Army. But to be appointed a recruiting agent was apparently rare. Mary Ann Shadd Cary relished this unique new role and left her children under her family's care in Chatham to take up the challenge. She spent much of her time canvassing in the Midwest. In the 1860s, this was an especially daunting—and even dangerous—task for any black person. The Midwest was a bastion of white supremacy second only to the South, and was the site of discriminatory laws, race riots, and anti-black activities including threats, intimidation, and violence. Immediately after the war, William Wells Brown wrote that the stringent blacks laws established in this region were an attempt to drive out contraband slaves from neighboring states, as well as free blacks deemed to be troublemakers.[52]

In the early 1850s, Iowa, Illinois, and Indiana passed legislation forbidding blacks to settle in their states. These and other parts of the Midwest embraced numerous laws that prevented blacks from obtaining an education, serving on juries, voting, or marrying outside their race. Indiana boasted a particularly inhospitable climate for African Americans at the outbreak of the Civil War. At least one scholar has identified Indiana as "the most conservative when it came to state policies related to blacks" in the Midwest. Democratic officials from the state were in the forefront of opposing the recruitment of black soldiers, and as the Emancipation Proclamation became a reality, local communities violently reacted to the prospect of a massive influx of former slaves from the South. Although Republicans and other supporters of black rights controlled the Indiana legislature in the 1860s, the state was so conservative that they could not overturn its black codes.[53]

Despite—or perhaps because of—these conditions, Delany set up a recruiting base in New Albany, Indiana, just minutes across the Ohio river from Louisville, Kentucky, which was neutral territory in the war but a slave state. New Albany was one of the largest cities in Indiana with more than 8,000 residents, and it had the largest proportion of blacks—7.5 percent—in the state. It boasted a thriving steamboat-building industry, and its dependence on southern business created a tense and hostile environment during the Civil War. The town's proximity to slaveholding states also meant that there was a steady influx of African Americans during the war, which made it ripe for recruiting black troops but also a hot spot for racial strife.[54]

Here Mary Ann Shadd Cary spent several months drafting newly freed or escaped slaves, as well as long-time Indiana residents. She also likely aided some runaway slaves in making their way to Canada West. Her recruiting activities thrust Shadd Cary into the midst of the state's racial turmoil. Indiana's river towns along the Kentucky border feared they were rapidly "filling up with strange Africans," as one local newspaper reported, and the backlash frequently took a violent turn. In the summer of 1862, a thirty-hour anti-black riot in New Albany resulted in the death of one black man and numerous incidents of beatings and vandalism, ironically forcing a number of blacks to escape to Kentucky. In that same year Indiana troops threatened to shoot at a group of blacks fleeing across the Ohio River, and state authorities set up an outpost at New Albany to turn back fugitives from slavery. By the time she arrived two years later, white residents were more reconciled to the war but the racial climate was still strained.[55]

Evidence of the dangers she faced can be found among Shadd Cary's surviving papers, in a certificate from Indiana Governor Oliver P. Morton pledging to protect Delany and his agents as they recruited troops for the Connecticut regiment. The certificate also forbade them from recruiting Indiana's black residents, or to leave the state with "colored men belonging to the state," because Indiana had begun organizing its own black regiment, the Twenty-eighth Colored Infantry. Ironically, once the Emancipation Proclamation paved the way for the recruitment of black soldiers, officials in the Midwest abandoned their opposition to black troops and began recruiting them with the idea that sending them to fight in the South might reverse blacks' northward migration. In Indiana, state officials who had actively banned black immigration a year ago were now actively recruiting black residents so desperately needed for the war effort.[56]

The combined efforts of Delany's recruiters were successful, and the Twenty-ninth Colored Infantry was mustered in Connecticut in March 1864, to amass an outstanding record in combat. By April they were dispatched to the Department of the South for active duty. The Commander of Recruiting Services in Connecticut was so pleased with Shadd Cary's service that he hired her that same month to recruit for another regiment in his state. Lt. Col. Benjamin S. Pardee wrote:

> I have heard from them a most excellent report concerning you, and desire your services in another field. It is useless at present to attempt to do anything where men must pass through Ohio—I enclose a ticket for transportation. *There is no time to be lost*—I will pay you from now to May 1st $2 per day for your services, (sunday included,) and your expenses from the time you reach New Haven. . . . Should your efforts in the new field be successful I will then reward you handsomely, besides your regular pay.[57]

Shadd Cary lived an exciting and unpredictable life during her time as an Union Army recruiter. When summoned by Colonel Pardee she had to drop everything and make her way from New Albany to Cincinnati, where she took a train to New York City and then to New Haven, for a meeting at his headquarters. We can only guess at how Mary Ann Shadd Cary negotiated the hazards and restrictions of her sex and her race during these months. Even influential white military officers, like Brigadier General Edward Wild, were harassed and bullied by opponents when they attempted to recruit black soldiers. There was always the risk of running into enemy or renegade soldiers as she traveled, and she would have had to seek safety in the homes of charitable black and white families along the way. On occasion Mary Ann was accompanied by other agents, but there must have been many times when she forged ahead alone.[58]

Her precarious situation was highlighted in June 1864, when she was back in New Albany, Indiana, recruiting troops for Connecticut and raising funds for the Mission School in Chatham. A check she had just received from the American Missionary Association was stolen from

MARY ANN SHADD CARY

Abraham W. Shadd in Civil War uniform. During Reconstruction, Abraham earned a law degree from Howard University and became a lawyer and public official in Mississippi. (Raleigh Township Centennial Museum)

her basket as she tried to get it cashed at a local bank. In her usual determined fashion, she used some bullying tactics of her own to get the money back. "By prompt steps and a little bluster [the money] was drawn from its hiding place today where it had been put on the hope of getting it cashed privately, I suppose," she wrote to George Whipple. After fifteen years of engaging in nasty political battles, traveling in hostile territory, lecturing to unfriendly audiences, and withstanding insults, threats, and physical discomfort, Mary Ann Shadd Cary was not easily intimidated.[59]

Shadd Cary juggled several jobs as she remained in the States to help the war effort. In the spring of 1864, the Colored Ladies Freedmen's Aid Society invited her, whom they called "that active and assiduous worker," to serve as their traveling agent. The society, based in Chicago, was one of dozens of aid organizations that sent supplies to contrabands— or former slaves freed by the war—on the front lines. On at least one occasion, Shadd Cary crossed the river that separated Indiana from Louisville, Kentucky, to collect $89.55 from local churches on behalf of the society.[60]

But foremost on her mind was the Mission School in Chatham, which was hanging on by a slender thread. Support from the American Missionary Association had not been consistent, and she frantically searched for funding. In a plaintive appeal reminiscent of an earlier time, she complained to the association's corresponding secretary, George Whipple, that the only charitable donations she had raised were from the Refugee Home Society, and that wartime inflation had rendered the American dollars almost negligible by the time they reached Canada. In 1863 and 1864, 259 children and adults attended the school, and she reported a litany of troubles that added to the "mere drudgery of a school of the sort." The school was so crowded that students had to be turned away, prompting them to migrate among schools in the towns and rural areas that would have them. "The poverty of many parents obliging the older ones to work at times and the others to take their place," prevented any efforts at a continuous education, she complained. The school also owed back wages to a former teacher, and Mary Ann's younger sister Emaline Shadd Simpson was teaching for free while Amelia Shadd worked in the public school to pay off some of their debts. A month later Mary Ann received a check for $75 from the A.M.A., perhaps enough to stave off an emergency or pay another bill, but certainly not enough to keep the school going.[61]

As the war progressed even reluctant states like Indiana began to actively recruit black soldiers after they encountered difficulty filling their troop quotas with whites. Governor Morton initiated the formation of a black regiment despite considerable white opposition, because recruiting agents like Shadd Cary and Delany had successfully enticed Indiana blacks to serve for other states. As pressure increased on states to fill their Union Army quotas, even holdouts like Indiana took up the cause. Some white men in the state began to support black troop recruitment as a means of avoiding military service themselves; by late 1864 drafted men had furnished hundreds of black substitutes. One broadside published in the local press revealed whites' enthusiasm in sending blacks to the front:

> Indiana, at last, is to have credit for the colored troops raised in her border. . . . It is no longer a question whether we should use them. They have proved themselves patriotic and heroic, and, surely, any white man would . . . just as cheerfully see a colored man with only one arm as be in that fix himself.[62]

But black leaders chose to ignore these sentiments, focusing instead on the liberatory effects of black military participation. Mary Ann Shadd Cary was among a group of recruiting agents hired by Governor Morton to raise the Twenty-eighth United States Colored Infantry, based in Indianapolis. In this capacity, she could employ her own agents, as Delany had done, and she hired a relative to assist her. Recruiters published lengthy advertisements in newspapers across the state that appealed to black men's desire for recognition and status. They called on them to "show yourselves worthy soldiers, and the petty prejudices that weak and wicked men have endeavored to excite against you will be forever swallowed up in the gratitude of a nation that will own and applaud your heroic deeds."[63]

There was fierce competition among different counties to receive credit for each soldier recruited, and as it became increasingly difficult to find volunteers, slaves from Kentucky were enticed to enroll. Shadd Cary could have been among the recruiters who ventured across the river into Henderson, Kentucky, for this purpose, and she would have been paid an extra bounty to do so. The risks and hardships of these ventures included threats of violence from masters who lost their slaves to the Union Army. It has been estimated that anywhere from 800 to 1,500 black men from Indiana were recruited for various Union Army regiments, comprising at least ten percent of the state's black population. The soldiers went on to active duty that was heralded by the press, and several units, including the Twenty-eighth Colored Infantry, suffered heavy losses. Shadd Cary recruited troops through the fall of 1864, and returned to Canada West as the war entered its fierce final months. It must have been a relief to come home after more than a year on the road, eluding danger and being separated from her children and family. She could derive satisfaction from knowing that she aided in the Union Army victory and the empowerment of African American men. Her work as a recruiter also provided a steady income that was sorely needed at home.[64]

The community in Chatham that Mary Ann returned to, like most of Canada's black enclaves, was no longer the asylum that offered so much hope and promise. Once the Confederate Army surrendered in the spring of 1865, there were few social and political barriers to hold back those African Americans who wished to leave. While military service led some blacks in Canada to return to the United States, many fugitive slaves and black expatriates simply longed to go back to the places they considered home. The possibility of reuniting with lost relatives was one of the most powerful motivating factors that influenced the movement of African Americans during the post-emancipation years. The strong commitment to family ties often superseded the relative comfort and safety blacks had found in Canada West. The families most likely to remain in Canada were those whose extended families had emigrated, like the Shadds, or who had prospered so greatly that they had little incentive to leave. In nearby Raleigh Township, Mary Ann's father, Abraham

Shadd, was a successful farmer and was the first black person to hold elected office in Canada when he gained a seat on the Town Council in 1859. But in Chatham much of the black political leadership was drained away. Many African Americans left Canada's black communities but retained their land and homes, which they rented out with the expectation that they would return. Most eventually sold their Canadian holdings. Others tried without success to relocate groups of blacks living in Canada to confiscated lands in the South.[65]

The Shadd family was not immune to these trends. As early as the summer of 1863 Isaac Shadd toured black communities in northern California as he considered moving back to the United States. He had been restive about life in Canada West since his failed attempts to emigrate to Africa. Sometime after Mary Ann's return to Chatham, she and Amelia closed the Mission School. With the loss of Mary Ann's income as a recruiter, and the end of support from the American Missionary Association, there were no funds to keep it going. In 1870 Isaac and Amelia relocated to the United States, settling in Mississippi where he was elected to the state legislature and she taught in the freedmen's schools. Their younger brother Abraham Jr., who moved to Washington, D.C., after his discharge from the Union Army, eventually settled in Arkansas.[66]

One of Shadd Cary's closest associates, Martin Delany, had already returned to the United States by the end of the war. Delany was not content with his role as an army recruiter, and was determined to get into the fighting. In early 1865 he moved his family to Wilberforce, Ohio, where he left his four younger children with his wife, and he received a commission as Major of the 104th United States Colored Troops in South Carolina—the highest ranking black officer to lead a black regiment. The Civil War ended before Delany could carry out his plan for creating a Corps d'Afrique commanded by black officers. For several years he served as an Army officer for the Freedman's Bureau and was finally mustered out of the service in 1869. Delany's family eventually joined him in South Carolina, where they lived for another twenty years.[67]

Other African Americans left Canada because of the optimism and promise sparked by the beginnings of Reconstruction. Ministers in towns like Buxton urged educated blacks to return to the southern United States in the service of the freedmen. The region's black professionals and intellectuals hoped that with the changes brought on by Radical Reconstruction they might be able to practice their skills and acquire political power unheard of a decade before. As one historian has noted, "With the end of the war, black hopes and expectations seemed almost boundless."[68]

Mary Ann Shadd Cary found herself in the middle of these competing perspectives and desires. On the one hand, her family was already in Canada, and their participation in the care and support of her two children was paramount. She had worked closely with some of her siblings, and many in the extended Shadd family shared her political and intellectual interests. After the demise of the Mission School in Chatham, she may have lived with her family or on her own farm in Raleigh Township. On the other hand, Shadd Cary was among the black elite whose dreams of financial and political success had been thwarted by racism and segregation in both antebellum America and Canada. She had played an active role in the Civil War, and expected to reap some of the benefits that trickled down to the black populace in the United States.[69]

Shadd Cary's prospects in Canada were dim. The country's schools, which would be her best option for employment, remained racially segregated until well into the 1870s, and government support for black education remained limited. While African Americans were celebrating their liberation in the United States, race relations in Canada worsened. Open manifestations of racism became common in both individual behavior and public culture. "Canadian blacks, once individuals to many whites, now became the stock figures they had been in Southern mythology," noted historian Robin Winks. Shadd Cary must have been disheartened by the loss of many of Canada's influential black activists, as well as the demise of the *Provincial Freeman* and the Mission School.[70]

In 1865, Mary Ann Shadd Cary was not yet ready to relinquish her identity as a Canadian. Two months before Lee's surrender at Appomattox, she was issued a Canadian passport with the following description: height—five feet, six inches; color of hair—black; complexion—mulatto; nose—pug; general appearance—slight figure; age—thirty-five years. She falsified her age—in 1865 she would have been forty-two years old— perhaps out of vanity, or out of a desire to erase the years in Canada that had taken such a toll on her life. But at least for a while, she clung to the quasi-freedom and security that Canada had provided her for almost fifteen years.[71]

SEVEN

Reconstructing a Life—
Reconstructing a People

Mary Ann Shadd Cary emerged from the Civil War years with grand expectations. She was representative of the African Americans who had developed and sharpened their leadership skills and political ideology in the expatriate communities they built across Canada West. Mary Ann had arrived in Toronto fifteen years earlier as an angry and exuberant foe of slavery and champion of black emigration. By the late 1860s, she was a seasoned activist who bore the scars from the personal and political battles of that era. Now that emancipation was a reality, it was time to discover the meanings and implications of the antislavery struggle she helped wage from Canada. Mary Ann viewed this period of rapid advances for black rights as the culmination of her years of labor and self-sacrifice as an abolitionist, journalist, educator, and Civil War recruiter. Mary Ann, her brothers Isaac and Abraham, and Martin Delany were among those who were determined to participate in, and benefit from, the changes in America's racial order that were wrought by Reconstruction. They would all pursue new careers with varying success—Mary Ann seeking to become the first black woman lawyer in the land.

Mary Ann cautiously evaluated the events of early Reconstruction by reading newspapers and hearing accounts from her friends in the States. It would take two years before she was convinced that black Americans' political status had improved significantly. Abolitionists and Radical Republicans agitated for black suffrage, but the deeds of President Andrew Johnson lagged far behind their expectations. Johnson feared that to impose black suffrage on the South would create a "war of races," and he angered Radicals with his interest in the rehabilitation of the Confederates. The President, who was to preside over African Americans' enfranchisement, revealed deep-seated racism and a belief that blacks lacked the capacity for full citizenship. By 1866 some abolitionists were calling for the President's impeachment, after he moved to pardon the Confederates. But beginning in July 1866 each state began voting on the 14th Amendment, and despite wholesale opposition in the South, the measure was ratified in 1868. Finally, black Americans were guaranteed citizenship by national law.[1]

The passage of the 14th Amendment represented to many African Americans a legal commitment to Reconstruction policies, and a step toward redressing their history of discrimination and subjugation. This inspired Mary Ann to make the break with her Canadian past, an inevitable move if she was going to be a true participant in this era of reform. For her this was a period of transition and reinvention—one in which she had to renounce her claim on the Canadian utopia she fought so hard to establish, and revert to an identity as an American citizen that she had at one time rejected. She was an abolitionist in a world that no longer needed abolitionists; an emigrationist for a people who no longer sought a new homeland. But her abilities as an organizer, educator, and journalist made her valuable to African Americans in the midst of Reconstruction, and the changes in the States held out promise for her own advancement.

Shadd Cary found it difficult to leave her family and friends because they provided solace and support for herself and her children. Her parents and many of her younger siblings were content to continue running the family farm in Raleigh Township and enjoy the extended community they established through hard work and marriage. But Mary Ann was too restless to watch the developments in Reconstruction America from a distance, and her options for employment in Canada West were dismal. Many of black Canadians' vital institutions—churches, schools, and benevolent societies—were shrinking or disappearing. Blacks in Canada were, according to Winks, "sliding down an inclined plane from mere neglect to active dislike." Whites in Canada West generally viewed Reconstruction with skepticism and racial animosity, and doubted the freedmen's ability to function as citizens.[2]

Black emigrationists made a deliberate shift toward the United States that underscored the lessening importance of the emigrationist/nationalist ideology that had so dominated their political consciousness. The spark of emigration did not die out entirely during the postwar years. By 1868 Martin Delany was already convinced that Reconstruction was faltering, and he began promoting expeditions to Africa sponsored by the American Colonization Society. Until his death in 1885, Delany clung to his nationalist dreams of resettlement in Africa, despite his years of working for the Freedman's Bureau, and as a public official in South Carolina. Mary Ann professed little interest in emigration during the final decades of her life. Instead, she threw in her lot among the faithful and the hopeful who lived on American soil. Her first step was to relocate just a few miles away in Detroit. We will never know the exact date of her move, but her Canadian passport enabled her to cross the border freely and she had many friends and contacts in the city, so she likely traveled back and forth until settling in Detroit sometime in 1867.[3]

Detroit, like other northern U.S. cities, appeared to be a new promised land in comparison to the simmering racial animosities in Canada. Michigan was solidly Republican, and in 1867 the state legislature outlawed school segregation, barred discrimination in public accommodations, and took the first steps toward black suffrage. Since the early 1860s, blacks could vote in school meetings, public school education was free of cost, and public funds were ostensibly spent equally on black and white children. It seemed that Detroit offered all that Shadd Cary had hoped for when she first arrived on Canadian soil more than fifteen years earlier.[4]

Shadd Cary's move to Detroit was inspired by economic as well as political opportunity. In the postwar years, the city's proximity to the Great Lakes and railroads aided its development as a commercial and manufacturing center. There was growth in the lumber and mining industries, and factories rapidly appeared on the city's landscape. The resulting jobs attracted a sizable black influx, including numerous Canadians who eventually made up fifteen percent of the city's black population. While many former slaves and freedmen from Canada West migrated to southern states, to their former homes and families, others sought their fortunes in Detroit, which boasted the largest proportion of blacks in the Great Lakes area. In the 1860s, the number of African Americans living in Detroit increased by fifty percent.[5]

When Shadd Cary returned to the United States, she banked on her oldest and most employable skill—teaching. In the summer of 1868, Mary Ann was awarded a teacher's certificate from the Detroit Board of Education that certified her ability to teach reading, writing, arithmetic, geography, and English grammar in city schools. This signaled the possibility for guaranteed employment as a teacher once the school term commenced in the fall. At the age of forty-five, Shadd Cary could look forward to life without begging and scraping for funds to support her private ventures, whether they were her newspaper or schools. Education was the cornerstone of Reconstruction activities; newly freed and enfranchised black Americans had to be prepared for their role as citizens, and education was essential to the rebuilding of the nation's economy and political structure. Blacks who had been free before the war, as well as white abolitionists, were in the forefront of Reconstruction education efforts. In the South, the Freedman's Bureau, the American Missionary Association, and other freedmen's aid organizations made it a priority to provide at least rudimentary schooling for the ninety percent of the region's blacks who were illiterate. In the North, Reconstruction promised to open the school doors for thousands of African Americans who had been crowded into impoverished segregated schools, or had been socially, financially, and legally prevented from obtaining an education. Mary Ann had left the States in 1851, when the conditions in New York City's colored schools were intolerable; she returned with the expectation that educational reform was underway.[6]

Legislative change in northern cities occurred rapidly because of Republican political clout. But social stratification and racial segregation generally remained intact. Since the beginning of the decade, most of Detroit's black population lived in a small enclave on the near east side, intermixed with poor and working-class whites. Mary Ann and her children lived among the majority of Detroit's black residents on Woodbridge Street. Blacks were not a dominant presence in the city, comprising only about three percent of the overall population. Nevertheless, in 1863 Detroit exploded in a violent racial clash between blacks and mainly Irish immigrants who resented black labor competition. The riot resulted in the death of two blacks, with numerous injuries and the destruction of many black residents' homes. After the Civil War, racial tensions and segregation of the races continued. The Detroit *Free Press* printed regular diatribes against Reconstruction policies that it said encouraged lazy blacks to migrate to northern cities and that promoted equality between the races. The paper was particularly outraged by the state's school desegregation measure.[7]

Not surprisingly, Mary Ann Shadd Cary continued her penchant for activism by becoming involved in local politics. She formed friendships with influential figures, including two white Republican leaders, D. Bethune Duffield and William A. Howard. She knew Duffield well enough to entrust him with the management of her property, and she sought his help in borrowing money after she left Detroit. Both Duffield and Howard wrote glowing job references for Shadd Cary several years later. She also had friends and associates among Detroit's black elite: a small clique of old families who often lived outside the black enclave, attended white churches, formed exclusive social clubs, and gained public office. As a teacher, journalist, and well-known activist, Shadd Cary was a rarity in Detroit—only about one percent of the city's black women worked in any profession, with the vast majority engaged in domestic service. Virtually all of the city's black leadership came from the tiny cadre of black professionals and entrepreneurs committed to social reform. Among them was Samuel C. Watson, a successful black physician and pharmacist whom Shadd Cary probably knew when they both lived in Chatham in the 1850s. In 1863 Watson left Canada and moved to Detroit where he opened a pharmacy and joined the legions of Radical Republicans. In late 1869 he was instrumental in nominating Shadd Cary to represent Detroit's black workers at the Colored National Labor Union Convention.[8]

Shadd Cary's high hopes for Reconstruction were not to be realized through opportunity in Detroit's public school system. Despite Michigan's desegregation ruling, the city's schools remained segregated and the white population powerfully resisted any efforts at change. Black children had the option of attending one of two poorly equipped primary schools, and they were barred from attending the sole high school. In 1868–69, when Shadd Cary was certified to teach in the public schools, the options for both black faculty and students were dismal. After two years of protest and agitation by black citizens, the school board grudgingly opened a new segregated black school, but little else changed until the 1870s, by which time Shadd Cary had moved on. Women were also at the lowest rungs of Detroit's school employees, earning a third of a male teacher's salary, restricted to primary schools, and enduring crowded classrooms and poor working conditions. In fact, there is no evidence to suggest that Shadd Cary ever taught in Detroit's schools, although she was certified to do so. She is not listed as a teacher in the city directory nor mentioned in a study of the eleven black female teachers who served in Detroit's schools prior to 1871. There simply may have not been any positions for a new black teacher in the small, segregated school system. Or, Shadd Cary may have taught temporarily, but left Detroit before becoming established in the city. Little else is known about her brief stay in Detroit. She lived there long enough to purchase a house which she kept and rented out after she left the city. But her next, and final, destination—after a lifetime of migration—was Washington, D.C.[9]

Mary Ann arrived in the nation's capital sometime in 1869, and she immediately lent her voice to one of the key issues of the period—the efforts of black labor to gain a foothold in the economy. During her stay in Detroit, she had observed rampant racial segregation in the city's trades and industries. The same factors that induced blacks to migrate to northern cities—the prospect of jobs and economic opportunity—inflamed the fears and prejudices of white workers. Racist politicians predicted a widespread labor crisis in cities like Detroit, and white workers and burgeoning labor unions closed ranks to resist this threat. Thus, black men could only find work as day laborers, dock workers, servants, or waiters. Prevented from joining the white unions that were indifferent to their concerns, Detroit's black workers began to show interest in organizing on their own. The national movement of black workers to form independent associations was initiated by a group of Baltimore ship caulkers who purchased their own shipyard, obtained government contracts, and established a trade union in 1866. Blacks' labor protests spread throughout the South and in northern cities like Philadelphia and New York. When black workers were rebuked by the white-only National Labor Union, Isaac Myers, leader of the Baltimore union, led the call for a black labor convention to meet in Washington, D.C., in 1869.[10]

Black workers across the United States held local meetings and assemblies to nominate their delegates to the national convention. Mary Ann Shadd Cary was selected to represent the state of Michigan by Samuel Watson and her other Detroit associates. She had the political acumen to represent their interests, and she had already relocated to Washington. Although Mary Ann had little direct involvement with unionization, the Colored National Labor Union was a gathering of the nation's most distinguished black leaders, rather than of the black rank-and-file. Thus, she was ideally suited for this role. After the convention, Watson and another of Detroit's prominent black men, George DeBaptiste, held a meeting in a rented hall for forty black local workers to hear the results of the convention. Watson wrote Mary Ann that they were delighted with the convention's activities, and he praised her efficiency as their delegate. When the CNLU met again in 1871, DeBaptiste attended as Detroit's representative, and a resolution encouraged the formation of black labor unions in the state of Michigan. But there were few tangible results for Detroit's black workers from these early labor conventions. Perhaps it provided a psychological lift for the city's black servants and longshoremen to know that they were counted among the growing legions of African Americans who sought to control their labor and livelihood. But Detroit's trades and businesses resisted unionization and it would not be until the early twentieth century that a significant number of the city's black workers were organized.[11]

Mary Ann Shadd Cary was among 214 representatives at the Colored National Labor Union meeting, which began a national campaign to break down the color barriers to employment across the nation. The gathering focused on issues of civil rights and economic progress as well as the formation of cooperative labor organizations. This middle-class emphasis has been attributed to the participation of well-educated black elites like Shadd Cary, who were more removed from the interests of southern tenant farmers or urban stevedores. Mary Ann, one of only a handful of women in attendance, rose to prominence when she was elected to the executive committee—the only woman to hold office in the organization. The convention's delegates enthusiastically endorsed the principles of cooperation between capital and labor, of the necessity of education and training for black Americans, of the right for men and women to have work according to their ability, and of targeting intemperance as the foe of the working class. In these tumultuous times, African Americans clung to the dream of upward mobility; the Colored National Labor Union conference promoted the notion that even the poorest black workers could become capitalists.[12]

Mary Ann Shadd Cary extended this promise to black women when, on the third day of the gathering, she gave a lengthy speech on the rights of women and their role in the black labor movement. The following day she delivered her report as chair of the Committee on Female Suffrage, which underscored "unjust discrimination" against working women, and urged the gathering of African Americans to avoid the "mistakes heretofore made by our white fellow citizens in omitting women as coworkers in such societies." Joining Mary Ann on the committee were prominent white abolitionists Josephine Griffing and Belva Lockwood. The committee's report denounced the ways in which black women's vocations were limited to work as seamstresses, laundresses, teachers, clerks, and domestic servants. The report also heralded the accomplishments of the handful of black women who were attempting careers in the arts, medicine, and government. Black women were called upon to "learn trades, to engage in whatever pursuits women of the most highly favored classes now pursue, and to . . . enlarge their sphere and influence of labor." Mary Ann had a particular self-interest in this agenda as well, since she intended to train as a lawyer. The Colored National Labor Union's inclusion of black women's concerns was shaped by Shadd Cary's exhortations at the conference, as well as the support of women's rights by several male attendees. The work of her committee injected a much stronger position on women than was customary in the era's allwhite, all-male labor federations.[13]

This speech signaled Mary Ann's revived, and more visible commitment to, women's rights. Her address to the CNLU, with its frequent references to the progress of "women of the favored classes," indicates she was profoundly influenced by the activities of the white women's equal rights movement, which was building momentum in the postwar era. Throughout the later years of her life she would labor for black women's inclusion in African Americans' political agenda. Her battles for legitimacy within the male-centered networks of antebellum reformers and journalists had taught her that politics based purely on race or on gender could not serve the interests of black women. By raising the specter of black women's rights and progress at this forum, she refused to be complicit with the marginalization of black women in Reconstruction ideology. Mary Ann Shadd Cary had no intention of taking a back seat in these debates.

Mary Ann's comments at the CNLU also underscored her educational philosophy, which linked formalized learning to the acquisition of skills. During the years in Canada, she maintained that blacks' collective actions were necessary for the development of employment opportunities and vocational training. Three years after the labor convention, she pursued this issue in the pages of Washington's black newspaper, the *New National Era*. She complained that the "indifference on the part of leading colored men, and the death-like silence of colored women," as well as racial discrimination, had contributed to a scarcity of jobs for blacks.

In the first of her series of articles, Shadd Cary revealed the personal nature of her concern: that as the mother of a son, Linton, who was entering his teens, there were literally no opportunities for him to learn or practice a trade or profession. She argued that despite the political advances of Reconstruction—particularly the election of black men to public office—the black community had ignored the necessity of establishing a foundation for social and economic progress. While immigrants were gaining a foothold in the factories, she lamented, African Americans were still relegated to the most menial labor. She called on the black elite, including women, to forge a labor movement that would address this need. Not surprisingly, Shadd Cary easily adapted the self-help ideology she preached among Canada's black fugitives to address the economic problems of twenty years later. In a subsequent article, she proposed specific action that promoted self-help and community consciousness: black businesses should demand patronage from shops where they spent money; blacks should hire and patronize their own over white tradesmen and merchants; black politicians should be lobbied to serve their constituencies. Shadd Cary's direct involvement in the black labor movement waned after the 1869 convention; she did not play a role in subsequent conventions and only served on the executive committee for one year. But she would retain a lifelong interest in the issues confronting black workers.[14]

Shadd Cary was determined to promote the interests of black women in the course of her work for racial progress. And she was equally determined to reap the benefits of Reconstruction that were slowly trickling down to black citizens. If Detroit offered a modicum of improvement over the deteriorating race relations in Canada West, Washington, D.C., extended to African Americans the possibility of real headway in the political and economic spheres. Mary Ann was not in Washington simply to attend the CNLU convention. She had arrived in the city as early as September 1869 to begin a new life. She found employment as a teacher in the city's growing school system for blacks, and hoped to be among those African American women she encouraged to move beyond conventional boundaries to attain success in a high-status profession. The nation's capital was the logical place for her to carry out these aspirations.

Washington was the true hotbed of Reconstruction activity. The sixty-nine-square-mile federal District of Columbia was governed by a mayor, a board of aldermen, and a common council. But as the nation's capital, Congress had legislative power over the district. This enabled Radical Republicans to create laws that would serve as a model for the reconstructed South. By the time Mary Ann Shadd Cary moved to the city at the end of the 1860s, sweeping legislative changes had been initiated that would later be applied to the rest of the country. Black male suffrage became law in the city in 1867—two years before the introduction of the 15th Amendment—leading to significant black participation in local politics. Black Americans used public places of entertainment without threat of discrimination, black men served on juries, and Congress erased the word "white" in the city's charters and laws, all within two years. A handful of ambitious and educated African Americans started their own businesses and obtained appointments in the federal government as the legal restraints to black progress were eliminated. Some bought their own homes, placed their savings in the Freedmen's Savings and Trust Company, and took advantage of the opportunities for a university education provided by the newly established Howard University. All of these developments were enticements to blacks like Shadd Cary, who sought a tangible transformation of antebellum society.[15]

Washington was also a magnet for ex-slaves fleeing the southern states, who believed "that since the capital was the seat of the emancipation, it was likewise a haven for the freedmen." This contributed to a rapid growth in the city's black population, which jumped from 60,000 to 100,000 during the 1860s. While blacks in Detroit and most northern cities were a tiny proportion of the whole, in Washington they became a visible and increasingly powerful influence. But just like the fugitives from slavery who congregated in the towns of Canada West, the freedmen who thronged to Washington relied heavily on housing, food, and other relief provided by the Freedmen's Bureau and private philanthropy. Many of the ex-slaves lived in squalid conditions on the streets and in shanty towns, but were reluctant to leave the city because of the protection afforded by Congress and the Freedmen's Bureau. During the early years of Reconstruction, Washington's black community became strikingly stratified—on the one end desperately poor and on the other end increasingly prosperous and elite.[16]

Washington, D.C., was the "Capital of the Colored Aristocracy" throughout the nineteenth century, and this distinction crystallized during Reconstruction. This group was comprised of about a hundred "old" families, generally well-educated, economically secure, fair-skinned, and politically influential within their own circles. The city's black gentry, particularly those of the former free black community, isolated themselves socially from the freedmen and preferred to send their children to private schools. As an elite segment of an aggrieved community, their relationship to the masses of blacks was contradictory; at the same time that many of the District's "upper tens" labored for civil rights and racial equality, they also avoided contact with the less fortunate. Their fragile status was as dependent on the largesse and good will of whites as it was on their own skills and courage. Yet many held out hope of one day being assimilated into white society.[17]

Mary Ann's extended family had roots among the city's black elite, a fact that may have aided in her settlement there. Her uncle, Absolom Shadd, had opened a hotel and restaurant in Washington in the late 1830s, placing the Shadds among the city's older established free black families, just as they had been in Delaware. Absolom sold his business for $25,000 in the 1850s and joined his brother, Abraham D. Shadd—Mary Ann's father—in Canada West, where he bought a farm. But the next generation was not content to remain in Canada during Reconstruction. Absolom's son, Furman J. Shadd, returned to Washington to attend Howard University at about the same time as his cousin Mary Ann, who may have served as his chaperone during his teen years. A young man of only 16 when he first arrived in the city, Furman Shadd eventually earned a medical degree, married, and later was counted among Washington's most distinguished black leaders.[18]

A more distant but perhaps more useful Washington connection was provided by her brother-in-law, Isaac N. Cary. In the 1830s and 1840s Isaac, her husband Thomas's brother, owned a barbershop in Washington and was party to a legal dispute in which the city tried to restrict him from selling perfume. Isaac Cary emigrated to Canada West, married the former Mary Bibb, and during Reconstruction settled in Brooklyn, New York. But he visited Washington frequently during the 1870s, and lived there in the early 1880s when he was appointed a Deputy United States Marshal. Thus the Shadds and the Carys were no strangers to the nation's capital.[19]

Once Mary Ann was settled in Washington, she encouraged members of the Shadd clan to join her in this city of promise. Her younger brother, Abraham W. Shadd, moved to Washington in 1870 following his service in the Union Army. About a year later, they were followed by niece Mattie Shadd, age 21, who participated in literary organizations and sought work as a teacher. At the same time their sister Eunice P. Shadd, age 29, left Canada West to join their extended household. Eunice also worked as a teacher, sold subscriptions for the *New National Era,* and became a fixture in Washington's black community. Mary Ann's children, Sarah and Linton, who would have been 13 and 9 in 1870, were presumably living with their mother, although her friend William Still inquired about their whereabouts, saying "I hope they are a comfort to you." The assorted family members undoubtedly contributed to the children's care. Another comfort was the 1873 arrival of one of her closest siblings, Amelia Shadd Williamson, who had helped with the operations of the *Provincial Freeman* and in whose Canada West home Mary Ann and Thomas Cary were married. Amelia's husband, David T. Williamson, opened a jewelry store and they settled into life in the United States. The Shadds, with Mary Ann as family matriarch, became an established entity in Washington. During the early 1870s, she lived a rather unsettled life, changing residences almost every year, and struggling to hold on to her meager resources. Nevertheless her home was always open to her extended family, and she helped to launch many into successful careers. By the end of the nineteenth century, the Shadd name would be on any short list of the city's most influential black residents.[20]

Shadd Cary's move was part of a convergence of black activists, emigrationists, religious leaders, and distinguished scholars into the nation's capital. Many were her old friends and compatriots from the busy struggles of the antebellum years. Among them was John Sella Martin, befriended by Mary Ann in 1856 when both were traveling across the Midwest to campaign against slavery. He aided her in public meetings in Chicago and became an agent for the *Provincial Freeman.* By 1868 he was the pastor of a church in the District, and he became publisher and editor of the *New Era* (later the *New National Era*), a newspaper endorsed by the CNLU that would serve as the voice of the African American community. Others in Washington's network of black activists included George Vashon, John Mercer Langston, Henry Highland Garnet, and Frederick Douglass, who bought a half-interest in the *New Era* in 1870 and was permanently settled in the city by 1872.[21]

Mary Ann arrived in Washington during the tail end of the city's "philanthropic period" of black education. The years 1861–72 marked a transformation from a loose network of private and sabbath schools to a publicly funded and operated system. Unlike Detroit, where there were scant educational opportunities for blacks before the Civil War and strong resistance during Reconstruction, black education in Washington had been a fact of life throughout the century. Between 1807 and 1861, more than sixty black schools had been established in the district. Most were small private institutions which offered a primary education for the few pupils who could pay tuition—ranging from five cents to one dollar per month—or a handful of free parochial schools.[22]

The flood of freedmen into the District during the Civil War prompted benevolent societies to respond with relief services, including education. The American Missionary Association was one of the first philanthropic societies to promote black public education in Washington. Beginning in 1862, the AMA sent teachers to the capital, which was considered to be a showcase for impressing federal officials. They were quickly followed by a wide array of evangelical and secular organizations—by one count 26—which established free schooling for the city's black masses. The first black public school opened in 1864, and in that same year Congress passed a law requiring the city to fund the black schools in proportion to the number of black school-age children in the population. The district government was ordered to pay an equal amount to black schools and white schools from funds gathered through collection of debts. In 1865, the Freedmen's Bureau reported that there were 45 schools in the district handling more than 5,000 students, operated by the American Tract Society, the American Missionary Association, the National Freedmen's Relief Association, and other organizations. The Freedmen's Bureau role was to "systematize, facilitate, and supplement" the schools of the benevolent societies until these functions could be taken over by local government. The Bureau also paid for rent or construction of school buildings, and for furniture and supplies.[23]

But by the end of the 1860s, when Mary Ann Shadd Cary joined the district's school system, educational funding from freedmen's aid societies was drying up and the Freemen's Bureau had exhausted its school funds. The AMA gradually closed its schools in the District of Columbia once government resources were mandated for the purpose, although they continued to contribute some resources to schools in the early 1870s. The district's Board of Trustees of Colored Schools took over administration of the schools while grappling to meet the increasing need. In 1870 it served about 3,000 black students in 66 schools across the district, but two times as many black children lacked an access to education. Funds were necessary to replace the inadequate military barracks where many of the schools were located, and the Trustees complained that "while a portion [of the school buildings] are tolerable . . . there is not one that, in respect to convenience, healthfulness, or general adaptation . . . is worthy of the present time, or creditable to the capital of an enlightened nation."[24]

Mary Ann was first appointed as a teacher in Washington's black schools on September 1, 1869. Her twenty-year relationship with the American Missionary Association may have aided her in securing the job. The Trustees of the Colored Schools were committed to hiring educat-

Reconstructing a Life—Reconstructing a People

The Lincoln School, Washington, D.C., where Mary Ann
Shadd Cary served as teacher and principal from 1869 to
1871, from *The History of Public Schools in Washington, D.C.*
(District of Columbia Public Library)

ed and qualified teachers regardless of their race, and all applicants had to
take a "rigid examination" before appointment. They must have been delighted to have an experienced and well-known educator in their midst,
as many teachers had only rudimentary training. Within two years Shadd
Cary had been appointed principal of the Lincoln Mission School in the
Third District, where she both taught students and supervised the staff.[25]

The Lincoln Mission School had been established by the American Missionary Association in 1867 as an industrial school, and in 1869 it
was a thriving night school for adults. Shadd Cary's salary was reported
at $800 a year, making her the highest paid teacher in the Third District
and among the highest paid in the city's system. The Lincoln school was
also in one of the system's better facilities—a new brick building on
the corner of Second and C Streets, S.E. She had finally attained a level
of success and financial security that had been out of reach during the
years of teaching in wretched antebellum schools in the North and in
the crude missions of Canada West. And she was among the fortunate
3 percent of the city's blacks (or 6 percent of mulattos) who found employment in lower-level professional occupations.[26]

All of Mary Ann's skills as an educator, administrator, and community leader were required for her role as a principal in Washington's Reconstruction-era schools. Between February and June of 1871 she supervised twenty-five teachers and assistants at the Lincoln school, which served an average of 150–200 mostly adult students each month. She had to combat chronic absenteeism among a student body preoccupied with providing for their families. Many of the teachers were little more than "young girls not out of their teens," who desperately needed training themselves. The students in Shadd Cary's school received instruction in reading, geography, arithmetic, grammar, writing, and sewing. This was a first line of defense against the poverty and inequality that confronted most of the city's black residents. The basic curriculum equipped the students to function, if only marginally, in a rapidly changing society. Only a small portion of the graduates might move on to a high school or normal school education. Some of the students belied the myth that the black population was wholly comprised of illiterate former slaves. In her monthly reports to the Freedmen's Bureau, Mary Ann noted that as many as half of the pupils had a rudimentary grasp of reading and spelling, and that nearly 20 percent of them had been free before the war. This school was in the trenches of the freedmen's education battle. Because of the efforts of northern-born black educators like Mary Ann, education was, in the words of W. E. B. Du Bois, the "crowning accomplishment of the era."[27]

The Lincoln Mission School's aims reflected Mary Ann's experiences teaching in antebellum northern cities and in Canada West and her interest in preparing African Americans for a trade or profession to help them escape the ranks of the highly exploited unskilled workforce. At the same time, Shadd Cary believed that the acquisition of knowledge and the ability to converse in the discourse of Western ideas was vital to black advancement. Mary Ann fervently believed in the ability of African Americans to transcend the disabilities of slavery and deprivation to become participants in the worlds of commerce, government, and the professions. Across the country, the freedmen's schools were demonstrating black Americans' hunger for learning and their capacity for intellectual progress, proving the correctness of Reconstruction policies. "These children must be educated or the country can scarcely stand. How can you build the house of which you have never laid the foundation?" asked the nation's first Commissioner of Education, Henry Barnard.[28]

The progress of the district's black schools was tempered by the realities of segregation and white resistance, however. Throughout Mary Ann's career as a teacher, she had labored in separate and unequal facilities that demonstrated the resolve of whites to prevent race mixing.

These sentiments prevailed and worsened as the black population grew in Washington, despite the support of Congress' Republican leadership. The city council was reluctant to follow the Congressional mandate to adequately fund the city schools, so that teachers' salaries were frequently paid late. This also delayed construction of new schools, which led to severe overcrowding. Many whites in the District blocked the construction of black schools in their neighborhoods, vehemently opposed integrated schools, and thwarted the Trustees' efforts to collect the funding promised by law. In 1871, the Trustees bemoaned the unfairness of segregated schools and recommended legislation to abolish the practice, arguing that the policy "tends to perpetuate a cruel, unreasonable, and unchristian prejudice, which has been and is the source of untold wrong and injustice." By 1871, the hesitant support for black schools was a source of anger and political friction within Washington's black communities. The *New National Era* declared that the efforts to withhold funding for black education were "born of a desire to cripple those schools, and also to pander to the prejudices of the old citizens and pro-slavery class" in the city.[29]

Mary Ann found herself in the center of a controversy which symbolized African Americans' uphill struggle to implement and benefit from the legislative accomplishments of Radical Republicanism. Nevertheless, the city's black schools were her best option for employment, and she continued working in the segregated school system for more than a decade. In 1872–73 she was appointed principal of the Second District Grammar School in the John F. Cook Building on O Street, N.W., in an older building that had been erected in 1867 by the Freedmen's Bureau. She remained in this position for at least three years, and perhaps longer. During this period she supervised from 5 to 13 other teachers in a regular day school in the 12-room schoolhouse. The next year she received a raise that brought her salary to $850 annually.[30]

Mary Ann's position as a principal also afforded her some public visibility and a voice through which she could advance a variety of causes. She benefited greatly from the positive attention she received in the pages of the *New National Era,* which was under the control of her old nemesis Frederick Douglass. Time had erased the contentious battles the two had fought over emigration, and each expressed mutual respect for the other. Douglass was deeply committed to preserving the memory of the abolitionist struggle, the Union victory, and emancipation, and Shadd Cary was representative of the accomplishments and potential of the race. He used the paper's editorial page to educate readers about Shadd Cary's contributions as a pioneering abolitionist, journalist, and educator who "vindicated the mental dignity and capacity of colored women." At the opening of the 1871 school term the newspaper

Mary Ann was appointed principal of the John F. Cook School,
Washington, D.C., in 1872. From *The History of Public Schools in
Washington, D.C.* (District of Columbia Public Library)

described her as presiding over a "new school-house on Capital Hill"
for 500 students who faced the daunting task of dispelling the myths of
"negro-haters" that black children lacked the capacity to learn. Shadd
Cary was portrayed as part of the vanguard of the city's black educators.
When complaints about the competency of the black school system's
administration were leveled in the white press, the *Era* cited Shadd
Cary's reputation as "a sufficient guaranty that the results of her prin-
cipalship will be gratifying to all interested in the welfare of the race."[31]

The exchange of praise between Douglass and Shadd Cary was beneficial to each. In the summers of 1871 and 1872 Mary Ann resurrected
her skills as a fund raiser to tour the countryside on behalf of the *Era*.
As a subscription agent for the paper, Mary Ann could rely on her old
persona as the publisher of the *Provincial Freeman,* and accrue the attention and credit she so actively sought. Douglass was delighted to use
her experience and contacts to extend the circulation of the struggling
newspaper outside the confines of Washington. He instructed her to
reassure other African American editors that he did not intend the *Era*
to be their competitor in local markets, but rather a national publica-

tion. Douglass promoted her excursion with effusive praise, calling her "a pioneer among colored women" who demonstrated "the possibilities of her sex and her class." Shadd Cary, armed with this endorsement, was able to return to the public speaking platform while supplementing her income. She traveled to nearby cities, including Baltimore and her home town of Wilmington, Delaware, to lecture among the freedmen and evaluate their progress firsthand. She also promoted the reelection of President Grant, who was strongly endorsed by the *Era*, in Pennsylvania, Ohio, and Michigan. Douglass viewed Shadd Cary's mission as an embodiment of the black elites' responsibility for their struggling brethren. He wrote her a warm and encouraging letter that urged her to "go to the South, my friend, go with words of cheer—go with words of wisdom to our newly emancipated people and help them in their travels through the wilderness."[32]

In her travels below the Mason-Dixon line Mary Ann found newly enfranchised African Americans who were prospering and seizing opportunities for education and investment. She proudly described the "growth and enterprise at every hand" that she encountered in the city of her birth. "The young men and women are an example," she wrote; "they have stock companies, a Christian association, and an Abraham Literary Society; besides which, the doors are thrown open to the active, sex being no barrier." Yet, she observed that African Americans' every success was threatened by "rabid Democrats, luke-warm Republicans, and timid . . . colored people," as well as the excesses of the "Ku-Klux anti-faith." Obstacles to improving black education were her particular target: "But woe the poor negro! Buy him and sell him in slavery; manage him, educate independence and aspiration out of him in freedom," she complained. In Baltimore she was outraged that northern-educated black teachers were blocked from employment in the public schools while "rebel" teachers easily found employment teaching black children. In Wilmington blacks were denied even modest government funding for their education. The white backlash to blacks' meager gains in the border states was indicative of the fragile status of Reconstruction policies. Mary Ann's assessments underscored her ideology of self-help and black community solidarity. Racial progress required bridging the gaps between freeborn and the freed, between northern and southern, between affluent and poor, and between male and female.[33]

Mary Ann seized every opportunity to preserve her legacy and to remind others of the intense struggle for black freedom that had been waged during her lifetime. This was a common response among black activists of her generation, particularly Frederick Douglass, who was deeply concerned that the nation not lapse into historical amnesia regarding the Civil War. Shadd Cary also sought to promote recognition and remembrance for herself and for the antebellum battles. This was achieved in small measure by the homage paid to her in the abolitionist histories written after the war. By 1871 her old friend and compatriot William Still was busy at work on his documentary project, *The Underground Rail Road.* Still boasted to Shadd Cary that he had more narratives, letters, and facts on the subject than any other veteran of the movement. The 780-page book recounted the stories of slave escapes and rescues, the harboring of fugitives, and the assorted heroic deeds of both slaves and conductors on the railroad. The final chapter celebrated the deeds of a select group of activists, including Frances E. W. Harper.[34]

But Shadd Cary did not appear in Still's book as a heroine of abolition. Instead, he viewed her as an authoritative source when he requested that she provide him with background information on the Christiana uprising in Pennsylvania. This 1851 incident, in which several dozens blacks in the Pennsylvania town confronted a group of southern slave catchers and killed a white man, was important in the annals of resistance to the Fugitive Slave Law. William Parker, a leader of the Christiana rebels, eluded federal officers and fled to Canada West where he apparently met Shadd Cary. "Did you not take down one time the account of the affair from the hero himself?" Still asked her. But Mary Ann never responded to his query; the section on Christiana that finally appeared in the book was taken from another source. It may be that Still was mistaken and Mary Ann did not have the information he sought, or she may have simply decided to save it for her own purposes.[35]

Given her entrepreneurial bent it is not surprising that Mary Ann became a sales agent for *The Underground Rail Road,* which Still published privately. He gave her the exclusive rights to sell the book in the Washington, D.C., area, providing Mary Ann yet another opportunity to earn a few dollars while doing a favor for a friend. Selling the book provided her an opportunity to hold meetings and lectures to commemorate abolitionism. But Mary Ann found the job difficult and unremunerative. While Still commended her for her sales and marketing abilities, she complained that "money is no where in Washington," and that numerous obstacles prevented her enterprise from becoming very lucrative.[36]

William Wells Brown, another abolitionist veteran and writer, was putting together his fourth volume on African American history when he asked Still to write a sketch of Mary Ann Shadd Cary in 1873. Finally, she was to be immortalized among a list of "leading colored men and women." Ironically, the entry on Shadd Cary was intended to be a last-minute replacement for a profile of another woman, Fanny M. Jackson, a principal in Philadelphia. Still asked Mary Ann to furnish him with biographical material that could be used in the piece. Following a frenzied exchange of letters between Brown, Still, and Shadd Cary, the four-paragraph profile was written and rushed to the typesetter in time for publication. In it, Still emphasized her strength, determination, and ability to "mingle much in the society of men," and it is possible that he used her own wording in the description. Shadd Cary was aptly portrayed as a formidable woman who remained active in the "real service for the moral, social, and political elevation of the colored race."[37]

Occasional public recognition—whether from Douglass, Still, or Brown —did not satisfy Mary Ann's desire to control her image and to disseminate her ideas. Her cordial relationship with the *New National Era* soured by late 1873, when she wrote Still that she was not happy with the paper's content and direction. She may have clashed with Douglass's sons Frederick Jr. and Lewis, who took over most of the paper's daily operations that year, and who may not have been as receptive as their father to Shadd Cary's contributions. Perhaps she felt that her efforts to expand the paper's circulation had not been appreciated. The *Era* was in deep financial trouble and it folded in 1874 after the elder Douglass reported that he had lost ten thousand dollars on the venture. So Mary Ann was constantly searching for other outlets for her writing. She missed the stimulation of seeing her words in print, and the sense of power derived from having her ideas read by a large audience. She implored William Still to help her find a "paying place on some newspaper." It was a futile inquiry, however. Still confessed that he had no contacts that would help her find such a position. Mary Ann's expectations of earning a living through journalism always seemed beyond her grasp.[38]

If she could not find employment at a newspaper, perhaps she could join other African American writers like Still, Brown, and Frances E. W. Harper by writing and publishing her own books. But while novelists like Brown and Harper sought to reach a wide audience through fiction, Shadd Cary fashioned herself as a journalist-historian-philosopher who had firsthand experience with her subjects. *The Underground Rail Road* was selling well enough to prompt Still to consider putting out additional books, and he encouraged Mary Ann to compile a "very elaborate" work. But she was already several steps ahead of him. Mary Ann had developed at least two book ideas: a text titled "Modern Civilization—Our Relations and Duty," and another on the life and times of John Brown. She scribbled out sketchy outlines for these projects on a scrap of notebook paper—all that remains of her literary aspirations. The first project was a vague treatise on the failure of racial progress in the New World. She planned to expound on "the dominating tendency of the Saxons," which, in her view was "inconsistent with religion and reason."[39]

Mary Ann envisioned the John Brown book as an account of the

Chatham convention where the Harpers Ferry raid was planned, and an analysis of his contribution to the national struggle for human rights. The topics were to include: "His acts in their relation to us of today," and "Lessons of endurance, of charity, of humanity, of zeal in a good cause." The proposal also elucidated Shadd Cary's commitment to the memory of abolitionism as an embodiment of democratic ideals and social reform. Her interest in celebrating the victories of abolition overshadowed lingering resentments with the movement's gender discrimination and factionalism. "The antislavery work invited all ages and sexes," was to be the subject of the book's final section. This act of recovering the legacy of John Brown was directly linked to Mary Ann's efforts to have an imprint on the history of abolitionism. She had been an observer, a participant, and a leader of this crusade, and considered herself a legitimate standard-bearer of the era.[40]

The proposed books never found their way into print. Mary Ann completed at least one manuscript during the early 1870s; it could have been from among the ideas outlined. She submitted the book to Harper and Brothers, based in New York City, signing her correspondence M. A. S. Cary, Esq. to hide her gender, just as she had done fifteen years earlier in the *Provincial Freeman*. In the fall of 1874, the manuscript was rejected and returned to her with a letter addressed to "Dear Sir." The subterfuge had been successful, but not her attempt to secure a publisher, which was undoubtedly a source of great frustration. There is no evidence that she and William Still ever pursued the idea of publishing her book. If she tried again in later life to produce her own book, the results were the same. Thus, Mary Ann Shadd Cary was forever limited in her ability to preserve her historical memory. Nor was she able to effectively rescript the past. She had hoped to construct a narrative to serve as a lesson for future generations of African Americans on the efficacy of collective action and organized resistance. But this dream was never realized.[41]

Mary Ann was clearly troubled by what she perceived to be African Americans' inattention to the famous people and events of the antebellum struggles. An example was the neglect of Osborne Perry Anderson, the only black survivor of the Harpers Ferry raid, who died alone and a pauper. Anderson, her friend and compatriot from Canada West, lay "dangerously ill" somewhere in Washington, in June 1862, reported the *New National Era*. Six months later he was dead. At a civil rights gathering held a week later, Mary Ann was among a group of local blacks who called for "the rights due American citizens." At the end of the meeting she spoke to the crowd about Anderson's importance and took up a collection to pay for his funeral. She must have been saddened and outraged over the disregard for Anderson as a community

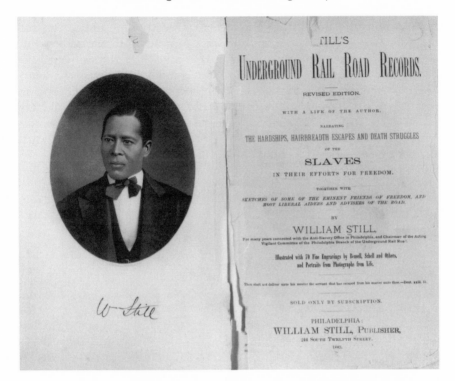

William Still, frontispiece to *The Underground Rail Road*
(Philadelphia, 1883).

hero. Despite her efforts, his body languished in a vault for months
awaiting burial because of insufficient funds.[42]

Mary Ann Shadd Cary's return to the United States was symptomatic
of African Americans' yearnings for redress and remembrance during Reconstruction. She clearly expected that the legislative victories of
the late 1860s would lead to more and better jobs, housing, land, and
business opportunities for blacks, and access to the political sphere. Black
elites such as herself would pave the way and serve as examples for
the masses of freedmen. The government would make reparations, and
African Americans, unfettered by chattel slavery and legally sanctioned
discrimination, would quickly demonstrate their capacity for advancement. The memories of the Civil War would remain ever-present in the
national consciousness, serving as a caution against a return to the old
racial order.

But the granting of individual rights in the 13th, 14th, and 15th

Amendments did not redress the legacy of subjugation and racism suffered by African Americans, and did little to stifle white backlash. While Mary Ann obtained reliable employment as a teacher, and witnessed the progress of her race on many fronts, each symbol of progress was tempered by her knowledge of the fragility of blacks' hard-won freedoms. To revel in past victories and remain fixed in an old identity would not promote the forward movement she expected of herself and her people, and contradicted her spirit of adventure. So, true to her life's pattern, while she became ensconced within Washington's black establishment, she was also forging ahead with new professional and political ambitions.

EIGHT

Law and Reform in the Nation's Capital

Mary Ann Shadd Cary's life did not proceed in a linear fashion during and after the Reconstruction years. She was part of a whirlwind of activity that concentrated on freedmen's education, public speaking and writing, and the pursuit of a career in law. Mary Ann believed that as an attorney she could have a direct impact on the political issues closest to her heart—women's suffrage, blacks' equal access to education and employment, and the elimination of legally sanctioned discrimination. This was an understandable step for someone who considered herself a race woman, and who was dissatisfied by the limitations she encountered in her work as a journalist and educator. Her dream was made possible by the establishment of Howard University, and the creation of the university's law school, which pledged to admit students regardless of sex or color. Congress authorized the incorporation of Howard University in the spring of 1867 as the first higher education institution below the Mason-Dixon line with a biracial faculty and student body.

Howard Law School began instruction in January 1869, and by the end of the first term in June there were 21 students in the class. Because there were no entrance requirements for applicants to the school, this first session was devoted to remedial instruction to prepare the students for the law curriculum. Mary Ann Shadd Cary joined the first bona fide law class in September 1869 and was one of 46 hopeful lawyers who began the rigorous two-year program. One of her classmates was her brother Abraham W. Shadd, her junior by 20 years. By all accounts, she was the first African American woman to gain admission to a law school, and one of the first American women of any race to embark on this professional goal. Mary Ann was fully intent on blazing a trail for women in the law, just as she had "broken the editorial ice" for black women as a newspaper editor and publisher. This was yet another example of the intersections between her personal life and her political rhetoric. At the same moment that she called upon the Colored Naional Labor Union to support black women's ascent into the professions, she was actively moving in that direction.[1]

Mary Ann kept up a demanding pace. She continued her work as a teacher and principal during the day and attended law classes each evening from five to nine P.M. Most students at the law school worked as clerks and messengers in federal agencies, or, like Shadd Cary, in the freedmen's schools, to pay for their tuition and living expenses. Indeed, the federal government subsidized the school through direct grants and by employing large numbers of Howard Law School's students. The university also provided housing to students, including Mary Ann, who reported living on campus from 1870 to 1873. In addition to studying classic legal texts like Blackstone's *Commentaries,* Mary Ann and her classmates met on Thursday evenings for instruction in debating, public speaking and the writing of legal essays. Attendance at Sunday Bible study classes was expected, as well. Somehow, in the midst of all of this activity, she also had to care for her two children and manage her financial affairs.[2]

At the end of each school term the faculty of Howard University sponsored public presentations and oral examinations to demonstrate their students' progress and expertise. In early July 1870 the law students performed before a large gathering, and the *New National Era* praised them for "exhibiting the most satisfactory progress during the past year, and ability of a high order." Among the speakers was Mary Ann Shadd Cary, whose home state was listed as Michigan. A local reporter commented on her presence as the only woman in the group, and proclaimed the event proof of "the capacity of the freed people for all the duties of the highest citizenship." The writer singled out Mary Ann's thesis on corporations as "not copied from the books but from her brain, a clear, incisive analysis of one of the most delicate legal questions." Some historians have mistakenly attributed this description to Charlotte Ray, who began attending Howard Law School the next year. But in 1870 there was only one female law student—Shadd Cary—and her paper, titled "The Origin and Necessity of Corporations," can be found among her surviving papers. The thesis, which marked her debut as a legal scholar, was a lengthy discussion of the history, development, and role of corporations in modern society. "Among the provisions of the Law designed to further the welfare of man, in establishing and maintaining enterprises of national and individual interest, none are of greater importance than those which respect corporations," she wrote. Mary Ann demonstrated her ability to absorb and analyze her course work effectively, quoting Blackstone and other legal scholars. By all appearances, she was on her way to successfully completing her law degree.[3]

But somehow, the plan went awry. Eight months later, on February 3, 1871, the first commencement of the law school was held at the First Congregational Church of Washington. Visibly absent from the list of graduates was Mary Ann Shadd Cary. Among the ten graduates of Howard University Law school was her brother Abraham, who gave a presentation titled "Popular Prejudices" as part of the graduation exercises. Mary Ann did not attend the ceremonies, and her brother sent her a copy of the program with a cheery note: "Dear Sis, I may be down your way ere long. I was admitted to the bar on Saturday—4th and now am *attorney at-law."* Shortly after his graduation, Abraham Shadd moved South and simultaneously gained admission to the bars in Arkansas and Mississippi. He established a law practice in Washington County, Mississippi, where he was able to take advantage of blacks' growing political strength in the state. He was appointed clerk of the county court, and eventually ran for office in the Mississippi Legislature. But the future did not promise such an illustrious career for his determined sister. When the Trustees of Howard University shifted the schedule for the law school, another small group of students were allowed to graduate that summer, in July 1871. Again, Mary Ann Shadd Cary was not among them.[4]

Shadd Cary's initial failure to graduate from Howard University Law School has been the subject of speculation and curiosity. One pair of authors have contended that school officials deliberately prevented her from graduating in 1871 because they were reluctant to put forward a woman for admission to the bar. They have argued that it was impossible to disguise Shadd Cary's gender from the District courts because she was already a well-known figure in the city. Shadd Cary apparently told one of her contemporaries that she was "refused graduation on account of her sex," but gave no details of the events surrounding this decision. It is certainly a plausible explanation. Race and gender discrimination in the legal profession was a fact of life in the nineteenth century. African American men had only recently broken the race barrier in the practice of law. The tiny handful of black male lawyers in the United States in the years preceding and following the Civil War had to confront hostile white lawyers and judges, and reluctant clients, in their efforts to work in their profession. Nevertheless, the founders of Howard University's law school expected that its graduates would be in the vanguard of pressing for civil rights in the courts. "Yourselves must strike the blow, not by violence, but in every mode known to the Constitution and law," Sen. Charles Sumner told that first graduating class.[5]

But the issues preventing women—white or black—from becoming lawyers were even more contentious. Prior to the 1870s, it was both custom and legal precedent to exclude women from serving as attorneys. This was rooted in English common law, which maintained that women were ineligible for admission to the bar. A handful of women had been permitted to practice law in various states but during the Reconstruction era the courts generally banned women from the profession. In the nineteenth-century United States, numerous arguments upheld this position: state statutes governing the bar specified eligibility only for male citizens; menstruation, child-bearing, and child-rearing constituted disabilities that made women unfit for the position; and married women were, by law, unable to enter into contracts or other legal arrangements without their husbands' permission. In 1869 at least seven women in different states, including Mary Ann Shadd Cary, challenged these assumptions by applying for admission to law schools and the bar. Like Shadd Cary, several gained entry to law school although not all were permitted to graduate. In that same year a white woman, Arabella Mansfield, was admitted to the Iowa bar. But other women, including Myra Bradwell in Illinois, had their petitions to the bar rejected. In Bradwell's case, the Illinois Supreme Court ruled that her marital status prevented her from practicing law, and that the state legislature would have to change the legal status of women to enable them to conduct business without their husbands' consent. When the case was appealed to the Supreme Court of the United States, the high court ruled in 1873 that U.S. citizenship did not give one the right to practice law, and that women's role and responsibility should be that of wife and mother. These prohibitions occurred on a state-by-state basis, and as more women graduated from law schools, challenges to these barriers became more numerous. But many women of both races, like Myra Bradwell, were thwarted from making careers as attorneys.[6]

The District of Columbia may have had similar restrictions against women practicing law, but that was changed in 1871 when an order of the Supreme Court of the District of Columbia allowed graduates of Howard to practice in district courts once they earned their diploma and had the recommendation of a lawyer in good standing. This ruling ostensibly overrode any statutory or legislative impediments for women to be admitted to the bar, although it was probably assumed that only men would be taking advantage of this opportunity. It was first tested by Charlotte Ray, who graduated from the Howard University law school in 1872. Ray's father, Charles Ray, was a well-known Congregational minister and abolitionist in New York and was editor of the *Colored American* in the early 1840s. He had known Mary Ann since her days in New York City, and was part of the controversial committee of the American Missionary Association that revoked her teaching position in Windsor. In 1869 Charlotte, then age 19, moved to Washington and began teaching in the normal school at Howard University. She joined the student body of the law school in the fall of 1870, a year after Shadd Cary. In two years Charlotte Ray had successfully completed the course of study and became the first woman to graduate. In February 1872, the *New National Era* proudly announced: "The first colored lady in the world to graduate in law graduated from Howard University," and went on to praise her "bravery and perseverance" in reaching that goal. Some informant, very likely Shadd Cary herself, told a legal magazine that Ray gained admission to the bar only because her name was submitted along with her classmates as C. E. Ray. This is interesting, but if Howard University was attempting to mask Ray's gender from public scrutiny, the strategy had little success because her name and references to her sex appeared in the local press. Nevertheless, Ray was admitted to the district bar on March 6, 1872, with little fanfare, and proceeded with the difficult task of establishing a law practice.[7]

It is certainly possible that in Shadd Cary's case, officials at Howard University feared reprisal for recommending a woman to practice law in the district. The university was under constant scrutiny from Democrats and Southerners in Congress who opposed public funding of the institution, and deemed it a breeding ground of miscegenation. "The very existence of Howard University in the nation's capital was . . . an outrage to the South," noted one historian. As a mother Shadd Cary may have been considered unfit for legal practice, although as a widow she would not face restrictions based on her marital status. Mary Ann— the fighter and activist—was not likely to have accepted this fate quietly. She may have raised such a fuss about gender discrimination that when Ray approached graduation the next year, school officials softened their position. But none of these theories explains why school officials would deliberately contradict one of its founding principles— equal opportunity to higher education regardless of gender or race.[8]

It is also possible that Shadd Cary simply could not complete the demanding two-year program. It is unlikely that she was intellectually incapable of passing her courses and final examinations, given her initial success in the program. Her education and work experience made her better prepared than most to tackle challenging academic work. But age and physical infirmity may also have contributed to her problems. In 1871 Mary Ann was 48 years old, and her difficult life in Canada West and her ceaseless travels were already taking their toll. Just two years later she was incapacitated by a bout with rheumatism which prevented her from traveling to Philadelphia. Her close friend William Still sympathized with her malady, noting that "if I had the means of affording instant relief, you may rest assure I would do so in double quick time." Other life demands may have also forced Shadd Cary to slow down in her pursuit of a law degree, or to quit altogether. In 1871 she was the principal of a night school for freedmen. If she was appointed to this post in the beginning of the 1870–71 school year, it would have been impossible for her to attend night classes in her final term of law school. Mary Ann Shadd Cary—the sole supporter of her children—may have had to choose between losing her source of income or postponing her law career.[9]

In the summer of 1870 Mary Ann tried in vain to secure a daytime civil service job—like those held by her law school classmates—that would enable her to continue her studies. She asked two influential white Michigan Republicans whom she had known in Detroit, attorney D. Bethune Duffield and William A. Howard, to use their influence on her behalf. The two men wrote U.S. senators I. M. Howard and Zachariah Chandler, urging them to hire her for "any position in Government Service to which she may aspire and feel herself qualified to fill." Senator Chandler, a wealthy Michigan merchant, abolitionist, and influential Radical Republican, had been instrumental in aiding Detroit blacks in getting federal jobs. In his letter, Duffield highlighted the public notices about Shadd Cary's presentation on corporations at the Howard Law School exercises, and proclaimed her "a well balanced, well cultivated and soundheaded woman, who would I think make an energetic and reliable person in the service of government." Howard attached a brief note recommending her as "a very respectable and intelligent colored woman" who would be qualified for any clerical position. Despite their efforts, such an opportunity was not offered. Compared to the masses of blacks in Washington who were glad to get jobs as day laborers or domestics, Shadd Cary was fortunate to have the prestige and security of regular employment as a teacher. But she aspired to the office jobs in Congress and assorted federal agencies—the spoils of living in Reconstruction Washington—that were given to a small cadre of educated black men. There was a dramatic increase in the number of federal workers in Washington following the Civil War, and government clerkships were highly coveted positions among whites and blacks. But Mary Ann Shadd Cary was not to share in this seeming prosperity.[10]

Not earning the law degree must have been a source of profound disappointment for Mary Ann. She had to watch as her much younger brother became an attorney, and then a year later, as her classmate Charlotte Ray, barely in her twenties, was heralded as the first woman to graduate from Howard Law School and be accepted to the District of Columbia bar. Unlike many of her white female contemporaries who were struggling to launch careers in the law, Shadd Cary had no husband in the profession to provide connections or financial support that would facilitate her goal. But she did not entirely give up on becoming a lawyer. Months after the first Howard Law School graduation was held, her longtime friend William Still inquired about her progress with "exploring Blackstone and teaching at the same time," which suggests that she may have continued to study law on a part-time basis. But the final interruption likely occurred between 1873 and 1877 when a nationwide economic depression, the closing of the Freedmen's Bureau, and the failure of the Freedmen's Bank where much of Howard's monies were invested, led to a crisis at the University. The law school's dean, John Mercer Langston, resigned and law school classes were disrupted or canceled. The school did not fully recuperate and resume a full-scale program until the end of the 1870s.[11]

Mary Ann did not shrink away in anonymity as her quest for a law degree faltered. In fact, she was so busy with other activities that she may have considered the law school's circumstances only a temporary setback. The fight for women's suffrage became a central activity in her life, and she emerged as an important advocate for African American women. The right to vote was not an end in itself, but would enable women to engage directly in politics. Mary Ann must have watched with a mixture of pride and frustration as the men in her life used their education and experience to establish themselves in the politics of the Reconstruction South. Isaac Shadd joined his younger brother Abraham in Mississippi in 1871, where he was elected to the state House of Representatives and chaired several committees. He served as Speaker of the House in 1874–75, and was described in the *New National Era* as "one of the best prepared members of the House." Martin Delany became an important fixture in South Carolina's Republican Party, holding several minor positions and losing a bid for governor in 1874. Without such opportunities at her disposal, Mary Ann began to apply the rights arguments formulated by white women suffragists to the needs of black women. Shortly after arriving in Washington she began attending women's suffrage meetings and she seized numerous opportunities to rally on behalf of black women's rights.[12]

During the Civil War years, Shadd Cary publicly focused on emigration, abolition, and the war effort, pushing her interest in women's rights to the background. Her silence on gender issues paralleled the stagnation of the women's movement in that period. Women's rights activism evolved through the framework of abolitionism. During the war, antislavery feminists generally subordinated their own interests to the causes of emancipation and a Union Army victory. Once the war was over, white feminists believed they should be included in the quest for suffrage. During Reconstruction the abolitionist-feminist coalition was permanently damaged when the antislavery leadership put their emphasis on passage of the 14th Amendment to the Constitution, which simultaneously granted black male suffrage while denying white women's right to vote. The Republican leadership in Congress made it clear that women's rights would not be part of the Reconstruction agenda. Wendell Phillips typified this position when he said in 1865, "One question at a time. This hour belongs to the negro."[13]

African American women like Sojourner Truth and Frances E. W. Harper were active participants in the formation of postwar suffrage alliances including the American Equal Rights Association. The E.R.A. was organized to promote universal suffrage, but eventually collapsed over the issue of race. Truth garnered the most attention for her impassioned speeches and tireless advocacy for civil rights, yet Painter has reminded us that white activists were particularly enamored by Truth's "exotic character of the slave woman." By contrast, Harper, Shadd Cary and other free-born educated black women were relegated to the periphery of the white women's suffrage movement; often denied membership, seats at conventions, or positions of power and influence within the organizations. In the late 1860s the Equal Rights Association attempted to champion the cause of black women's double disfranchisement, but this strategy languished. Proponents of black male suffrage like Frederick Douglass argued that black women's endangered position in American society was due to their color, not their gender. Hopes for a biracial coalition promoting black and white women's concerns faded and the visibility of black women receded to the background of the movement.[14]

The sharpest blow to white feminists was passage in February 1869 of the 15th Amendment to the Constitution, which forbade racial discrimination in the granting of voting rights. In May of that year, Elizabeth Cady Stanton, Susan B. Anthony, and other ardent feminists left the Equal Rights Association in a move that formally separated them from the abolitionist and radical Republican communities. Their new organization, the National Women's Suffrage Association, devoted its attention to women's rights and spurned any association with the cause of black suffrage. These feminist leaders adopted an increasingly racist tactic to promote their cause as they argued that educated white women were better suited to vote than illiterate black males. This further alienated black women from the women's rights arena. For example, Frances E. W. Harper, an active member of the Equal Rights Association, decried the racist discourse of the suffragists and stated that gender was not necessarily the dominant issue facing black women. She agreed with Frederick Douglass that activists should concentrate their energies on securing passage of the 15th Amendment, and scolded the 1869 annual meeting of the ERA because "the white women go all for sex, letting race occupy a minor position."[15]

Mary Ann Shadd Cary, unlike many of her black feminist counterparts, found the arguments of the NWSA compelling despite their racist overtones, and she was a supporter of the group from its inception. Her speech to the Colored National Labor Union revealed her admiration for white women's progress in the professions and their tenacity in fighting the political establishment. Mary Ann celebrated the accomplishments of women like the British astronomer and mathematician Mary Somerville, whom she held up as the embodiment of achievement against all odds. "The difficulties overcome by [Somerville] in the pursuit of that and other great studies are equal in every respect to any that we're acquainted with among the most celebrated men," she wrote in an unpublished essay. Mary Ann's discourse on rights was firmly rooted in the Enlightenment concepts of equality, individualism, and natural rights. She used elite women's achievements to exemplify the principle that when given equal opportunities, all persons will rise to the extent of their abilities. African Americans and women faced social and cultural impediments to the realization of their natural rights, and their rights were also blocked by decree of the government.[16]

Mary Ann probably attended the National Women's Suffrage Association's annual meetings in Washington at the beginning of the 1870s, but one of her earliest endorsements of the organization appeared in the pages of the *New National Era* in 1874. She described the gathering as "the most harmonious and the most practical in every way of any of the many gatherings ever held here," and used the editorial "they" as she reported on the proceedings rather than including herself as a participant. Shadd Cary heaped praise on the work of Stanton, Anthony, and other leaders at the meeting and proclaimed the District of Columbia to be the center of the feminist movement. "No city in the country possesses more workers in the cause of woman suffrage or any other positive moral need of human society," she wrote. Shadd Cary played the role of interpreter and journalist, explaining the women's suffrage agenda to a black community wounded by the racially inflammatory rhetoric of the feminists. "They want the word male stricken from the organic law," she reported, "because they want woman to have rights and to be enabled to help protect herself throughout the nation." She hoped this was a political agenda which African Americans might identify with and support.[17]

Shadd Cary took pains not to reveal any racial discord within the organization. Her silence may have been uncharacteristic for someone known to be combative and contentious, but it also suggests that in the world of white women activists she was deliberately careful and judicious. She used her involvement in the NWSA to lobby for the inclusion of black women in the suffrage agenda. In January 1874 a group of women petitioned the Judiciary Committee of the House of Representations on behalf of 600 women in the District of Columbia who sought enfranchisement. Mary Ann prepared an address for presentation at the Committee hearing, but it was never recorded in the public transcript. In her speech, Mary Ann gently demanded that the wants and needs of "colored women" be considered in the Congressional debates over civil rights. She was careful not to supersede the prominence of white suffrage leaders as she displayed unusual modesty: "I am not vain enough to suppose, for one moment, that words of mine could add one iota of weight to the arguments of these learned and earnest women," she wrote. Yet, she argued, as a citizen, a resident of the District, a taxpayer, an African American, and a woman, she believed she had a legitimate claim to be heard. Shadd Cary endorsed the position, promoted by Victoria Woodhull and other suffrage leaders, that the 14th and 15th Amendments guaranteed the rights of citizenship and suffrage to all persons born or naturalized in the United States. Black women, she maintained, shared with black men the responsibilities of freedom, and thus had a legitimate claim on the franchise:

> The colored women of this country though heretofore silent, in great measure upon this question of the right to vote . . . have neither been indifferent to their own just claims under the amendments, in common with colored men, nor to the demand for political recognition.

Shadd Cary wanted to put white and black leaders on notice that African American women had a stake in the suffrage movement and would assert their rights at the same time that they worked in other areas of reform.[18]

Despite the opposition of feminists, passage of the 15th Amendment was greeted with jubilation in the city's black wards. Numerous parades, festivals, and meetings were held across the city to celebrate this hard-won victory. The *New National Era*'s front page highlighted President Grant's address to Congress, in which he announced that the amendment "makes at once four million of the people voters who were heretofore declared, by the highest tribunal in the land, not citizens of the United States." Passage of the measure was the culmination of six years of agitation and politicking in the District, beginning with petitions by local blacks seeking voting rights in 1864. Whites consistently opposed any measure allowing black suffrage, voting overwhelmingly against the bill in two public referendums. African American men were immediate and enthusiastic participants in Washington's stormy political scene. They registered to vote in large numbers, becoming the majority of voters in several districts, and they emerged as important players in Washington politics. In 1868 two African Americans won elected office—one to the board of alderman, the other to the common council—and in the following year, blacks won seats on the council representing each of the city's seven wards. Black voters had become a force with whom whites had to reckon.[19]

In the spring of 1871, Mary Ann Shadd Cary sought to merge feminists' quest for citizenship with this growing black political clout when she attempted to register as a voter in the Second district. The opportunity to cast one's ballot was a tantalizing prospect for the newly enfranchised community and it was promoted in the pages of the black press and in black churches, schools and social institutions. Shortly after passage of the 15th Amendment, groups like the National Executive Committee of Colored Men were formed, a constant reminder of black women's increasingly marginal position. On April 14, Shadd Cary arrived at the City Hall where she appeared before a seven-member Board of Registration to present her name and proof of residency. Among the registrars were two black men who probably knew Shadd Cary and her local reputation: John F. Cook, a long-time black educator who was elected alderman in 1869, and John S. Crocker, who was elected alderman in 1870. She demanded that her name be listed as a registered voter, but her arguments did not hold sway and she was summarily refused by the panel. Nevertheless, her symbolic action signaled black women's demands for the vote in the District.[20]

Shadd Cary's registration attempt was part of a burgeoning civil disobedience strategy among women's rights advocates. She was one of sixty-three women in the District who protested their subordinate status by attempting voter registration that year. Following the protest she wrote a report titled "A First Vote Almost," which outlined the movement's ideological framework. Including women in the provisions of the 14th and 15th Amendments was a politically prudent strategy for the Republican Party, which faced increasing opposition from the Democrats. Republicans' refusal to seriously consider women's suffrage capitulated to the Democrats' position that the amendments were invalid. Denying women the vote was, in Mary Ann's view, "a virtual admission of the rebel claim that there is nothing in those amendments by which the people should be bound and is more potent as an element of future success to the democratic party than all else." She articulated feminists' frustration with their failure to gain suffrage, noting that "the refusal [to register] was and is a bitter pill to swallow."[21]

Mary Ann's sarcastic description of the registration attempt placed men in two categories: those who supported women's suffrage, and those at the other extreme, who wallowed in patriarchal righteousness. Among the former group was a man who asked, "Did they not let you register? Very short-sighted policy," and others who stood around the polling places offering words of encouragement. She recalled several such men: "'Let me compliment your bravery,' was said at one precinct with many other pleasant allusions and approbative remarks . . . indications were many strong & favorable that the rank & file are accessible to right and reason," she wrote. Opponents to women's suffrage were in evidence on this day as well. Mary Ann singled out one man who exemplified the unenlightened position: "The big grocer is shocked at the 'brass' of them women who could go through a crowd of men, ought to be 'hoss' whipped, hand cuffing & 'hoss whipping' women having been an old vocation, he sighs for a return of the good old times." Her zeal for the women's rights struggle remained strong despite the government's stubborn refusal to take seriously women's demands for enfranchisement.[22]

A year later, Susan B. Anthony led a group of 14 women who successfully registered to vote in her home town of Rochester, New York. Each cast her ballot as a Republican in the November 1872 elections, and then was arrested under an obscure provision of the 1870 Civil Rights Act. After being released on bail, Anthony seized the opportunity to campaign for women's voting rights as she awaited trail on the charges. In June 1873 Anthony was found guilty; in an especially harsh decision, the U.S. Circuit Court judge ruled that "Miss Anthony knew that she was a woman, and that the constitution of this state prohibits her from voting." She was fined $100 and court costs. The charges against the other women who voted on that day were dropped, Anthony never paid the fine, and the case faded from public view. Mary Ann Shadd Cary must have contemplated filing a lawsuit in her battle for voting rights in the District of Columbia; in 1874 she had a sworn statement notarized charging that she had been wrongfully denied the right to register three years earlier. There is no record that such a case was ever filed.[23]

Shadd Cary witnessed the judicial and legislative setbacks to women's rights which characterized what one historian has called a period of blatant constitutional discrimination. This was an exceedingly disappointing period for feminists; little headway was made in the quest for suffrage in the 1870s and 1880s. Nevertheless, the NWSA maintained a regular schedule of meetings and national conventions that kept up the movement's visibility and provided momentum. Mary Ann Shadd Cary was a persistent, if not always recognized, figure in this world. In 1876, after Anthony and other NWSA members were prevented from participating in the centennial commemoration in Philadelphia, they issued a "Women's Declaration of Rights" that demanded impeachment of all federal officials and full civil and political rights. Shadd Cary wrote to the NWSA on behalf of ninety-four black women in the District, requesting that their names be added to a list of signers to the Declaration at the organization's annual meeting in New York.[24]

When the NWSA met in Lincoln Hall in Washington in January 1877, the organization had shifted its agenda away from voter registration based on provisions in the 14th and 15th Amendments. The new focus was to be on passage of a 16th constitutional amendment that would guarantee women's right to vote. Mary Ann attended the meeting in her home town as a vocal and visible participant among the handful of African American women present. She was appointed to a seven-person business committee which gave her unprecedented, if only brief, influence in the organization. When the suffrage association gathered in Washington again in 1878, Shadd Cary addressed the gathering and declared that "colored women would support whatever party would allow them their rights, be it Republican or Democratic." Some black leaders like Frederick Douglass remained fiercely loyal to the Republicans or had their own fortunes tied to the G.O.P. But Mary Ann was among those black Americans who were abandoning their traditional allegiance to the Republican party as the gains of Reconstruction eroded. In the convention's annals, Mary Ann was heralded as "the first colored woman that ever edited a newspaper in the United States," and as a feminist who had been committed to the cause for twenty years. She could be grateful, at least, that her pioneering legacy had not been forgotten altogether.[25]

The temperance movement provided another outlet through which Mary Ann could deploy her dual interests in feminism and racial progress. The formation of the national Woman's Christian Temperance Union in 1874 signaled the resurgence of a national crusade that combined religious and moral ideology with the quest for women's rights. Late nineteenth century temperance activism reflected the simmering anger and resentment of white women of the middle classes. It provided a platform through which women could critique male behavior while exercising their power over the domestic realm. For Mary Ann, like many of the black elite, the eradication of alcohol was a crucial element in the veneer of respectability they presented to white America. Black American activists—particularly those with an evangelical background —had viewed drinking as an obstacle to racial uplift since the days of the antebellum black conventions. Temperance had been deeply embedded in Mary Ann's political roots from the time of her father Abraham Shadd's involvement in the American Moral Reform Society in the 1830s. Many of her abolitionist colleagues, including Samuel Ringgold Ward and Frederick Douglass, incorporated temperance into their ideology of black self-sufficiency. After the Civil War, temperance, piety, and Victorian morality were part of the cultural code that black educators and missionaries dictated to freedmen in the Reconstruction South. Mary Ann had occasionally targeted intemperance in editorials she wrote for the *Provincial Freeman* and in her abolitionist speeches, but it was not until the 1870s that the issue took on greater importance in her political life.[26]

Mary Ann was a consistent champion of black temperance activities during her years in Washington. In 1873 she upbraided the *New National Era* for failing to write about a local group called the Moral Education Society, whose purpose was to educate black youth in the dangers of alcohol, tobacco, and the use of profanity. This organization may have been an early attempt at interracial cooperation in the temperance movement. Shadd Cary's article suggested that the Society's message appealed "to colored people with peculiar force," but that their main audience was white women. But there is no indication that the Moral Education Society survived or that its efforts to reach black youth had any lasting effect.[27]

Mary Ann's interest in temperance was closely linked to her daily work in freedmen's education. In the black schools of Washington she witnessed the struggles of the freedmen's children to overcome social and personal obstacles to self-improvement. She considered intemperance, like other moral lapses, to be a vestige of slavery that prevented black Americans' assimilation into the mainstream. She wrote in the *New National Era* that "the 'peculiar institution' was not choice in its methods—no warning voice was raised against tobacco, profanity, or intemperance, on the score of refinement or Christianity." Blacks' worst enemies, she reminded her readers, were those who criticized their character on the one hand, and then encouraged them to drink on the other.[28]

By the late 1870s, the Women's Christian Temperance Union was actively organizing segregated black unions in the South, and there were sporadic efforts in states like New Jersey and Connecticut to allow black and white women to join forces. In the District of Columbia, however, racial segregation seemed the rule in the temperance movement. Frances E. W. Harper was the most visible black woman associated with the organization. In 1881 she was the sole black delegate to the WCTU convention in Washington. In the mid-1880s Harper served as Superintendent of Colored Work in Pennsylvania, and later as Superintendent for the national organization. Like Shadd Cary, Harper found temperance a compelling reform issue and she remained active in the WCTU through the early 1890s.[29]

Frances Harper was one of very few African American women to play a significant role in the Women's Christian Temperance Union. Mary Ann Shadd Cary had no connection to the organization and fashioned herself as an independent temperance activist who linked prohibition to other causes such as women's suffrage, sexual morality, education. Temperance became a prominent theme in Mary Ann's lectures on women's issues and racial uplift as she sought to integrate, rather than compartmentalize, these pressing concerns. She penned temperance songs which were published in the *Christian Recorder,* organ of the A.M.E. Church, and she sang them with vigor at the start of her public appearances. Members of the audience were exhorted to sign a temperance pledge while she belted out: "Thus the rozy morn arising, Mark the cheerful song, thousands bear on high the banner, hail the sturdy temp'rance throng." In 1885 the *New York Freeman* described Mary Ann as a "lecturer on Temperance and other reforms," who was greeted by "frequent rounds of hearty applause." In 1888 she was still giving temperance lectures with gusto when the *Washington Star* praised her as "one of the most talented colored women of the country." The approach of old age—by this time she was in her 60s—did not seem to staunch Mary Ann's thirst for an audience or for political engagement.[30]

The temperance cause's framework of religion and family provided Mary Ann with a vehicle through which she tried to mobilize black women to public activism. Her writing in the *New National Era* had consistently called upon the women of the black elite to take greater responsibility for the progress of their communities. But it was temperance, along with black women's work in church and educational societies, that formed a crucial stepping stone to the late nineteenth century club movement. Mary Ann's spectrum of experience as an activist, teacher, and parent led her to realize the possibilities of all-women's associations more than a decade before the club movement emerged in the city with the founding of the Colored Women's League of Washington.

The Colored Women's Progressive Franchise Association, formed by Shadd Cary in 1880, was the manifestation of these various interests. It focused on the need for young women to obtain vocational training, and for black women to learn to invest their money and promote business ventures. This multi-purpose organization hoped to promote women's political and economic rights, encourage black women as workers and entrepreneurs, serve as a clearing house for information on black business and labor, and generally foster religious and moral values among the district's black population.[31]

On at least one occasion the association gathered at Mt. Pisgah Chapel on R Street, and the church's pastor Rev. J. Nichols presided over the meeting, suggesting at least some local church support for black women's self-help and reform activities. Indeed, many of the black women who started the club movement developed their organizing and leadership skills in church activities. Shadd Cary, however, had honed these skills through forty years of advocacy and conflict in abolition, emigration, and women's rights organizations. Her confrontational style had not mellowed; the organization's charter underscored her frustrations with multiple forms of discrimination. Mary Ann listed the points she planned to present to the association's first gathering in her handwritten notes appended to the meeting's minutes: "1. Our leaders do not take the women into consideration; 2. The men furnish an example in that they have committees and clubs to give information . . . 3. The men need light . . . 4. Thirty or forty occupations for white women; half a dozen for colored ones," she wrote. She offered several anecdotes that established a rationale for the creation of an autonomous black women's organization: for example, there were only two African Americans among the 2,000 attendees at a recent suffrage convention in Washington.[32]

The proposed Colored Women's Progressive Franchise Association moved beyond the maternal, family-centered rhetoric of temperance and other women's reform movements. In many respects, Mary Ann's plan openly confronted the gender ideologies of post-Reconstruction America. Black women, she suggested, should be able to function independently and successfully in the public sphere at the same time that they were mindful of their domestic duties. She insisted that black men relinquish some of their authority so that women might participate with them on equal footing in the political, intellectual, and economic realms. Scholars have noted black Americans' movement toward increasingly restrictive gender roles during this period. While some black leaders supported women's suffrage, much of their political and cultural discourse on the subject sought to keep elite black women in their place. This was a source of extreme frustration and consternation for Shadd Cary, as her notes reveal; black women were simultaneously excluded from the fragile power held by black men, and from the gradual advances made by the white women's movement.[33]

Washington's black newspaper, the *People's Advocate*, was neither generous or supportive in its review of the association's activities. It passed off the session as "another woman suffrage meeting," ignoring the discussion of substantive issues. The article focused on Shadd Cary's comments, in which she complained that the needs and potential of black girls were ignored by "our leading men of color." She allegedly blamed the failure of a sewing program at the Lincoln Mission school on the fact that it was managed by men. According to the newspaper, she ridi-

culed the idea of men in such an enterprise. The brief article concluded on a doubtful tone: "What these meetings will bring forth does not
yet appear." Such ambivalence toward black women's independent endeavors also appeared during the meeting, when one man in attendance refused to support women's suffrage, saying that the ballot was
useless for women.[34]

Nevertheless, Shadd Cary laid out an ambitious plan for the association using her legal expertise. The group was to form a joint stock company that would invest in small businesses, "and thus enable poor persons
to get a start in business of either sex." Among the favored investments
were land for farming and development, a dry goods and millinery store,
a men's clothing store, and grocery stores, all of which would be potential employers of young black women and men. For thirty years Shadd
Cary had remained consistent in her calls for black self-sufficiency and
economic development. Also embedded in this project was her renewed
quest for a public voice. She proposed the establishment of "a paper or
papers unbiased by sex restrictions and jealousies," suggesting that she
was experiencing such discrimination in the city's existing black press.
This was a reprise of Mary Ann's long-standing complaint that gender
conventions restricted her access to avenues of public expression.[35]

The surviving papers of Mary Ann Shadd Cary reveal her persistent longing for a journalistic forum. During the 1870s and 1880s she
wrote numerous unpublished reports and essays on her observations
of the changing world around her. She was envious that white women
seemed to have made inroads into the newspaper profession, particularly in the nation's capital. And the national press had grown as a site
of power second only to the government. Why was she, a black women
with far greater experience in the field, denied the same opportunity?
On the last day of the 43rd Congressional session, she sat in the gallery
as the thermometer hit 107 degrees inside, and wrote out her frustrations in assorted fragments:

> The men and women of the newspaper world—that most potential
> of dynasties—have become of late of especial wonder and admiration
> to the uninitiated: from no perceptible beginnings, they seem to have
> come full-grown into the most satisfying completeness of permanence
> and power. At the extreme limits of every other legitimate pursuit the
> gentler sex has halted and hesitated, or at most pled to enter in depre-
> cating protest. . . . In this unique department of letters and labor she
> begs not place, but is confessedly an equal; an honored member of the
> guild.[36]

But on the same occasion, she contradicted these sentiments in
a tongue-in-cheek sketch she wrote about two fictional women reporters struggling to gain recognition in the male-dominated press. This

humorous account was a thinly veiled exposition of her own disappointments—editor's rejection of women's articles, and the inability of wom-
en professionals to stick together under the withering scrutiny of
their male counterparts. The 15-page piece, written during the long
hours sitting at the Capitol, concludes on an ironic note. Mary Ann
created a woman character who had been observing the female reporters as they worked. Described as "a grave looking lady in quiet colors, who had been almost stationary for hours," the woman scornfully
labeled the presswomen "abominable creatures," and accused them of
producing "tiresome conversation" and "just backbiting every body."
The "lady" said of the reporters: "I never heard so much gossip in so
short a time. Tut! Tut! What is the country coming to!" In Mary Ann's
fictional world, as well as the real, professional women were reduced to
gossiping harpies not to be taken seriously. This narrative rearticulated
Mary Ann's oft-cited lament that women were as guilty as men when it
came to ridiculing and devaluing women's work. Mary Ann had found
a friendly vehicle in Frederick Douglass's *New National Era,* which ran
her letters and articles on the front page and hailed her work in the
district's schools. But Douglass and Shadd Cary were compatriots from
another generation, and their mutual admiration was based on decades
of work in common struggles. When the *Era* folded in 1874 Shadd Cary
lost her only reliable medium.[37]

The *People's Advocate,* a newspaper founded by black Washingtonian John Wesley Cromwell in 1876, was not as willing to furnish her a forum. The *Advocate* never published any of the letters or articles Mary
Ann wrote during its eight years of publication. Cromwell had graduated from Howard University's law school in 1874, and as an attorney,
teacher, and entrepreneur was an established member of Washington's black elite. He used his newspaper to encourage civil rights efforts
through the courts and legislative action, rather than through radical
protest. The *People's Advocate* argued that affluent and educated black
citizens should be engaged in helping the less fortunate of the community. Yet, the *Advocate* chose to ignore those same principles when they
were espoused by the Colored Women's Franchise Association—perhaps because of its clearly feminist identity. In the light of such treatment, Mary Ann hoped for a newspaper "controlled by those not opposed to equal rights for the sexes," and one that would highlight the
advancement of black women.[38]

There is no evidence that the newspaper or any of the other schemes
of the Colored Women's Franchise Association ever reached fruition.
Shadd Cary's idea for a black women's periodical would not be realized
until the creation of *Women's Era* in Boston by Josephine St. Pierre Ruffin more than ten years later. But she continued to promote the efficacy

of black women's organizations. Mary Ann attended a meeting of the Association for the Advancement of Women in New York in 1887, and reported in the *New York Age* that women's clubs were "a means for a broader and more worthy citizenship, and as a means to develop a higher moral and economic excellence for us." The Colored Women's Franchise Association had failed, but Mary Ann remained convinced that black women's activism would have greater influence through regional clubs with a specific interest in reform and philanthropy. "A thousand capable colored women are on hand, not one or two only," she wrote, referring to the "educated colored women, North and South." These women, who would later be counted among the talented tenth, should be the backbone of the quest for racial improvement, Mary Ann concluded.[39]

The speaker's platform, rather than the press, provided Mary Ann with the most consistent opportunities for public expression. African American lecturers were an important bulwark against cultural isolation for a community with limited resources and education. The nation's most famous black orator, Frederick Douglass, deemed public communication a vital component of racial progress: "Press, platform, pulpit should continue to direct their energies to the removal of the hardships and wrongs which continue to be the lot of colored people," he wrote in 1870.[40]

The founding of the Bethel Literary and Historical Association provided Mary Ann with an ideal outlet that supplemented her own lecture tours. Bethel, organized by A.M.E. Bishop Daniel Payne in 1881, was Washington's central gathering place for black intellectuals and public figures. Mary Ann Shadd Cary became a regular fixture of the association, which attracted the nation's distinguished African Americans to discuss the pressing issues of race and society, as well as science and letters. She gave public talks—one was titled "Heroes of the Anti-Slavery Struggles"—and often participated in discussions from the floor. When *People's Advocate* editor Cromwell published a history of the Bethel Association in 1897, his posthumous acknowledgment of Mary Ann's contributions was more generous than his earlier commentary. Cromwell praised her oratorical abilities when he described her as "a speaker whose clear, high treble voice and epigrammatic sentences were a signal for death-like stillness and oracular sayings that nearly always met with popular approval."[41]

The Bethel Literary and Historical Association cultivated a flourishing high-brow culture for local African Americans that served as an antidote to the decidedly philistine press. In the 1880s and 1890s Washington's public black discourse was controlled by a newspaper whose publisher "obviously thought scandal and malicious gossip sold better than other news," noted one historian. The *Washington Bee* was founded in 1882 by Calvin Chase, and after the demise of the *People's Advocate*, the *Bee* developed a reputation for using invective and "methods approaching blackmail" that were a far cry from the genteel advocacy of the antebellum black press. The *Bee*'s motto was "Honey for Friends, Stings for Enemies," and Chase vacillated between denouncing the city's black upper class and reporting on the minutiae of their social activities. The *Bee*, like the *People's Advocate*, was not as willing to entertain the ideological musings of an older generation, as represented by Shadd Cary, and it never published any of her writing.[42]

The black press grew dramatically in the late nineteenth century, particularly in the South where improved literacy and growing political engagement created a large black audience. This new generation of periodicals was influenced by the commercial and editorial practices of the mainstream press, including the use of sensationalism, and professionalized news gathering practices. Many of these newspapers were focused on the internal life of the black communities they served and avoided political risks or strident positions. Mary Ann found these changes abhorrent. In one of her numerous unpublished essays written during this period, she characterized these newspapers as a grave disappointment. "It is truly painful to observe some of their 'staggers' at general improvement," she wrote. "The fitness of things does not commend itself to young enthusiasts among the colored people. That is seen in the Press in their hands." She was scathing in her review of the "innumerable muscular, lazy, ambitious unskilled young people" who comprised this generation, and she determined that with the exception of the old *New National Era* and "one or two non-partizan papers," the black press was incompetent and served to worsen the image of the black community.[43]

This was not an entirely fair assessment, although there was some truth to it. There were many exceptions, among them a young editor and writer named T. Thomas Fortune who began his career at the *People's Advocate* before moving to New York in 1881, where he took over the helm of the New York *Globe* (later the *Freeman*, and then the *Age*). Fortune toiled to make his paper a national forum for African American writers and political figures. He argued that the role of the black press was to speak out against the outrages perpetrated against his people. Fortune's papers earned him a reputation as an uncompromising advocate for civil rights, but like Mary Ann and an earlier generation of black journalists, he had to make frequent pleas for financial sustenance. Fortune declared that "the only way we can hope ever to win our fight is to arm ourselves as our opponents do, support those newspapers alone that support us."[44]

Despite the increase in the number of black newspapers, none found-ed before the 1880s survived until 1914. Even strong political organs like Harry C. Smith's *Cleveland Gazette* often resorted to petty squab-bling with local black leaders and a preoccupation with "high society" and popular culture. This content, particularly as it appeared in Wash-ington's newspapers, offended all of Shadd Cary's moral and intellec-tual standards. She was incensed that the black press served up "the vilest material that can pander to or feed gross appetites, as the pabu-lum wherewith to advance their people."[45]

At the same time Mary Ann complained bitterly that her contribu-tions had been turned down by the local black press. In the months preceding the election of 1888 she courted the Washington *Post,* the city's new Democratic newspaper, with the hope that it might publish regular correspondence from "a reporter who knows colored people in and out." She presented herself as a writer who identified with black independents and Democrats—a position she had announced at the women's rights convention ten years earlier—and who scorned blacks' loyalty to the Republicans. The postwar Republican stronghold on the White House had been broken by the election of Grover Cleve-land in 1884, and the *Post* was actively promoting his reelection. Shadd Cary appealed to the paper's self-interest with the claim that it would aid Cleveland's presidential bid if "it be known that the organ at the Capital was open to a colored 'democrat,'" and she maintained that many blacks in Washington had switched to the Democratic party but that this fact had been overshadowed by the claims of black Republi-can elected officials.[46]

Mary Ann's rhetoric was indicative of the changing political terrain in the post-Reconstruction United States. During the Civil War, lead-ers of one black convention characterized the Democrats—party of the slaveocracy—as the body where "all the worst elements of Ameri-can Society fraternize," and they resolved that blacks "need not expect a single voice from that quarter for justice, mercy, or even decency." But by the late 1870s, many blacks were disillusioned with the Republi-cans and were examining their options among the Democrats and inde-pendent parties. The debate over blacks' party loyalties was fierce. In 1883 the Washington *Bee* branded all black independents "traitors to the race," who left themselves open to the worst political attacks. Three years later, Harry C. Smith of the *Cleveland Gazette* wrote, "The Negro sees precisely what has been accomplished for his race through the agency of the Democratic party and it amounts to zero." But at the same time, the influence of Radical Republicanism had disappeared, and there was little evidence of Republicans' commitment to black civil rights. In Washington, this retrenchment took the form of provisions in the Or-

ganic Act of 1878, which ended suffrage in the nation's capital, eliminated all elected offices, and turned over the city's governance to feder-
ally authorized commissions, effectively disfranchising all citizens. The
Republican-dominated Congress, according to one historian, "knowing-
ly handed enemies of black suffrage a substantial symbolic victory."
Just a few years earlier Mary Ann had eagerly sought the voting rights
facilitated by Radical Reconstruction. Now she was searching for a new
political identity. "I know scores of good people here who have changed
their views but the colored republican-nothing if not in office, decries
the moral and social standing of the negro independent to the Democrats, to keep their place," she argued, clearly placing herself at odds
with the black political establishment that included Frederick Douglass and the *Bee*'s Calvin Chase.[47]

Mary Ann's letter to the Democrats' newspaper was cloaked in secrecy. She requested that the paper keep her correspondence confi-
dential because she did not want "any negro to suspect me," and she
adopted the pseudonym "St. Anthony." The accompanying article she
submitted for publication, titled "Music in the Air!" was a diatribe in
true Shadd Cary fashion. She weighed in on a local controversy in
which a member of the black gentry named Mathews was denied
a political appointment by the Republican-controlled Senate. Shadd
Cary claimed that Kansas Senator John J. Ingalls, a Republican, opposed Mathews because he was free born rather than a former slave.
She saw the issue as symbolic of politicians' attempts to weaken the
city's black elite, "to belittle men of free birth," and to promote
"the monstrous doctrine, that slave birth and degradation were fitter
qualifications for office for negroes than free birth." In the 1850s Mary
Ann had used the pages of the *Provincial Freeman* to criticize Henry
Bibb for favoring fugitive slaves over free blacks in the policies of the
Refugee Home Society. Forty years later she asked the white press to
help her wage a similar campaign. In her view, the Republicans easily
stooped to the lowest forms of expedient politics.[48]

It is possible that this correspondence with the *Post* was purely opportunistic. In her desire to be published Shadd Cary may have written what she thought would appeal to a Democratic newspaper. But
her writing suggests she was keenly aware of the tyranny of the nation's
two-party system, which had effectively blocked African American participation. While she might not wholeheartedly embrace the Democrats, she could not trust the Republicans either. Her article stated
this clearly, when she wrote that black people were "working away at
the knotty end of a stubborn fact both parties are slow to learn . . . the
word 'Republic'—can should [*sic*] be no more the fetish that blinds
than the term "Democrat" should be the scarecrow to demoralize." As

the nation's civil rights pendulum began to swing back toward slavery, in the words of Du Bois, there was little to lose from such arguments. Perhaps this letter was nothing more than an exercise in futility; she may have never actually mailed it to the newspaper. It was never published in the *Post,* which probably took little interest in the ravings of an aging black woman.[49]

In the last decade of her life, Shadd Cary remained an energetic and articulate advocate for civil rights. But her embittered and angry rhetoric told the story of a life that was constantly beaten back from insurmountable barriers. At times she seemed to succumb to the increasingly popular thesis of social Darwinism that argued blacks' inability to compete in a white world. Her critiques of the African American character showed the enduring influence of early black nationalist ideology on her own thinking. A generation earlier, David Walker lamented that the black masses were "ignorant and treacherous creatures" who seemed unable to raise themselves from their wretchedness. Lewis Woodson worried in the 1840s that the majority of African Americans existed "in a most degraded condition, and this has stamped the character of degradation upon the whole race." A quarter century after the Civil War, Mary Ann found the same disabilities still lurking in the African American community. While the sons of European immigrants were making great strides in politics and business, African Americans seemed, in her view, to be on an endless backward slide. "The negro alone of all American natives rejects unification as a social or other basis," she complained. There were "great colored men" like Alexandre Dumas, Ira Aldridge, and Frederick Douglass, but even they could not "be free from the peculiarities of their race, in the conspicuous absence of social and tribal co-hesion," Mary Ann wrote.[50]

She complained of blacks' apparent lack of unity, and their inability—or unwillingness—to learn from the lessons of the past. She offered the following anecdote as a tragic example of what she believed to be blacks' ignorance and lack of racial pride:

> Said a young colored man after years of training in our best colleges, and with a remarkably good class standing: "Who ever heard of colored men of talent and were there any? . . . I was never of the opinion that much could be made of the colored people, and think still that the race must run out."

Why were the Dutch immigrant, the Jew, and the Arab, as well as native-born whites, so much better at functioning collectively and acting in their own self interest? Mary Ann asked. She concluded that "the young colored people disregard and ignore the presence and counsel of the old people with a lingering remnant of fetichism [*sic*]." She undoubtedly included herself among those whose wisdom was being cast off or ignored. It is perhaps a tribute to the reformer's consciousness that she always held unreasonably high hopes for her brethren to obtain an education, shed all vices, develop ambition and entrepreneurial talents, and display constant pride and vigilance in the face of threats of violence—both emotional and physical—that shaped black life in the late nineteenth century.[51]

But the decline in social and political conditions for blacks in the District of Columbia, as elsewhere in the nation, was a real and distressing fact. As the gains of Reconstruction waned, whites in Washington shed any pretense of tolerance for or acceptance of their black neighbors. Blacks were uniformly ignored or denigrated by the white press, civil rights laws were repealed, public facilities became increasingly segregated, and even the most affluent blacks were subjected to constant harassment and indignities. The city of Washington, so recently the model of Reconstruction, was now a place were blacks were routinely arrested and beaten by police without cause, and where jobs paying a livable wage were scarce although the city boasted the largest number of educated and professionally trained African Americans in the nation. The number of federal jobs held by blacks—a long-standing benefit from Reconstruction—had eroded dramatically, and there was a severe shortage of homes available to those blacks who could afford to buy them. African Americans in the District of Columbia were, like their counterparts throughout the South, a group under siege, and Mary Ann Shadd Cary experienced this reality firsthand.[52]

Mary Ann Shadd Cary's writing from this period provides an a penetrating analysis of the system of economic exploitation, lawlessness, and political discrimination which stripped away the fruits of Reconstruction. She was impatient with what appeared to be blacks' acquiescence to these conditions, but she fully recognized the hegemonic forces against which African Americans had to struggle. Blacks had been rendered impotent and invisible through a conscious campaign to deny them power. "By common consent the negro is conceded to be out of politics," she observed during this period of disfranchisement. Black Americans were "regarded as out of the national concern, not as a component part of the nation." White Americans were more interested in examining the lives of Indians and Mexicans through romanticized and stereotyped imagery in the popular press, she contended. "The greaser or Indian on the border thus becomes to be better known in his tribal and class relation, than the colored servant behind the chair of the Cabinet officer, or the negro minister to foreign sable nationalities."[53]

Once black life was rendered invisible, she reasoned, black Americans' enemies could unleash their hatred and wrath without fear of retribution. "Thousands of colored men and women are whipped and murdered in the south and sneers and incredulity meet one on every hand," she wrote. If a black man is accused of a crime "the country is aroused to suppress 'negro outlaws,'" but meanwhile, "nameless outrages are committed upon colored women and children in the presence of bound and helpless fathers, sons and brothers." Mary Ann's condemnation of lynching and the sexual mythologies that supported the practice, was a precursor to the powerful indictments of another black woman journalist, Ida Wells-Barnett, who would publish her exposes in the New York *Age* in the 1890s. Sadly, Mary Ann would not live to see the courageous journalism of Wells-Barnett as it attacked the core of southern racism and northern paternalism that allowed the lynching of blacks to go unpunished. Once again, Mary Ann was ahead of her time; the black press was not yet ready to publish such controversial and inflammatory ideas. These comments were part of a series of articles, probably written in the 1880s, which Mary Ann wrote under the pseudonym "Pix." They were never published.[54]

Mary Ann did enjoy one belated victory despite these generally worsening conditions—the completion of her law degree in 1883 at the age of 60. She was awarded the Bachelor of Law at a June graduation ceremony at the city's Congregational Church, whose members had been among the founders of Howard University. The *People's Advocate* made note of the fact that Mary Ann was the only black woman in the class, which also graduated three white women. Hers was a quiet presence; she did not read a paper or thesis, as did the other graduates, nor did her work attract any special attention. At this moment, perhaps, it was simply enough to finally earn the degree. By the mid 1880s, Mary Ann had retired from her teaching posts and the degree allowed her to shed her life-long identity as an educator to belatedly take up a career in the law. She continued her lecturing on women's rights and temperance, but now appended the cherished professional title to her name, such as when she visited Mississippi in 1885 to give a talk on "Race Pride and Co-operation." She was M. A. Shadd Cary, Esq., "a colored lady lawyer."[55]

Within three years of earning the degree, Mary Ann was practicing law in Washington, and she began advertising her services in the business pages of the city directory. It is likely that Mary Ann's fledgling legal practice met with only limited success. Her predecessor Charlotte Ray practiced law in Washington into the 1890s but was always hampered by race and gender prejudice. Ray eventually moved back to New York City where she worked as a schoolteacher for the remaining years of her life. Mary Ann and her colleagues faced enormous obstacles in Washington's legal community. The white-only District of Columbia Bar Association denied blacks membership and prohibited them from using its law library. This meant that most black attorneys, who lacked the money to purchase their own law books, could not adequately prepare their cases. The handful of active black lawyers in the city generally had other jobs in federal agencies, as teachers, or in business, and practiced law in their spare time. The District bar association's grievance committee was controlled by white lawyers who seized every opportunity to exclude or disbar black lawyers at the slightest hint of impropriety. It was not until 1918 that the District of Columbia Colored Bar Association was formed (succeeded by the Washington Bar Association between 1925 and 1944), a group that would finally force the white-only association to allow blacks' access to its library in 1941 and membership in 1958.[56]

Shadd Cary's hard-won professional status held more symbolic than literal meaning. She was the embodiment of what she believed should be African Americans' aspirations—to be hard-working, well-educated, respected, and committed to social change. Yet the impoverished state of most of Washington's black residents, combined with enduring resistance to women in the law, meant that she had difficulty finding paying clients. Sources suggest that Charlotte Ray earned a reputation as an effective attorney in the District's courts, but there is little evidence that Mary Ann Shadd Cary had such opportunities. A survey of the dockets of the Supreme Court of the District of Columbia found that she never argued any cases in that court. Among her remaining papers are some handwritten documents that indicate she may have worked on civil cases, such as a claim against the property of a local couple. But she was unable to earn a living as an attorney.[57]

In the last ten years of her life, Mary Ann lived with one or both of her children, who took on an increasingly larger share of their household's finances. In the 1870s her son, Linton Cary, while still in his teens, found work in the cloakroom and as a messenger in the House of Representatives. He was fortunate to be among the few black workers who could count on reliable government employment instead of uncertain, unskilled labor, the only alternative for many of his contemporaries. Mary Ann's daughter, Sarah Cary, initially followed in her mother's footsteps as a teacher until about 1885, when she started her own dressmaking business—an example, perhaps, of Mary Ann's efforts to shepherd black women into entrepreneurial activities.[58]

The Carys were a transient family, often living together but always on the move. From 1881 to 1886 they all lived in a two-story brick house on W Street in the city's northwest quadrant, their longest stay at a single residence. Thereafter impermanence seemed to dictate their living situation. In 1886, for example, Linton and Sarah lived together on 17th St. N.W., while their mother lived two blocks away on 15th Street. By 1888 Sarah was married and living on her own, while Mary Ann began running her legal practice out of her home, which she seemed to move annually. More Shadds arrived in Washington to live with their well-established relative, including a niece, Aurelia L. Shadd, who stayed for about a year until she found work as a teacher in nearby Maryland. The Carys were reunited for the last time in 1892, when Linton died in his sister's home four days before Christmas. Mary Ann's final heartbreak was the loss of her 32-year-old son, who was described by a local newspaper as "the support of his aged mother and sister." Just six months later, she succumbed to stomach cancer at age 70.[59]

On the day Mary Ann died, the nation seemed preoccupied with matters far removed from her world of racial and gender politics. President Cleveland and his cabinet grappled with a national fiscal crisis, and the trial of Lizzie Borden began in New Bedford, Massachusetts. Her death attracted little fanfare—a couple of death notices in the local press, and an obituary in the Washington *Bee* that bid her a kindly but dubious farewell:

> Mrs. M. S. Carey [sic] one of the best known women in this country died at her residence on last Monday morning at 4:50 A.M. Mrs. Carey was a woman of excellent traits of character and loved by all who knew her. While she may have been excentric [sic] at times, she was a woman of kind disposition.[60]

Her funeral was held at Israel Metropolitan A.M.E. Church, one of the city's oldest black churches, and home to the Bethel Literary and Historical Association, where she had often held forth in public lectures. She was finally laid to rest in the District's Harmony Cemetery. Mary Ann died without a will and with few worldly goods. When her daughter Sarah petitioned the courts to become the administrator of her mother's estate, her property was estimated at $150. Her most valued possessions were her books, including a collection of legal texts. She undoubtedly spent her few dollars on the essential tools for her work as a lawyer, writer, and educator, rather than on more material possessions. Mary Ann had lived as she preached—scorning conspicuous consumption and a lack of thrift for herself as well as for all black Americans. The fact that she did not employ her hard-won legal skills to craft her own will suggests that, true to her stubborn and defiant spirit, Mary Ann had no intention of dying.[61]

A Life Spent Fighting
at the Margins

**From the very first it has been the educated
and intelligent of the Negro people that have led
and elevated the mass, and the sole obstacles
that nullified and retarded their efforts were
slavery and race prejudice.**   W. E. B. Du Bois[1]

The District of Columbia in the late nineteenth century was a locus for privileged black women to carry on the work begun by Mary Ann Shadd Cary. Many of the wives and daughters of the city's most influential black men, like Charlotte Forten Grimké and Josephine Bruce, began to appreciate the necessity of organizations that integrated a commitment to racial and gender equality. Gradually they claimed visibility and authority within Washington's black world. In 1892 Mary Church Terrell, an Oberlin graduate and the wife of a black judge, became the first female President of the Bethel Literary and Historical Association. During the same period educator and author Anna Julia Cooper would, like Shadd Cary, become an influential teacher and later principal of Washington's only black secondary school, the M. Street School. Out of this network emerged a community of black women intellectuals who would analyze and resist the varied forms of race and gender discrimination that shaped and limited their lives.[2]

Just a year before Mary Ann's death, these women organized the National Colored Women's League in Washington, ushering in what one scholar has called an era of "black bourgeois feminism." The group's goals were racial uplift, education and training for black youth, support for black women's interests, and the encouragement of a club movement at the national level—all part of the platform Mary Ann had tried to advance more than a decade earlier. The League's Constitution noted that "lack of unity and organization" contributed to African Americans' vulnerability and oppression. This organization has been credited with promoting the development of a national network of black women's clubs which would come to fruition in 1896 with the formation of the National Association of Colored Women, headed by Terrell. Spearheading these developments was the courageous and enterprising young journalist, Ida Wells-Barnett, who urged the clubs to protest black women's exclusion from the 1893 World's Columbian Exposition in Chicago. This new cohort of female activists clearly followed Shadd Cary's lead, yet there is no clear lineage between her work and theirs. She undoubtedly crossed paths with Terrell, Cooper, and the others during her final years in black Washington's political, literary, and social circles. Forty years later, the N.A.C.W. would include Mary Ann in a compilation of black foremothers, briefly noting her accomplishments in journalism and law. But there is no sense that her presence was felt or acknowledged in the early days of this burgeoning club movement. Instead, she was overshadowed by the accomplishments of the generation she helped to inspire.[3]

By 1890 Mary Ann had already begun to retreat from the public sphere as she invested her declining energies in her struggling legal practice. She withdrew from public life in an era of profound strife for African Americans—what Rayford Logan identified as their nadir. This period was marked by a campaign of judicial and legislative actions, coupled with fraud, intimidation, and violence, designed to preserve African Americans' second-class status. The next generation of black intellectuals and activists would have to muster their resources to confront this onslaught against their rights. Many, like W. E. B. Du Bois, Ida Wells-Barnett, Booker T. Washington, and Mary Church Terrell, were born or came of age after the Civil War. They entered the struggle for rights and justice at the end of the century as the grand old abolitionists and nationalists like Shadd Cary, Martin Delany, and Frederick Douglass died off. This generation carried on the agenda of racial progress that Mary Ann had championed throughout her life.[4]

Mary Ann Shadd Cary helped pave the way for the African American women's club movement, and demanded that the black public sphere be accessible to both men and women. At the same time she carved out a space for black women in the overwhelmingly white women's suffrage movement. She cultivated and sustained a voice for the black nationalist impulse for self-sufficiency and community consciousness. She promoted the use of the press and speaker's pulpit as a forum for political discourse. Through example, she demonstrated women's ability to engage in professional and leadership activities in journalism, education, and the law. But the United States in the nineteenth century was not yet ready for a black female editor or lawyer; consequently she spent her life struggling for recognition and fending off insolvency and failure. Nevertheless, she openly confronted the boundaries of race and gender, and parlayed a small education and limited means into a wide-ranging and influential career as a public figure.

Mary Ann Shadd Cary may best be remembered as an outspoken feminist at a time when male hegemony dictated the leadership of black organizations and communities. While there was often a partnership between the sexes, women were expected to play an auxiliary —and sometimes submissive—role. As Manning Marable has noted, the primacy of race, rather than class or gender, was a heuristic principle organizing black Americans' social and political relations. Mary Ann was among a tiny group of nineteenth-century African American women who possessed the education, economic mobility, and courage necessary to engage in public life. But their endeavors were circumscribed by the extent to which African Americans clung to patriarchal models of family, community, and politics. This has been interpreted as a reflection of African Americans' desire to emulate Victorian gender roles, and to counteract the mythologies that constructed the black family as dysfunctional and black sexuality as abnormal and promiscuous.[5]

Scholars have contended that the grip of male authority in African American communities became more apparent over time, so that by the late nineteenth century "sexism had increased significantly among educated blacks." This was put most eloquently by Anna Julia Cooper, who wrote in 1892 that "while our men seem thoroughly abreast of the times on almost every other subject, when they strike the woman question they drop back into sixteenth-century logic." After emancipation, elite black women bore a heavy responsibility for racial improvement at the same time that they encountered increasingly restrictive gender conventions. Mary Ann accepted these obligations imposed on her sex, but her feminism kept her estranged from the sites of black power.[6]

Part of Mary Ann's uniqueness can be found in the ways she resisted the prevailing assumption that racial liberation and improvement were dependent on black men's assertion of patriarchal authority. She did not sidestep the problems of gender or attempt to mollify black male anxieties. Rather, she outwardly challenged male authority and defiantly entered into professions that restricted women's involvement. When the pressures for gender conformity were too great—such as in the early days of the *Provincial Freeman*—she adopted elaborate strategies to retain her power while supporting men in leadership roles. Numerous educated black women in Mary Ann's circle—Frances E. W. Harper, Charlotte Forten, Sarah Douglass, among them—professed feminist tendencies and were actively engaged in public activities. But she was alone in her willingness to openly challenge men. Not since the public speeches of Maria Stewart had a black woman taken such social and political risks.[7]

Mary Ann's gender politics were also reflected in the choices she made in her personal life. The cult of true womanhood assumed that all women would care for a husband and children, yet black women could not assume that marriage would bring them a measure of financial security or safety. It was not uncommon for antebellum black women to postpone marriage, live with men out of wedlock, remain single, or enjoy the autonomy of widowhood. Refraining from marriage—even among the elite in Boston, Philadelphia, and other cities—allowed some black women to have greater control over their lives and property. Both Frances Harper and Sarah Mapps Douglass, like Mary Ann Shadd Cary, chose to wait for marriage until middle age. In each case these women married men considerably older than themselves, and like Shadd Cary they all outlived their husbands.[8]

Mary Ann Shadd Cary's decision to postpone marriage freed her from household duties and childrearing in her twenties and early thirties so that she could devote her energies exclusively to the *Freeman,* and her work as an educator and reformer. But what she gained in time and autonomy she lost in social status and respectability. Her virtue was an easy target for those seeking to discredit her, and at least some of the opposition to her work as a newspaper editor stemmed from the fact that many found it improper for a single woman to be such a public figure. It is not surprising that decades after Thomas Cary's death, Mary Ann continued to claim the privileges of marriage by identifying herself as a widow in public records, although she rarely used the courtesy title Mrs. Thomas F. Cary.

Mary Ann's and Thomas's marriage was more than a convenient hedge against the perils of spinsterdom, however. It was a relationship that brought companionship and affection to her life. Having children created much greater financial and emotional burdens for Mary Ann, although motherhood did not seem to curtail her activities. Shadd Cary defied the standards of Victorian motherhood, which required that she devote most of their time and energy to her children's well-being. It is impossible to know the details of her relationship with her daughter and son, but it is clear that she left them in the care of relatives for long periods. Nevertheless, they were a close-knit family unit and Mary Ann created a household that welcomed extended family members.

She also maintained close ties with many of her siblings, as well as her far-flung network of friends and supporters. Her daughter, Sarah Cary Evans, revealed a steadfast pride in her mother's life and accomplishments when she wrote a celebratory essay about Mary Ann for Hallie Quinn Brown's *Homespun Heroines*, published in 1926.[9]

The responses to Mary Ann's unwavering feminism were varied. There were many black male leaders, including Frederick Douglass, William Still, and Martin Delany, who championed her right to speak in public, publish a newspaper, or study the law. Delany, for example, touted Mary Ann's accomplishments with pride. He "delighted in introducing her at lectures and in writing about her, for she personified all he had expressed concerning the intellectual potential of his people, both female and male," notes one of Delany's biographers. But others were clearly offended by Mary Ann's gender politics, using them to undermine her political activities and public expression.[10]

It is no coincidence that in the early days of her career as an activist, as well as at the end of her life, the term "eccentric" was used to characterize her personality. Mary Ann's open defiance meant that even in the twentieth century, she would be described in ambivalent, if not hostile, terms. The leading authority on blacks in Canada claimed that "Mary Shadd served meat strong even for the time, and few cared to digest it." The double standard is clear; in an era in which political speech was filled with argument and invective, women activists were nevertheless expected to remain ladylike and decorous. This was an expectation with which Mary Ann simply could not comply. She was too passionate about her causes, too committed to social change, and too angry about the injustices she experienced and observed. Above all, she was exceedingly stubborn.[11]

Mary Ann's political development began amid the debates and traditions of the antebellum black convention movement and early black nationalism. She became an established political figure through a combination of selfless effort and deliberate self-promotion. There was little room in this political culture for expressions of overt feminism. Her early activism was focused on the pressing problems of slavery, disfranchisement, and discrimination although she occasionally addressed the problem of gender in her speeches and editorials. As a black woman she had to reconcile her own ambitions and frustrations with the androcentric nature of black American politics. The concept of manhood, as articulated by figures like Douglass and Garnet, represented the integrity of the black community and the potential for violent resistance to oppression. Many of Mary Ann's activist contemporaries "saw the crucial test of black fitness to be whether or not black men were . . . considered 'manly.'" Many in the next generation would continue to associate manhood with black liberation. Du Bois made this abundantly clear when he asserted in 1903: "The Negro race, like all races, is going to be saved by its exceptional men. . . . Men we shall have only as we make manhood the object of the work of the schools."[12]

The emphasis on a masculine ideal was especially true within the small community of black nationalist-emigrationists. Mary Ann's friend and ally Martin Delany was among the first black nationalists to directly equate black patriarchy with racial progress and cohesiveness. Black women, in Delany's view, should be educated to take on the Victorian roles of mother, teacher, and transmitter of moral values. That Delany eventually welcomed Mary Ann into the fold of black nationalist-emigrationists suggests that her tenacity and influence overcame any misgivings he may have had about her participation. But her leadership in the movement was clearly exceptional. The only other woman to frequent the 1850s emigration conventions was Mary Bibb, who was a powerful spokeswoman in her own right although she was recognized mostly as a stand-in for her deceased husband. Henry Bibb, James Theodore Holly, and Canadian emigrationists were always uncomfortable with Mary Ann's influence and openly disapproved of her visibility in the movement.[13]

Mary Ann was drawn to Canada and emigrationist ideology because of her disillusionment with the worsening racial climate in the United States on the one hand, and her adventurer's optimism on the other. It was a place where she could find both a political and physical space for herself, unlike the narrow black political establishment in the northern United States. Mary Ann's bourgeois nationalism represented a merger of the racial uplift theories she developed in free black communities in the North, with more radical ideals of black autonomy and self-sufficiency honed on the Canadian frontier. Her politics reflected her experiences as a privileged free person of color who felt responsible for the less fortunate of her race. She saw no contradictions between her support of integrated public institutions in white Canada and her calls for a black nationality. Shadd Cary, unlike Delany, Bibb, and Holly, had no particular romance with blackness or an idealized "fatherland" in Africa or the Caribbean. She was a pragmatic nationalist—interested in finding a homeland where African Americans could flourish without the constant oppression of racism. But after the Civil War she learned that there was no escape from racial tyranny, either in the United States or Canada, in the North or South.

During the heyday of Reconstruction, black nationalists and integrationists alike invested their energies in traditional politics as the surest route for advancement. But political engagement through voting and public office were beyond Mary Ann's reach—this was the province of men like her brothers Isaac and Abraham. As she encountered gender barriers to equal participation in the political arena, Mary Ann had to fall back on the philosophy of reform, self-help and economic development that she first articulated in *Hints to the Colored People of the North* in 1849, and later reprised at the Colored National Labor Union convention. Over time, she developed a political ideology that bridged her early nationalism with an increasingly militant feminism. Thus, Mary Ann's politics during the latter half of her life were predicated on the dual quests for racial and gender justice through alternative public spheres. One issue was not given primacy over the other; instead, she called for a racial politics that was gender inclusive, and a platform for women's rights that foregrounded racial discrimination.

Mary Ann, like other postbellum black leaders, tended to blame African Americans for their condition even as they recognized the exigencies of racial oppression. Throughout her political life, she believed that black people bore the primary responsibility for improving their lot and changing their social position. Her notions of elitist reform were a precursor to the identification of a talented tenth by figures like Du Bois and Alexander Crummell. She made considerable personal and economic sacrifices to demonstrate blacks' ability to rise to the top of Western civilization. By the end of her life, the meaning of racial uplift itself had become a subject of debate among black leaders. She would likely have applauded Crummell's establishment of the American Negro Academy in 1897 despite its exclusion of women. It was designed as an intellectual haven in which the black elite could forge a new "domestic nationalism" based on many of the principles she had championed. Mary Ann would undoubtedly have joined other black leaders in their criticism of Booker T. Washington's strategy of racial progress through manual labor and vocational training, rather than through a classical education that led to professional pursuits. His program of conciliation with and appeasement of white America would have gone against the grain of Mary Ann's understanding of political agitation and protest. Nevertheless, the new generation of black leaders such as Washington, Crummell, and Du Bois owed much to her early formulations of racial solidarity and economic improvement.[14]

Shadd Cary's life also tells us a great deal about class and color in nineteenth-century black communities of the North. As a light-skinned, free-born person of color, she had access to a social and intellectual world that set itself apart from the darker-skinned masses. Mary Ann's family followed a familiar pattern of marrying within a color caste and she traveled easily within the networks of the light-skinned black elite of many northern cities. Unlike many of her lighter-skinned contemporaries, however, Mary Ann showed no public ambivalence about her racial heritage. Her political discourse focused on racial unity and a recognition of the shared plight of black Americans. Mary Ann's experiences as a teacher of fugitive slaves and freedmen may have shaped these beliefs; she had close, daily contact with blacks of all castes and colors throughout her working life. And her upbringing in an activist household and training by Quakers probably instilled a fundamental appreciation for equality and a disdain for cliquishness and snobbery. Yet, it is difficult to know if she deliberately placed social distance between herself and darker-skinned blacks, particularly in her private life. Many of her closest friends and associates, such as Samuel Ringgold Ward, Martin Delany, and William Still, articulated pride in their dark-skinned visage. If Mary Ann's rhetoric offers some insight into her closely held ideas, it suggests that she was more influenced by displays of breeding and intelligence than by skin color in evaluating a person's character.[15]

Mary Ann became part of an educated, professional elite that assumed its position as the talented tenth envisioned by Du Bois. Yet she was without money, her own home, possessions, or other outward symbols of middle-class comfort. At the beginning of her life, the Shadd family lived on the margins of Philadelphia's small black upper class—geographically, socially, and economically. Mary Ann benefited from being part of this intellectual and political world, but her daily existence was far removed from the families of the wealthy entrepreneurs who defined the city's black elite. Mary Ann's education and political instincts were her ticket into the middle class. But this did not translate into an ideal life of true womanhood. Free black women lucky enough to obtain an education neither had extensive leisure time, nor were they pampered housewives with servants to help with child rearing and household labor. A study of Boston's black nineteenth-century communities highlighted this gap: "The romanticization of womanhood which left females free from the necessities of employment was as inapplicable [to black women] as it was for poor women generally."[16]

As a teacher, Mary Ann lived a significant step above domestic employment, but her financial situation was always precarious. In Canada West, she courted poverty as she begged for money and scraped for jobs. She accepted the job of Union Army recruiter, in part, because it offered a way to make money. In her final years in Washington, she still functioned on the fringes of the black aristocracy, with their receptions and debutante balls, social clubs and trips to Europe, fancy attire and what Gatewood has termed their "genteel performance." It was her far more prosperous cousin, the doctor Furman Shadd, who was at the helm of Washington's black bourgeoisie. In 1895 Furman Shadd was listed among the city's ten wealthiest black men. Mary Ann's family connections gave her access to this world, but fundamentally, she was not a part of it.[17]

Throughout her life, Mary Ann was preoccupied with gaining and maintaining a public voice. This was essential for her self-described roles as a reformer and race woman. Inadvertently, perhaps, her quest for access to the press placed Shadd Cary in the forefront of a developing African American print culture in the United States. From the era of David Walker's "Appeal to the Colored Citizens of the World" in the 1830s through Reconstruction, pamphlets, newspapers, and periodicals were essential for public communication and political discourse within the varied African American communities. The debates over citizenship, abolition, and emigration would have been muted and indistinct without the struggling print media that gave them a voice. Mary Ann actively contributed to this discourse through her early pamphlets *Hints to the Colored People of the North* and *Notes of Canada West,* as well as her articles and letters to the press. But it was her newspaper, the *Provincial Freeman,* which helped construct an imagined community for black Americans in Canada and England, as well as in the North, by providing them with a shared experience in the act of reading. As Benedict Anderson has argued, the simultaneous consumption of newspapers and other print media across broad geographic areas has been instrumental in facilitating collective identities that become the basis for emergent nationalisms.[18]

The newspapers of Henry Bibb and Mary Ann Shadd Cary were vital institutions in the efforts to build a sense of black nationalism in Canada West. As black-controlled publications they exemplified the nationalist values of self-determination and self-sufficiency. Within the pages of these newspapers, Canada's black population could find information that specifically addressed their needs and circumstances, and have a vehicle for public expression. These publications also served an important external function by promoting the emigrationist agenda, and informing readers in the United States about black life in Canada.

It has been suggested that the *Provincial Freeman* failed because of its small and fragmented audience, and because it fostered dissension among its black and white readers. This criticism reflects a fundamental misunderstanding about the paper's functions and about the history of the black press. Virtually all antebellum black newspapers reached a relatively small audience and were short-lived. They struggled to reach the often illiterate and impoverished black masses, a tiny black elite with limited resources, and potential advertisers who might be indifferent or openly hostile. That the *Freeman* remained active for seven years places it among a small group of influential publications, including Frederick Douglass's newspapers and the *Christian Herald*. In addition to its longevity, the *Provincial Freeman* contributed to the formation of a black public sphere by giving voice to the many factions of dissent among blacks in Canada and the United States. The presence of a newspaper and an opinionated editor in a small, secluded black community gave vitality to these debates and enabled multiple voices to be heard.[19]

As a journalist, Shadd Cary stretched the boundaries of the nineteenth century associational press to engage in investigative reporting and muckraking, practices usually attributed to the early twentieth century. She carried out lengthy investigations of the Refugee Home Society, the Dawn settlement, rival emigrationists, and a host of white and black figures whom she considered unscrupulous or immoral. Her editorials were clearly rhetorical devices, but they were frequently supported by observation, documents, and quotes. Like reporters fifty years later, she had no qualms about attacking revered institutions like the church, she decried hypocrisy and greed, and she sought to expose wrongdoing especially when she believed such actions exploited the black community. Mary Ann's journalism was an activist endeavor aimed at social change. Her work provided a blueprint for a future generation of black journalists such as Ida Wells-Barnett and T. Thomas Fortune by demonstrating that public expression could constitute a range of oppositional acts. Mary Ann was anxious to continue this work after the Civil War, but she never secured the funds or public support to do so.

Her efforts at cultivating a black public sphere, especially one which included women, extended well beyond the black press. Mary Ann Shadd Cary was deeply committed to engaging in rational political discourse beginning with her early involvement in the convention and emigration movements, through her ceaseless speaking tours and her efforts at securing women's suffrage. From the *Provincial Freeman* to the Colored Women's Professional Franchise Association, she exhorted black women to claim a public voice and work collectively. Some nineteenth-century black women were successful in promoting a distinct counter-public in which they could establish authority in their communities without overtly challenging black male hegemony. In the post-Reconstruction South, this frequently occurred within the structures of the black church. But this was not always an option for Mary Ann. The ideology of separate spheres was firmly entrenched in the older and more established black elite of Washington. Mary Ann also had a complicated, and not always friendly, relationship with black religion beginning with her condemnation of the A.M.E. church in the 1850s. Through her community organizing and temperance work she revealed a powerful spiritual and intellectual engagement with Christianity. But she also had great disdain for what she saw as the low-brow trappings of black evangelical religion, and black ministers were some of her frequent targets. Thus, Mary Ann did not turn to the church as a route to public expression. At the same time, she did not have access to benevolent societies like the Independent Order of Saint Luke, which provided a site for black women's organizing in Virginia at the turn of the century. Nor could she turn to the black women's clubs that would crop up shortly after her death. Mary Ann had set her sights on a secular public sphere that was concerned with economic and political development—she had the foresight, but not the critical mass, necessary to forge such alliances.[20]

Mary Ann may have suffered considerable disappointment in her efforts to support herself as a journalist, but ultimately she will be remembered as a pioneer in the field. She was acutely aware of her status as a trailblazer. When she reminded African American women that she had "broken the editorial ice" in journalism, she was also urging them to follow in her footsteps. But it took thirty years before black women had any active involvement with the press. One analyst found that forty-six black women—mostly from the South—worked as writers and editors between 1883 and 1905. This dramatic increase was attributed to the rapid rise of the black press during this period, improved educational opportunities for women, and the emergent women's club movement. These women were praised by their male colleagues and they played a visible role in national press conventions. But by the time black women began to claim a place in journalism, Mary Ann was putting her waning energy into her legal work.[21]

Just two years before her death, in 1891, the first history of the black press was published by a young educator named I. Garland Penn. One chapter singled out more than a dozen black women who were making their mark as freelance writers, reporters, and editors for both black and white-owned newspapers and magazines. The only mention of Mary Ann was a brief paragraph citing her editorship of the *Provincial Freeman,* which misspelled her name. Journalist and clubwoman Gertrude Mossell wrote an essay for Penn's volume that reviewed women's status in the black press. She complained that the handful of women listed were the exception to the rule: "Few have become independent workers in this noble field of effort, being yet satellites, revolving round the sun of masculine journalism." Mossell's assessments could have been a page out of Shadd Cary's own writing. In particular she echoed Shadd Cary's views—expressed decades earlier—that black women should be given the opportunity to prove themselves as competent as any man.[22]

The growing attention to black women's accomplishments was reflected in a spate of celebratory books and articles like Penn's published in the 1890s. These texts were intended to elevate black women's status amid the unrelenting assaults on their character and bodies; they were a calculated response to the racist campaigns seeking to denigrate black women's advancement. One such author, Monroe Majors, embraced Victorian rhetoric to ennoble black women—"I regard a true woman as the best, the grandest of all God's human creatures"—and went on to entertain the possibility that "our leading women have cleared the culminating point and out-distanced our great men." Major's book *Noted Negro Women: Their Triumphs and Activities* included Mary Ann among a list of nearly three hundred individuals. The entry, published in the year of her death, reproduced Bishop Payne's recollections of Mary Ann's work in Canada West and her editorship of the *Provincial Freeman*. It is clear that Majors knew nothing about her post-Civil War career. He referred to her as Miss Mary A. Shadd and only discussed her work in the 1850s. Similarly, a lecturer at the Brooklyn Literary Union in New York briefly mentioned Mary Ann's skill as a public speaker in a speech titled "Some Afro-American Women of Mark," given in 1892. Two years later, Gertrude Mossell identified Mary Ann as one of three black female lawyers in the nation when she published *The Work of the Afro-American Woman,* but the book failed to address her work in the black press, or as an educator.[23]

Thirty years after her death, W. E. B. Du Bois chose to resurrect Shadd Cary's legacy in an essay titled "The Damnation of Women," which pleaded for the elevation of black women in the national imagination. Du Bois captured many of Shadd Cary's achievements and characteristics as he painted her in a romantic, almost ethereal light.

> She was tall and slim, of the ravishing dream-born beauty,—that twilight of the race which we call mulatto. Well-educated, vivacious, with determination shining from her sharp eyes, she threw herself single-handed into the great Canadian pilgrimage. . . .

Du Bois' brief tribute celebrated her work as an editor, teacher, and lecturer who "tramped afoot through winter snows" and held forth at public meetings, culminating with her role as a Union Army recruiting agent. But, what of the rest of her life? Du Bois presented both the substance and folklore surrounding Mary Ann Shadd Cary. She was beautiful, tenacious, and a powerful symbol for the cause of racial uplift. But despite Mary Ann's best efforts at defining her legacy, others would compartmentalize her by career or era. Who she was and what she did could not be neatly packaged in a brief biographical sketch. Perhaps Shadd Cary paid a price for her divided energies. Her many interests meant that she would never be associated with a singular accomplishment or role. Ultimately, Shadd Cary became obscured in the history of a people intent on preserving memories that would venerate leaders and exemplify the aptitude and abilities of the race. So many in the generations that followed her would know nothing about Shadd Cary's work or her struggles. It would take one hundred years from the time of her death, and a renewed commitment to uncovering the forgotten, before her story would be reclaimed.[24]

NOTES

Abbreviations

AMA = American Missionary Association Archives, Amistad Research Center, New Orleans

MASC/MS = Mary Ann Shadd Cary Papers, Moorland-Spingarn Research Center, Howard University, Washington, D.C.

MASC/NAC = Mary Ann Shadd Cary Papers, National Archives of Canada, Ottawa

MASC/OPA = Mary Ann Shadd Cary Papers, Ontario Provincial Archives, Toronto

Introduction

1. *Frederick Douglass' Paper*, 4 July 1856; for more on Douglass see William S. McFeeley, *Frederick Douglass* (New York: W. W. Norton, 1991), and Benjamin Quarles, *Frederick Douglass* (Washington, D.C.: Associated Publishers, 1948).

2. James W. Carey, "The Problem of Journalism History," *Journalism History* 1 (Spring 1974): 5. Shadd Cary has been generally ignored in the annals of journalism history, with one notable exception: Rodger Streitmatter, *Raising Her Voice: African-American Women Journalists Who Changed History* (Lexington: University Press of Kentucky, 1994). Most recently, Robert S. Levine, *Martin Delany, Frederick Douglass, and the Politics of Representative Identity* (Chapel Hill: University of North Carolina Press, 1997) relies heavily on the *Provincial Freeman* as a source.

3. Floyd Miller, *The Search for a Black Nationality: Black Emigration and Colonization, 1787–1863* (Urbana: University of Illinois Press, 1975); and C. Peter Ripley, ed., *The Black Abolitionist Papers, Vol. II, Canada 1830–1865* (Chapel Hill: University of North Carolina Press, 1986). More recently Shirley J. Yee, *Black Women Abolitionists: A Study in Activism, 1828–1860* (Knoxville: University of Tennessee Press, 1992), and Carla L. Peterson, *"Doers of the Word": African-American Women Speakers and Writers in the North (1830–1880)* (New York: Oxford University Press, 1995) suggest Shadd Cary is part of a larger network of black women activists.

4. On Douglass, see David W. Blight, *Frederick Douglass' Civil War: Keeping*

226

Notes for Pages xvi–xviii

Faith in Jubilee (Baton Rouge: Louisiana State University Press, 1989); and Levine, *Martin Delany, Frederick Douglass, and the Politics of Representative Identity.*

5. Peterson, *"Doers of the Word,"* 8–18; also see James Oliver Horton and Lois Horton, "Violence, Protest, and Identity: Black Manhood in Antebellum America," in James Oliver Horton, *Free People of Color: Inside the African American Community* (Washington, D.C.: Smithsonian Institution Press, 1993). The debate over the proper behavior of nineteenth-century women activists can be traced to Catharine Beecher's 1837 assertion that women should appeal to the public through love and an absence of confrontation. Although abolitionist women like Angelina Grimké opposed this ideal, it remained a popular position. See Jean Fagan Yellin, *Women and Sisters: The Antislavery Feminists in American Culture* (New Haven: Yale University Press, 1989), 29–50. Shadd Cary has not been included in some works, such as Beverly Guy-Sheftall, ed., *Words of Fire: An Anthology of African-American Feminist Thought* (New York: New Press, 1995).

6. See Nell Painter, "Sojourner Truth in Life and Memory: Writing the Biography of an American Exotic," *Gender and History* 2 (Spring 1990): 10.

7. See Deborah Gray White, "Mining the Forgotten: Manuscript Sources for Black Women's History," *Journal of American History* 74 (June 1987): 237–42.

8. Ira Berlin, *Slaves without Masters: The Free Negro in the Antebellum South* (New York: Pantheon Books: A Division of Random House, 1974), xiv.

9. These early references include Sylvia Dannett, *Profiles of American Negro Womanhood,* vol. I (New York: M. W. Lads, 1964); Elsie M. Lewis, "Mary Ann Shadd Cary," in Edward T. James, ed., *Notable American Women* (Cambridge: Cambridge University Press, 1971), 300–1; Eleanor Flexner, *Century of Struggle* (Cambridge: Harvard University Press, 1975), 98; Gerda Lerner, *Black Women in White America: A Documentary History* (New York: Vintage Books, 1973), 323–24; Bettina Aptheker, *Woman's Legacy: Essays on Race, Sex, and Class in American History* (Amherst: University of Massachusetts Press, 1982), 38; Michelle Cliff, *Free Enterprise* (New York: Dutton, 1993); for a study of the cultural representations of Pleasant, see Lynn M. Hudson, "When 'Mammy' Becomes a Millionaire: Mary Ellen Pleasant, An African-American Entrepreneur" (Ph.D. diss., Indiana University, 1996).

10. Evans identified herself as a "paralytic" in the Mary Ann Shadd Cary Papers, Moorland-Spingarn Research Center, Howard University, Washington, D.C., hereafter MASC/MS. Among those who relied heavily on Evans's biographical sketch are Robin Winks, "Mary Ann Shadd," in *The Dictionary of American Negro Biography,* Rayford W. Logan and Michael R. Winston, eds. (New York: W. W. Norton, 1982), 552–53; Sylvia Dannett, "Mary Ann Shadd Cary: Newspaper Woman, Canadian Pioneer, and Lawyer," 150–57; and Marianna W. Davis, *Contributions of Black Women to America,* vol. 1 (Columbia, S.C.: Kenday Press, 1982), 432, 211–14.

11. Alexander L. Murray, "The *Provincial Freeman*: A New Source for the History of the Negro in Canada and the United States," *Journal of Negro History* 43 (April 1959): 123–35. For studies of blacks in Canada, see Robin Winks, *The Blacks in Canada* (New Haven: Yale University Press, 1971); Donald G. Simpson, "Negroes in Ontario from Early Times to 1970" (Ph.D. diss., University of Western Ontario, 1971); and Jason Silverman, *Unwelcome Guests: Canada West's Response to American Fugitive Slaves, 1800–1865* (Millwood, N.Y.: Associated Faculties Press,

1985). Quotes are from Harold B. Hancock, "Mary Ann Shadd: Negro Editor, Educator, and Lawyer," *Delaware History* 15 (1973): 187–94; and Lerner, *Black Women in White America: A Documentary History*, 323. See also Miller, *The Search for a Black Nationality: Black Emigration and Colonization, 1787–1863* (Urbana, Ill.: University of Illinois Press, 1975). Jim Bearden and Linda Jean Butler, *Shadd: The Life and Times of Mary Shadd Cary* (Toronto: NC Press Ltd., 1977).

12. In addition to articles in the black press, sources include correspondence between Shadd Cary and several well-known figures including Douglass, Delany, and Still. On Watkins Harper, see Frances S. Foster, *A Brighter Coming Day: A Frances Ellen Watkins Harper Reader* (New York: Feminist Press, 1990). Foster, p. 14, for example, claims Shadd Cary and Watkins Harper were friends, but there is nothing to support this contention.

13. *The Toronto Star*, 28 April 1987; for reproductions of her work see, for example, *Tiger Lily: Journal by Women of Colour* Amistad Research Center 9/10 (1991): 14–25.

14. Audre Lorde, "Age, Race, Class, and Sex: Women Redefining Difference," in *Sister Outsider: Essays and Speeches* (Trumansburg, N.Y.: Crossing Press, 1984), 123.

ONE / The Making of an Activist

1. Amelia C. Shadd Williamson and A. T. Shadd Williamson, *Record of the Shadd Family in America*, 21 August 1905, Shadd Family Papers, Tulane University, New Orleans; a copy of this family history is also in the Regional Collection, D. B. Weldon Library, University of Western Ontario; *Shadd Family Tree*, 1977, Raleigh Township Centennial Museum, North Buxton, Ontario; Albert R. Schmitt, "'The Hessians and Who?' A Look at the Other Germans in the American War of Independence," *Yearbook of German-American Studies* 18 (1983): 41–61; Rodney Atwood, *The Hessians: Mercenaries from Hessen-Kassel in the American Revolution* (Cambridge: Cambridge University Press, 1980), 12–21.

2. Mill Creek Hundred tax lists of 1775, 1785, and 1798, Division of Historical and Cultural Affairs, Department of State, Dover, Delaware. Over the years, Hans's name became Americanized to Hance Shad in some public records. Also see Amelia C. Shadd Williamson and A. T. Shadd Williamson, *Record of the Shadd Family in America*; John A. Munroe, *History of Delaware*, 2nd ed. (Newark: University of Delaware Press, 1984), 16–20, 57, 96–100; U.S. Census, 1790.

3. Elizabeth Montgomery, *Reminiscences of Wilmington, in Familiar Village Tales, Ancient and New* (Philadelphia: T. K. Collins, Jr., 1851; rept. Port Washington, N.Y.: Kennikat Press, 1972), 251–52.

4. Record of Marriages, Holy Trinity Church, 1785–86, Division of Historical and Cultural Affairs, Department of State, Dover, Delaware; Amelia C. Shadd Williamson and A. T. Shadd Williamson, *Record of the Shadd Family in America*, Shadd Family Papers, Tulane University; also see another version of the Shadd family record in the Regional Collection, D. B. Weldon Library, University of Western Ontario; Montgomery, *Reminiscences of Wilmington*, 252.

5. Letter to Mrs. Shadd, 26 February 1928, Regional Collection, D. B. Weldon Library, University of Western Ontario; the letter recounts the tales of an old

Wilmington businessman recited to a member of the Shadd family in the late nineteenth century; Ira Berlin, "The Structure of the Free Negro Caste in the Antebellum United States," *Journal of Social History* 9 (Spring 1976): 309–11.

6. *Return of the Whole Number of Persons within the Several Districts of the United States, 1800* (House of Representatives); Loren Schweninger, *Black Property Owners in the South, 1790–1915* (Urbana: University of Illinois Press, 1990), 74–75, 108–12; Inventory and Probate Records of Jeremiah Shad, New Castle County, 1819, 1820, 1823, Division of Historical and Cultural Affairs, Department of State, Dover, Delaware. Note that the family name was altered from Schad.

7. On Harriet Shadd, see U.S. Census, Enumeration for the County of West Chester, 1850 (Washington, D.C., 1851); 1800, 1810, 1820, 1830 Census of North Carolina, Wilson Library, North Carolina Collection, University of North Carolina, Chapel Hill; the state census only lists heads of households until 1850 and birth/death records were not kept in North Carolina before 1913. On Abraham Shadd, see New Castle County Tax Records, 1825, 1827, 1830 and New Castle County Apprentice Indenture Book, 1829–31, Division of Historical and Cultural Affairs, Department of State, Dover, Delaware; for a thorough discussion of the shoemaking trade, see Mary H. Blewett, *Men, Women and Work: Class, Gender, and Power in the New England Shoe Industry, 1780–1910* (Urbana: University of Illinois Press, 1990).

8. The handful of photographs of the Shadd relatives support the assumption that the family was very fair-skinned. A number of scholars have discussed the role of skin color in the formation of a caste system among antebellum blacks. See Berlin, "The Structure of the Free Negro Caste in the Antebellum United States," 305; Willard B. Gatewood, *Aristocrats of Color: The Black Elite, 1880–1920* (Bloomington, Ind.: Indiana University Press, 1990), 7–29; and James Oliver Horton, *Free People of Color*, 122–44.

9. Ira Berlin, *Slaves without Masters*, 15–16, 45.

10. U.S. Census, 1790–1840; for discussion of factors that contributed to Delaware's relatively mild form of slavery see Munroe, *History of Delaware*, 96–99, and John A. Munroe, "The Negro in Delaware," *South Atlantic Quarterly* 56 (Autumn 1957): 428; also see Bruce Bender, "Securing One of the Blessings of Liberty: Black Families in Lower New Castle County, 1790–1850," *Delaware History* 25 (1993–94): 237–52.

11. See Patience Essah, "Slavery and Freedom in the First State: The History of Blacks in Delaware from the Colonial Period to 1865" (Ph.D. diss., University of California, Los Angeles, 1985), 55–77; Carol E. Hoffecker, *Delaware: A Bicentennial History* (New York: W. W. Norton, 1977), 90–95; Munroe, "The Negro in Delaware," 428–44; quote from Barbara J. Fields, *Slavery and Freedom on the Middle Ground: Maryland during the Nineteenth Century* (New Haven: Yale University Press, 1985), 209 n.3.

12. William Yates, "Slavery and Colored People in Delaware," *The Emancipator*, 5 August 1837, reprinted in *Delaware History*, 14 (April 1971): 205–16. Fears of slave revolts were induced with Gabriel Prosser's revolt in 1800 and the insurrection led by Denmark Vesey in 1822, and peaked in 1831 with the Nat Turner rebellion in Southampton County, Virginia, in which sixty whites and more than 100 blacks were killed.

13. See Essah, "Slavery and Freedom in the First State," 205–11; and Yates letter for extensive description of these legal proscriptions, including references to Delaware statutes.

14. Berlin, *Slaves without Masters,* 91–92; also see Yates letter; Hancock, "Not Quite Men," 323.

15. Hancock, "Not Quite Men," 328; Berlin, *Slaves without Masters,* 69; Munroe, *History of Delaware,* 92–95; Record of Marriages, Holy Trinity Church, 1785–86, Division of Historical and Cultural Affairs, Department of State, Dover, Delaware.

16. Lewis V. Baldwin, "Festivity and Celebration: A Profile of Wilmington's Big Quarterly," *Delaware History* 19 (1981): 197–211; quoted from Montgomery, *Reminiscences of Wilmington,* 252.

17. Carter G. Woodson, *The Education of the Negro Prior to 1861* (1919; rpt., New York: Arno Press, 1968), 103; also see Jacqueline J. Halstead, "Practical Christianity: The Delaware Association for the Moral Improvement and Education of the Colored People," *Delaware History* 15 (April 1972): 19–40; Berlin, *Slaves without Masters,* 75; Yates, "Slavery and Colored People in Delaware," 210.

18. Abraham Shadd's correspondence indicates a high degree of intelligence, but poor spelling and grammar skills suggest no formal schooling. On education for blacks, see Yates letter; and Patience Essah, "Slavery and Freedom in the First State," 146–50, 199–200; quote from Sarah Cary Evans, "Mrs. Mary Ann Shadd Cary, 1823–1893, The Foremost Colored Canadian Pioneer in 1850," in *Homespun Heroines and Other Women of Distinction,* ed. Hallie Q. Brown (1926; rpt., New York: Oxford University Press, 1988), 92.

19. See P. J. Staudenraus, *The African Colonization Movement, 1816–1865* (New York: Columbia University Press, 1961); for extensive discussion on the ASC and Liberia, see Miller, *The Search for a Black Nationality,* 45, 55–74; on blacks' response, see Benjamin Quarles, *Black Abolitionists* (New York: Oxford University Press, 1975), 3–22; and Jane H. Pease and William Pease, *They Who Would Be Free: Blacks' Search for Freedom, 1830–1861* (New York: Athenaeum, 1974), 4–6.

20. The Seventh Annual Report of the American Society for Colonizing the Free People of Colour of the United States, February 1824, Washington, D.C.; *The African Repository and Colonial Journal,* January 1826, 335, 343, 346.

21. *Tenth Annual Report of the American Society for Colonizing the Free People of Colour of the United States,* February 1827, Washington, D.C.

22. "The First Colored Convention," *Anglo-African Magazine,* October 1859; quote on Shadd from Martin Delany, *The Condition, Elevation, Emigration and Destiny of the Colored People of the United States* (1852; rpt., New York: Arno Press, 1968), 15; Howard H. Bell, *A Survey of the Negro Convention Movement, 1830–1861* (New York: Arno Press, 1969), 13–14; and Leon Litwack, *North of Slavery: The Negro in the Free States, 1790–1860* (Chicago: University of Chicago Press, 1965), 235.

23. See Winks, *Blacks in Canada,* 178–81, 159–60; and C. Peter Ripley, *The Black Abolitionist Papers,* vol. II, *Canada 1830–1865* (Chapel Hill: University of North Carolina Press, 1986), 9; Bell, *Survey of the Negro Convention Movement,* 13; *Minutes and Proceedings of the First Annual Convention of Free Persons of Color* (Philadelphia: 1831), Africana Library, Cornell University.

24. *Minutes and Proceedings of the First Annual Convention of the Free People of*

Colour at the Wesleyan Church, Philadelphia, July 6, 1831 (Philadelphia, 1831); Bell, *Survey of the Negro Convention Movement,* 30; and Howard Bell, ed., *Proceedings of the National Negro Conventions, 1830–1864* (New York: Arno Press, 1969).

25. *The Liberator,* 24 September 1831.

26. William Lloyd Garrison, *Thoughts on African Colonization* (1832; rpt. New York: Arno Press, 1968), 36–40; Quarles, *Black Abolitionists,* 20.

27. *Minutes and Proceedings of the Second Annual Convention for the Improvement of the Free People of Color in These United States* (Philadelphia: Martin and Boden, 1832), 8–10; Bell, *Proceedings of the National Negro Conventions.*

28. Bell, *Survey of the Negro Convention Movement,* 33; Delany, *The Condition, Elevation, Emigration and Destiny of the Colored People of the United States,* 24.

29. Charles W. Heathcote, *History of Chester County* (West Chester, Pa.: Horace Temple Printer, 1926); and W. W. Thomson, ed., *Chester County and Its People* (Chicago: Union Historical Company, 1898), both from Historical Society of Pennsylvania, Philadelphia.

30. Bell, *Proceedings of the National Negro Conventions.*

31. Quarles, *Black Abolitionists,* 25; for a discussion of Garrisonian ideology and the rise of moral suasion see Gerald Sorin, *Abolitionism: A New Perspective* (New York: Praeger, 1972), 56–75; and Ronald G. Walters, *The Antislavery Appeal: American Abolitionism after 1830* (New York: W. W. Norton, 1978), 3–18; Bell, *Proceedings of the National Negro Conventions.*

32. Charles L. Blockson, *The Underground Railroad* (New York: Prentice Hall, 1987), 166–67; see, for example, William Still, *Underground Rail Road Records* (Philadelphia: William Still, 1883), 223–34.

33. R. C. Smedley, *History of the Underground Railroad in Chester and the Neighboring Counties of Pennsylvania* (1883; rpt., New York: Negro Universities Press, 1968), 33, 337; Shadd is also mentioned in J. Smith Futhey and Gilbert Cope, *History of Chester County, Pennsylvania* (1881), 426–27, Chester County Archives and Records Services, West Chester, Pennsylvania; and in Edward Raymond Turner, *The Negro in Pennsylvania: Slavery—Servitude—Freedom, 1639–1861* (1911; rpt., New York: Arno Press, 1969), 240.

34. West Chester County Tax Lists, 1836 and 1850; and West Chester Septennial Census, 1835 and 1842, Chester County Historical Society, West Chester, Pennsylvania; Commissioner's Tax Index, 1833 to 1854; and West Chester Recorder of Deeds, 1839, 1848, 1853, 1854, Chester County Archives and Records Services, West Chester, Pennsylvania; quote from Quarles, *Black Abolitionists,* 149.

35. U.S. Department of State, *Sixth Census* (Washington: 1841), 24–27; Turner, *Negro in Pennsylvania,* 79–88; Gary B. Nash, *Forging Freedom: The Formation of Philadelphia's Black Community, 1720–1840* (Cambridge: Harvard University Press, 1988), 212–14.

36. Julie Winch, *Philadelphia's Black Elite: Activism, Accommodation, and the Struggle for Autonomy, 1787–1848* (Philadelphia: Temple University Press, 1988), 4–25; Joseph Wilson, *Sketches of the Higher Classes of Colored Society in Philadelphia* (Philadelphia: Merrihew and Thompson, Printers, 1841).

37. Emma Jones Lapsansky, "Friends, Wives and Strivings: Networks and Community Values among Nineteenth-Century Philadelphia Afroamerican Elites,"

Pennsylvania Magazine of History and Biography 108 (January 1984): 3–19; Wilson, *Sketches of the Higher Classes.*

38. Theodore Hershberg, "Free Blacks in Antebellum Philadelphia: A Study of Ex-Slaves, Freeborn, and Socioeconomic Decline," *Journal of Social History* V (Winter 1971–72): 191; and Nash, *Forging Freedom,* 223–27.

39. Woodson, *Education of the Negro Prior to 1861,* 145–9; W. E. B. Du Bois, *The Philadelphia Negro* (1899; rpt., Millwood, N.Y.: Kraus-Thomson Organization Limited, 1973), 83–87; Nash, *Forging Freedom,* 208–11, 267–71.

40. *The Minutes and Proceedings of the First Meeting of the American Reform Society* (Philadelphia: Merrihew and Gunn, 1837), 17; Sixth Census; Sarah Cary Evans, "Mrs. Mary Ann Shadd Cary," 92; and biographical sketch by David T. Williamson Shadd, 29 June 1960, Mary Ann Shadd Cary Papers, National Archives of Canada, Ottawa, Canada, hereafter MASC/NAC; Abraham Shadd Ledger, Shadd Family Papers, Raleigh Township Centennial Museum, North Buxton, Ontario; Futhey and Cope, *History of Chester County,* 427. More recent accounts assert that she attended Price's Boarding School in West Chester, based on the findings in Sylvia Dannett, *Profiles of Negro Womanhood* (New York: M. W. Lads, Inc., 1964). This is also purely speculative. Other sources, including Thomas Woody, *Early Quaker Education in Pennsylvania* (New York: Teachers College, Columbia University, 1920); and Vincent P. Franklin, *The Education of Black Philadelphia* (Philadelphia: University of Pennsylvania Press, 1979), confirm the existence of Price's Boarding School but no school run by Darlington.

41. Woodson, *The Education of the Negro Prior to 1861,* 4–11.

42. Bell, *Survey of the Negro Convention Movement,* 34; Howard Bell, "The American Moral Reform Society, 1836–1841," *Journal of Negro Education* 27 (Winter 1958): 34–40; see also the *Minutes and Proceedings of the First Meeting of the American Moral Reform Society;* and Winch, *Philadelphia's Black Elite,* 83–84.

43. Wilson, *Sketches of the Higher Classes;* James Oliver Horton, "Freedom's Yoke: Gender Conventions among Antebellum Free Blacks," *Feminist Studies* 12 (Spring 1986): 106–8; see also Ira V. Brown, *The Negro in Pennsylvania History* (University Park, Pa.; Pennsylvania Historical Association, 1970), 37–39; Turner, *Negro in Pennsylvania,* and Du Bois, *The Philadelphia Negro,* both rely on the following sources for this data: *Register of the Trades of the Colored People in the City of Philadelphia and Districts* (Philadelphia: 1838); and *A Statistical Inquiry into the Condition of the People of Colour of the City and Districts of Philadelphia* (Philadelphia: Society of Friends, 1849).

44. Linda Perkins, "Black Women and Racial 'Uplift' Prior to Emancipation," in Filomina Chioma Steady, ed., *The Black Woman Cross-Culturally* (Cambridge, Mass.: Schenckman Publishing, 1981), 317; also see Perkins, "The Impact of the Cult of True Womanhood on the Education of Black Women," *Journal of Social Issues* 39 (1983): 3.

45. *The Colored American,* 15, 22 August 1840; the article mentions a Capt. J. N. Shadd present at the program; this could have been Abraham's brother Jacob, who was four years his junior.

46. This contention appears in Evans's entry in *Homespun Heroines,* and in Sylvia Dannett, *Profiles of Negro Womanhood,* 151; *The North Star,* 5 January 1849.

47. Mary Ann's brief residence in Norristown is suggested in a biographical sketch by David T. W. Shadd, June 29, 1960, MASC/NAC. Sources are limited on blacks in Norristown and Trenton during this era. No city directories are available for the 1840s and local histories give scant reference to black residents or schools. See *Directory of the Boroughs of Norristown and Bridgeport, 1860–61* (1860), and Rev. Theodore Heysham, *Norristown, 1812–1912* (1913), both at Historical Society of Pennsylvania, Philadelphia; A. D. Shadd to Mary Ann Shadd, 8 December 1844, MASC/MS.

48. *Minutes of the State Convention of the Coloured Citizens of Pennsylvania, convened at Harrisburg, December 13th and 14th, 1848,* in Philip S. Foner and George E. Walker, eds., *Proceedings of the Black State Conventions, 1840–1865* (Philadelphia: Temple University Press, 1979), 119–35, 149; Turner, *Negro in Pennsylvania,* 169–93, gives an extensive account of the campaign to deny blacks in the state the right to vote. The state constitution passed in 1873 finally enfranchised black males; also see Gary Nash, *Forging Freedom,* 217–23.

49. *North Star,* 23 March 1849.

50. Ibid.

51. Mary Ann Shadd to George Whipple, 27 November 1851, American Missionary Association Archives, Amistad Research Center, New Orleans, hereafter AMA; on Woodson, see Sterling Stuckey, *The Ideological Origins of Black Nationalism* (Boston: Beacon Press, 1979); also see Miller, *The Search for a Black Nationality,* 95–105.

52. *North Star,* 8 June 1849.

53. Ibid.; Delany, *The Condition, Elevation, Emigration and Destiny of the Colored People of the United States,* 131.

54. *The Anglo-African Magazine,* February 1859.

TWO / Emigration Furor and *Notes of Canada West*

1. For discussion on early racial uplift, see Frederick Cooper, "Elevating the Race: The Social Thought of Black Leaders, 1827–50," *American Quarterly* 24 (December 1972): 604–25; and Kevin K. Gaines, *Uplifting the Race: Black Leadership, Politics, and Culture in the Twentieth Century* (Chapel Hill: University of North Carolina Press, 1996), 1–4. Frances Ellen Watkins Harper (1825–1911) began teaching in Ohio and Pennsylvania in the 1850s and became a well-known anti-slavery lecturer. She wrote articles, prose and poetry for the *Liberator* and other newspapers and became an important literary figure after the Civil War. Sarah Mapps Douglass (1806–1882) was a leader in Philadelphia's antislavery and black literary organizations, one of the first female contributors to the *Liberator,* and founder of a high school for black girls in that city.

2. Mary Ann Shadd to George Whipple, November 27, 1851, AMA; Carlton Mabee, *Black Education in New York State: From Colonial to Modern Times* (Syracuse: Syracuse University Press, 1979), 63–67; Mabee notes that in 1853, the New York City Board of Education absorbed both black and white schools and public support for black education gradually improved; on black education in urban settings, see Leonard P. Curry, *The Free Black in Urban America 1800–1850* (Chicago: University of Chicago Press, 1981), 147–50.

3. Mabee, 77, notes that while comparisons between black and white teachers' salaries are difficult, most evidence points to a pattern of lower salaries for teachers in black schools, which did not change in New York City until after the Civil War. On networks among free blacks, see James Oliver Horton, *Free People of Color*, 32–31, 41–51, and 153–54.

4. Curry, 101, 244–45, 246, 260, 267; quote from *Frederick Douglass' Paper*, 9 November 1855.

5. Curry, 267–69; Litwack, *North of Slavery*, 153–86.

6. Ibid., 247–63. Massachusetts, Maine, New Hampshire, Vermont, and Rhode Island granted the franchise to black males; Illinois, Indiana, Iowa, and Oregon passed laws against black entry between 1850–57.

7. United States Statutes at Large, 9:462–65; Stanley W. Campbell, *The Slave Catchers: Enforcement of the Fugitive Slave Law, 1850–1860* (Chapel Hill: University of North Carolina Press, 1968), 4.

8. Ibid., 24–25; see also Litwack, *North of Slavery*, 248.

9. *North Star*, 31 October 1850; *Liberator*, 14 May 1852.

10. Campbell, 49; *North Star*, November 16, 1849.

11. Fred Landon, "The Negro Migration to Canada after the Passing of the Fugitive Slave Act," *Journal of Negro History* 5 (January 1920): 22–36; Quarles, *Black Abolitionists*, 200; William H. Pease and Jane H. Pease, *Black Utopia: Negro Communal Experiments in America* (Madison, Wis.: State Historical Society, 1963), 8; *Liberator*, 13 December 1850.

12. William Renwick Riddell, "Slavery in Canada," *Journal of Negro History* 5 (July 1920): 261–377; also see discussion in Jason Silverman, *Unwanted Guests: Canada West's Response to American Fugitive Slaves, 1800–1865* (Millwood, N.Y.: Associated Faculty Press, 1985), 1–7.

13. Winks, *Blacks in Canada*, 111, 129; Silverman, 9–12; for discussion on the roots of Canadian abolitionism, see Allen P. Stouffer, *The Light of Nature and the Law of God: Antislavery in Ontario, 1833–1877* (Baton Rouge: Louisiana State University Press, 1992), 12–18.

14. Winks, *Blacks in Canada*, 144–48.

15. Winks, *Blacks in Canada*, 155–57; *Liberator* 17 September 1831; between 1841 and 1867 the region known today as Ontario Province was called Canada West, and present-day Quebec Province was called Canada East.

16. Winks, *Blacks in Canada*, 178–79; Alexander Murray, "Canada and the Anglo-American Anti-Slavery Movement: A Study in International Philanthropy" (Ph.D. diss., University of Pennsylvania, 1960), 79–90, 97–116; Pease and Pease, *Black Utopia*, 63–83, 102–8.

17. Winks, *Blacks in Canada*, 233–40, gives an exhaustive analysis of the problems in pinpointing the exact size of the Canadian black population. Murray, 23, and Winks note these figures were inflated for propaganda value. See also "Proceedings of the Cazenovia Fugitive Slave Law Convention, August 21–22, 1850," reprinted in Philip S. Foner and George E. Walker, eds., *Proceedings of the Black State Conventions, 1840–1865* (Philadelphia: Temple University Press, 1979), 43. Michael Wayne, "The Myth of the Fugitive Slave: The Black Population of Canada West on the Eve of the American Civil War: A Reassessment Based on the Manuscript Census of 1861," *Histoire Sociale/Social History* 56 (Nov. 1995): 465–85.

18. The Canada Mission was the representative of the American Missionary

Association, formed in 1846 by several Christian denominations to coordinate and distribute funds to the missionary efforts among black settlers in Canada West. See Winks, *Blacks in Canada*, 224–26; Murray, 403–4; *North Star*, 23 February 1849.

19. *North Star*, 10 November 1848 and 7 April 1849; for discussion on antislavery rhetorical strategies that rendered the slave helpless and prostrate, see Yellin, *Women and Sisters*, and Karen Sanchez Eppler, "Bodily Bonds: The Intersecting Rhetorics of Feminism and Abolition," *Representations* 44 (Fall 1988): 28–59; on Canadian antislavery activities, see Stouffer, *The Light of Nature and the Law of God*, 82.

20. Miller, *The Search for a Black Nationality*, 111–12; "Proceedings of the North American Convention, convened at St. Lawrence Hall, Toronto, Canada West, Sept. 11–13, 1851," reprinted in Ripley, *Black Abolitionist Papers*, 149–57. Although it is likely that women attended the convention only men were listed as delegates. Several biographical sketches of Mary Ann Shadd claim she moved to Canada in 1850 following passage of the Fugitive Slave Act. For example, see Robin W. Winks, "Mary Ann Shadd Cary," in Rayford W. Logan and Michael R. Winston, eds., *Dictionary of American Negro Biography* (New York: W. W. Norton, 1982), 552–53. But her own correspondence confirms her presence in New York City until the summer of 1851; on early racial uplift, see Quarles, *Black Abolitionists*, 90–115.

21. Ripley, *Black Abolitionist Papers*, 17; Dan Hill, "The Blacks in Toronto," in Robert F. Harney, ed., *Gathering Place: Peoples and Neighbourhoods of Toronto, 1834–1945* (Toronto: Multicultural History Society of Ontario, 1985), 87; "Proceedings of the North American Convention," 154; her minutes appeared in *The Christian Herald*, September 1851, and in the *Voice of the Fugitive*, 29 January 1852. Henry Bibb and John Scoble addressed the Buffalo meeting, which was presided over by Rev. Israel Campbell, all of whom attended the Toronto convention.

22. Mary Ann Shadd to Isaac Shadd, 16 September 1851, Mary Ann Shadd Cary Papers, Ontario Provincial Archives, Toronto, Ontario, Canada, hereafter MASC/OPA; Mary Ann Shadd to George Whipple, 21 June 1852, AMA. Shadd said she had been offered a job in Toronto but was persuaded by Bibb to move to Windsor.

23. Henry Bibb, *The Narrative of the Life and Adventures of Henry Bibb, An American Slave* (1849; rpt., Miami: Mnemosyne, 1969); Fred Landon, "Henry Bibb, a Colonizer," *Journal of Negro History* 5 (October 1920): 437–47; Ripley, *Black Abolitionist Papers*, vol. II, 109–10; Roger W. Hite, "Voice of a Fugitive: Henry Bibb and Ante-bellum Black Separatism," *Journal of Black Studies* 4 (March 1974): 269–84.

24. See discussion in Silverman, *Unwanted Guests*, 105–10; and Donald George Simpson, "Negroes in Ontario from Early Times to 1870" (Ph.D. diss., University of Western Ontario, 1971), 143–53; also Bernell E. Tripp, "Mary Miles Bibb: Education and Moral Improvement in the *Voice of the Fugitive*" paper presented to Association for Education in Journalism and Mass Communication, August 1993; *Voice of the Fugitive*, 1 January 1851.

25. Benjamin Drew, *The Refugee: A North-side View of Slavery* (1856; rpt. Reading, Mass.: Addison-Wesley, 1969), 225; *Frederick Douglass' Paper*, 7 August 1851; Mary Ann Shadd to George Whipple, 27 October 1851, AMA.

26. Mary Ann Shadd to George Whipple, 27 October 1851, AMA; Clara Merritt

DeBoer, *Be Jubilant My Feet: African American Abolitionists in the American Missionary Association*, 1839–1861 (New York: Garland Publishing, 1994), 154–56.

27. Jason H. Silverman and Donna J. Gillie, "'The Pursuit of Knowledge under Difficulties': Education and the Fugitive Slave in Canada," *Ontario History* 74 (June 1982): 95–112; Hildreth H. Spencer, "To Nestle in the Mane of the British Lion: A History of Canadian Black Education, 1820–1870" (Ph.D. diss., Northwestern University, 1970); see also Winks, *Blacks in Canada*, 362–89; Fred Landon, "The Work of the American Missionary Association among the Negro Refugees in Canada West," *Ontario Historical Society Papers and Records* 21 (1921): 198–205.

28. Mary Ann Shadd to George Whipple, 27 November 1851, AMA.

29. Ibid.

30. Ibid.; Alexander McArthur to George Whipple, 27 November 1851, AMA; DeBoer, *Be Jubilant My Feet*, 155.

31. Ibid.

32. *Voice of the Fugitive*, 19 November 1851 and 29 January 1852.

33. Alexander McArthur to George Whipple, 9 January 1852, and Mary Ann Shadd to George Whipple, 14 February 1852, AMA.

34. Mary Ann Shadd to George Whipple, 14 February 1852, AMA.

35. Mary Ann Shadd to George Whipple, 3 April 1852, AMA.

36. Ibid.

37. Ibid.; see also Mary Ann Shadd to George Whipple, 22 April 1852, and Alexander McArthur to George Whipple, 24 May 1852, AMA; for discussion on black opposition to white missionaries, see in DeBoer, *Be Jubilant My Feet*, 158–61.

38. Pease and Pease, *Black Utopia*, 109–22; Landon, "Henry Bibb, a Colonizer," 443–47; the constitution and bylaws of the Refugee Home Society are reprinted in Ripley, *Black Abolitionist Papers*, vol. 2, 208.

39. David Walker's pamphlet "Appeal to the Colored Citizens of the World," published in 1830, is considered to be one of the earliest and most eloquent formulations of a black nationalist ideology. Rev. Lewis Woodson contributed to this developing school of thought in a series of letters to the black press published between 1837 and 1841. See discussion in Stuckey, *The Ideological Origins of Black Nationalism*, and in Miller, *The Search for a Black Nationality*, 93, 103–4; Bibb's quote in *Voice of the Fugitive*, 26 February 1852.

40. On the Antislavery Society of Canada, see Stouffer, *The Light of Nature and the Law of God*, 82.

41. Mary Ann Shadd, *A Plea for Emigration or, Notes of Canada West, in Its Moral, Social and Political Aspect: with Suggestions Respecting Mexico, West Indies, and Vancouver's Island, for the Information of Colored Emigrants* (Detroit: George W. Pattison printing, 1852) [hereafter referred to as *Notes of Canada West*], MASC/NAC.

42. Carla Peterson, *"Doers of the Word,"* 88–118.

43. *Voice of the Fugitive*, 3 June 1852 and 17 June 1852.

44. Mary Ann Shadd to George Whipple, 21 June 1852, AMA.

45. Ibid.

46. Ripley, *Black Abolitionist Papers*, vol. II, 108, 113–15; Henry Bibb to American Missionary Association, 14 April 1851, AMA; Spencer, "To Nestle in the Mane of the British Lion," 198, suggests that white supporters of the Refugee Home

Society may have been engaged in writing for and editing the paper; also see Bernell Tripp, "Mary Miles Bibb," 7, 24.

47. Mary Ann Shadd to George Whipple, 21 June 1852, AMA; *The Pennsylvania Freeman*, 3 July 1852; Receipt from George W. Pattison to Rev. Mr. McArthur, 22 July 1852, MASC/OPA.

48. Delany, *The Condition, Elevation, Emigration and Destiny of the Colored People of the United States;* also see Dorothy Sterling, *The Making of an Afro-American: Martin Robison Delany, 1812–1885* (New York: Da Capo Press, 1996), 136–58; and Victor Ullman, *Martin R. Delany: The Beginnings of Black Nationalism* (Boston: 1971).

THREE / Trouble in "Paradise"

1. Edwin C. Guillet, *Early Life in Upper Canada* (1933; rpt. University of Toronto Press, 1963), 148–52, 322–23; William Lloyd Garrison to H. E. Garrison, 17 October 1853, William Lloyd Garrison Papers, Boston Public Library; Winks, *Blacks in Canada*, 244–46.

2. *Voice of the Fugitive*, 17 June 1852; *Village Record* (West Chester, Pa.), 6 July 1852.

3. *The Pennsylvania Freeman*, 26 February 1852. Although some accounts suggest that Abraham Shadd moved to Canada as early as 1851, the evidence points to late 1852; see Assessment Roll, Township of Raleigh, County of Kent, 1852–1866 (Raleigh Township Centennial Museum, North Buxton, Ontario); Colin A. Thomason, "Doc Shadd," *Saskatchewan History*, 30 (Spring 1977): 41.

4. *Voice of the Fugitive*, 3 June 1852; in addition to a short article on Holly's arrival, both Bibb and Holly's names appear as editors of the paper beginning with this issue; Holly quote from *Voice of the Fugitive*, 1 June 1851; also see Miller, *The Search for a Black Nationality*, 110.

5. Michael F. Hembree, "The Question of 'Begging': Fugitive Slave Relief in Canada, 1830–1865," *Civil War History* 37 (December 1991): 314–27, argues that Bibb advanced a more agrarian ideology while Shadd's was focused on the needs of urban blacks.

6. *Voice of the Fugitive*, 15 July 1852; see discussion in Shirley Yee, *Black Women Abolitionists: A Study in Activism, 1828–1860* (Knoxville: University of Tennessee Press, 1992), 40–59; quote from James Oliver Horton, "Freedom's Yoke," 51–76; Pease and Pease, *Black Utopia*, 116.

7. *Voice of the Fugitive*, 29 July 1852; Ripley, *Black Abolitionist Papers*, vol. II, 276; Proceedings of the Public Meeting held at Windsor, Canada West, 20 July 1852, AMA.

8. Mary Ann Shadd to George Whipple, 21 July 1852, *The Western Evangelist*, n.d., report of the Missionary Society of Illinois conference held 5 June 1852, and Alexander McArthur to George Whipple, 20 July 1852; and *Sixth Annual Report of the American Missionary Association* (1852), AMA; Winks, *Blacks in Canada*, 207, says Hiram Wilson persuaded the AMA not to hire McArthur.

9. Mary Ann Shadd to George Whipple, 21 July 1852; Pease and Pease, *Black Utopia*, 121.

10. Mary Ann Shadd to George Whipple, n.d., AMA.

11. Reprinted in *The Pennsylvania Freeman*, 3 June 1852; *Frederick Douglass' Paper*, 17 June 1852.

12. See Frankie Hutton, *The Early Black Press in America, 1827 to 1860* (Westport, Conn.: Greenwood Press, 1993), ch. 4; *Voice of the Fugitive*, 22 April, 20 May 1852.

13. *Voice of the Fugitive*, 12 August 1852.

14. Ibid.

15. Reprints were not found in the *Liberator*, the *Pennsylvania Freeman*, *Frederick Douglass' Paper*, or the *Christian Recorder*.

16. Samuel J. May to Lewis Tappan, 3 August 1852, AMA. Notations in Whipple's handwriting indicate that the letter, written at the end of May's trip, was passed on to Whipple and the AMA's Executive Committee; a report of May's visit also appears in the *Voice of the Fugitive*, 29 July 1852.

17. Mary Ann Shadd to George Whipple, 18 August, 6 September 1852, AMA; *Voice of the Fugitive*, 26 August 1852.

18. Sources on Ward include: Ronald K. Burke, "Samuel Ringgold Ward: Christian Abolitionist" (Ph.D. diss., Syracuse University, 1975); Robin Winks, unpublished biographical sketch of Ward, Robin Winks Collection, Schomburg Center for Research in Black Culture, New York Public Library; and S. R. Ward, *Autobiography of a Fugitive Negro: His Anti-Slavery Words and Labors in the United States, Canada, and England* (1855; rpt., New York: Arno Press, 1968).

19. Ward, *Autobiography of a Fugitive Negro*, 83–84; also see Stouffer, *The Light of Nature and the Law of God*, 120–30.

20. Samuel Ringgold Ward to George Whipple, 13 and 24 October 1851, AMA; also see Alexander Murray, "Canada and the Anglo-American Anti-Slavery Movement: A Study in International Philanthropy" (Ph.D. diss., University of Pennsylvania, 1960), 216–18.

21. *The Pennsylvania Freeman*, 18 September 1852; Ward, *Autobiography*, 205–6.

22. *The Liberator*, 15 October 1852; contemporary scholars use Refugee Home Society as the correct reference to this organization but during the period in question some used Refugees Home Society, Refugees' Home Society, or Refugees' Home Association; see DeBoer, *Be Jubilant My Feet*, 156–61.

23. *Voice of the Fugitive*, 21 October; and the *Liberator*, 10 December 1852.

24. Mary Ann Shadd to William Lloyd Garrison, 5 October 1852, William Lloyd Garrison Papers, Boston Public Library.

25. *The Liberator*, 29 October 1852.

26. Maria Stewart, Address of the African Masonic Hall, Boston, February 27, 1833, in *Productions of Mrs. Maria W. Stewart, Presented to the First African Baptist Church and Society, of the City of Boston* (Boston: Friends of Freedom and Virtue, 1835).

27. *Voice of the Fugitive*, 21 October 1852; as the debate heated up, the article was reprinted in *The Liberator*, 5 November 1852; also see *The Liberator*, 12 November 1852.

28. *The Pennsylvania Freeman*, 18 November 1852; see Stouffer, *The Light of Nature and the Law of God*, 119–20.

29. *The Liberator,* 10 December 1852; reprinted in *Frederick Douglass' Paper,* 17 December 1852.

30. *Voice of the Fugitive,* 21 October, 18 November 1852; see Stouffer, *The Light of Nature and the Law of God,* 123; and Ripley, *Black Abolitionist Papers,* vol. II, 222.

31. Mary Ann Shadd to George Whipple, 24 October, 5 December 1852, AMA.

32. *The Liberator,* 12 December 1852; reprinted in *Frederick Douglass' Newspaper,* 14 January 1853.

33. Samuel Ringgold Ward to George Whipple, 15 December 1852, Alexander McArthur to George Whipple, 22 December 1852, AMA.

34. Alexander McArthur to George Whipple, 22 December 1852, AMA.

35. Mary Ann Shadd to The Executive Committee of the American Missionary Association, n.d., AMA.

36. Mary Ann Shadd to George Whipple, 28 December 1852, AMA.

37. Mary Ann Shadd to George Whipple, 13 January 1853, AMA.

38. Copy of letter, Horace Hallock to Rev. C. C. Foote, 12 January 1853, AMA.

39. Minutes of the Committee on Canada Missions of the American Missionary Association, 14 January 1853, AMA; also see Mary Ann Shadd to George Whipple, 27 November 1851, AMA.

40. Sixth Annual Report of the American Missionary Association (1852), AMA; also see Landon, "Work of the American Missionary Association," 202–3.

41. Mary Ann Shadd to George Whipple, 7 February 1853, AMA.

42. Ibid.

43. *The Liberator,* 4 March 1853.

44. Mary Ann Shadd to George Whipple, 28 March 1853, AMA.

FOUR / "We Have 'Broken the Editorial Ice'"

1. *Voice of the Fugitive,* 16 December 1852; on Jones see Ripley, *Black Abolitionist Papers,* vol. II., 133–35.

2. Letter to Mary Ann Shadd, 1852, MASC/OPA. Portions of the letter are torn and barely legible; however, its content, the fact that its author was based in Toronto, and similarities in handwriting indicate it was written by Ward; also see Mary Ann Shadd to Samuel Ringgold Ward, n.d., MASC/OPA. The timing of the letter can be pinpointed to early 1853 because it suggests that plans for the paper are under way but that the first issue has not yet been published.

3. Handwritten copy from *The Religious Recorder* (Syracuse, N.Y.), 22 February 1849, Onondaga Historical Association, Syracuse, N.Y.; *New York Tribune,* 17 July 1850.

4. *The Impartial Citizen,* 14 November 1849; *Voice of the Fugitive,* 5 November 1851; the charges were launched by Jermain W. Loguen, an African Methodist Episcopal Zion minister and escaped slave, who fled to Canada with Ward after both were involved in the Syracuse fugitive slave rescue. Their long association notwithstanding, Loguen charged that Ward absconded with subscription payments for the *Impartial Citizen.* See *Voice of the Fugitive,* 29 July 1852.

5. *Pennsylvania Freeman,* 17 February, 17 March 1853. Ward's term "Hollyism" refers to James Theodore Holly, coeditor of the *Voice.*

6. *Voice of the Fugitive,* 22 February, 8 March 1853; *Provincial Freeman,* 24 March 1853.

7. *Provincial Freeman,* 24 March 1853; on newspapers, see Hazel Dicken-Garcia, *Journalistic Standards in Nineteenth-Century America* (Madison: University of Wisconsin Press, 1989), 26, 39–40; the publication committee was comprised of H. Brown, of Hamilton, and W. P. Francis, of Windsor; Thomas Jones, of Windsor, was a fugitive slave and consistent Shadd supporter; James M. Jones, of Chatham, was an American-born black gunsmith; A. Beckford Jones, of London, was a fugitive slave and prominent activist; John W. Lindsay was a freeborn American and leading figure in St. Catherine's politics; Thomas W. Stringer of Buxton was a prominent fugitive who returned to the United States after the Civil War and became a member of the Mississippi Senate; see Ripley, *Black Abolitionist Papers,* vol. II, 44, 260–62.

8. *Provincial Freeman,* 23 March 1853.

9. Day, founder of the *Aliened American,* was a freeborn African American from Ohio who was active in abolitionism and the black convention movement. Eventually he would join the emigrationist movement and relocate in Canada West; quote from *Aliened American,* 9 April 1853; Samuel Ringgold Ward, *Autobiography of a Fugitive Negro: His Anti-Slavery Words and Labors in the United States, Canada and England* (1855: rpt., New York: Arno Press, 1968), 227.

10. *Frederick Douglass' Paper,* 8 April 1853; reprinted in the *Liberator,* 22 April 1853.

11. Ibid.

12. *Pennsylvania Freeman,* 7, 21 April 1853; *The Anti-Slavery Bugle,* 16 April 1853.

13. Mary Ann Shadd to George Whipple, 27 April 1853, AMA.

14. Purvis, president of the Pennsylvania Anti-Slavery Society 1845–1850, was a college-educated black entrepreneur who worked with Abraham Shadd as a leader of the early black convention movement and the American Moral Reform Society. Several branches of the Shadds' extended family lived in Philadelphia; see 1850 U.S. Census.

15. Donald M. Scott, "The Popular Lecture and the Creation of a Public in Mid-Nineteenth-Century America," *Journal of American History* 66 (March 1980): 791–809, quote from 797; *Pennsylvania Freeman,* 26 May 1853.

16. *Pennsylvania Freeman,* 26 May 1853.

17. *Pennsylvania Freeman,* 8 September 1853.

18. See Mary Ryan, *Women in Public: Between Banners and Ballots, 1825–1880* (Baltimore: Johns Hopkins University Press, 1990), 132–36; on Truth's lecturing, see Nell Irvin Painter, *Sojourner Truth: A Life, A Symbol* (New York: Norton, 1996), 114–19; on Harper, see Shirley J. Yee, *Black Women Abolitionists,* 112–13; and Quarles, *Black Abolitionists,* 179.

19. *Pennsylvania Freeman,* 29 September 1853.

20. See David Howard-Pitney, "The Enduring Black Jeremiad: The American Jeremiad and Black Protest Rhetoric, From Frederick Douglass to W. E. B. Du Bois,

1841–1919," *American Quarterly* 38 (1986): 481–92; Moses quoted from 483; and Celeste Michelle Condit and John Louis Lucaites, *Crafting Equality: America's Anglo-African Word* (Chicago: University of Chicago Press, 1993), 77–97.

21. On the financial status of antebellum newspapers, see Dicken-Garcia, *Journalistic Standards in Nineteenth-Century America*, 39–40.

22. Winks, *Blacks in Canada*, 245–46; as noted earlier, faulty census data makes it impossible to pinpoint the numbers of black residents in Canada during this period. Estimates come from several observers in the field, including missionary Isaac Rice and reformer-activist Samuel Gridley Howe; also see Daniel Hill, "The Blacks in Toronto," in *Gathering Place*, 89–91; quote from *Voice of the Fugitive*, 8 October 1851.

23. William Lloyd Garrison to H. E. Garrison, 17 October 1853, William Lloyd Garrison Papers, Boston Public Library, Boston; Ripley, *Black Abolitionist Papers*, vol. II, 112, and Winks, *Blacks in Canada*, 396, say publication of the *Voice of the Fugitive* was suspended following the fire; other sources avoid pinpointing the date. Copies of the paper found at the Burton Historical Collection, Detroit Public Library, only go through late 1852. However, issues of the *Voice* dating to 24 December 1853 were found in the Slavery Collection, Rare Books Division, Olin Library, Cornell University, Ithaca, New York; *The Liberator*, 28 October 1853.

24. William Still to Mary Ann Shadd, 1854, MASC/OPA; although there is no stated month and day, this was obviously written prior to the appearance of the *Provincial Freeman* in March.

25. William S. McFeely, *Frederick Douglass* (New York: W. W. Norton, 1991), 152–53; Mary Ann Shadd, "Report of the Affairs of the Provincial Freeman Association," n.d., MASC/MS; *Rowsell's City of Toronto and County of York Directory, 1850–51* (Toronto: Henry Rowsell, 1850); Toronto General Directory and Auctioneer of Real Estate (Toronto, 1856).

26. *Brown's Toronto General Directory* (W. R. Brown: Toronto, 1856); *Provincial Freeman*, 25 March 1854; three regular contributors were listed in the first issue, with the note that more would be added later. They were A. B. Jones of London (Canada West), who had been on the first publication committee, investor Rev. J. B. Smith, and John J. Cary, brother of Mary Ann's future husband, Thomas Cary. Four subscription agents, all based in Toronto, were also named. Ultimately all of these individuals had a relatively minor role in the paper's operations, except for John Dick.

27. None of the editorials in the early issues of the *Freeman* were signed, but Shadd and her staff established a covert method of identification beginning with this first issue. An asterisk following an editorial or article indicated that Shadd was the author; a D identified the writer as John Dick. As other writers joined the paper, their initials would be added.

28. Mary Kelley, *Private Woman, Public Stage: Literary Domesticity in Nineteenth-Century America* (New York: Oxford University Press, 1984), 111.

29. *Provincial Freeman*, 24 March 1854.

30. Ibid.; on the association of Shadd with the Garrisonians, see, for example, Kristin Hoganson, "Garrisonian Abolitionists and the Rhetoric of Gender, 1850–1860," *American Quarterly* 45 (December 1993): 558–95.

31. *Provincial Freeman*, 24 March 1854.

32. See Miller, *The Search for a Black Nationality*, 137–50; and Ullmann, *Martin Delany*, 160–64; *Provincial Freeman*, 24 March 1854.

33. *Frederick Douglass' Paper*, 26 August 1853; *Provincial Freeman*, 15 April 1854.

34. *Provincial Freeman*, 15 April 1854.

35. On ideologies of nationalism, see Alphonso Pinkney, *Red, Black and Green: Black Nationalism in the United States* (London: Cambridge University Press, 1976), 1–12; Benedict Anderson, *Imagined Communities: Reflections on the Origin and Spread of Nationalism* (London: Verso, 1983), 11–16; and Wilson Jeremiah Moses, *The Golden Age of Black Nationalism, 1850–1925* (Hamden, Conn.: Archon Books, 1978), 15–30.

36. *Provincial Freeman*, 22 April, 17 June 1854.

37. Agreement made between M. A. Shadd and Abraham McKinney, 29 August 1854, MASC/MS.

38. *Provincial Freeman*, 29 April 1854.

39. *Provincial Freeman*, 27 May 1854.

40. *Provincial Freeman*, 3 June 1854.

41. Ibid.; on Douglass and Julia Griffiths, see William S. McFeeley, *Frederick Douglass*, 163–82.

42. *Provincial Freeman*, 10 June 1854. Thomas Henning was the first Secretary of the Anti-Slavery Society of Canada, formed in 1851, and was on the editorial staff of the *Toronto Globe*, which took a strong anti-slavery position in the 1850s. Henning's wife, Isabella, was a founder of the Ladies' Association. See Winks, *Blacks in Canada*, 253–55.

43. *Provincial Freeman*, 10 June 1854.

44. *Provincial Freeman*, 17 June 1854.

45. *Provincial Freeman*, 29 April 1854.

46. *Provincial Freeman*, 23 September, 4 November 1854.

47. *Provincial Freeman*, 29 April, 13 May 1854.

48. *Provincial Freeman*, 10 June 1854.

49. Amelia C. Shadd to David Williamson, 25 July 1854, MASC/NAC. Amelia Cisco Shadd was the sixth child born to Abraham and Harriet Shadd, and was about 23 years old when she arrived in Canada.

50. *Provincial Freeman*, 22 July 1854.

51. Ibid.

52. Minutes of meeting in *Provincial Freeman*, 19 August 1854. A copy of the *Constitution of the Provincial Union* is in the MASC/NAC.

53. *Provincial Freeman*, 26 August 1854.

54. *Provincial Freeman*, 26 August, 2 September 1854.

55. *Proceedings of the National Emigration Convention of Colored People; Held at Cleveland, Ohio on Thursday, Friday and Saturday, the 24th, 25th and 26th of August, 1854* (Pittsburgh: A. A. Anderson, Printer, 1854). See discussion in Miller, *The Search for a Black Nationality*, 144–56; and Ullman, *Martin Delany*, 161–62.

56. *Provincial Freeman*, 14, 21 October 1854.

57. Sometime in late 1854 Ward stopped working for the Anti-Slavery Society of Canada. He continued to freelance as a lecturer in Britain although it was uncertain for whom he was raising funds. In 1855 he left Britain for Jamaica, where he

settled without his wife and six children, who were left stranded in Toronto. He died in Jamaica in about 1866. See Alexander Murray, "Canada and the Anglo-American Anti-Slavery Movement: A Study in International Philanthropy" (Ph.D. diss., University of Pennsylvania, 1960), 274–77; *Provincial Freeman,* 28 October 1854, 17 February 1855.

58. *Provincial Freeman,* 28 October 1854.

59. *Provincial Freeman,* 24 March 1855.

60. *Provincial Freeman,* 5 May, 9 June 1855.

61. *Provincial Freeman,* 30 June 1855.

FIVE / The Chatham Years

1. William Wells Brown, "The Colored People of Canada," The *Pine and Palm,* 28 September 1861, reprinted in C. Peter Ripley, *The Black Abolitionist Papers,* vol. II, 470.

2. Walter Lippmann, *Public Opinion* (1922; rpt., New Brunswick, N.J.: Transaction Publishers, 1991), 328.

3. *Provincial Freeman,* 23 June 1855; on the economics of nineteenth-century newspapers, see Gerald J. Baldasty, *The Commercialization of News in the Nineteenth Century* (Madison: University of Wisconsin Press, 1992), 36–50; and Dicken-Garcia, *Journalistic Standards in Nineteenth-Century America,* 39.

4. *Provincial Freeman,* 23 June 1855; Winks, *Blacks in Canada,* 493, notes Chatham had the third largest concentration of blacks in Canada during the period. Colin Thomson, "Doc Shadd," *Saskatchewan History* 30 (Spring 1977): 42, states that in the mid-1850s there were nearly 1,600 blacks in Chatham, or a quarter of the town's population; Drew, *The Refugee: A North-side View of Slavery,* 164.

5. On Abraham Shadd, see Thomson, "Doc Shadd"; Emaline Shadd was the seventh of the thirteen Shadd children, born in 1835, thus was about twenty years old at the time. See *Provincial Freeman,* 8 November 1855; and "Short History of the Shadd Family," Metropolitan Toronto Library Board, Toronto.

6. *Provincial Freeman,* 22, 29 August 1855.

7. Ibid.

8. Winks, *Blacks in Canada,* 206; also see Sherriff J. R. Gemmill, "Historical Sketch of the Press of Chatham," *Kent Historical Society Papers and Addresses* 2 (1915): 30–37; *Provincial Freeman,* 22 August 1855.

9. *Provincial Freeman,* 22 August 1855.

10. Drew, *The Refugee: A North-side View of Slavery,* 164–65; *Provincial Freeman,* 26 July 1856.

11. *Provincial Freeman,* 22 August 1855.

12. Ibid.; on the Dawn settlement, see Winks, *Blacks in Canada,* 181–96; and Stouffer, *The Light of Nature and the Law of God,* 70–72.

13. *Provincial Freeman,* 8 September 1855.

14. *Provincial Freeman,* 22 September 1855.

15. *Provincial Freeman,* 8 November 1855.

16. A circular published in *Provincial Freeman,* 18 February 1857, sought dona-

tions to finance the suit over the Dawn lands. No further notices appeared in the paper. See Alexander Murray, "Canada and the Anglo-American Anti-Slavery Movement: A Study in International Philanthropy" (Ph.D. diss., University of Pennsylvania, 1960), 469–74; and Hembree, "The Question of 'Begging,'" 322; and Winks, *Blacks in Canada*, 195–204.

17. *Provincial Freeman*, 6 October 1855.

18. *Provincial Freeman*, 3 November 1855.

19. *Provincial Freeman*, 3 November and 22 December 1855.

20. *Provincial Freeman*, 3 November 1855; *Proceedings of the Colored National Convention* held in Franklin Hall, Sixth Street, Philadelphia, Pennsylvania, October 16, 17, 18th, 1855 (Salem, N.J.: *National Standard* Office, 1856).

21. Ibid, 10; and Vincent Harding, *There Is a River: The Black Struggle for Freedom in America* (New York: Random House, 1983), 137.

22. *Frederick Douglass' Paper*, 9 November 1855. William J. Watkins wrote regularly to Douglass' newspaper under the pseudonym "Ethiop."

23. Ibid.; *Provincial Freeman*, 3 November 1855.

24. See Harry C. Silcox, "The Black 'Better Class' Political Dilemma: Philadelphia Prototype Isaiah C. Wears," *Pennsylvania Magazine of History and Biography* CXIII (January 1981): 46–66; *Provincial Freeman*, 22 December 1855. See also Ira V. Brown, *The Negro in Pennsylvania History* (University Park, Pa.: The Pennsylvania Historical Association, 1970), 41.

25. *Provincial Freeman*, 1 December 1855.

26. Ibid,; on Bowers, see Julie Winch, *Philadelphia's Black Elite: Activism, Accommodation, and the Struggle for Autonomy, 1787–1848* (Philadelphia: Temple University Press, 1988), 155–56.

27. *Provincial Freeman*, 8 December 1855.

28. *Provincial Freeman*, 22 and 29 December 1855; see Fred Landon, "The Work of the American Missionary Association among the Negro Refugees in Canada West, 1848–1864," *Ontario Historical Society Papers and Records* 21 (1921): 198–205; and Drew, *The Refugee: A North-side View of Slavery* 165–66.

29. Bishop Daniel Alexander Payne, *Recollections of Seventy Years* (1883: rpt. New York: Arno Press, 1968), 126–27.

30. David T. W. Shadd, "Biographical Sketch," 29 June 1960, MASC/NAC; and "Census of 1861, Canada West," *Census of Canada, 1665–1871* (Ottawa, 1876). The Census was probably in error about Thomas Cary's age since his eldest child was born in 1842; see Ripley, 2:396–97 for brief biography of Cary based on scant primary and secondary sources. It is unclear whether the Cary brothers were free born or escaped slaves; brothers George and John J. Cary were born in the early 1800s, lived in Virginia during their youth, and moved to Cincinnati before emigrating to Canada. It is possible that this was Thomas's background as well.

31. James Oliver Horton, "Freedom's Yoke," 51–77.

32. For a detailed biography of Day, see R. J. M. Blackett, *Beating against the Barriers: The Lives of Six Nineteenth-Century Afro-Americans* (Ithaca: Cornell University Press, 1989), 299–317; also see Miller, *The Search for a Black Nationality*, 142.

33. *Provincial Freeman*, 19 January 1856.

34. *Provincial Freeman*, 2 February 1855; Robert L. Harris, Jr., "H. Ford Doug-

lass: Afro-American Antislavery Emigrationist," *Journal of Negro History* 62 (July 1977): 217–34. Also see Blackett, *Beating against the Barriers*, 298.

35. Hereafter, the subject will be identified by her married name, Shadd Cary; see *Provincial Freeman*, 26 January and 2, 9 February 1855.

36. *Provincial Freeman*, 9 February 1855.

37. *Provincial Freeman*, 1 March 1856.

38. *Provincial Freeman*, 8 March 1856.

39. Ibid., *Provincial Freeman*, 26 April 1856.

40. *Provincial Freeman*, 5 April 1856.

41. *Provincial Freeman*, 13 October 1855; also see Miller, *The Search for a Black Nationality*, 157–60.

42. *Provincial Freeman*, 23 February, 10 May 1856; see Sterling, *Martin Robeson Delany*, 160–66; and McFeely, *Frederick Douglass*, 151–52; "Historical Guide to Blacks in Chatham," Raleigh Township Centennial Museum, North Buxton, Ontario.

43. *Provincial Freeman*, 1 March, 19 April 1856; and Ripley, 289–90n.

44. Research notes for Daniel Hill's *Freedom Seekers*, Ontario Provincial Archives, Toronto; and Ripley, 2:428n.

45. *Provincial Freeman*, 24 May 1856.

46. *Provincial Freeman*, 7 June 1856; for a thorough discussion see Marva Banks, "*Uncle Tom's Cabin* and Antebellum Black Response," in *Readers in History: Nineteenth-Century American Literature and the Contexts of Response*, James L. Machor, ed. (Baltimore: Johns Hopkins University Press, 1993), 209–27.

47. *Provincial Freeman*, 5 July 1856.

48. *Frederick Douglass' Paper*, 4 July 1856; *Provincial Freeman*, 12 July 1856.

49. On the convention, see Miller, *The Search for a Black Nationality*, 165–66; the *Afric-American Repository* was planned as a general interest periodical to showcase black literary talent. It was supposed to begin publication in July 1857 if at least $500 could be raised for the venture and 1,000 subscribers were committed. A printing company was formed to produce the journal, and production was postponed for one year. There is no evidence that it was ever published. See Penelope L. Bullock, *The Afro-American Periodical Press, 1838–1909* (Baton Rouge: Louisiana State University Press, 1981), 20–21.

50. *Provincial Freeman*, 27 December 1856.

51. *Provincial Freeman*, 25 November 1856.

52. *Provincial Freeman*, 6 December 1856; 31 January 1857.

53. *Provincial Freeman*, 31 January 1857.

54. Mary A. S. Cary, H. F. Douglass, and I. D. Shadd, "Slavery and Humanity," circular published by the *Provincial Freeman*, February 1857. MASC/MS.

55. *Provincial Freeman*, 28 February 1857.

56. *Provincial Freeman*, 31 February 1857.

57. David Hotchkiss to George Whipple, 6 March 1857 and 25 April 1857, AMA. See discussion in Murray, "Canada and the Anglo-American Anti-Slavery Movement," 456–58.

58. *Provincial Freeman*, 4, 18 April and 2 May 1857; Benjamin C. Howard, *Report of the Decision of the Supreme Court of the United States in the Case of Dred Scott v. Sanford* (Washington, 1857).

59. H. Ford Douglass to Mary A. S. Cary, n.d., MASC/OPA; *Provincial Freeman,* 20 June 1857.

60. *Provincial Freeman,* 11 July 1857.

61. *Provincial Freeman,* 20 June, 25 August 1857.

62. *Provincial Freeman,* 18 July 1857.

63. Ibid.

64. Thomas F. Cary to Mary A. S. Cary, 21 May and 11 June 1857, MASC/OPA.

65. *Provincial Freeman,* 12 September 1857.

66. H. Ford Douglass to Mary A. S. Cary, 23 November 1857, MASC/OPA.

67. Thomas F. Cary to Mary A. S. Cary, 17 December 1857 and 21 January 1858, MASC/OPA.

68. William Still to Mary A. S. Cary, 30 January 1858, MASC/OPA.

69. Chatham, Canada West, Petition, 4 March 1858, MASC/MS.

70. The paper halted publication on Sept. 12, 1857, vol. 4. no.1, and the extant copy of January 1859 was vol. 4. no. 16 indicating that sixteen issues were published sometime in 1858 on either a weekly or bi-monthly basis, or that volume and issue numbers were skipped between these periods; Isaac Shadd Diary, Shadd Family Papers, University of Western Ontario, London, Ontario; *Provincial Freeman,* 18 June 1859.

71. Handwritten draft of sermon by Mary Ann Shadd Cary, 6 April 1858, MASC/OPA.

72. Osborne P. Anderson, *A Voice from Harpers Ferry* (Boston: 1861), 37–43; Isaac Shadd Diary in Abraham D. Shadd Ledger, Raleigh Township Centennial Museum, North Buxton, Ontario.

73. Winks, *Blacks in Canada,* 267–68; "Journal of the Provisional Constitutional Convention, May 8–10, 1858, Chatham, Canada West," *Select Committee on the Harpers Ferry Invasion,* U.S. Senate, Rep. Com. No. 278 (June 15, 1860); Fred Landon, "Canadian Negroes and the John Brown Raid," *Journal of Negro History,* 6 (April 1921): 174–82; on William Howard Day's participation see Blackett, *Beating against the Barriers,* 313; Isaac Shadd Diary.

74. William Wells Brown, *The Rising Son; or, The Antecedents and Advancement of the Colored Race* (1874; rpt., Miami: Mnemosyne, 1969), 540; also see Isaac Shadd Diary; Hallie Q. Brown, *Homespun Heroines,* 95.

75. William Howard Day to Gerrit Smith, 21 June 1858, Gerrit Smith Papers, George Arents Research Library, Syracuse University, Syracuse, N.Y.; also see Blackett, *Beating against the Barriers,* 312–13; and Miller, *The Search for a Black Nationality,* 180.

76. Isaac Shadd to Thomas Cary, 25 June 1858, MASC/OPA.

77. Mary Ann Shadd Cary to Thomas F. Cary, n.d., MASC/MS.

78. Ibid.; Sarah Shadd was the ninth of Abraham and Harriet Shadd's thirteen children. She was approximately nineteen years old at the time. Shadd Family sketch, D. T. W. Shadd, 29 June 1960, MASC/NAC.

79. Miller, *The Search for a Black Nationality,* 179–81; also see Blackett, *Beating against the Barriers,* 314; and Howard Bell, "Negro Nationalism: A Factor in Emigration Projects, 1858–1861, *Journal of Negro History,*" 68 (January 1962): 42–53.

80. *Gerrit Smith Banner,* 28 October 1858. Articles on the case also appeared in the *New York Tribune* and the *National Anti-Slavery Standard.*

81. Elizabeth J. Williams to Mary A. S. Cary, 2 November 1858, MASC/OPA.

82. *Provincial Freeman*, 28 January 1859.

83. *Provincial Freeman*, 18 June 1859.

84. Ibid.

SIX / Civil War and the End of the Canadian Sojourn

1. *Weekly Anglo-African*, 14 July 1860; for discussion on economy in Chatham, see Jonathan William Walton, "Blacks in Buxton and Chatham, Ontario, 1830–1890: Did the 49th Parallel Make a Difference," 87.

2. "Census of 1861, Canada West," *Censuses of Canada, 1665 to 1871* (Ottawa, 1876); *Weekly Anglo-African*, 29 December 1860.

3. *Weekly Anglo-African*, 29 December 1860.

4. James McPherson, *Battle Cry of Freedom* (New York: Oxford University Press, 1988).

5. For an exhaustive analysis of the impact of the Civil War on Canada, see Robin W. Winks, *Canada and the United States: The Civil War Years* (Baltimore: Johns Hopkins Press, 1960), 12–21, 216–19; Walton, 131.

6. *Weekly Anglo-African*, 14 September 1861; and *Douglass' Monthly*, May 1861.

7. Chatham *Planet*, 15 January 1861.

8. For discussion on Delany's Niger River plan, see R.J.M. Blackett, *Building an Antislavery Wall: Black Americans in the Atlantic Abolitionist Movement, 1830–1860* (Ithaca: Cornell University Press, 1983), 175–78; 184–85; also in Winks, *Blacks in Canada*, 167–68.

9. Moses, *The Golden Age of Black Nationalism*. 45.

10. For discussion of Delany's ideology, see Moses, *The Golden Age of Black Nationalism*, 36–37, 45; for reports on Delany's lectures, see *Chatham Tri-Weekly Planet* 8 September 1858, 29 November 1859, 8, 14 January 1861; Mary Ann Shadd Cary to George Whipple, 26 February 1861, AMA; on the AMA, see Augustus Field Beard, *A Crusade of Brotherhood: A History of the American Missionary Association* (1909: rpt. New York: Kraus, 1970), 38–48; also see discussion in Miller, *The Search for a Black Nationality*, 250–63.

11. *Provincial Freeman*, 5 July 1856, 29 January, 18 June 1859. On Delany's Niger Valley plan see Winks, *Blacks in Canada*, 167–68; Miller, *The Search for a Black Nationality*, 250–61.

12. See David M. Dean, *Defender of the Race: James Theodore Holly, Black Nationalist and Bishop* (Boston: Lambeth Press, 1979); Miller, *The Search for a Black Nationality*, 232–41.

13. *Weekly Anglo-African*, 28 September, 19 October, 26 October 1861; see John R. McKivigan, "James Redpath, John Brown, and Abolitionist Advocacy of Slave Insurrection," *Civil War History* 37 (December 1991): 293–313.

14. *Weekly Anglo-African*, 7 December 1861.

15. *Weekly Anglo-African*, 28 September, 7 December 1861.

16. *Weekly Anglo-African*, 19 October 1861; Miller, *The Search for a Black Nationality*, 242.

17. *Weekly Anglo-African,* 19 October, 9 November, 7 December 1861.

18. *Pine and Palm,* 28 September 1861; see William E. Farrison, *William Wells Brown: Author and Reformer* (Chicago: University of Chicago Press, 1969), 341–51; *Weekly Anglo-African,* 9 November 1861.

19. *Douglass' Monthly,* May 1861; for thorough discussion of Douglass' ideological conflicts during the secession crisis, see David W. Blight, *Frederick Douglass' Civil War: Keeping Faith in Jubilee* (Baton Rouge: Louisiana State University Press, 1989), 77–79, 131–35; Miller, *The Search for a Black Nationality,* 239.

20. *Weekly Anglo-African,* 26 October 1861; Winks, *Blacks in Canada,* 164–65.

21. *Pine and Palm,* 14 September 1861; Winks, *Blacks in Canada,* 164; we know from the 1861 Census of Canada that Mary Ann's three stepchildren lived with Thomas's brother, George Cary, in the town of Camden before he set sail for Haiti.

22. Farrison, *William Wells Brown,* 351–52; Miller, *The Search for a Black Nationality,* 257–58.

23. Jason Silverman coined the term "unwelcome guests" in his book of the same title. Winks, *Blacks in Canada,* and Walton, "Blacks in Buxton and Chatham, Ontario," generally agree with this assessment.

24. Quoted in Silverman, *Unwanted Guests,* 37; Samuel Ringgold Ward also recounted this incident in the *Voice of the Fugitive,* 21 October 1852; quoted in Howard Law, "Self-Reliance Is the True Road to Independence": Ideology and the Ex-Slaves in Buxton and Chatham," *Ontario History* 77 (June 1985): 109.

25. *Voice of the Fugitive,* 5 November 1851.

26. For discussion on black employment, see Jean Burnet, *Ethnic Groups in Upper Canada* (Toronto: Ontario Historical Society, 1972).

27. See Reginald Horsman, *Race and Manifest Destiny: The Origins of American Racial Anglo-Saxonism* (Cambridge: Harvard University Press, 1981), 62–77.

28. *Voice of the Fugitive* 4 November 1852; *Provincial Freeman,* 18 June 1859; for discussion of migration patterns in Ontario between 1850–1870, see J. M. Bumsted, *The Peoples of Canada: A Pre-Confederation History* (Toronto: Oxford University Press, 1992), 342–43; and Fred Landon, *Western Ontario and the American Frontier* (Toronto: Ryerson; New Haven: Yale University Press, 1941), 46–61; Montreal editor quoted in Winks, *Canada and the United States,* 217.

29. See Helen I. Cowan, *British Emigration to North America: The First Hundred Years* (Toronto: University of Toronto Press, 1961), 179–200; Bumsted, *The Peoples of Canada,* 284–85, 340–45; on black and Irish competition, see Silverman, *Unwelcome Guests,* 62; and Jean Burnet, "Occupational Differences and Class Structure," in Douglas Francis and Donald B. Smith, eds., *Readings in Canadian History* (Toronto: Holt, Rinehart and Winston, 1986), 257–67.

30. David R. Roediger, *The Wages of Whiteness: Race and the Making of the American Working Class* (London: Verso, 1991), 137, 149–50; on black and Irish competition, see Jason Silverman, *Unwanted Guests,* 62; *Provincial Freeman,* 18 June 1859.

31. *Voice of the Fugitive,* 1 January 1851; Takaki, *Iron Cages,* 113–16; for discussion of political uses of miscegenation in the 1860s, see Roediger, *Wages of Whiteness,* 155–56; Allen P. Stouffer, "A 'Restless Child of Change and Accident': The Black Image in Nineteenth Century Ontario," *Ontario History* 76 (June 1984): 128–49.

32. See Marjorie Griffin Cohen, *Women's Work, Markets, and Economic Development in Nineteenth-Century Ontario* (Toronto: University of Toronto Press, 1988), 45–54; Constance Backhouse, *Petticoats and Prejudice: Women and Law in Nineteenth-Century Canada* (Toronto: Women's Press, 1991), 177; and Bettina Bradbury, "Surviving as a Widow in Nineteenth-Century Montreal," *Urban History Review* 17 (February 1989): 148–60.

33. "Census of 1861, Canada West," *Censuses of Canada, 1665 to 1871* (Ottawa, 1876). Although the accuracy of the 1861 census' counting of blacks has been questioned, Abraham Shadd was the census enumerator for Raleigh Township and was likely very precise about his own family. On the independence of black widows, see Suzanne Lebsock, "Free Black Women and the Question of Matriarchy: Petersburg, Virginia, 1784–1820," *Feminist Studies* 8 (Summer 1982): 271–87.

34. Suzanne Morton, "Separate Spheres in a Separate World: African-Nova Scotian Women in late 19th-Century Halifax County," *Acadiensis* 22 (Spring 1993): 61–83; and Cohen, *Women's Work, Markets and Economic Development*, 147–48.

35. Walton, "Blacks in Buxton and Chatham," 77–79; Silverman, *Unwelcome Guests*, 139; George Cary to James Redpath, 14 September 1861, *Pine and Palm*; Isaac Shadd to George Whipple, 7 December 1862, AMA.

36. *The Weekly Anglo-African*, 28 December 1861. Also see C. C. Foote to George Whipple, 19 February 1864, AMA.

37. *Weekly Anglo-African*, 6 April 1862; Walton, 78; Winks, *Blacks in Canada*, 366–76; Handwritten circular, n.d., MASC/MS.

38. *Weekly Anglo-African*, 28 December 1861, 6 April 1862; Silverman, *Unwelcome Guests*, 139.

39. See Richardson, *Christian Reconstruction*, 3, 22; and Beard, *Crusade of Brotherhood*, 61.

40. See discussion in Leon F. Litwack, *Been in the Storm So Long: The Aftermath of Slavery* (New York: Vintage, 1980), 65–67; and in Dudley Taylor Cornish, *The Sable Arm: Negro Troops in the Union Army, 1861–1865* (New York: Norton, 1966), 10–15.

41. McPherson, *Battle Cry of Freedom*, 500. Lincoln quoted in Litwack, *Been in the Storm So Long*, 66. For discussion of early use of black troops see Cornish, *Sable Arm*, 33–50.

42. McPherson, *Battle Cry of Freedom*, 557–59; Litwack, *Been in the Storm So Long*, 70; Winks, *Blacks in Canada*, 289.

43. *Weekly Anglo-African*, 6 April 1862; Naturalization Papers for Mary Ann Shadd Cary, County of Kent, Canada West, 9 September 1862. MASC/NAC.

44. Hamilton in *Weekly Anglo-African*, 17 January 1863; Douglas in *Weekly Anglo-African* 9 June 1863.

45. For extensive discussion on the early months of black troop recruitment and the Massachusetts 54th, see Cornish, *Sable Arm*, 105–28; and James M. McPherson, *The Negro's Civil War* (New York: Pantheon Books, 1965), 170, 173–78; also Litwack, *Been in the Storm So Long*, 77.

46. See Litwack, *Been in the Storm So Long*, 77–86; Martin R. Delany to Edwin M. Stanton, 15 December 1863, "The Negro in the Military Service of the United States, 1639–1886," National Archives, Washington, D.C.

47. McPherson, *Negro's Civil War*, 170–73; Martin Delany to Mary A. S. Cary, 7 December 1863, MASC/MS.

48. Walton, *Blacks in Buxton and Chatham,* 158–59 and Winks, *Blacks in Canada,* 288–89, and Silverman, *Unwelcome Guests,* 159 all refer to the "great exodus" of blacks from Canada. More recently, Wayne, "The Myth of the Fugitive Slave," argues that no mass migration of blacks occurred. On Abraham and Gabriel Shadd, see Shadd Family memorabilia on display at the Raleigh Township Centennial Museum, North Buxton, Ontario; on Toussaint L'Overture Delany, see M. Delany to William Coppinger, 18 August 1880, Library of Congress; on H. Ford Douglass, see Ripley, *Black Abolitionist Papers* 5:166–68; on Delany see Cornish, *Sable Arm,* 216–17.

49. Hondon B. Hargrove, *Black Union Soldiers in the Civil War* (Jefferson, N.C.: McFarland, 1988), 78. Recruitment Authorization for Connecticut Volunteers, signed by Martin Delany, 24 February 1864, MASC/MS.

50. See Frank Moore, *Women of the War; Their Heroism and Self-Sacrifice* (Hartford: S. S. Scranton, 1866), iv, and Elizabeth D. Leonard, *Yankee Women: Gender Battles in the Civil War* (New York: W. W. Norton, 1994); on women abolitionist's activities, see Wendy Hamand Venet, *Neither Ballots nor Bullets: Women Abolitionists and the Civil War* (Charlottesville: University Press of Virginia, 1991), 94–110; on women in active battle, see Richard Hall, *Patriots in Disguise: Women Warriors of the Civil War* (New York: Paragon House, 1993).

51. There is little comprehensive data on the role of black women in the Civil War. For an overview, see Dorothy Sterling, *We Are Your Sisters: Black Women in the Nineteenth Century* (New York: W. W. Norton, 1984); Mary Elizabeth Massey, *Bonnet Brigades* (New York: Alfred. A. Knopf, 1966), 266–77; Catherine Clinton, *The Other Civil War,* 87–89; Truth quoted in Carlton Mabee, *Sojourner Truth: Slave, Prophet, Legend* (New York: New York University Press, 1993), 92; also see Nell Painter, *Sojourner Truth,* 179, 182–83.

52. V. Jacque Voegeli, *Free but Not Equal: The Midwest and the Negro during the Civil War* (Chicago: University of Chicago Press, 1967) 1–2, 34; William Wells Brown, *The Negro in the American Rebellion* (1867; rpt. New York: Johnson Reprint Corp, 1968), 142–46.

53. Quoted from William R. Forstchen, "The Twenty-Eighth United States Colored Troops: Indiana's African Americans go to War, 1863–1865" (Ph.D. diss., Purdue University, 1994), 44; Voegeli, *Free but Not Equal,* 73–90, 98, 170.

54. Lawrence M. Lipin, *Producers, Proletarians, and Politicians: Workers and Party Politics in Evansville and New Albany Indiana, 1850–87* (Urbana: University of Illinois Press, 1994), 10, 17; and Emma Lou Thornbrough, *The Negro in Indiana* (Indianapolis: Indiana Historical Bureau, 1957), 141, 184.

55. Quoted in Thornbrough, *Negro in Indiana* 184, 185–86; also see Voegeli, *Free but Not Equal,* 88.

56. Certificate of protection from O. P. Morton, Gov. of Indiana, 19 February 1864, MASC/MS; Forstchen, "The Twenty-Eighth United States Colored Troops," 74–75. Also see Hargrove, *Black Union Soldiers in the Civil War* 83; and Voegeli, *Free but Not Equal,* 107.

57. Lt. Col. Robert N. Scott, *The War of the Rebellion: A Compilation of the Official Records of the Union and Confederate Armies* (Washington, D.C., 1891), series I, vol. 23, 804; Benjamin S. Pardee to Mary A. S. Cary, March 3, 1864. MASC/MS; Hargrove, *Black Union Soldiers in the Civil War* 83.

58. Richard Reid, "General Edward A. Wild and Civil War Discrimination,"

Historical Journal of Massachusetts (1985) 13: 14–29; for discussion on draft riots, see McPherson, *Negro's Civil War,* 493, 507, 609.

59. Mary Ann Shadd Cary to George Whipple, 22 June 1864, AMA.

60. *Christian Recorder,* 24 October 1863, 12 March 1864.

61. Mary Ann Shadd Cary to George Whipple, 17 May 1864; Mary Ann Shadd Cary to George Whipple, 22 June 1864, AMA; on Amelia Freeman Shadd, see Walton, "Blacks in Buxton and Chatham," 138.

62. W. H. H. Terrell, *Indiana in the War of the Rebellion: Report of the Adjutant General* (Indiana Historical Society, 1960), 77–79, 100; *Daily Journal* (Indianapolis), 4 December 1863.

63. Recruiting Permit, State of Indiana, 15 August 1864, MASC/NAC; and Certification of Authorization for W. G. Shadd, 17 August 1864, MASC/MS; Recruiting Broadside, "Men of Color to Arms," Leon Gardiner Collection, Historical Society of Pennsylvania, Philadelphia.

64. For a detailed discussion on the Indiana Twenty-eighth's battle record, see Fortstchen, 167–210; Terrell, *Indiana in the War of the Rebellion: Report of the Adjutant General,* 562; Thornbrough, *The Negro in Indiana,* 191–99.

65. Litwack, *Been in the Storm So Long,* 229–35; Ripley, *Black Abolitionist Papers,* 2:40–42; Walton, "Blacks in Chatham and Buxton," 166–67; on Abraham Shadd, see *Weekly Anglo-African,* 14 December 1861, and Winks, *Blacks in Canada,* 215.

66. On Isaac Shadd's visit to California, see *San Francisco Pacific Appeal,* 22 August 1863.

67. Martin Delany to William Coppinger, 18 August 1880, copy in records of Canadian Black Studies Project, Regional Collections, D. B. Weldon Library, University of Western Ontario, London, Ontario. Also see Ripley, *Black Abolitionist Papers,* 397.

68. Litwack, *Been in the Storm So Long,* 515.

69. An historical marker at the Raleigh Township Centennial Museum, North Buxton, Ontario, suggests Shadd Cary owned her own farm for a period, but no public documents confirm this fact.

70. On post-emancipation education, see Winks, *Blacks in Canada,* 374–76; quote from Winks, 290.

71. Canadian Passport, February 28, 1865. MASC/NAC.

SEVEN / Reconstructing a Life—Reconstructing a People

1. See discussion in James M. McPherson, *The Struggle for Equality: Abolitionists and the Negro in the Civil War and Reconstruction* (Princeton, N.J.: Princeton University Press, 1964), 308–40, 369; Eric Foner, *Reconstruction: America's Unfinished Revolution, 1863–1877* (New York: Harper and Row, 1988), 251–80; and W. E. B. Du Bois, *Black Reconstruction* (1935; rpt. Millwood, N.Y., Kraus-Thomson Organization, 1976), 325–35.

2. Allen Stouffer, "A 'Restless Child of Change and Accident,'" 134–40; Ripley, *Black Abolitionist Papers,* II:42–43; quote from Winks, *Blacks in Canada,* 292.

3. On Delany see Miller, *The Search for a Black Nationality,* 265–66; and Eric

Foner, *Reconstruction*, 288–89; Shadd Cary's name is absent from the 1864–65 Chatham city directory, but she does not appear in the Detroit directory until 1868; *Kent County Gazetteer for 1864–65* (R. R. Sutherland, Publishers: Ingersoll, Canada West, 1864); and *Detroit City Directory, 1868–69*, Microfilm Division, Library of Congress.

4. Katzman, 84; U.S. Commissioner of Education, *History of Schools for the Colored Population* (1871; rpt. New York: Arno Press, 1969), 357; Miller, *The Search for a Black Nationality*, 264–67.

5. Silas Farmer, *The History of Detroit and Michigan* (Detroit, 1884); David M. Katzman, *Before the Ghetto: Black Detroit in the Nineteenth Century* (Urbana: University of Illinois Press, 1973), 26–28, 62, 84; Eric Foner, *Reconstruction*, 460–64.

6. Teaching certificate, Board of Education, Detroit, Michigan, 1 July 1868, MASC/MS; for discussion on the ideology of reconstruction education, see Ronald E. Butchart, *Northern Schools, Southern Blacks, and Reconstruction: Freedmen's Education, 1862–1875* (Westport, Conn.: Greenwood Press, 1980), 13–31; and Eric Foner, *Reconstruction*, 96–100.

7. See Forest G. Wood, *Black Scare: The Racist Response to Emancipation and Reconstruction* (Berkeley: University of California Press, 1968), 20–21; 138; also see Katzman, *Before the Ghetto*, 44–47, 62–63, 75; Detroit City Directory, 1868–69.

8. Mary Ann Shadd Cary to D. B. and H. M. Duffield, Esqs., 16 May 1871; and from D. Bethune Duffield and W. A. Howard to Hons. I. M. Howard and Z. Chandler, 29 July 1870, MASC/MS; also see Gatewood, *Aristocrats of Color*, 124–26; on Samuel Watson, see William Wells Brown, "The Colored People of Canada," 7 September 1861, *Pine and Palm*; and Katzman, *Before the Ghetto*, 127; Samuel C. Watson to Mary Ann Shadd Cary, 26 December 1869, MASC/MS.

9. John B. Reid, "'A Career to Build, A People to Serve, a Purpose to Accomplish': Race, Class, Gender, and Detroit's First Black Women Teachers, 1865–1916," *Michigan Historical Review* 18 (Spring 1992): 1–25; Farmer, *History of Detroit and Wayne County and Early Michigan*, 751; Katzman, *Before the Ghetto*, 84–90.

10. Wood, *Black Scare*, 20–25; Katzman, *Before the Ghetto*, ch. 4; see Philip S. Foner, *Organized Labor and the Black Worker, 1619–1973* (New York: International Publishers, 1974), 17–29.

11. Samuel C. Watson to Mary Ann Shadd Cary, 26 December 1869, MASC/MS; Katzman, *Before the Ghetto*, 124–26; Philip S. Foner and Ronald Lewis, eds., *The Black Worker during the Era of the National Labor Union* (Philadelphia: Temple University Press, 1978), 82–92.

12. *Proceedings of the Colored National Labor Union Convention Held in Washington, D.C.*, December 6, 7, 8, 9, 10, 1869, reprinted in Philip S. Foner and Ronald L. Lewis, eds., *Black Workers: A Documentary History from Colonial Times to the Present* (Philadelphia: Temple University Press, 1989), 165–89; on class themes of convention, see August Meier and Elliot Rudwick, "Attitudes of Negro Leaders toward the American Labor Movement from the Civil War to World War I," in Julius Jacobson, ed., *The Negro and the American Labor Movement* (New York: Anchor Books, 1968), 31.

13. Foner and Lewis, *The Black Worker during the Era of the National Labor Union*, 55–56; Philip S. Foner, *Women and the American Labor Movement: From*

Colonial Times to the Eve of World War I (New York: Free Press, 1979), 139, ironically, Foner wrongly identifies Shadd Cary as a white delegate to the CNLU Convention; for constitution of Colored National Labor Union and list of officers, see *New National Era,* 7 April 1870; also see Eric Foner, *Reconstruction,* 446–49.

14. "Letter to the People," *New National Era,* 21 March, 11 April 1872.

15. Eric Foner, *Reconstruction,* 272; Alan Lessoff, *The Nation and Its City: Politics, 'Corruption,' and Progress in Washington, D.C., 1861–1902* (Baltimore: Johns Hopkins University Press, 1994), 15–35; Constance McLaughlin Green, *The Secret City: A History of Race Relations in the Nation's Capital* (Princeton, N.J.: Princeton University Press, 1967), 80, 89, 93–94; Melvin Roscoe Williams, "Blacks in Washington, D.C., 1860–1870" (Ph.D. diss., Johns Hopkins University, 1975), 5, 136, 191–92.

16. William Henry Jones, *The Housing of Negroes in Washington, D.C.: A Study in Human Ecology* (Washington, D.C.: Howard University Press, 1929), 27–33, quote from 30; Green, *Secret City,* 81–82; James Oliver Horton, "Race, Literacy and Occupation in Reconstruction Washington, D.C.," in *Free People of Color: Inside the African American Community* (Washington, D.C.: Smithsonian Press, 1993), 185–87; Litwack, *Been in the Storm So Long,* 513–14.

17. For a thorough discussion on Washington's black elite, see Gatewood, *Aristocrats of Color,* 39–68; Gatewood coined the term "Capital of the Colored Aristocracy."

18. Gatewood, *Aristocrats of Color,* 39–45; Mrs. Amelia C. Shadd and A. T. Shadd, "Record of the Shadd family in America" (unpublished manuscript, Regional Collection, D. B. Weldon Library, University of Western Ontario, London, Ontario, 1905); Green, *Secret City,* 43.

19. On Isaac Cary, see Letitia Woods Brown, *Free Negroes in the District of Columbia, 1790–1846* (New York: Oxford University Press, 1972), 134–35; *Boyd's Directory of Washington, Georgetown, and Alexandria* (Washington, D.C., 1882); *New National Era,* 5 September 1872.

20. *Boyd's Directory of Washington, Georgetown, and Alexandria* (Washington, D.C., 1870–71, 1881–84); *New National Era,* 2 May, 15 August 1872; Shadd Family Tree, Raleigh Township Centennial Museum, North Buxton, Ontario, 1977; William Still to Mary Ann Shadd Cary, 8, 26 August 1873; Gatewood, *Aristocrats of Color,* 40–41.

21. Green, *Secret City,* 97–98; for a detailed study of John Sella Martin, see Blackett, *Beating against the Barriers,* 188–89, 253–61.

22. Lillian G. Dabney, *The History of Schools for Negroes in the District of Columbia, 1807–1947* (Washington, D.C.: Catholic University of America Press, 1949), 5, 29–34.

23. Melvin R. Williams, "A Blueprint for Change: The Black Community in Washington, D.C., 1860–1870," *Records of the Columbia Historical Society* 48 (1971–72): 369–77; Joel M. Richardson, *Christian Reconstruction: The American Missionary Association and Southern Blacks, 1861–1890* (Athens: University of Georgia Press, 1986), 22–25, 110; Ronald Butchart, *Northern Schools, Southern Blacks, and Reconstruction,* 94; Robert C. Morris, *Reading, 'Riting, and Reconstruction: The Education of Freemen in the South, 1861–1870* (Chicago: University of Chicago Press, 1981), 43; Dabney, *The History of Schools for Negroes in the District of Columbia, 1807–1947,* 45–52, 82–85.

24. Dabney, *The History of Schools for Negroes in the District of Columbia, 1807–1947*, 84, 111–16; Richardson, *Christian Reconstruction*, 110; Williams, "A Blueprint for Change," 376–77; *Report of the Board of Trustees of Colored Schools of Washington and Georgetown, District of Columbia* (Washington, 1871), 9, 19–22, 32, Daniel Murray Pamphlet Collection, Rare Book Division, Library of Congress.

25. *Special Report of the Commissioner of Education on the Improvement of Public Schools in the District of Columbia, 1871* (rpt. New York: Arno Press, 1969), 256–57.

26. *Annual Report of the Superintendent of Colored Schools of Washington and Georgetown, 1871–72* (Washington: National Republican Job Office Printer, 1873), Washingtonia Section, District of Columbia Public Library; Dabney, *The History of Schools for Negroes in the District of Columbia, 1807–1947*, 47, 91–92; Horton, "Race, Occupation, and Literacy," 191–93.

27. Mary Ann Shadd Cary, "Teacher's Monthly Report to Bureau of Refugees, Freedmen, and Abandoned Lands," March, April, May 1871, AMA; quote from *Report of the Board of Trustees of Colored Schools of Washington and Georgetown, D.C.* (Washington, 1871), 29; The Lincoln School received some financial support from the American Missionary Association, as well as the local School Board, and black citizens; Du Bois, *Black Reconstruction*, 637.

28. Quoted from *Special Report of the Commissioner of Education on the Improvement of Public Schools in the District of Columbia, 1871*, 258.

29. Green, *Secret City*, 100; Dabney, *The History of Schools for Negroes in the District of Columbia, 1807–1947*, 87–88; *New National Era*, 9 November 1871; quote from *Report of the Board of Trustees of Colored Schools of Washington and Georgetown, D.C.*, 10; *New National Era*, 8 November 1871.

30. *Annual Report of the Superintendent of Colored Schools of Washington and Georgetown, 1872–73* and *1873–74*.

31. *New National Era*, 13 July, 7 September 1871; on Douglass see Blight, *Frederick Douglass' Civil War*, chs. 9 and 10.

32. Frederick Douglass to Mary Ann Shadd Cary, 4 July and 5 July 1871, MASC/MS; *New National Era*, 8 August 1872.

33. *New National Era*, 10, 31 August 1871.

34. William Still to Mary Ann Shadd Cary, 13 April 1871, MASC/MS.

35. William Still to Mary Ann Shadd Cary, 13 April 1871, Leon Gardiner Collection, Historical Society of Pennsylvania, Philadelphia; William Still, *The Underground Railroad*, rev. ed. (Philadelphia: Wm. Still, 1883), 348–57.

36. Ibid.; and William Still to Mary Ann Shadd Cary, 8 and 26 August, 27 October 1873, Leon Gardiner Collection, Historical Society of Pennsylvania.

37. William E. Farrisen, *William Wells Brown*, 437–39; William Wells Brown, *The Rising Son*, 539–40.

38. William Still to Mary Ann Shadd Cary, 8 August 1873, Leon Gardiner Collection, Historical Society of Pennsylvania; on Douglass and the *Era*, see McFeely, *Frederick Douglass*, 272–73, 297; and Blight, *Frederick Douglass' Civil War*, 204.

39. William Still to Mary Ann Shadd Cary, 9 September 1873, Leon Gardiner Collection, Historical Society of Pennsylvania; Miscellaneous notes, n.d., MASC/MS.

40. Miscellaneous notes, n.d., MASC/MS.

41. R. R. Sinclair to M. A. S. Cary, 3 September 1874, MASC/MS; for discussion of historical memory see Robert E. McGlone, "Rescripting a Troubled Past: John Brown's Family and the Harpers Ferry Conspiracy," *Journal of American History,* 75 (March 1989): 1179–1200.

42. *New National Era,* 6 June, 19 December 1872, 19 June 1873.

EIGHT / Law and Reform in the Nation's Capital

1. Green, *Secret City,* 89; Maxwell Bloomfield, "John Mercer Langston and the Rise of Howard Law School," *Records of the Columbia Historical Society* (1971–72): 428–30; Walter Dyson, *Howard University: The Capstone of Negro Education, A History: 1867–1940* (Washington, D.C.: Graduate School of Howard University, 1941), 229–33.

2. Bloomfield, "John Mercer Langston and the Rise of Howard Law School," 430–31; *Boyd's Directory of Washington, Georgetown, and Alexandria* (Washington, D.C., 1870, 1873).

3. Dyson, *Howard University,* 231; *New National Era,* 7 July 1870; reporter for Washington *Sunday Chronicle* quoted in *Third Annual Report of Howard University,* July 1870, 7–8; "Thesis on Corporations," MASC/MS; these comments wrongly attributed to Charlotte Ray have been published numerous times, most recently in Darlene Clark Hine, ed., *Black Women in America: An Historical Encyclopedia* (Brooklyn: Carlson Publishing, 1992), 965.

4. Dyson, *Howard University,* 233; *New National Era,* 2, 9 February 1871; Howard University Law Department commencement program, 3 February 1871 with note from A. W. Shadd, MASC/MS; J. Clay Smith, Jr., *Emancipation: The Making of the Black Lawyer, 1844–1944* (Philadelphia: University of Pennsylvania Press, 1993), 290, 323.

5. Bearden and Butler, *Shadd: The Life and Times of Mary Shadd Cary,* 212–13, advance the idea that Shadd Cary was deliberately prevented from graduating because of her gender, although they rely on scanty evidence. Judge Macon B. Allen was probably the first black attorney to have access to the courts when he was admitted to the Maine Bar in 1844. Ten years later, John Mercer Langston, who would become the Dean of the Howard University law school, was admitted to the Ohio bar. The New England abolitionist John S. Rock was the first African American admitted to practice before the Supreme Court in 1865. George B. Vashon, an Oberlin College graduate and long-time abolitionist, was the first black lawyer admitted to the bar in the District of Columbia in October 1869. On early black lawyers see Kenneth S. Tollett, "Black Lawyers, Their Education, and the Black Community," *Howard Law Journal* 17 (1972): 328–9; and Smith, *Emancipation,* 129; Sumner quoted in Bloomfield, "John Mercer Langston and the Rise of Howard Law School," 431; Shadd Cary's claims published in Leila J. Robinson, "Women Lawyers in the United States," *The Green Bag* 2 (1890): 10–32.

6. Ada M. Bittenbender, "Women in Law," in Annie Nathan Meyer, ed., *Woman's Work in America* (New York: Henry Holt, 1891), 218–21; Nancy T. Gilliam, "A Professional Pioneer: Myra Bradwell's Fight to Practice Law," *Law and History*

Review 5 (1987): 105–33; Sadie T. M. Alexander, "Women as Practitioners of Law in the United States," *National Bar Journal* 1 (July 1941): 58–59; D. Kelly Weisberg, "Barred from the Bar: Women and Legal Education in the United States, 1870–1890," in *Women and the Law: A Social Historical Perspective,* vol. II (Cambridge, Mass.: Schenkman Publishing, 1982), 231–45; also see extensive discussion in Joan Hoff, *Law, Gender, and Injustice: A Legal History of U.S. Women* (New York: New York University Press, 1991), 161–70.

7. See Bloomfield, "John Mercer Langston and the Rise of Howard Law School," 431; Dyson, *Howard University,* 233; Alexander, "Women as Practitioners of Law in the United States," 59; Robinson, "Women Lawyers in the United States," 28; *New National Era* 2 February, 14 March 1872; another female graduate of Howard Law School, Eliza Chambers, made similar allegations in the 1880s, but none of these claims have ever been substantiated.

8. Robinson, 28; on opposition to Howard University, see James H. Whyte, *The Uncivil War: Washington during the Reconstruction, 1865–1878* (New York: Twayne Publishers, 1958), 261.

9. William Still to Mary Ann Shadd Cary, 30 July 1873, Leon Gardiner Collection, Historical Society of Pennsylvania, Philadelphia.

10. D. Bethune Duffield and W. N. Howard to Hons. I. M. Howard and Z. Chandler, 29 July 1870, MASC/MS; Katzman, *Before the Ghetto,* 4, 179; Eric Foner, *Reconstruction,* 233, 485; Green, *Secret City,* 93–94; Alan Lessoff, *The Nation and Its City: Politics, "Corruption," and Progress in Washington, D.C., 1861–1902* (Baltimore: Johns Hopkins University Press, 1994), 18–19.

11. William Still to Mary Ann Shadd Cary, 13 April 1871, MASC/MS; Bloomfield, "John Mercer Langston and the Rise of Howard Law School," 432–36; Dyson, *Howard University,* 60–61.

12. On Isaac Shadd, see New National Era, 13 March 1873; Eric Foner, *Freedom's Lawmakers: A Directory of Black Officeholders during Reconstruction* (New York: Oxford University Press, 1993), 192; and Robert F. Holtzclaw, *Black Magnolias: A Brief History of the Afro-Mississipian, 1865–1980* (Shaker Heights, Ohio: Keeble Press, 1984), 44; on Delany, see Sterling, *Martin Robison Delany,* 290–98; on Shadd's feminist politics, see Rosalyn Terborg-Penn, "Afro-Americans in the Struggle for Woman Suffrage" (Ph.D. diss., Howard University, 1977), 109.

13. For extensive discussion see Ellen Carol DuBois, *Feminism and Suffrage: The Emergence of an Independent Women's Movement in America, 1848–1869* (Ithaca: Cornell University Press, 1978); quoted in Du Bois, *Black Reconstruction,* 59.

14. Nell Painter, "Difference, Slavery, and Memory: Sojourner Truth in Feminist Abolitionism," in Jean Fagan Yellin and John C. Van Horne, eds., *The Abolitionist Sisterhood: Women's Political Culture in Antebellum America* (Ithaca: Cornell University Press, 1994), 157; DuBois, *Feminism and Suffrage,* 68–71, 174; Hoff, *Law, Gender and Injustice,* 147.

15. DuBois, *Feminism and Suffrage,* 162–65, 174; Terborg-Penn, "Afro-Americans in the Struggle for Woman Suffrage," 58–59, 100–9; Rosalyn Terborg-Penn, "Discrimination against Afro-American Women in the Woman's Movement, 1830–1920," in Steady, ed., *The Black Woman Cross-Culturally,* 305; on Harper, see Hazel Carby, *Reconstructing Womanhood: The Emergence of the Afro-American Woman Novelist* (New York: Oxford, 1987), 66–70.

16. Untitled manuscript, n.d., MASC/MS; on Somerville see entry in Jennifer S. Uglow, ed., *The International Dictionary of Women's Biography* (New York: Continuum, 1982), 435.

17. *New National Era,* 5 February 1874; a handwritten draft of the article is in the MASC/MS.

18. *Hearing before the Judiciary Committee of the House of Representatives, January 21, 1874* (Washington, D.C.: Gibson Brothers Printers, 1874); the transcript indicates several white women made comments during the hearing. Speech to Judiciary Committee, n.d., MASC/MS; Catherine Clinton, *The Other Civil War,* 93–96; Hoff, *Law, Gender and Injustice,* 170–77.

19. *New National Era,* 7 April 1870; "Although they accepted emancipation, most white Washingtonians found black suffrage obnoxious," notes one scholar. When the Republican-led Congress finally passed legislation in 1867 that allowed blacks to vote in District elections, it was vetoed by President Andrew Johnson who maintained that the measure ignored whites' concerns. Congress mustered enough votes to override the veto and it became law; see Williams, "A Blueprint for Change," 377–93; Lessoff, *The Nation and Its City,* 40–41, 52.

20. Sworn oath by Mary A. S. Cary, 19 April 1874, MASC/MS; Williams, "Blueprint for Change," 383–85; *New National Era,* 7 April 1870.

21. "A First Vote Almost," n.d., MASC/MS.

22. Ibid.

23. Hoff, *Law, Gender, and Injustice,* 152–61; Sworn oath by Mary A. S. Cary, 19 April 1874, MASC/MS.

24. Joan Hoff uses this term extensively, see *Law, Gender and Injustice,* 178–80; Elizabeth Cady Stanton, Susan B. Anthony, and Matilda Joslyn Gage, eds., *History of Woman Suffrage,* vol. 3. (1881, rpt. New York: Source Book Press, 1970), 17–19; Terborg-Penn, "Afro-Americans in the Struggle for Woman Suffrage," 60, makes this claim about Shadd Cary's request to the NWSA.

25. Stanton, et al., *History of Woman Suffrage,* 3:61, 72–73.

26. Barbara L. Epstein, *The Politics of Domesticity: Women, Evangelism, and Temperance in Nineteenth-Century America* (Middletown, Conn.: Wesleyan University Press, 1981), 1–9; 117–23. Little has been written on the black temperance movement, with the exception of Donald Yacovone, "The Transformation of the Black Temperance Movement, 1827–1854: An Interpretation," *Journal of the Early Republic* 8 (Fall 1988): 281–97. On temperance ideology among black women activists see Evelyn Brooks Higginbotham, *Righteous Discontent: The Women's Movement in the Black Baptist Church, 1880–1920* (Boston: Harvard University Press, 1993), 43, 193; and Dorothy Salem, *To Better Our World: Black Women in Organized Reform, 1890–1920* (Brooklyn, N.Y.: Carlson, 1990), 75.

27. *New National Era,* 27 February 1873.

28. Ibid.

29. Ruth Bordin, *Women and Temperance: The Quest for Power and Liberty, 1873–1900* (Philadelphia: Temple University Press, 1981), 83–84. On Frances Harper, see Margaret Hope Bacon, "'One Great Bundle of Humanity': Frances Ellen Watkins Harper," *Pennsylvania Magazine of History and Biography* 113 (January 1989): 21–43; Foster, *A Brighter Coming Day,* 21; and Carby, *Reconstructing Womanhood,* 68.

30. *Christian Recorder* 30 August 1877; *New York Freeman,* 11 April 1885; clipping from *Washington Star* 1888, MASC/MS.

31. Statement of purpose of the Colored Women's Progressive Franchise Association, MASC/MS.

32. See Higginbotham, *Righteous Discontent,* 16–17; Minutes of the first meeting, Colored Women's Professional Franchise Association, Moorland-Spingarn Research Center, Howard University, Washington, D.C.

33. Minutes of the first meeting, Colored Women's Professional Franchise Association, Moorland-Spingarn Research Center, Howard University, Washington, D.C.; for discussion of late nineteenth-century black gender conventions, see Beverly Guy-Sheftall, *Daughters of Sorrow: Attitudes toward Black Women, 1880–1920* (Brooklyn, N.Y.: Carlson, 1990), 91–112; and Higginbotham, *Righteous Discontent,* 67–73.

34. *People's Advocate* 21 February 1880.

35. Minutes of the first meeting, Colored Women's Professional Franchise Association, Moorland-Spingarn Research Center, Howard University, Washington, D.C.; Green, *Secret City,* 118.

36. "The Last Day of the 43 Congress," n.d., MASC/MS.

37. Untitled manuscript, n.d., MASC/MS.

38. On Cromwell, see Smith, *Emancipation: The Making of the Black Lawyer,* 132–33; Green, *Secret City,* 122.

39. *New York Age,* 19 November 1887.

40. *New National Era,* 6 October 1870.

41. Green, *Secret City,* 123, 150; John W. Cromwell, *History of the Bethel Literary and Historical Association* (Washington, D.C., 1897), 6.

42. The *People's Advocate* and the Washington *Bee* overlapped for two years, between 1882 when the *Bee* was founded and 1884 when the *Advocate* folded. See Green, *Secret City,* 143; quoted from Gatewood, *Aristocrats of Color,* 56–60; and from Thornbrough, *T. Thomas Fortune,* 30; also see David Howard-Pitney, "Calvin Chase's Washington *Bee* and Black Middle-Class Ideology, 1882–1900," *Journalism Quarterly* 63(Spring 1986): 89–97.

43. "Letter No. 5," n.d., MASC/MS.

44. See Emma Lou Thornbrough, *T. Thomas Fortune: Militant Journalist* (Chicago: University of Chicago Press, 1972), 29, 44–60, quoted from 46.

45. Emma Lou Thornbrough, "American Negro Newspapers, 1880–1914," *Business History Review* 40 (Winter 1966): 468; Summer E. Stevens and Owen V. Johnson, "From Black Politics to Black Community: Harry C. Smith and the *Cleveland Gazette,*" *Journalism Quarterly* 67 (Winter 1990): 1090–1102; "Letter No. 5," n.d., MASC/MS.

46. "Music in the Air," n.d., MASC/MS.

47. Proceedings of National Convention in Syracuse, N.Y., October, 1864, as quoted in Du Bois, *Black Reconstruction,* 232; *Washington Bee,* 10 February 1883; Lessoff, *The Nation and Its City,* 118–22, quote from 103; and Howard Gillette Jr., *Between Justice and Beauty: Race, Planning, and the Failure of Urban Policy in Washington, D.C.* (Baltimore: Johns Hopkins University Press, 1995), 66–70; *Cleveland Gazette,* 10 July 1886.

48. Ibid.

49. Foner, *Reconstruction*, 548–49, 592–93; Du Bois, *Black Reconstruction*.

50. For the text of David Walker's "Appeal" and the letters of Lewis Woodson, see Stuckey, *The Ideological Origins of Black Nationalism*, 39–117, 118–48.

51. "Letter No. 2" n.d., MASC/MS.

52. Green, *Secret City*, 119–44; Gatewood, *Aristocrats of Color*, 66–67; Gillette, *Between Justice and Beauty*, 67–68.

53. "Letter No. 1" n.d., MASC/MS.

54. Ibid.

55. *Directory of Graduates, Howard University, 1870–1963* (Washington, D.C., 1967), 67; *People's Advocate*, 2 June 1883; *New York Freeman*, 11 April 1885.

56. Lelia J. Robinson, "Women Lawyers in the United States," 28–30; Smith, *Emancipation*, 134, 141, 576–78.

57. "Washington Case," MASC/MS.

58. *Washington Evening Star*, 22 December 1892; *Boyd's Directory of the District of Columbia* (Washington, D.C.: Wm. H. Boyd, 1884–1892).

59. *Washington Evening Star*, 22 December 1892, 5 and 6 June 1893; *Boyd's Directory of the District of Columbia* (Washington, D.C.: Wm. H. Boyd, 1881–1893); clipping from *Washington Star*, 1888, Mary Ann Shadd Cary Papers; Certificate of Death, Mrs. Mary A. S. Cary, Vital Records Division, Department of Public Health, District of Columbia.

60. *Washington Bee*, 10 June 1893; *Washington Evening Star*, 5 June 1893.

61. Green, *Secret City*, 25; Estate of Mrs. Mary A. S. Cary, Supreme Court of the District of Columbia, 8 December 1893, National Archives.

Conclusion

1. W. E. B. Du Bois, "The Talented Tenth," in Nathan Huggins, ed., *The Writings of W. E. B. Du Bois* (New York: Library of America, 1986), 842.

2. See Dorothy Salem, "To Better Our World: Black Women in Organized Reform, 1890–1920," 18–30; Cynthia Neverdon-Morton, *Afro-American Women of the South and the Advancement of the Race, 1895–1925*, 191–93; Hazel Carby, "'On the Threshold of Woman's Era': Lynching, Empire, and Sexuality in Black Feminist Theory," in Henry Louis Gates, ed., *Race, Writing and Difference* (Chicago: University of Chicago Press, 1986), 301–16; Willard Gatewood, *Aristocrats of Color*, 241–46; Green, *Secret City*, 127.

3. Elizabeth L. Davis, *Lifting as They Climb* (Washington: National Association of Colored Women, 1933), 294; Sharon Harley, "Beyond the Classroom: The Organizational Lives of Black Female Educators in the District of Columbia, 1890–1930," *Journal of Negro Education* 51 (1982): 254–65; Moses, *The Golden Age of Black Nationalism*, 103–31.

4. Rayford W. Logan, *The Negro in American Life and Thought: The Nadir, 1877–1901* (New York: Collier Books, 1965), 15–22, 62.

5. Manning Marable, *Black American Politics: From the Washington Marches to Jesse Jackson* (London: Verso, 1985), 41–48; James Oliver Horton and Lois E. Horton, "Violence, Protest, and Identity: Black Manhood in Antebellum America," in *Free People of Color*, 95–96; George M. Fredrickson, *The Black Image in*

the White Mind: The Debate on Afro-American Character and Destiny, 1817–1914
(New York: Harper and Row, 1971), 256–82.

6. Quoted from Linda Perkins, "Impact of the Cult of True Womanhood," 25;
Anna Julia Cooper, *A Voice from the South*, 75.

7. I am arguing against James Oliver Horton's assertion that Shadd Cary "never
directly tackled gender roles," which ignores her rhetoric and behavior; see
"Freedom's Yoke," 73; see Sterling, *We Are Your Sisters;* and Emma Jones Lapsansky, "Feminism, Freedom, and Community: Charlotte Forten and Women Activists in Nineteenth-Century Philadelphia," *Pennsylvania Magazine of History and
Biography* 1 (January 1989): 3–19; see, for example, Stewart's speech of 27 February 1833, in Marilyn Richardson, ed., *Maria W. Stewart: America's First Black
Woman Political Writer* (Bloomington: Indiana University Press, 1987), 56–64.

8. Suzanne Lebsock, *The Free Women of Petersburg: Status and Culture in a
Southern Town, 1784–1860* (New York: W. W. Norton, 1985), 87–111; also see
James Oliver Horton, *Freedom's Yoke*, 64–69; and Sterling, *We Are Your Sisters*,
131–32.

9. Hallie Q. Brown, ed., *Homespun Heroines*, 92.

10. Victor Ullman, *Martin R. Delany*, 187–88.

11. Winks, *Blacks in Canada*, 396.

12. Richard Yarborough, "Race, Violence, and Manhood: The Masculine Ideal in
Frederick Douglass's 'The Heroic Slave,'" in Eric J. Sundquist, *Frederick Douglass:
New Literary and Historical Essays* (New York: Cambridge University Press, 1990),
167–68; W. E. B. Du Bois, "The Talented Tenth," in *Writings*, 842.

13. On Delany's patriarchal ideology, see Paul Gilroy, *The Black Atlantic: Modernity and Double Consciousness* (Cambridge, Mass.: Harvard University Press,
1993), 19–27.

14. On Crummell, see Moses, *The Golden Age of Black Nationalism*, 72–73; for
discussion of black Washingtonian's response to Booker T. Washington, see Green,
Secret City, 167–68.

15. See Gatewood, *Aristocrats of Color*, 149–81; James Oliver Horton nicely
summarizes this scholarship in "Shades of Color: The Mulatto in Three Antebellum Northern Communities," in *Free People of Color*, 122–44.

16. James Oliver Horton and Lois E. Horton, *Black Bostonians: Family Life and
Community Struggle in the Antebellum North* (New York: Holmes and Meier,
1979), 20.

17. Gatewood, *Aristocrats of Color*, 44; in Green, *Secret City*, illustration no.
20, Furman Shadd is identified as hosting elaborate parties and receptions.

18. Benedict Anderson, *Imagined Communities: Reflections on the Origin and
Spread of Nationalism* (New York: Verso, 1987), 38–39, 62–63.

19. For an extensive discussion on this issue, see Jane Rhodes, "Race, Money,
Politics and the Antebellum Black Press," *Journalism History* 20 (Autumn-Winter
1994): 95–106.

20. Elsa Barkley Brown, "Negotiating and Transforming the Public Sphere:
African American Political Life in the Transition from Slavery to Freedom," *Public Culture* 7 (1994): 107–46, contends that black women in Richmond, Va., of
the 1880s and 1890s retained a public authority through an internal political arena
within the black church; Higginbotham, *Righteous Discontent*, makes similar

assertions; also see Brown, "Womanist Consciousness: Maggie Lena Walker and the Independent Order of Saint Luke," *Signs* 14 (Spring 1989).

21. Gloria Wade-Gayles, "Black Women Journalists in the South, 1880–1905," *Callaloo* 11–13 (Feb.–Oct. 1981): 138–51.

22. I. Garland Penn, *The Afro-American Press and Its Editors* (1891; rpt. New York: Arno Press, 1969), 427, 487–91; Penn spelled her name Crary.

23. Gertrude Mossell, *The Work of the Afro-American Woman* (1894; rpt. New York: Oxford University Press, 1988), 19; S. Elizabeth Frazier, "Some Afro-American Women of Mark," *A.M.E. Church Review,* April 1892; Monroe Majors, *Noted Negro Women: Their Triumphs and Activities* (Chicago: Donohue and Henneberry, 1893), 112–13.

24. W. E. B. Du Bois, *Darkwater: Voices from within the Veil* (New York: Harcourt, Brace, 1920), ch. 7.

BIBLIOGRAPHY

Manuscript Collections and Archives

American Missionary Association Archives. Amistad Research Center, Tulane University, New Orleans

Anti-Slavery Collection. Rare Books Division, Cornell University, Ithaca

Chatham-Kent Museum, Chatham Cultural Centre, Chatham, Ontario.

Chester County Historical Society, West Chester, Pennsylvania

Chester County Archives and Records Services, West Chester, Pennsylvania

Daniel Murray Pamphlet Collection. Rare Books Division, Library of Congress, Washington, D.C.

Delaware State Archives, Dover, Delaware.

Gerrit Smith Papers. George Arents Research Collection, Syracuse University, Syracuse

History Department, Metropolitan Toronto Reference Library, Toronto, Ontario

Leon Gardiner Collection. Historical Society of Pennsylvania, Philadelphia

Mary Ann Shadd Cary Papers. Moorland-Spingarn Research Center, Howard University, Washington, D.C.

Mary Ann Shadd Cary Papers. National Archives of Canada, Ottawa, Ontario

Mary Ann Shadd Cary Papers. Ontario Provincial Archives, Toronto, Ontario

North American Black Historical Museum and Cultural Centre, Amherstburg, Ontario

Old Military Section: Negro in Military Service of the United States, 1639–1886, Colored Troops Division, National Archives of the United States, Washington, D.C.

Reference Section, Library of Congress, Washington, D.C.

Regional Collection. D. B. Weldon Library, University of Western Ontario, London, Ontario

Robin W. Winks Blacks in Canada Collection. Schomberg Center for Research in Black Culture, New York Public Library, New York.

Samuel Ringgold Ward Papers. Onondaga Historical Society, Syracuse

Shadd Family Collection. Raleigh Township Centennial Museum, North Buxton, Ontario

Shadd Family Papers. Amistad Research Center, Tulane University, New Orleans

Southern Historical Collection, University of North Carolina, Chapel Hill.

Washingtonia Division, District of Columbia Public Library, Washington, D.C.
William Lloyd Garrison Papers. Boston Public Library, Boston.

Documents, Reports, and Pamphlets

Anderson, Osborne P. *A Voice from Harpers Ferry*, 1859. 1861. Reprint. Atlanta: World View Publishers, 1980.
Annual Report of the American Society for Colonizing the Free People of Colour of the United States. Washington, D.C. 1824–27.
Annual Report of the Board of Trustees of Public Schools in and for the District of Columbia and Superintendent of Colored Schools of Washington and Georgetown. 1873–74. Washington, D.C.: 1875.
Annual Report of the Superintendent of Colored Schools of Washington and Georgetown. 1871–72 and 1872–73. Washington, D.C.: National Republican Job Office Printers, 1873.
Bibb, Henry. *Narrative of the Life and Adventures of Henry Bibb, an American Slave*. 1850. Reprint. Miami: Mnemosyne Publishers, 1969.
Brown, Hallie Q. *Homespun Heroines and Other Women of Distinction*. 1926. Reprint. New York: Oxford University Press, 1988.
Brown, William Wells. *The Negro in the American Rebellion*. 1867. Reprint. New York: Johnson Reprint, 1968.
———. *The Rising Son; or, The Antecedents and Advancements of the Colored Race*. 1874. Reprint. Miami: Mnemosyne Publishers, 1969.
"Census of 1861, Canada West." *Censuses of Canada, 1665 to 1871*. Ottawa: 1876.
Cromwell, John W. *History of the Bethel Literary and Historical Association*. Washington, D.C.: 1897.
Delany, Martin. *The Condition, Elevation, Emigration, and Destiny of the Colored People of the United States, Politically Considered*. 1852. Reprint. New York: Arno Press, 1968.
Drew, Benjamin. *A North-Side View of Slavery—The Refugee: or the Narratives of Fugitive Slaves in Canada*. 1856. Reprint. Reading, Mass.: Addison-Wesley, 1969.
First Annual Report of the Superintendent of Colored Schools for Washington and Georgetown, D.C., for the Year Ending June 30, 1868. Washington, D.C.: Judd and Detweiler, 1870.
Garrison, William Lloyd. *Thoughts on African Colonization*. 1832. Reprint. New York: Arno Press, 1968.
Hearing before the Judiciary Committee of the House of Representatives. Washington, D.C.: Gibson Brothers Printers, 1874.
Howe, Samuel Gridley. *The Refugees from Slavery in Canada West: Report to the Freedmen's Inquiry Commission*. 1864. Reprint. New York: Arno Press, 1969.
Minutes and Proceedings of the First Annual Convention of the Free Persons of Color. Philadelphia: 1831.
Minutes and Proceedings of the First Annual Convention of the People of Colour at the Wesleyan Church, Philadelphia, July 6, 1831. Philadelphia: 1831.
Minutes and Proceedings of the Second Annual Convention for the Improvement of the Free People of Color in These United States. Philadelphia: Martin and Boden, 1832.

Bibliography

Minutes of the District of Columbia Board of Trustees of Public Schools. June 1880, Nov. 1880, Dec. 1880. District of Columbia Archives, Washingtonia Division, District of Columbia Public Library.

"Minutes of the State Convention of the Coloured Citizens of Pennsylvania, convened at Harrisburg, December 13th and 14th, 1848." *In Proceedings of the Black State Conventions, 1840–1865,* ed. Philip S. Foner and George E. Walker. Philadelphia: Temple University Press, 1979.

Montgomery, Elizabeth. *Reminiscences of Wilmington, in Familiar Village Tales, Ancient and New.* Philadelphia: T. K. Collins, Jr., 1851. Reprint. Port Washington, N.Y.: Kennikat Press, 1972.

Payne, Bishop Daniel Alexander. *Recollections of Seventy Years.* 1883. Reprint. New York: Arno Press, 1968.

"Proceedings of the Cazenovia Fugitive Slave Law Convention, August 21–22, 1850." In *Proceedings of the Black State Conventions, 1840–1865.*

Proceedings of the Colored National Convention held in Franklin Hall, Sixth Street, Philadelphia, Pennsylvania, October 16, 17, 18th, 1855. Salem, N.J.: National Standard Office, 1856.

"Proceedings of the Colored National Labor Union Convention Held in Washington, D.C., December 6, 7, 8, 9, 10, 1869." *In Black Workers: A Documentary History from Colonial Times to the Present,* ed. Philip S. Foner and Ronald L. Lewis. Philadelphia: Temple University Press, 1989.

Proceedings of the National Emigration Convention of Colored People; Held at Cleveland, Ohio on Thursday, Friday and Saturday, the 24th, 25th and 26th of August, 1854. Pittsburgh: A. A. Anderson, Printer, 1854.

Report of the Board of Trustees of Colored Schools of Washington and Georgetown, District of Columbia. Washington, D.C. 1871.

Return of the Whole Number of Persons within the Several Districts of the United States. House of Representatives, 1800.

Scott, Lt. Col. Robert N. *The War of the Rebellion: A Compilation of the Official Records of the Union and Confederate Armies.* Washington, D.C.: Government Printing Office, 1891.

Shadd, Mary Ann. *A Plea for Emigration or, Notes of Canada West, in its Moral, Social and Political Aspect: with Suggestions Respecting Mexico, West Indies, and Vancouver Island, for the Information of Colored Emigrants.* Detroit: George W. Pattison Printing, 1852.

Special Report of the Commissioner of Education on the Improvement of Public Schools in the District of Columbia, 1871. Rare Books Collection, Library of Congress.

Special Report of the Superintendent of Colored Schools of Washington and Georgetown, 1871–72. Washington, D.C.: National Republican Job Office Printer, 1873.

Stanton, Elizabeth Cady, Susan B. Anthony, and Matilda Joslyn Gage, eds. *History of Woman Suffrage.* Vol. 3. 1881. Reprint. New York: Source Book Press, 1970.

Still, William. *The Underground Rail Road.* Philadelphia: William Still, 1883.

Terrell, W. H. H. *Indiana and the War of the Rebellion: Report of the Adjutant General.* 1869. Reprint. Indiana Historical Society, 1960.

The Minutes and Proceedings of the First Annual Meeting of the American Moral Reform Society. Philadelphia: Merrihew and Gunn, 1837.

United States Commissioner of Education. *History of Schools for the Colored Population.* 1871. Reprint. New York: Arno Press, 1969.

United States Department of State. *Sixth Census.* Washington, D.C., 1841.

United States Senate. Select Committee on the Harpers Ferry Invasion. *Journal of the Provisional Constitutional Convention, May 8–10, 1858, Chatham, Canada West.* Rpt. 278. (June 15, 1860).

Ward, Samuel Ringgold. *Autobiography of a Fugitive Negro: His Anti-Slavery Words and Labors in the United States, Canada and England.* 1855. Reprint. New York: Arno Press, 1968.

Wilson, Joseph. *Sketches of the Higher Classes of Colored Society in Philadelphia.* Philadelphia: Merrihew and Thompson Printers, 1841.

Yates, William. "Slavery and Colored People in Delaware." 1837. Reprint. *Delaware History* 14 (April 1971): 205–16.

Newspapers and Periodicals

African Repository and Colonial Journal (1824–60)
Aliened American (1853–56)
Anglo-African Magazine (1859)
Anti-Slavery Bugle (1845–61)
Christian Recorder (1854–1902)
Cleveland Gazette (1883–1945)
Colored American (1837–42)
Douglass' Monthly (1859–63)
Frederick Douglass' Paper (1851–59)
Liberator (1831–65)
New National Era (1870–74)
North Star (1847–51)
Pennsylvania Freeman (1838–54)
People's Advocate (1876–1884)
Pine and Palm (1861–2)
Provincial Freeman (1852–60)
Voice of the Fugitive (1851–53)
Washington Bee (1882–1922)
Weekly Anglo-African (1859–65)

Secondary Sources

Alexander, Sadie T. M. "Women as Practitioners of Law in the United States." *National Bar Journal* 1 (July 1941): 58–59.

Anderson, Benedict. *Imagined Communities: Reflections on the Origin and Spread of Nationalism.* New York: Verso, 1987.

Aptheker, Bettina. *Women's Legacy: Essays on Race, Sex and Class in American History.* Amherst: University of Massachusetts Press, 1982.

Atwood, Rodney. *The Hessians: Mercenaries from Hessen-Kassel in the American Revolution.* Cambridge: Cambridge University Press, 1980.

Backhouse, Constance. *Petticoats and Prejudice: Women and Law in Nineteenth-Century Canada.* Toronto: Women's Press, 1991.

Bacon, Margaret Hope. "'One Great Bundle of Humanity': Frances Ellen Watkins Harper." *Pennsylvania Magazine of History and Biography* 113 (January 1989): 21–43.

Baldasty, Gerald J. *The Commercialization of News in the Nineteenth Century.* Madison: University of Wisconsin Press, 1992.

Baldwin, Lewis V. "Festivity and Celebration: A Profile of Wilmington's Big Quarterly." *Delaware History* 19 (1981): 197–211.

Banks, Marva. "Uncle Tom's Cabin and Antebellum Black Response." In *Readers in History: Nineteenth-Century America Literature and the Contexts of Response,* ed. James L. Machor. Baltimore: Johns Hopkins University Press, 1993.

Beard, Augustus Field. *A Crusade of Brotherhood: A History of the American Missionary Association.* 1909. Reprint. New York: Kraus, 1970.

Bearden, Jim and Linda Jean Butler. *Shadd: The Life and Times of Mary Shadd Cary.* Toronto: N. C. Press Ltd., 1977.

Beaseley, Maurine and Sheila Gibbons, eds. *Women in Media: A Documentary Source Book.* Washington, D.C.: Women's Institute for Freedom of the Press, 1981.

Bell, Howard H. *A Survey of the Negro Convention Movement, 1830–1861.* New York: Arno Press, 1969.

———, ed. *Minutes of the Proceedings of the National Negro Conventions, 1830–1864.* New York: Arno Press, 1969.

———. "The American Moral Reform Society, 1836–1841." *Journal of Negro Education* 27 (Winter 1958): 34–40.

———. "The Negro Emigration Movement, 1849–1854: A Phase of Negro Nationalism." *Phylon* 20: 132–42.

———. "Negro Nationalism: A Factor in Emigration Projects, 1858–1861." *Journal of Negro History* 67 (January 1962): 42–53.

———. "Expressions of Negro Militancy in the North, 1840–1860." *Journal of Negro History* 65 (January 1960): 11–20.

Bender, Bruce. "Securing One of the Blessings of Liberty: Black Families in Lower New Castle County, 1790–1850." *Delaware History* 25 (1993–94): 237–52.

Bender, Thomas. *Community and Social Change in America.* Baltimore: John Hopkins University Press, 1978.

Berlin, Ira. *Slaves without Masters: The Free Negro in the Antebellum South.* New York: Pantheon Books, 1974.

———. "The Structure of the Free Negro Caste in the Antebellum United States." *Journal of Social History* 9 (Spring 1976): 297–318.

Bittenbender, Ada M. "Women in Law." In *Woman's Work in America,* ed. Annie Nathan Meyer. New York: Henry Holt, 1891.

Blackett, R. J. M. *Beating against the Barriers: The Lives of Six Nineteenth-Century Afro-Americans.* Ithaca: Cornell University Press, 1986.

———. *Building an Antislavery Wall: Black Americans in the Atlantic Abolitionist Movement, 1830–1860.* Ithaca: Cornell University Press, 1989.

Blewett, Mary H. *Men, Women and Work: Class, Gender, and Power in the New England Shoe Industry, 1780–1910.* Urbana: University of Illinois Press, 1990.

Blight, David W. *Frederick Douglass' Civil War: Keeping Faith in Jubilee.* Baton Rouge: Louisiana State University Press, 1989.

Blockson, Charles L. *The Underground Railroad.* New York: Prentice Hall, 1987.

Bloomfield, Maxwell. "John Mercer Langston and the Rise of Howard Law School." *Records of the Columbia Historical Society* (1971–72): 428–30.

Bordin, Ruth. *Women and Temperance: The Quest for Power and Liberty, 1873–1900.* Philadelphia: Temple University Press, 1981.

Bradbury, Bettina. "Surviving as a Widow in Nineteenth-Century Montreal." *Urban History Review* 17 (February 1989): 148–60.

Brown, Elsa Barkley. "Negotiating and Transforming the Public Sphere: African American Political Life in the Transition from Slavery to Freedom." *Public Culture* 7 (1994): 107–46.

———. "Womanist Consciousness: Maggie Lena Walker and the Independent Order of Saint Luke." *Signs* 14 (Spring 1989).

Brown, Hallie Q., ed. *Homespun Heroines and Other Women of Distinction.* 1926. Reprint. New York: Oxford University Press, 1988.

Brown, Ira V. *The Negro in Pennsylvania History.* University Park, Pa.: Pennsylvania Historical Association, 1970.

Brown, Letitia Woods. *Free Negroes in the District of Columbia, 1790–1846.* New York: Oxford University Press, 1972.

Bryan, Carter. "Negro Journalism in America before Emancipation." *Journalism Monographs* 12 (September 1969).

Bullock, Penelope. *The Afro-American Periodical Press, 1838–1909.* Baton Rouge: Louisiana State University Press, 1981.

Bumsted, J. M. *The Peoples of Canada: A Pre-Confederation History.* Toronto: Oxford University Press, 1992.

Burnet, Jean. *Ethnic Groups in Upper Canada.* Toronto: Ontario Historical Society, 1972.

———. "Occupational Differences and Class Structure." In *Readings in Canadian History,* ed. Douglas Francis and Donald B. Smith. Toronto: Holt, Rinehart and Winston, 1986.

Butchart, Ronald E. *Northern Schools, Southern Blacks, and Reconstruction: Freedmen's Education, 1862–1875.* Westport, Conn.: Greenwood Press, 1980.

Campbell, Stanley W. *The Slave Catchers: Enforcement of the Fugitive Slave Law, 1850–1860.* Chapel Hill: University of North Carolina Press, 1968.

Canadian Press Association. *A History of Canadian Journalism, 1859–1908.* Toronto: 1908.

Carby, Hazel. *Reconstructing Womanhood: The Emergence of the Afro-American Woman Novelist.* New York: Oxford University Press, 1987.

———. "'On the Threshold of Woman's Era': Lynching, Empire, and Sexuality in Black Feminist Theory." In *Race, Writing and Difference,* ed. Henry Louis Gates. Chicago: University of Chicago Press, 1986.

Cary, James W. "The Problem of Journalism History." *Journalism History* 1 (Spring 1974): 3–5, 27.

Clinton, Catherine. *The Other Civil War: American Women in the Nineteenth Century.* New York: Hill and Wang, 1984.

Cohen, Marjorie Griffin. *Women's Work, Markets, and Economic Development in Nineteenth-Century Ontario.* Toronto: University of Toronto Press, 1988.

Condit, Celeste Michelle and John Louis Lucaites. *Crafting Equality: America's Anglo-African Word*. Chicago: University of Chicago Press, 1993.

Cooper, Anna Julia. *A Voice from the South*. 1892. Reprint. New York: Oxford University Press, 1988.

Cooper, Frederick. "Elevating the Race: The Social Thought of Black Leaders, 1827–50." *American Quarterly* 24 (December 1972): 604–25.

Cornish, Dudley Taylor. *The Sable Arm: Negro Troops in the Union Army, 1861–1865*. New York: Norton, 1966.

Covert, Catherine L. "Journalism History and Women's Experience: A Problem in Conceptual Change." *Journalism History* 8 (1981): 2–5.

Cowan, Helen I. *British Emigration to North America: The First Hundred Years*. Toronto: University of Toronto Press, 1961.

Curry, Leonard P. *The Free Black in Urban America, 1800–1850*. Chicago: University of Chicago Press, 1981.

Dabney, Lillian G. *The History of Schools for Negroes in the District of Columbia, 1807–1947*. Washington, D.C.: Catholic University of America Press, 1949.

Dann, Martin. *The Black Press, 1827–1890: The Quest for a National Identity*. New York: G. P. Putnam and Sons., 1971.

Dannett, Sylvia. *Profiles of Negro Womanhood*. Vol. 1. New York: M. W. Lads, 1964.

Davis, Angela Y. *Women, Race and Class*. New York: Random House, 1981.

Davis, Elizabeth Lindsay. *Lifting as They Climb*. Washington, D.C.: National Association of Colored Women, 1933.

Davis, Marianna W. *Contributions of Black Women to America*. Vol. 1. Columbia, S.C.: Kenday Press, 1982.

Dean, David M. *Defender of the Race: James Theodore Holly, Black Nationalist and Bishop*. Boston: Lambeth Press, 1979.

DeBoer, Clara Merritt. *Be Jubilant My Feet: African American Abolitionists in the American Missionary Association, 1839–1861*. New York: Garland Publishing, 1994.

———. *His Truth Is Marching On: African Americans Who Taught the Freedmen for the American Missionary Association, 1861–1877*. New York: Garland Publishing, 1995.

de Tocqueville, Alexis. *Democracy in America*, ed. Richard D. Heffner. New York: New American Library, 1956.

Dicken-Garcia, Hazel. *Journalistic Standards in Nineteenth-Century America*. Madison: University of Wisconsin Press, 1989.

Dill, Bonnie Thornton. "The Dialectics of Black Womanhood." *Signs* 4 (Spring 1979): 543–55.

Directory of Graduates, Howard University, 1870–1963. Washington, D.C.: 1967.

DuBois, Ellen Carol. *Feminism and Suffrage: The Emergence of an Independent Women's Movement in America, 1848–1869*. Ithaca: Cornell University Press, 1978.

Du Bois, W. E. B. *The Philadelphia Negro*. 1899. Reprint. Millwood, N.Y.: Kraus-Thomson, 1973.

———. *Darkwater: Voices from within the Veil*. New York: Harcourt, Brace, 1920.

———. *Black Reconstruction*. 1935. Reprint. Millwood, N.Y.: Kraus-Thomson, 1976.

————. "The Talented Tenth." In *The Writings of W. E. B. DuBois,* ed. Nathan Huggins. New York: Library of America, 1986.

Dyson, Walter. *Howard University: The Capstone of Negro Education, A History, 1867–1940.* Washington, D.C.: Graduate School of Howard University, 1941.

Eppler, Karen Sanchez. "Bodily Bonds: The Intersecting Rhetorics of Feminism and Abolition." *Representations* 44 (Fall 1988): 28–59.

Epstein, Barbara. *The Politics of Domesticity: Women, Evangelism, and Temperance in Nineteenth Century America.* Middletown, Conn.: Wesleyan University Press, 1981.

Farmer, Silas. *The History of Detroit and Wayne County and Early Michigan.* Detroit: Silas Farmer, 1890.

Farrison, William E. *William Wells Brown: Author and Reformer.* Chicago: University of Chicago Press, 1969.

Fields, Barbara J. *Slavery and Freedom on the Middle Ground: Maryland during the Nineteenth Century.* New Haven: Yale University Press, 1985.

Filler, Louis. *The Crusade against Slavery, 1830–1860.* New York: Harper and Row, 1960.

Flexner, Eleanor. *Century of Struggle.* Cambridge: Harvard University Press, 1975.

Foner, Eric. *Reconstruction: America's Unfinished Revolution, 1863–1877.* New York: Harper and Row, 1988.

Foner, Philip S. *Organized Labor and the Black Worker, 1619–1973.* New York: International Publishers, 1974.

————. *Women and the American Labor Movement: From Colonial Times to the Eve of World War I.* New York: Free Press, 1979.

———— and Ronald Lewis, eds. *The Black Worker during the Era of the National Labor Union.* Philadelphia: Temple University Press, 1978.

Foster, Frances Smith, ed. *A Brighter Coming Day: A Frances Ellen Watkins Harper Reader.* New York: Feminist Press, 1990.

Franklin, John Hope and Alfred A. Moss. *From Slavery to Freedom: A History of Negro Americans.* 6th ed. New York: Alfred A. Knopf, 1988.

Franklin, Vincent P. *The Education of Black Philadelphia.* Philadelphia: University of Pennsylvania Press, 1979.

————. *Black Self-Determination: A Cultural History of the Faith of the Fathers.* Westport, Conn.: Lawrence Hill, 1984.

Frederickson, George W. *The Black Image in the White Mind: The Debate on Afro-American Character and Destiny, 1817–1914.* New York: Harper and Row, 1971.

Futhey, J. Smith and Gilbert Cope. *History of Chester County, Pennsylvania with Genealogical and Biographical Sketches.* Philadelphia: Louis H. Everts, 1881.

Gaines, Kevin K. *Uplifting the Race: Black Leadership, Politics, and Culture in the Twentieth Century.* Chapel Hill: University of North Carolina Press, 1996.

Gatewood, Willard B. *Aristocrats of Color: The Black Elite, 1880–1920.* Bloomington: Indiana University Press, 1990.

Gemmill, Sherriff J. R. "Historical Sketch of the Press of Chatham." *Kent Historical Society Papers and Addresses* 2 (1915): 30–37.

Giddings, Paula. *When and Where I Enter: The Impact of Black Women on Race and Sex in America.* New York: William Morrow, 1984.

Gillette, Howard Jr. *Between Justice and Beauty: Race, Planning, and the Failure of Urban Policy in Washington, D.C.* Baltimore: Johns Hopkins University Press, 1995.

Gilliam, Nancy T. "A Professional Pioneer: Myra Bradwell's Fight to Practice Law." *Law and History Review* 5 (1987): 105–33.

Gilroy, Paul. *The Black Atlantic: Modernity and Double Consciousness.* Cambridge, Mass.: Harvard University Press, 1993.

Green, Constance McLaughlin. *The Secret City: A History of Race Relations in the Nation's Capital.* Princeton: Princeton University Press, 1967.

Guillet, Edwin C. *Early Life in Upper Canada.* 1933. Reprint. Toronto: University of Toronto Press, 1963.

Guy-Sheftall, Beverly. *Daughters of Sorrow: Attitudes toward Black Women, 1880–1920.* Brooklyn: Carlson Publishing, 1990.

Hall, Richard. *Patriots in Disguise: Women Warriors of the Civil War.* New York: Paragon House, 1993.

Halstead, Jacqueline J. "Practical Christianity: The Delaware Association for the Moral Improvement and Education of the Colored People." *Delaware History* 15 (April 1972): 19–40.

Hancock, Harold B. "Mary Ann Shadd: Negro Editor, Educator, and Lawyer." *Delaware History* 15 (1973): 187–94.

———. "Not Quite Men: The Free Negroes in Delaware in the 1830s." *Civil War History* 17 (December 1971): 320–31.

Harding, Vincent. *There Is a River: The Black Struggle for Freedom in America.* New York: Random House, 1983.

Hargrove, Hondon B. *Black Union Soldiers in the Civil War.* Jefferson, N.C.: McFarland, 1988.

Harley, Sharon. "Beyond the Classroom: The Organizational Lives of Black Female Educators in the District of Columbia, 1890–1930." *Journal of Negro Education* 51 (1982): 254–65.

Harris, Robert L. "H. Ford Douglass: Afro-American Antislavery Emigrationist." *Journal of Negro History* 62 (July 1977): 217–34.

Heathcote, Charles W. *History of Chester County.* West Chester, Pa.: Horace Temple Printer, 1926.

Hembree, Michael F. "The Question of 'Begging': Fugitive Slave Relief in Canada, 1830–1865." *Civil War History* 37 (December 1991): 314–27.

Hershberg, Theodore. "Free Blacks in Antebellum Philadelphia: A Study of Ex-Slaves, Freeborn, and Socioeconomic Decline." *Journal of Social History* 5 (Winter 1971–72): 191.

Higginbotham, Evelyn Brooks. "Beyond the Sound of Silence: Afro-American Women in History." *Gender and History* 1 (Spring 1989): 50–67.

———. *Righteous Discontent: The Women's Movement in the Black Baptist Church, 1880–1920.* Boston: Harvard University Press, 1993.

Hill, Daniel G. *The Freedom Seekers: Blacks in Early Canada.* Agincourt, Canada: Book Society of Canada, 1981.

———. "The Blacks in Toronto." In *Gathering Place: Peoples and Neighbourhoods of Toronto, 1834–1945,* ed. Robert F. Harney. Toronto: Multicultural History Society of Ontario, 1985.

Hine, Darlene Clark. "Lifting the Veil, Shattering the Silence: Black Women's History in Slavery and Freedom." In *The State of Afro-American History: Past, Present and Future*. Baton Rouge: Louisiana State University Press, 1986.

———, ed. *Black Women in America: An Historical Encyclopedia*. Vol. 1. Brooklyn: Carlson Publishers, 1992.

Hite, Roger W. "Voice of a Fugitive: Henry Bibb and Ante-Bellum Black Separatism." *Journal of Black Studies* 4 (March 1974): 269–84.

Hoff, Joan. *Law, Gender, and Injustice: A Legal History of U. S. Women*. New York: New York University Press, 1991.

Hoffecker, Carol E. Delaware: *A Bicentennial History*. New York: W. W. Norton, 1977.

Hoganson, Kristin. "Garrisonian Abolitionists and the Rhetoric of Gender, 1850–1860." *American Quarterly* 45 (December 1993): 558–95.

Horsman, Reginald. *Race and Manifest Destiny: The Origins of American Racial Anglo-Saxonism*. Cambridge: Harvard University Press. 1981.

Horton, James Oliver. *Free People of Color: Inside the African American Community*. Washington, D.C.: Smithsonian Institution Press, 1993.

———. "Freedom's Yoke: Gender Conventions among Antebellum Free Blacks." *Feminist Studies* 12 (Spring 1986): 51–75.

———and Lois E. Horton. *Black Bostonians: Family Life and Community Struggle in the Antebellum North*. New York: Holmes and Meier Publishers, 1979.

Howard-Pitney, David. "The Enduring Black Jeremiad: The American Jeremiad and Black Protest Rhetoric, from Frederick Douglass to W. E. B. DuBois, 1841–1919." *American Quarterly* 38 (1986): 481–92.

———. "Calvin Chase's *Washington Bee* and Black Middle-Class Ideology, 1882–1900." *Journalism Quarterly* 63 (Spring 1986): 89–97.

Howe, E. W. "Country Newspapers." Century 42 (September 1891): 777.

Hutton, Frankie. *The Early Black Press in America, 1827–1860*. Westport, Conn.: Greenwood Press, 1993.

Jones, William Henry. *The Housing of Negroes in Washington, D.C.: A Study in Human Ecology*. Washington, D.C.: Howard University Press, 1929.

Jordan, Winthrop D. *The White Man's Burden: Historical Origins of Racism in the United States*. New York: Oxford University Press, 1974.

Katzman, David M. *Before the Ghetto: Black Detroit in the Nineteenth Century*. Urbana: University of Illinois Press, 1973.

Kelley, Mary. *Private Woman, Public Stage: Literary Domesticity in Nineteenth-Century America*. New York: Oxford University Press, 1984.

Kessler, Lauren. *The Dissident Press*. Berkeley: Sage, 1984.

Kinshasa, Kwando M. *Emigration vs. Assimilation: The Debate in the African American Press, 1827–1861*. Jefferson, N.C.: McFarland, 1990.

Landon, Fred. *Western Ontario and the American Frontier*. Toronto: Ryerson; New Haven: Yale University Press, 1941.

———. "The Negro Migration to Canada after the Passing of the Fugitive Slave Act." *Journal of Negro History* 5 (January 1920): 22–36.

———. "Records Illustrating the Condition of Refugees from Slavery in Upper Canada before 1860." *Journal of Negro History* 13 (April 1928): 199–207.

———. "Canadian Negroes and the John Brown Raid." *Journal of Negro History*. 6 (April 1921): 174–82.

———. "From Chatham to Harpers Ferry." *Canadian Magazine* 3 (October 1919): 441–48.

———. "The Work of the American Missionary Association among the Negro Refugees in Canada West, 1848–1864. *Ontario Historical Society Papers and Records* 21 (1924): 198–205.

———. "Social Conditions among the Negroes in Upper Canada before 1865." *Ontario Historical Society Papers and Records* 22 (1925): 144–61.

———. "Abolitionist Interest in Upper Canada." *Ontario History* 64 (1952): 165–77.

———. "Henry Bibb, A Colonizer." *Journal of Negro History* 5 (October 1920): 437–47.

Lapsansky, Emma Jones. "Friends, Wives and Strivings: Networks and Community Values among Nineteenth-Century Philadelphia Afroamerican Elites." *Pennsylvania Magazine of History and Biography* 108 (January 1984): 3–25.

———. "Feminism, Freedom, and Community: Charlotte Forten and Women Activists in Nineteenth-Century Philadelphia." *Pennsylvania Magazine of History and Biography* 113 (January 1989): 3–19.

Law, Howard. "Self-Reliance Is the True Road to Independence: Ideology and the Ex-Slaves in Buxton and Chatham." *Ontario History* 77 (June 1985): 107–20.

Lebsock, Suzanne. *The Free Women of Petersburg: Status and Culture in a Southern Town, 1784–1860.* New York: W. W. Norton, 1985.

———. "Free Black Women and the Question of Matriarchy: Petersburg, Virginia, 1784–1820." *Feminist Studies* 8 (Summer 1982): 271–87.

Leonard, Elizabeth D. *Yankee Women: Gender Battles in the Civil War.* New York: W. W. Norton, 1994.

Lerner, Gerda. *Black Women in White America. A Documentary History.* New York: Vintage Books, 1973.

———. *The Majority Finds Its Past.* New York: Oxford University Press, 1979.

Lessoff, Alan. *The Nation and Its City: Politics, 'Corruption,' and Progress in Washington, D.C., 1861–1902.* Baltimore: Johns Hopkins University Press, 1994.

Lewis, Elsie M. "Mary Ann Shadd Cary." In *Notable American Women.* Vol. 2., ed. Edward T. James. Cambridge: Harvard University Press, 1971.

Lipin, Lawrence M. *Producers, Proletarians, and Politicians: Workers and Party Politics in Evansville and New Albany, Indiana, 1850–87.* Urbana: University of Illinois Press, 1994.

Lippman, Walter. *Public Opinion.* 1922. Reprint. New Brunswick, N.J.: Transaction Publishers, 1991.

Litwack, Leon F. *North of Slavery: The Negro in the Free States, 1790–1860.* Chicago: University of Chicago Press, 1965.

———. *Been in the Storm So Long: The Aftermath of Slavery.* New York: Vintage Press, 1980.

Logan, Rayford W. *The Negro in American Life and Thought: The Nadir, 1877–1901.* New York: Collier Books, 1965.

Mabee, Carlton. *Black Education in New York State: From Colonial to Modern Times.* Syracuse: Syracuse University Press, 1979.

——— with Susan Mabee Newhouse. *Sojourner Truth: Slave, Prophet and Legend.* New York: New York University Press, 1993.

Majors, Monroe. *Noted Negro Women: Their Triumphs and Activities*. Chicago: Donohue and Henneberry, 1893.

Marable, Manning. *Black American Politics: From the Washington Marches to Jesse Jackson*. London: Verso, 1985.

Marzolf, Marion. *Up from the Footnote: A History of Women Journalists*. New York: Hastings House, 1977.

Massey, Mary Elizabeth. *Bonnet Brigades*. New York: Alfred A. Knopf, 1966.

McFeely, William S. *Frederick Douglass*. New York: W. W. Norton, 1991.

McGerr, Michael E. *The Decline of Popular Politics: The American North, 1865–1928*. New York: Oxford University Press, 1986.

McGlone, Robert E. "Rescripting a Troubled Past: John Brown's Family and the Harpers Ferry Conspiracy." *Journal of American History* 75 (March 1989): 1179–1200.

McKivigan, John R. "James Redpath, John Brown, and Abolitionist Advocacy of Slave Insurrection." *Civil War History* 37 (December 1991): 293–313.

McPherson, James M. *Battle Cry of Freedom: The Civil War Era*. New York: Oxford University Press, 1988.

——. *The Negro's Civil War*. New York: Pantheon Books, 1965.

——. *The Struggle for Equality: Abolitionists and the Negro in the Civil War and Reconstruction*. Princeton: Princeton University Press, 1964.

Meier, August and Elliot Rudwick. "Attitudes of Negro Leaders toward the American Labor Movement from the Civil War to World War I." *In The Negro and the American Labor Movement*, ed. Julius Jacobson. New York: Anchor Books, 1968.

Miller, Floyd J. *The Search for a Black Nationality: Black Emigration and Colonization, 1787–1863*. Urbana: University of Illinois Press, 1975.

Moore, Frank. *Women of the War: Their Heroism and Self-Sacrifice*. Hartford: S. S. Scranton, 1866.

Morris, Robert C. *Reading, 'Riting, and Reconstruction: The Education of Freedmen in the South, 1861–1870*. Chicago: University of Chicago Press, 1981.

Morton, Suzanne. "Separate Spheres in a Separate World: African-Nova Scotian Women in late 19th-Century Halifax County." *Acadiensis* 22 (Spring 1993): 61–83.

Moses, Wilson Jeremiah. *The Golden Age of Black Nationalism, 1850–1925*. Hamden, Conn.: Archon Books, 1978.

Mossell, Gertrude. *The Work of the Afro-American Woman*. 1894. Reprint. New York: Oxford University Press, 1988.

Munroe, John A. "The Negro in Delaware." *South Atlantic Quarterly* 56 (Autumn 1957): 428–44.

——. *History of Delaware*. 2nd ed. Newark: University of Delaware Press, 1984.

Murray, Alexander L. "The *Provincial Freeman*: A New Source for the History of the Negro in Canada and the United States." *Journal of Negro History* 43 (April 1959): 123–35.

Nash, Gary B. *Forging Freedom: The Formation of Philadelphia's Black Community, 1720–1840*. Cambridge: Harvard University Press, 1988.

Neverdon-Morton, Cynthia. *Afro-American Women of the South and the Advancement of the Race, 1895–1925*. Knoxville: University of Tennessee Press, 1989.

Nord, David Paul. "Tocqueville, Garrison and the Perfection of Journalism." *Journalism History* 13 (Summer 1986): 56–63.

———. "William Lloyd Garrison." In *Dictionary of Literary Biography*. Vol. 29. Detroit: Gale Research, 1984.

Painter, Nell Irvin. "Sojourner Truth in Life and Memory: Writing the Biography of an American Exotic." *Gender and History* 2 (Spring 1990): 3–16.

———. "Difference, Slavery, and Memory: Sojourner Truth in Feminist Abolitionism." In *The Abolitionist Sisterhood: Women's Political Culture in Antebellum America*, ed. Jean Fagan Yellin and John C. Van Horne. Ithaca: Cornell University Press, 1994.

———. *Sojourner Truth: A Life, A Symbol*. New York: Norton, 1996.

Pease, William H. and Jane H. Pease. *Black Utopia: Negro Communal Experiments in America*. Madison: State Historical Society of Wisconsin, 1963.

———. *They Who Would Be Free: Blacks' Search for Freedom, 1830–1861*. New York: Atheneum, 1974.

———. "The Negro Convention Movement." In *Key Issues in the Afro-American Experience*, ed. Nathan Huggins, Martin Kilson, and Daniel M. Fox. San Diego: Harcourt Brace Jovanovich, 1971.

———. *Ladies, Women and Wenches: Choice and Constraint in Antebellum Charleston and Boston*. Chapel Hill: University of North Carolina Press, 1990.

Penn, I. Garland. *The Afro-American Press and Its Editors*. Springfield, Mass.: Willey, 1891.

Perkins, Linda M. "The Impact of the 'Cult of True Womanhood' on the Education of Black Women." *Journal of Social Issues* 39 (1983): 17–28.

———. "Black Women and Racial 'Uplift' Prior to Emancipation." In *The Black Woman Cross-Culturally*, ed. Filomina Chioma Steady. Cambridge, Mass.: Schenkman Publishing, 1981.

———. "The Black Female American Missionary Association Teacher in the South, 1861–1870." In *Black Americans in North Carolina and the South*, ed. Jeffrey J. Crow and Flora J. Hatley. Chapel Hill, N.C.: University of North Carolina Press, 1984.

Peterson, Carla L. *"Doers of the Word": African-American Women Speakers and Writers in the North, 1830–1880*. New York: Oxford University Press, 1995.

Quarles, Benjamin. *Black Abolitionists*. New York: Oxford University Press, 1969.

Reid, John B. "'A Career to Build, a People to Serve, a Purpose to Accomplish': Race, Class, Gender, and Detroit's First Black Women Teachers, 1865–1916." *Michigan Historical Review* 18 (Spring 1992): 1–25.

Reid, Richard. "General Edward A. Wild and Civil War Discrimination." *Historical Journal of Massachusetts* 13 (1985): 14–29.

Rhodes, Jane. "Mary Ann Shadd Cary and the Legacy of African-American Women Journalists." In *Women Making Meaning: New Feminist Directions in Communication*, ed. Lana F. Rakow. New York: Routledge, 1992.

———. "Race, Money, Politics and the Antebellum Black Press." *Journalism History* 20 (Autumn-Winter 1994): 95–106.

Richardson, Joel M. *Christian Reconstruction: The American Missionary Association and Southern Blacks, 1861–1890*. Athens: University of Georgia Press, 1986.

Richardson, Marilyn. *Maria W. Stewart: America's First Black Woman Political Writer.* Bloomington: Indiana University Press, 1986.

Riddell, William Renwick. "Slavery in Canada." *Journal of Negro History* 5 (July 1920): 261–377.

Ripley, C. Peter. *The Black Abolitionist Papers.* Vols. 1–5. Chapel Hill: University of North Carolina Press, 1986–92.

Robinson, Leila J. "Women Lawyers in the United States." *The Green Bag* 2 (1890): 10–32.

Roediger, David R. *The Wages of Whiteness: Race and the Making of the American Working Class.* London: Verso, 1991.

Ryan, Mary. *Women in Public: Between Banners and Ballots, 1825–1880.* Baltimore: Johns Hopkins University Press, 1990.

Salem, Dorothy. *To Better Our World: Black Women in Organized Reform, 1890–1920.* Brooklyn: Carlson Publishing, 1990.

Schmitt, Albert R. "'The Hessians and Who?' A Look at the Other Germans in the American War of Independence." *Yearbook of German-American Studies* 18 (1983): 41–61.

Schweninger, Loren. *Black Property Owners in the South, 1790–1915.* Urbana: University of Illinois Press, 1990.

Scott, Donald M. "The Popular Lecture and the Creation of a Public in Mid-Nineteenth-Century America." *Journal of American History* 66 (March 1980): 791–809.

Silcox, Harry C. "The Black 'Better Class' Political Dilemma: Philadelphia Prototype Isaiah C. Wears." *Pennsylvania Magazine of History and Biography* 113 (January 1981): 46–66.

Silverman, Jason H. *Unwelcome Guests: Canada West's Response to American Fugitive Slaves, 1800–1865.* Millwood, N.Y.: Associated Faculties Press, 1985.

———. "Mary Ann Shadd and the Search for Equality." In *Black Leaders of the Nineteenth Century,* ed. John Hope Franklin and August Meier. Urbana: University of Illinois Press, 1982.

——— and Donna J. Gillie. "The Pursuit of Knowledge Under Difficulties: Education and the Fugitive Slave in Canada." *Ontario History* 74 (June 1982): 95–112.

Smedley, R. C. *History of the Underground Railroad in Chester and the Neighboring Counties of Pennsylvania.* 1883. Reprint. New York: Negro Universities Press, 1968.

Smith, J. Clay. *Emancipation: The Making of the Black Lawyer, 1844–1944.* Philadelphia: University of Pennsylvania Press, 1993.

Sorin, Gerald. *Abolitionism: A New Perspective.* New York: Praeger, 1972.

Staudenraus, P. J. *The African Colonization Movement, 1816–1865.* New York: Columbia University Press, 1961.

Sterling, Dorothy. *We Are Your Sisters: Black Women in the Nineteenth Century.* New York: W. W. Norton, 1984.

———. *The Making of an Afro-American: Martin Robeson Delany, 1812–1885.* New York: Da Capo Press, 1996.

Stevens, Summer E. and Owen V. Johnson. "From Black Politics to Black Community: Harry C. Smith and the Cleveland Gazette." *Journalism Quarterly* 67 (Winter 1990): 1090–1102.

Stouffer, Allen P. *The Light of Nature and the Law of God: Antislavery in Ontario, 1833–1877.* Baton Rouge: Louisiana State University Press, 1992.

———. "A 'Restless Child of Change and Accident': The Black Image in Nineteenth-Century Ontario." *Ontario History* 76 (June 1984): 124–49.

Streitmatter, Rodger. *Raising Her Voice: African-American Women Journalists Who Changed History.* Lexington: University Press of Kentucky, 1994.

Stuckey, Sterling. *The Ideological Origins of Black Nationalism.* Boston: Beacon Press, 1970.

Takaki, Ronald. *Iron Cages: Race and Culture in 19th Century America.* New York: Oxford University Press, 1990.

Terborg-Penn, Rosalyn. "Discrimination against Afro-American Women in the Women's Movement, 1830–1920." In *The Black Woman Cross-Culturally,* ed. Filomina Chioma Steady. Cambridge, Mass.: Schenkman Publishing, 1981.

Thomason, Colin A. "Doc Shadd." *Saskatchewan History* 30 (Spring 1977): 41–55.

Thomson, W. W., ed. *Chester County and Its People.* Chicago: Union Historical Company, 1898.

Thornbrough, Emma Lou. *The Negro in Indiana.* Indianapolis: Indiana Historical Bureau, 1957.

———. "American Negro Newspapers, 1880–1914." *Business History Review* 40 (Winter 1966): 468.

———. *T. Thomas Fortune: Militant Journalist.* Chicago: University of Chicago Press, 1972.

Tollett, Kenneth S. "Black Lawyers, Their Education, and the Black Community." *Howard Law Journal* 17 (1972): 328–29.

Turner, Edward Raymond. *The Negro in Pennsylvania: Slavery-Servitude-Freedom, 1639–1861.* 1911. Reprint. New York: Arno Press, 1969.

Uglow, Jennifer S., ed. *The International Dictionary of Women's Biography.* New York: Continuum Press, 1982.

Ullmann, Victor. *Martin R. Delany: The Beginnings of Black Nationalism.* Boston: Beacon Press, 1971.

Venet, Wendy Hamand. *Neither Ballots nor Bullets: Women Abolitionists and the Civil War.* Charlottesville: University Press of Virginia, 1991.

Voegeli, V. Jacque. *Free But Not Equal: The Midwest and the Negro during the Civil War.* Chicago: University of Chicago Press, 1967.

Wade-Gayles, Gloria. "Black Women Journalists in the South, 1880–1905." *Callaloo* 11–13 (Feb.-Oct. 1981): 138–51.

Walters, Ronald G. *The Antislavery Appeal: American Abolitionism after 1830.* New York: W. W. Norton, 1978.

Wayne, Michael. "The Black Population of Canada West on the Eve of the American Civil War: A Reassessment Based on the Manuscript Census of 1861." *Histoire Sociale/Social History* 56 (Nov. 1995): 465–85.

Weisberg, D. Kelly. "Barred from the Bar: Women and Legal Education in the United States, 1870–1890." In *Women and the Law: A Social Historical Perspective.* Vol. II. Cambridge, Mass.: Schenkman Publishing, 1982.

Welter, Barbara. "The Cult of True Womanhood: 1820–1860." *American Quarterly* 18 (Summer 1966): 151–74.

White, Deborah Gray. "Mining the Forgotten: Manuscript Sources for Black Women's History." *Journal of American History* 74 (June 1987): 237–42.

Whyte, James H. *The Uncivil War: Washington during the Reconstruction, 1865–1878.* New York: Twayne Publishers, 1958.

Wilson, Clint C. *Black Journalists in Paradox: Historical Perspectives and Current Dilemmas.* New York: Greenwood Press, 1991.

Williams, Melvin R. "A Blueprint for Change: The Black Community in Washington, D.C., 1860–1870." *Records of the Columbia Historical Society* 48 (1971–72): 369–77.

Winch, Julie. *Philadelphia's Black Elite: Activism, Accommodation, and the Struggle for Autonomy, 1787–1848.* Philadelphia: Temple University Press, 1988.

Winks, Robin W. *The Blacks in Canada.* New Haven: Yale University Press, 1971.

———. "Mary Ann Shadd Cary." In *Dictionary of American Negro Biography,* ed. Rayford W. Logan and Michael R. Winston. New York: W. W. Norton, 1982.

———. "A Sacred Animosity: Abolitionism in Canada." In *The Antislavery Vanguard,* ed. Martin Duberman. Princeton: Princeton University Press, 1965.

———. *Canada and the United States: The Civil War Years.* Baltimore: Johns Hopkins University Press, 1960.

Wood, Forest G. *Black Scare: The Racist Response to Emancipation and Reconstruction.* Berkeley: University of California Press, 1968.

Woodson, Carter G. *The Education of the Negro Prior to 1861.* 1919. Reprint. New York: Arno Press, 1968.

Woody, Thomas. *Early Quaker Education in Pennsylvania.* New York: Teachers College, Columbia University, 1920.

Yacavone, Donald. "The Transformation of the Black Temperance Movement, 1827–1854: An Interpretation." *Journal of the Early Republic* 8 (Fall 1988): 281–97.

Yarborough, Richard. "Race, Violence, and Manhood: The Masculine Ideal in Frederick Douglass's 'The Heroic Slave'." In *Frederick Douglass: New Literary and Historical Essays,* ed. Eric J. Sundquist. New York: Cambridge University Press, 1990.

Yee, Shirley. *Black Women Abolitionists: A Study in Activism, 1828–1860.* Knoxville: University of Tennessee Press, 1992.

———. "Gender Ideology and Black Women as Community-Builders in Ontario, 1850–70." *Canadian Historical Review* 75 (March 1994): 53–73.

Yellin, Jean Fagin. *Women and Sisters: The Antislavery Feminists in American Culture.* New Haven: Yale University Press, 1989.

Unpublished Papers, Theses, and Dissertations

Burke, Ronald K. "Samuel Ringgold Ward: Christian Abolitionist." Ph.D. diss., Syracuse University, 1975.

Essah, Patience. "Slavery and Freedom in the First State: The History of Blacks in Delaware from the Colonial Period to 1865." Ph.D. diss., University of California, Los Angeles, 1985.

Forstchen, William R. "The Twenty-Eighth United Colored Troops: Indiana's African Americans Go to War, 1863–1865." Ph.D. diss., Purdue University, 1994.

Hudson, Lynn M. "When 'Mammy' Becomes a Millionaire: Mary Ellen Pleasant, a Nineteenth-Century African-American Entrepreneur." Ph.D. diss., Indiana University, 1996.

Johnson, Clifton. "The American Missionary Association, 1846–1861: A Study of Christian Abolitionism." Ph.D. diss., University of North Carolina, 1958.

Lewis, James K. "Religious Life of Fugitive Slaves and the Rise of Coloured Baptist Churches, 1820–1865, In What Is Now Known as Ontario." Bachelor's thesis, McMaster University, 1965.

Murray, Alexander L. "Canada and the Anglo-American Anti-Slavery Movement: A Study in International Philanthropy." Ph.D. diss., University of Pennsylvania, 1960.

Simpson, Donald G. "Negroes in Ontario from Early Times to 1870." Ph.D. diss., University of Western Ontario, 1971.

Spencer, Hildreth H. "To Nestle in the Mane of the British Lion: A History of Canadian Black Education, 1820–1879." Ph.D. diss., Northwestern University, 1970.

Terborg-Penn, Rosalyn. "Afro-Americans in the Struggle for Woman Suffrage." Ph.D. diss., Howard University, 1977.

Tripp, Bernell E. "Mary Miles Bibb: Education and Moral Improvement in the *Voice of the Fugitive*." Paper presented to the Association for Education in Journalism and Mass Communication, Kansas City, August 1993.

Williams, Melvin Roscoe. "Blacks in Washington, D.C., 1860–1870." Ph.D. diss., Johns Hopkins University, 1975.

INDEX

Aaron, Samuel, 20

Afric-American Quarterly Repository, 120

Africa, 9, 12, 28, 46, 80, 87, 133, 217, 137–139, 147, 160, 164; Liberia, 9–11, 13, 115, 119, 137; Niger Valley, 133

African Aid Society, 138

African Civilization Society of Canada, 133, 139

African Methodist Episcopal Church (Philadelphia), 7, 16, 22, 23, 38, 78, 100, 199; *see also* Richard Allen

African School Society (Wilmington), 8

African Schools, 8

African Union Church (Wilmington), 12

African Union Methodist Episcopal Church (Wilmington), 7

African Americans: education of, xvi, xvii, 8, 17, 20–27, 30–44, 92, 138, 148–149, 150, 155–156, 159, 161–162, 165, 166, 170–178, 185–208, 212–214, 218, 219, 222

Aliened American (Ohio), 76, 114

Allen, Richard, 7

American Colonization Society, 9, 10, 118, 137, 164

American Convention of Abolition Societies, 8

American Equal Rights Association, 192

American Missionary Association, xviii, 36–43, 47, 48, 49, 55–56, 59, 65, 67- 69, 105, 106, 138, 150, 166, 174

American Moral Reform Society, 18

American Negro Academy, *see* Alexander Crummell

American Revolution, 2, 5, 51

Amherstburg, 42, 43, 61, 74, 81, 112, 146

Anderson, Benedict, 220

Anderson, Osborne Perry, 118, 130, 131, 133, 138, 154, 182

Andrew, John, 152

Anthony, Susan B., 192, 193, 196

Antislavery, xviii, 18, 19, 34, 52, 56, 111, 116, 121, 125, 126, 128, 129, 182, 183, 191, 192, 198

Anti-Slavery Bugle (Ohio), 77

Anti-Slavery Society of Canada, 42, 56, 59, 60, 63, 75, 76, 81, 89

Association for Promotion of Interests of Colored People of Canada and United States, 132

Association for the Advancement of Women, 203

Banneker Institute of Philadelphia, 110

Barnard, Henry, 176

Berlin, Ira, xvii

Bethel Literary and Historical Association, 203, 211, 212

Bibb, Henry, xix, 34–35, 41–43, 52, 53, 63, 64, 65, 66, 71, 73, 76, 81–82, 95, 217; *see also Voice of the Fugitive*

Bibb, Mary, 34–35, 48–49, 63, 95, 143, 217

Black Church, 7, 221

Black Convention Movement: First Annual Convention of the Free Persons of Colour (June 6, 1831, Delaware), 10–11; Second Annual Convention of Free Persons of Colour (Philadelphia 1832), 12; Third Annual Convention for the Improvement of the Free People of Colour (Philadelphia 1833), 12–13

Black elites, 3–4, 5–18, 21, 22, 171, 172, 203, 219

Black expatriate communities of Canada, xiii, xvi

Black labor, 167, 168

Black masculinity, 98, 216

Black Women's Club Movement, 212, 213

Black women: as domestics, 148, 169, 170 as

workers, 169, 170; role in Civil War, 155; as teachers, 148, 149
Borden, Lizzie, 211
Bowers, John C., 111
Bradwell, Myra, 188
Brick Wesley Church (Philadelphia), 80
British American Institute (Chatham, Canada West), 30
British and Foreign Anti-Slavery Society, 107
Brown, George, 35
Brown, Hallie Q., 216
Brown, John, 118, 129, 130–132, 134, 140, 181, 182
Brown, William Wells, 100, 131, 142, 152, 156, 180, 181
Bruce, Josephine, 212
Buchanan, James, 121
Burney, James
Buxton, Ontario, xix

Canada West, 10, 137, 143, 145, 163; African Americans leaving, 160–162; economy, 127; as haven for blacks, 29- 33, 78, 133
Carey, James, xvi
Cary, George, 113, 136, 142, 143, 144
Cary, Isaac N., 112, 142, 143, 172
Cary, John J., 85, 96, 113, 133
Cary, Linton, 136, 173, 210, 211
Cary, Sarah Elizabeth, 127, 173
Cary, Mary Ann Shadd, 4, 6, 8, 13, 17- 18; on abolitionism, 88–89; absence in popular recognition, xvi–xvii; appearance in studies of early black nationalists and emigrationists, xiv– xv; on black ministers, 22–23; black women contemporaries, xvi; colonization, 78–80; contradictions of, xiii, xiv; participation in women's associational politics, xv; emigration, 80, 85–86; control over public representation, xv, 181; emigration, 217; death of, 211; exemplar of black educated women, xiii; feminism of, 216; as foremother, 213; gender struggles as editor, 53- 57, 66, 72–73, 77, 83–84, 91–92, 93, 95; gender boundaries in activist work, 116, 129; giving up editorship, 98; as lawyer, 209; literary aspirations, 181, 182; longing for journalistic forum, 201; nationalism of, 86–87, 216; as principal, 175–178, 190; pursuing law degree, 185, 190, 191; on racial uplift, 14–20; role in Civil War; relationships with black women, xix, 96, 99; 153–157; relationships with influential men, xvi, xix; school at Canada West, 34, 35; scholarly attention, xvii–xviii; school at Windsor, 35–41, 69; social darwinism, 207; status in modern Ontario, xix; as teacher 18, 19–20, 165; tours, 96–97; uneasy fit with folk mythology, xvi; as widow, 148; women's rights, 91, 191, 194–196, 200
Cary, Thomas F., 82, 85, 112, 113, 124, 127, 128, 131, 132, 135, 148, 215
Caste and color prejudice, 218–219
Chandler, Zachariah, 190
Chase, Calvin, 204, 206
Chatham Planet, 102, 103
Chatham, 101, 102, 103, 141, 143–146, 149, 150, 154, 155, 157, 159, 160, 161, 162, 182
Chicago, Illinois, 115, 154, 158, 173, 213
Cholera, 59, 64
Christian Herald, 221
Christian Recorder, 100
Christiana Uprising, 180
Civil War, xv, xvii, 1, 19, 20, 27, 31, 54, 92, 136, 142–147, 150–153, 155, 156, 166, 173, 174, 180, 183, 187, 190, 191, 198, 205, 205, 213, 217, 221, 223
Clay, Henry, 9
Cleveland Gazette, see Harry C. Smith
Colored American, see Charles Ray
Colored Ladies Freedmen's Aid Society, 158
Colored National Labor Union Convention, 167–169
The Colored American, 19
Colored National Labor Union, 167–169, 186, 218; Colored National Convention, 108, 109, 110
Colored Women's Progressive Franchise Association, 199, 200–203
Common School Act of Canada, 37
Compromise of 1850, 27–28
The Condition, Elevation, Emigration, and Destiny of the Colored People of the United States Politically Considered, 49
Conservative Party (Canada), 126, 127
Cook, John F., 195
Cooper, Anna Julia, 212, 214
Cornish, Samuel, 26, 38, 68
Crocker, John S., 195
Cromwell, John W., 202, 203
Crummell, Alexander, 218

Howard, I. M., 190
Howard, William A., 166, 190

The Impartial Citizen (Syracuse), 60, 71–72
Independent Order of Saint Luke, 222
Indiana, 154–160
Irish, 141, 146, 147, 166

Jackson, Fanny M., 180
Johnson, Andrew, 163, 164
Jones, A. B., 85
Jones, Thomas, 70–71

Keckley, Elizabeth, xvii
Kent Advertiser (Chatham), 102, 103, 127
King Street East, 83
King, William, 30, 144

Labor, xv, 6, 7, 11, 18, 29, 30, 125, 148, 166–170, 200, 210, 218; Black labor, 166–168, 200, 210, 218, 219; Black women's labor, 148, 169, 170; Labor unions, 167–168
Langston, John Mercer, 173, 191
Lawrence, George, 140
The Liberator, 12, 57, 62–63, 64
Lincoln Mission School, 175, 176, 200
Lincoln, Abraham, 136, 137, 142, 151
Lincoln, Mary Todd, 155
Lippmann, Walter, 100
Lockwood, Belva, 169
Loguen, Jermain W., 28, 118
Lorde, Audre, xx

Majors, Monroe, 223
Mansfield, Arabella, 188
Marable, Manning, 214
Marriage, 215
May, Samuel J., 58
McArthur, Alexander, 36, 38, 39, 41, 42, 55, 65–66, 71, 74, 83
McKinney, Abraham, 88
Michigan, 131, 149, 154, 155, 165, 167, 168, 179
Military: Fifty-Fourth Massachusetts Infantry, 152, 153, 154; recruitment of African Americans, 150, 151, 153, 154, 157, 159; Twenty-Eighth U.S. Colored Infantry of Indiana, 156, 157, 159–160; Twenty-Ninth Regiment of Connecticut Volunteers, 153, 157
Mission School (Chatham, Canada West), 150, 154, 159, 160, 162

Moral Education Society (Washington, D.C.), 198
Morton, Oliver P., 156, 159
Moses, Wilson J., 80, 138
Mossell, Gertrude, 222, 223
Mott, Lucretia, 20, 126
Myers, Isaac, 168

National Association of Colored Women, 213
National Colored Women's League, 212, 213
National Council of African-American Leaders, 108
National Emigration Convention, 86–87, 95, 115, 119, 132, 133
National Labor Union, 168
National Women's Suffrage Association, 192–194, 196, 197
Nationalism, 137, 164: Black nationalism, xvi, 22, 42, 47, 59–50, 87, 117, 137, 138, 216, 218
New National Era, 170, 173, 177, 178, 181, 182, 186, 198, 199, 202
New York Tribune, see Horace Greeley
New York, New York, 14, 26–27, 108, 146, 157, 166, 168, 172, 182, 188, 196, 197, 199, 203, 204, 209
Newman, William P., 99, 102–105, 108, 111, 114
Nichols, J., 199
North American League, 53
North Star, 21, 22, 23, 28, 82, 117
The Northern Star and Colored Farmer, 59
Noted Negro Women: Their Triumph and Activities, see Monroe Majors
Notes of Canada West, 43–47, 52, 56, 58, 78, 82, 105, 115, 220

Organic Act of 1878, 206

Painter, Nell, xvi, 192
Painter, Samuel, 15
Parker, William, 180
Patterson, Louis, 114
Payne, Daniel, 78, 112, 203, 223
Penn, I. Garland, 222
Pennsylvania: Philadelphia, 13–18, 10–11, 26, 27, 33, 65, 67, 77–79, 82, 88, 92, 109, 110, 111, 115, 126, 168, 190, 196, 215, 219; West Chester, 13–18, 52, 72, 78, 79, 80
Pennsylvania Freeman, 61, 64, 71, 72, 77, 78